LETTERS OF
ARNOLD BENNETT

Volume II

1889–1915

Arnold Bennett at the time of his wedding, 4 July 1907

LETTERS OF
ARNOLD BENNETT

Edited by
JAMES HEPBURN

VOLUME II

1889–1915

LONDON
OXFORD UNIVERSITY PRESS
NEW YORK   TORONTO
1968

Oxford University Press, Ely House, London W.1

GLASGOW NEW YORK TORONTO MELBOURNE WELLINGTON
CAPE TOWN SALISBURY IBADAN NAIROBI LUSAKA ADDIS ABABA
BOMBAY CALCUTTA MADRAS KARACHI LAHORE DACCA
KUALA LUMPUR HONG KONG TOKYO

Printed in Great Britain by R. & R. Clark Ltd., Edinburgh

CONTENTS

LIST OF ILLUSTRATIONS

ACKNOWLEDGEMENTS

To the editors of the Oxford University Press I am most especially obliged for their helpfulness during the preparation of this volume. I also owe particular thanks to the American Council of Learned Societies and the Penrose Fund of the American Philosophical Society for grants that made part of the work possible. And as with Volume I, I am deeply grateful to Dr. LaFayette Butler, and to his son Charles Tolhurst Butler, for their hospitality and generosity in allowing me to use the Arnold Bennett and George Sturt manuscripts in their home. Much of the research for this volume was made possible by these manuscripts.

The letters are reproduced with the kind permission of the owner of the copyright, Mrs. Dorothy Cheston Bennett. To the libraries and librarians, and to other public and private owners and holders of the letters themselves, I owe equal thanks:

Miss O. D. Becker, for letters to her aunt, Ida Meller.

County Record Office, Bedford, and Messrs. Brown and Merry of Leighton Buzzard, for letters to A. W. Merry.

University of Birmingham Library, and Rudolph Sauter, for a letter to John Galsworthy.

Brown University Library, for a letter to Wayland Williams. Christine D. Hathaway, Special Collections Librarian, provided me with information on Williams.

Sebastian H. Brown, for a letter to his father, James Brown, and for considerable information on George Sturt and other friends of his father.

Dr. LaFayette Butler, for letters to A. St. John Adcock, C. F. Cazenove, George H. Doran, John Drinkwater, Stanley Hazell, Edward Knoblock, A. R. Orage, Cedric Sharpe, and Charles Young.

University of California Library, Los Angeles, for letters to Edith Evors, Stanley and Florence Hazell, and Eden and Emily Phillpotts. Brooke Whiting, Literary Manuscripts Librarian, very kindly provided information on a few points.

Peter Cheeseman, for a letter to Mrs. H. H. Penrose.

Documents and Autographs Ltd., for a letter to Mrs. H. H. Penrose. I would like especially to thank Miss Alison Hill for her helpfulness in making this letter available to me.

Edinburgh University Library, for letters to J. M. Dent and Charles Sarolea. I am particularly obliged to C. P. Finlayson, Keeper of Manuscripts, for his helpfulness.

Fonds Gide, Bibliothèque Littéraire Jacques Doucet, Paris, for letters to André Gide.

Sir Rupert Hart-Davis, for letters to Douglas Baddeley. I am also obliged to Sir Rupert for providing transcripts of letters to Robert Ross.

Houghton Library, Harvard University, for letters to Colonel George Harvey and W. D. Howells.

Mrs. Hilda Hellman, for a letter to her, and for information about her friendship with Bennett.

Paul M. Herzog, for letters to his mother, Elsie Herzog, and to George H. Doran. Mr. Herzog very kindly gave me information on a number of points concerning the letters.

The Countess of Iddesleigh, for a letter to F. S. A. Lowndes.

University of Illinois Library, for letters to H. G. and Jane Wells. I am particularly grateful to Professor Harris Wilson, editor of the Bennett–Wells correspondence, for his courtesy in making these letters available to me.

University of Kansas Library, for a letter to T. L. Humberstone.

James Keddie, Jr., for letters to his father, James Keddie, and E. V. Lucas. I am especially obliged to Mr. Keddie for helping me on several occasions.

University of Keele Library, for letters to Holbrook Jackson and Mr. and Mrs. Frederick Marriott. I am very grateful to Stanley O. Stewart, University Librarian, and Ian H. C. Fraser, Archivist, for providing information and other help on several occasions.

Sir Allen Lane, for letters to Frederic Chapman and John Lane. Professor Curtis Page and Mr. Michael Rhodes very kindly supplied copies and transcripts of some of these letters.

Fonds Larbaud, Bibliothèque de la Ville de Vichy, for a letter to Valéry Larbaud.

Brotherton Library, University of Leeds, for letters to Edmund Gosse and Clement Shorter.

Lilly Library, Indiana University, Bloomington, for letters to Upton Sinclair and E. F. Spence.

University of Manchester Library, and Patrick Monkhouse, for letters to A. N. Monkhouse. Margaret M. Wright, in charge of Special Collections at the Library, provided some helpful information.

Central Library, Manchester Public Libraries, for a letter to Annie E. F. Horniman.

Merton College Library, Oxford, for a letter to Max Beerbohm.
Mrs. Wainwright Morgan, for a letter to her mother, Margaret
Hannah Marriott. I am very grateful to Mrs. Morgan for pro-
viding information about her parents and their friends.
Henry W. and Albert A. Berg Collection, New York Public Lib-
rary, Astor, Lenox, and Tilden Foundations, for letters to G. T.
Bagguley, W. M. Colles, F. M. (Hueffer) Ford, Violet Hunt,
Frederick Marriott, Cranstoun Metcalfe, (Sir) John Squire, and
George Sturt. I am deeply obliged to the late Dr. John D.
Gordan, Curator of the Berg Collection, and to Lola L.
Szladits, First Assistant, for their courtesy and helpfulness to
me on many occasions.
Fales Collection, New York University Library, for letters to Mrs.
Alcock, Frederic Chapman, W. M. Colles, T. L. Humberstone,
Eden Phillpotts, Lady St. Helier, T. B. Wells, and an unidenti-
fied correspondent.
University of Pennsylvania Library, and Professor T. E. M. Boll,
for a letter to May Sinclair. I am also deeply obliged to Pro-
fessor Boll for providing me with information on several occa-
sions.
Dorothy Rickard, for letters to her father, John Rickard. I am
especially indebted to Miss Rickard for giving me information
about her father and his friends.
J.-P. B. Ross, for letters to Robert Ross.
Society of Authors, for a letter to G. Herbert Thring.
Arnold Bennett Museum, Stoke-on-Trent, for letters to Lucie
Simpson, Hugh Walpole, Alfred Wareing, and R. W. Wright.
I am especially grateful to K. D. Miller, City Librarian, John
Ford, Deputy Librarian, and Norman Emery, Chief Biblio-
grapher, for their helpfulness on many occasions during the
past years. Several of the notes in this volume are drawn from
information provided by them.
Edwin A. Sy, Curator of Special Collections, State University of
New York at Buffalo, for a letter to E. V. Lucas.
Mayfield Library, Syracuse University, for letters to the *Daily
News* and *The Times*. I am particularly grateful to John S.
Mayfield, Curator of Manuscripts, for his generous helpfulness
on several occasions.
University of Texas Library, for letters to M. D. Calvocoressi,
F. S. Flint, F. M. (Hueffer) Ford, Edward Garnett, Frank
Harris, T. L. Humberstone, John Lane, Hugh Lunn, Lillah
McCarthy, W. L. Mathews, Stanley Service, and Arthur
Waugh. I am especially obliged to Mrs. Mary M. Hirth, Lib-
rarian, Academic Center, for her helpfulness on many occasions.

University College Library, University of London, for a letter to
W. L. Mathews.

Antony Waley, for a letter to Stanley Hazell.

Beinecke Library, Yale University, for letters to Mrs. George Day
and Frank Vernon.

This volume also includes eight letters and excerpts from several
other letters by George Sturt, which are used with the kind permission of G. F. Wright and F. O. Meddows Taylor of the George Sturt
Memorial Fund, and of Dr. LaFayette Butler; and a letter by Frank
Harris, which is used with the permission of Arthur Leonard Ross.

I would like to thank several people who put themselves to special
trouble to help me and to provide information that in several
instances I could not have obtained otherwise.

Christine Bowkay, for information about Charles Young and
Lamley's.

Gladys Hooley, for information on Arthur Hooley and his friends.

Mary Kennerley, for information about the Bennett family and
the Bennett–Marriott–Kennerley circle.

Officials of King's School, Canterbury, for letting me use copies
of letters from Edward Garnett to Bennett, and Roger Medill
of King's School for obtaining those copies.

Thomas R. Roberts, for information about the Five Towns.

Martin Secker, for information about Frederic Chapman and
Grant Richards.

Officials of the Society of Authors, for information about George
Paston and other friends of Bennett's.

Frank Swinnerton, for information on several points.

K. Williams, Headmaster of Wolstanton County Gramma
School, for information about R. W. Wright and the Baddeleys.

The late Gregory Hill provided information about his father, Joseph
Hill, and some of Bennett's other early friends in London.

I am also very much obliged to several people for information
leading to the location of letters: Dudley Barker, Robert Black,
Constance Bramley, Patricia Butler of A. P. Watt & Son, Alan
Denson, Marion Dudley, Professor Alfred Havighurst, Geoffrey
Hellman, Professor Dan Laurence, Peter Little, Patrick McCarthy,
Professor Frank MacShane, Morris Marples, Professor Arthur
Mizener, Winifred A. Myers of Winifred A. Myers Ltd., Eric Salmon,
and the officials of Sotheby and Co.

Several other people very kindly provided information on a
variety of points: R. M. Alcock, Agnes Arrowsmith, Ruth Bennett,
H. G. A. Booth, George Conway Brown, Frances Hankey, Margaret
Hazell, Alice Head, John Hullah-Brown, Winifred F. E. C. Isaac,
Rosalie Kersey, Charles Lacy, E. D. Mackerness, Dr. L. L. Pownall,

Professor Robert Scholes, Mrs. Cyril Shingler, and Ian Willison of the British Museum.

Lastly I owe special thanks to Mlle. Claudie Clément for advice on Bennett's French and assistance in obtaining letters in France; and to my typist, Mrs. E. L. Bird, for her care in transcribing difficult material.

Material from uncollected writings of Arnold Bennett is reprinted by permission of A. P. Watt & Son. Passages from *The Journal of Arnold Bennett*, copyright 1932, 1933, 1960, 1961 by the Viking Press, Inc., are reprinted by permission of the Viking Press, Inc., and also of A. P. Watt & Son. Quotations from letters by H. G. Wells to Arnold Bennett (in *Arnold Bennett and H. G. Wells*, ed. Harris Wilson) are reprinted by permission of Rupert Hart-Davis. The quotation from a letter by Wells to the editors of the *Daily Express* is reprinted by permission of A. P. Watt & Son and the Estate of H. G. Wells. Passages from Frederick Marriott's memoir of Bennett are reprinted by permission of the University of Keele Library. Cedric Sharpe very kindly gave permission for a letter of his to be printed; and Margaret Hazell generously permitted some song lyrics of her father, Stanley Hazell, to be printed. Two letters of Ford Madox (Hueffer) Ford are quoted by permission of David Higham Associates.

The photograph of Arnold Bennett is used with the permission of the city of Stoke-on-Trent Libraries, Museums, and Information Committee. The photograph of George Sturt is used with the permission of H. G. A. Booth and the Willmer House Museum, Farnham. The facsimile of the title page of Volume II of the manuscript of *The Old Wives' Tale* is reproduced with the permission of the Lilly Library, Indiana University, Bloomington, Indiana.

INTRODUCTION

This second volume of Arnold Bennett's letters is the first of two volumes of general correspondence—letters to friends, acquaintances, business associates, and strangers. It represents about one-sixth of such letters known to have survived from the years up to 1915, and a much smaller fraction of the presumed number that Bennett wrote during this period. Editorial principles have remained the same as in the first volume. Only a very few letters that were thought desirable to print have had to be omitted, and none of them would have altered the character of the volume. Of those printed, the following are printed with deletions: Numbers 2, 117, 182, and 418. In no case is the deletion of any material consequence to the collection; the longest is of thirty-three words. All other marks of omission are Bennett's own. In a few letters to Bennett from George Sturt and Frank Harris, deletions have been made of irrelevant material. Minor mistakes on Bennett's part—an *of* for a *to*, a repeated word, an omitted mark of punctuation—are silently corrected. Anything that Bennett crosses out is ignored unless it seems worth showing. Omitted words and dates are placed within brackets; a question mark preceding them indicates editorial uncertainty. A bracketed question mark alone indicates an unreadable word. The addresses from which Bennett wrote are given in full the first time, and thereafter abbreviated; no distinction is made between printed and written addresses. Presumed addresses and signatures on letters reproduced from copies are placed within brackets. In a few instances the presumed address is a substitute for an obviously wrong letterhead address. Punctuation and the printing of titles of short stories, novels, and periodicals have been standardized. The spelling of a few names has been made consistent. Otherwise all letters are reproduced exactly and in their entirety.

At the head of each letter appears information on its owner (or source) and character. The following list identifies the owners or sources in full.

ARNOLD BENNETT (*Arnold Bennett*, by Reginald Pound)
AUTHOR (Journal of the Society of Authors)
AUTHOR HUNTING (*Author Hunting*, by Grant Richards)
BECKER (Miss O. D. Becker)
BEDFORD (County Record Office, Bedford)
BERG (Henry W. and Albert A. Berg Collection, New York
  Public Library)
BIRMINGHAM (Birmingham University Library)
BOLL, PENNA (Professor T. E. M. Boll and the University
  of Pennsylvania Library)
BROWN (Brown University Library)
BUTLER (Dr. LaFayette Butler)
CALIF (University of California Library, Los Angeles)
CHEESEMAN (Peter Cheeseman)
DAILY NEWS
DOCUMENTS (Documents and Autographs Ltd.)
EDINBURGH (Edinburgh University Library)
FALES, NYU (Fales Collection, New York University Library)
FH TO AB (*Frank Harris to Arnold Bennett, Fifty-Eight Letters*)
GIDE (*Correspondance André Gide—Arnold Bennett*, ed. Linette
  F. Brugmans)
HART-DAVIS (Sir Rupert Hart-Davis)
HARVARD (Houghton Library, Harvard University)
HELLMAN (Mrs. Hilda Hellman)
HERZOG (Paul M. Herzog)
IDDESLEIGH (Countess of Iddesleigh)
ILLINOIS (University of Illinois Library)
KANSAS (University of Kansas Library)
KEDDIE (James Keddie, Jr.)
KEELE (University of Keele Library)
LANE (Sir Allen Lane)
LEEDS (Brotherton Library, University of Leeds)
L'EFFORT
LILLY (Lilly Library, Indiana University)
MANCHESTER (University of Manchester Library)
MANCHESTER GUARDIAN
MANCHESTER PL (Central Library, Manchester Public Lib-
  raries)
MAYFIELD, SYRACUSE (Mayfield Library, Syracuse Uni-
  versity)

MERTON (Merton College Library, Oxford)

NATION

NEW AGE

NEW STATESMAN

PALL MALL GAZETTE

PROCEEDINGS, A.L.A. (*Proceedings of the American Library Association*)

RICKARD (Miss Dorothy Rickard)

ROSS (J.-P. B. Ross)

S.A. (Society of Authors)

S. BROWN (Sebastian Brown)

SPECTATOR

STAFFORDSHIRE SENTINEL

STOKE (Arnold Bennett Museum, Stoke-on-Trent)

SY (Edwin A. Sy)

TEXAS (University of Texas Library)

T.P.'S WEEKLY

TWENTY LETTERS TO JOSEPH CONRAD

U.C. (University College Library, University of London)

VICHY (Bibliothèque de la Ville de Vichy, Fonds Larbaud)

WALEY (Antony Waley)

WESTMINSTER GAZETTE

W. MORGAN (Mrs. Wainwright Morgan)

YALE (Beinecke Library, Yale University)

The character of the text printed from, when it is not a book or periodical, is given thus: A.D. (autograph draft), MS. (manuscript), T.C. (typed copy), T.C.C. (typed carbon copy), T.D. (typed draft), TR. (transcript), TS. (typescript). The transcripts were supplied by the owners or holders of original manuscripts.

All footnoted information for a letter is given in a single note that bears the same number as the letter itself. Some letters have no notes, and relevant information may be found in succeeding letters and notes. Since this volume covers some of the same years as Volume I, but is independent of it, I have not hesitated to repeat certain small pieces of footnote information. When that information concerns the composition and publication of Bennett's writings, fuller information is usually to be found in Volume I.

Of the many letters that might have appeared in this volume

B

but are lost or unknown to the editor, the most important group are those to Pauline Smith. Bennett and Miss Smith met in 1908, and they quickly became friends and remained friends until Bennett's death. He was her literary and spiritual godfather, and he wrote to her at least once a week and sometimes as often as three times a week for more than twenty years. Upon his instruction, all his letters were burnt. No letters in the present volume have the character that one may guess belonged to this correspondence. Very likely some of the letters to Harriet Cohen in later years, and also to Marguerite Bennett and Dorothy Cheston Bennett, are somewhat the same. Another loss is a group of forty or more letters to George Sturt; but luckily the major part of the correspondence survives, and apparently the more important part. There are unknown losses of letters to several intimate friends of the nineties and later. In the case of Mrs. H. H. Penrose, there was apparently a fairly considerable correspondence, but only two letters are known to survive. With Edwin A. Rickards, no correspondence is known to have been written aside from the letter that is reproduced in part here, and it is only a surmise that what may have been lost was as valuable as the most valuable letters to Sturt. With Frederick Marriott, the years when correspondence between him and Bennett would have been most interesting were those when the two men spent much of their time under the same roof; but for a decade afterwards there is no surviving letter, and the few letters from subsequent years give little hint of the affectionate friendship between them. In two or three instances of this last sort, letters of no particular value are printed here because they are the chief memorials of close friendships.

Another sort of loss is of letters to a multitude of strangers who wrote to Bennett about his books, most especially about his pocket philosophies. He was characteristically concerned to reply to such correspondents, and he wrote to one of them on a number of occasions. Very few of these letters have come to the attention of the editor. There are also known losses among letters written to Joseph Conrad, John Galsworthy, Frank Harris, George Moore, Eden Phillpotts, and Maurice Ravel, but none of these men were intimate friends except for Harris and Phillpotts. Perhaps less than a quarter of the letters to

Harris survive, but it seems to be the most valuable quarter. The very few known letters to Phillpotts are doubtless the remains of a considerable and interesting correspondence. The two men quarrelled around 1907, and Bennett's letters may have been destroyed.

Arnold Bennett was almost twenty-two years old when he left the Potteries. The date was 2 March 1889. 'I came to London', he said, in a recollection of the occasion some thirteen years later, 'with no definite ambition, and no immediate object save to escape from an intellectual and artistic environment which had long been excessively irksome to me. Some achievement in literature certainly lay in the abyss of my desires, but I allowed it to remain there, vague and almost unnoticed.' His word is hardly to be doubted, for he came to London to be a shorthand clerk at the law offices of Le Brasseur and Oakley in Lincoln's Inn, and though during the preceding six months he had written a weekly paragraph or two for the Staffordshire Knot (gratis), it was another two years before he was urged by friends into writing a piece for Tit-Bits, and another three and a half years before he began writing his first novel. Doubtless he had glimmerings of the sort of world he wanted to escape into, but London was not precisely it. Likewise he was aware of the developing energies of his mind, but he did not regard them as creative and literary energies until he had been away from home for half a dozen years and more. He was merely a clever law clerk with a taste for order, form, and art. One day the managing clerk of Le Brasseur and Oakley said to him: 'You'd no business to be here. You ought to be doing something else. If I find you here when I visit town next, I shall look on you as a d——d fool. Don't forget what I say.' The first three letters in the present volume come from the months immediately after his arrival in London, the fourth from a few months before he abandoned the law office to become assistant editor of Woman. By the latter date he was earning three-pence an hour in his spare time writing cheap fiction and articles for the popular press, and he was ready to write his first serious story. Some sort of literary future lay ahead—as journalist, editor, critic.

HART-DAVIS / MS. / 1   Pendennis
(*To Douglas Baddeley*)   197 Coldharbour Lane
                                         SW.
                                         8/5/89
Dear Douglas,

I believe you have some feminine cousins or some such relatives up here. If you think they are my style, for God's sake send me up a letter or letters of introduction.

I & another man are at this present time absolutely in despair because we cannot find any *decent* girls. I turn to you for help. Write quick.

                              Yours ever, Arnold Bennett

P.S. If you will come up any time, e.g. Whitsuntide, shall be pleased to have you for a guest, & show you a few things.   A. B.

HART-DAVIS / MS. / 2   10 Cowley St.
(*To Douglas Baddeley*)   Westminster
                                         S.W.
                                         9th July 1889
My dear Douglas,

I am always willing to give advice. Change your note paper for goodness gracious power's sake. I have generally given you credit for good taste but that B is something overpoweringly awful; in fact too d——d awful.

I was waiting for you to write to me, with my usual angel patience.

You seem to have got a notion that I am a martyr up here. I have occasional flashes of fun, & see a few people. I am a member of one tennis Club but have not begun to play & shan't do this season, first because the people can't play &

---

1. Douglas Baddeley (1870–1929) was a nephew of Rowland Frank Baddeley, law partner of Bennett's father. He was born in London, where his father, Frederick Gerrard Baddeley, was a book-keeper for a pottery firm. Very likely the family was originally from Staffordshire, and they returned there presently, and the father went into business in Stoke-on-Trent as a confectioner. The son eventually succeeded him in the business. The friendship between Bennett and the young Baddeley seems to have arisen solely because of the law connection, and it does not seem to have survived the three letters printed here.

Bennett's address in Coldharbour Lane antedates the first London address—in Hornsey—given in the Chronology in Vol. I. He was here for two or three months.

second because it is too far away from my new place. I am very much obliged to the Sherwins & shall be glad of their assistance in joining a *good* Club next season.

I am in a few months going to remove to the North of London, Highgate, Finsbury or Wood Green, when I shall furnish my own rooms & you may bet I *shall* furnish them, too. When that happy time comes, I expect to settle down for a year or so at least, & make a few friends who are neighbours. Of course I know scores of fellows as it is but they are all over London. The place I live in now is moderately horrid, but it is cheap, & only temporary. You see what I want to know is some *families* not odd members. Twig?

How goes the Photography? You will remember that when you do come to London it only means your Ry fare & odd meals & I shall have pleasure in showing you a thing or two that I fancy the Sherwins haven't seen, especially in the dinner & supper line.

I hear that Frank looks very bad. Is this really so? If so, why so?

I heard a rumour that you & the great Edward had had a row. You are a chump, that is all I have to say on the matter.

The man I live with is engaged in a draper's shop. He introduced me to a lot of his shopgirls. They are good enough to amuse one, you understand.

He gave a little party on Saturday, which I shirked by means of an arranged telegram from a man at the office. Eight of the girls came, & the chorus was, I am told, where is Mr. Bennett? The telegram was pinned up on a curtain so that all might see I had been called away (ahem). Like a fool I ran into a lot of these girls afterwards & I caught it. This is what comes of sending off lying telegrams to yourself. However I avoided the party; the males are awful cads, as you may suppose.

I have only met one decent girl since I came up. She can talk, play, sing, dance, & looks *imm*ense, both face & figure. She is engaged at the Alhambra, one of the coryphées. Perhaps it would be as well not to blab this all over the place. It might get me talked about. Not that I care a gooseberry. . . .

Has RFB got sails to his boat? How is he going on? Remember me to him & also to your most important uncle. I hope to have the pleasure of coming over to Rudyard in September.

I went to the Alexandra Palace on Saturday. It is a rotten place, but the Fireworks are about the finest in the world. Baldwin parachutes here, but it is not much to see. Just at first he drops with a swish, but soon slows off. We got the best table d'hôte dinner there that we have had up to the present. I am getting rather a connoisseur in table d'hôtes. I know a French place where they will give you a dinner of 5 courses & half a bottle of Claret for 1/6, but I have not had courage to try it yet. Perhaps I may do, when I am *very* hungry.

I generally come down to the office from Westminster by steamer. This is rather fine, don't you think.

I find that real London fellows are much more demonstrative in their expressions of regard to each other. For instance fellows will think nothing of putting 'With best love' at the end of a letter to another man. I don't, I simply put

Thine, Arnold Bennett

2. Bennett's flat in Cowley Street and another flat in Raphael Street, Knightsbridge, where he stayed briefly some eighteen months later, were the models for Richard Larch's quarters in *A Man from the North* (1898):

'. . . a long, rather low room, its length cut by the two windows which were Mrs. Rowbotham's particular pride; between the windows a table with a faded green cloth, and a small bed opposite; behind the door an artfully concealed washstand; the mantelpiece, painted mustard yellow, bore divers squat earthenware figures, and was surmounted by an oblong mirror framed in rosewood; over the mirror an illuminated text, "Trust in Jesus", and over the text an oleograph, in collision with the ceiling, entitled, "After the Battle of Culloden". The walls were decorated with a pattern of giant pink roses; and here and there hiding the roses, were hung photographs of persons in their Sunday clothes, and landscapes hand-painted in oil, depicting bridges, trees, water, and white sails in the distance.'

Bennett left Cowley Street later in the year to go to live at 46 Alexandria Road, Hornsey, where he remained until early in 1891.

The Sherwins are unidentified. Frank is presumably Bennett's younger brother Francis Clayton (1868–1938). Edward is very likely Edward Harry Beardmore (1869–1932), older brother of Frank Beardmore (1870–1936), who married one of Bennett's sisters. Edward was later the model for Edwin Clayhanger, and his nickname of 'Darry' became 'Denry' in *The Card* (for Edwin Henry Machin).

RFB is presumably Rowland Frank Baddeley himself (1862–1910), who was rather nearer to Arnold's age and to Douglas's than to Enoch Bennett's. His partnership with Enoch could not have been many years old. He eventually died in a boat accident on Rudyard Lake. He had two brothers besides Douglas's father, one who went out to New Zealand at an unknown date and another who lived in Newcastle-under-Lyme. It is possible that Bennett's initials refer to another

HART-DAVIS / MS. / 3
(*To Douglas Baddeley*)

10 Cowley Street
3rd August 1889

My dear Douglas,

I am just writing to you to while away time this morning. Half of our fellows are away on their holidays. It is pouring cats & dogs. My holidays do not start till the 10th September, rather a long time to wait, but then I shall have the satisfaction of going when most of the other beggars have come back.

We had rather a jolly time when Pater & Mr. Gould were up here. While they were cheering Gladstone at the National Liberal Club, I & a man named Hill—artist, went to the Empire to pass the time till 11 o'clock when we had an appointment at Gatti's for supper with Pa & Gould. The ballet came on about 10.45. I had seen it before, but was more struck than ever with its marvellous beauty. Hill had never been either to the Empire or the Alhambra, & he was so utterly flabbergasted at its magnificence that I could not drag him away till 11.30. When we got to Gatti's of course the other two had gone & we had to lade in alone. This same Hill is a spiffing fellow, one of those quietly humorous men who make you roar without saying anything. I went down to his place (he bosses an artschool at Blackheath) on Monday night & had a rare time. He has some rather decent pictures. He wants me to go & live next door to him but I don't think I shall. To begin with you reach the place by the South Eastern Railway. Now the trains of the South Eastern Ry are considered deadly prompt if they get in within half an hour of advertised time. This kind of thing is apt to be annoying at times. There are other disadvantages, but against them it must be said that there is a tennis club, splendid country round about, artistic & musical people to live with.

I came up to Charing Cross Station this morning. People are going away in trillions. Without any exaggeration the large space at the head of the station is mountainous with luggage,

---

member of the Baddeley clan and that Rowland Frank is the most important uncle.

The Times of 8 June 1889 advertised 'Baldwin's Drop from the Clouds, 6 p.m.' Baldwin shared the clouds over the Alexandra Palace with a good many other ballooning enthusiasts.

rising as high as 10 feet. At Smith's bookstall there were five men raking in money & pitching out papers as hard as they could go. There seem to be trains to Paris every few minutes. It made me think it was high time I was off somewhere, & that September was an unconscionably long time in coming. The promenade concerts are beginning this next week. They are rather jolly things. Just the same *style* as the Alhambra etc, but concerts instead of a variety show.

Have you heard of the new dodge in the South Eastern Night Ry Carriages? There is an electric lamp fixed about each person's head. If you want to read, you stick a penny in a slot & the lamp burns for half an hour. Then it goes out & you stick another penny in if you want to go on reading. This is about the cutest thing going.

If you could pay me the instalments due to me on the 26th August & 26th September (according to your date) both on the 26th August, I should be glad, but I don't want you to put yourself about to do it. If you can't very well, I shall manage if you let me have them *prompt* on the days when they fall due. I suppose these will be the last two payments. Let me have the £1 due on the 26th July as soon as you can.

I only mention it because I am depending on them partially for my holidays, for which I am just starting to save up. Perhaps you would send me a line saying whether you can let me have the last £2 by the end of August, or whether it will be easier for you to pay them separately prompt on the 26th Augt & 26th Sept. Give the July instalment to Frank as usual.

If you are going to Llandudno in September you may see a fleeting vision of

Your humble servant, Arnold Bennett

3. Ebenezer Gould was for a time editor of the *Staffordshire Knot*, which Enoch Bennett (1843–1902) was backing and which Arnold contributed to before he went to London. The paper was absorbed by the *Staffordshire Sentinel* in 1892, which paper has thus been able to claim Bennett as one of its contributors.

Joseph Hill (d. 1894) was a Burslem man and an old friend of Bennett's father. He founded and directed the Blackheath School of Art and was art director at Goldsmiths' College.

Llandudno was the annual holiday resort of the Bennett family in these years.

BERG / MS. / 4
(*To George Sturt*)   6 Victoria Grove
                              Chelsea S.W.
                              24. V. 93

Dear Sturt,
     Thanks for your letter & the book. A word in reference to the former.
     I can't boast that I discovered what purports to be the 'central idea' of the novel for myself. I first heard of Barrès in an article by Edward Delille in the *Fortnightly*. Next I read a criticism of this very book in the latest volume issued of Anatole France's *La Vie Littéraire*. Lastly there was a rather striking article in a recent *Scribner* on new ideas in French literature generally in which the name of Barrès was prominent.
     So when I actually bought the book I knew just what to expect.
     As I understand the thing, the author is at direct variance with Flaubert, Zola & Guy de Maupassant, who at all costs aim at an impartial, impersonal presentment of life. He prefers to take a character & describe events and men solely in relation to their effect on that character. In a word, his novel is all hero. He cares nothing for absolute perspective. He interests himself in nothing but what affects his hero. Everything is described through the hero's eyes, & consequently everything is intentionally coloured & distorted. He utterly despises the 'one-eyed apathetic insight of the camera'.
     You mention his symbolism. I believe that the presence of numerous symbols & analogies in the actual writing is only a minor & unimportant manifestation of the symbolist theory. The whole book in its main outlines is a congeries of symbols. Philippe stands for the introspective type, intensely conscious of the refinement of its own personality. 'L'Adversaire' for the Philistinism which always rouses such active disgust in the Philippe-type. Bérénice for the utterly non-selfconscious, amiable, wilful animal in which by force of contrast, the Philippe-type delights. Compare Heine & his wife, & number-less other examples. And so on.
     At least that is my idea.
     I have just finished Guy de Maupassant's *Bel Ami*. One of the most obviously truthful, British-matron-shocking, disgusting, attractive, overwhelmingly-powerful novels I ever read. It

would be a good antidote to *Le Jardin de Bérénice*. Would you like it? Whenever you have any ideas to impart on things generally, I should be extremely glad to hear from you.

Believe me,

Sincerely yours, Arnold Bennett

BERG / MS. / 5
(*To George Sturt*)

6 Victoria Grove
24 April 94

My dear Sturt,

What pleasure hast thou given me during the last few days! First your letter, then your essay 'Fruit-Blossom Time' & then your nameless novel.

First as to your letter. I can't refer to it since Ken has collared it; & he is at Ealing. And this is not a reply to it, but a mere preliminary, sport*ive*, irrespons*ive* miss*ive*. I forget all the details—a habit of mine; only a vague impression remains that I agreed with most of it. I showed it to *my* brother Frank who was staying with me last week, & whose opinion I respect for the same reason that inspires your veneration for *your* brother Frank's opinions (only *my* Frank is younger than me by a year). He had never heard of your analytic self till then, I think—except perhaps casually; he said: 'I should like to see that beggar' (excuse his irreverence, it is customary). He rather laughed at your adventures with *Bel-Ami* and wondered how you would take Zola's *Confession de Claude*. However, I am not going into arguments now.

4. George Sturt (1863–1927), wheelwright and novelist, was Bennett's closest literary friend for several years. He began his career as a schoolteacher and was a master at Farnham Grammar School for a few years, but he was temperamentally unfitted for the work. He resigned in 1884, the year of his father's death, under the conviction that 'man's only decent occupation was in handicraft', and he took over his father's shop. He retained an interest in education, and in later years was a Governor of the Bourne Schools, Farnham. He and Bennett met perhaps not many months before the date of the present letter. The acquaintance came about through a mutual friend, W. W. Kennerley (1870–1965), a Burslem youth who had followed Bennett to London and who was now living in Fulham. Bennett himself had moved from Hornsey to 6 Victoria (now Netherton) Grove, Chelsea, in the spring of 1891.

The article by Edward Delille on Maurice Barrès (1862–1923) appeared in the *Fortnightly* on 1 September 1891.

You are too lenient with my work. But I entirely disagree with your dicta as to the *class* of topical fantastic *conte*, of which you have seen my vile specimens. I fail to see how you reach the conclusion that when a man has compassed grammar & luminosity, he has pushed this form of art to its furthest limit. On the contrary, I think this particular form offers a field in which even a great genius might not be ashamed to labour. I believe there is a future for that kind of thing. Certainly Paris Journalists have carried it far beyond our insular dreams. As a weapon for amusingly 'lashing the age', or as a sort of Kodak (with more than the 'one-eyed apathetic insight of the camera') for picturing society in snapshots (horrid word!) I think it is unequalled. What a field for the exercise of the divine virtues of compression and selection. My dear friend, do try to modify your opinion, it will ease my mind so much.

In some way, we must be looking at it from wholly different points of view. If there are degrees of badness, I cannot understand how you come to put 'A Political Crisis' at the bottom of the three of mine you have seen. I thought it most decidedly the least bad. And Low, the editor of the *St. James's*, wrote me to say how he liked it—not that *that* affects the question. But enough of this.

I am in a fever to finish the novel. Ken made me turn it up when I was at part ten. I shall, Sturto volente, animadvert at length upon it at a future date. Now, I will only say that I like it very much: Its calm, unabashed realism charms me. You find fault with Maupassant for his wealth of irrelevant (à vous entendre) detail. Frankly, I think you would do well to follow him some way in this. I don't think his detail *is* irrelevant. You have read *Anna Karenina*? Look at the mountains of detail there! It is only when you have finished the book that you find that there is not a line without conscious, special purpose. No, I believe in detail. It is the only way to create atmospheres, unless you happen to be a supreme poet. With reference to the first chapter of your novel, I think I perceive the intention of it, but it scarcely seems to me to reach the mark. It reminds me of some of Schumann's compositions, where you can feel that the composer had a hell of a lot to unload (excuse) but couldn't get rid of it quite happily—result, mistiness of impression on the hearer. Also I think there is a *leetle* too much girding at respectability and decorousness, for thorough Platonic, Matthew Arnoldish urbanity.

The essay was purely delicious. And after reading its record of convoluted, trebly-intricate impressions I understood better the amused contempt with which the writer of such a thing *must* view the commonplace obviousnesses of the author of e.g. 'A First Night'. But in one or two places the stress of metaphor has been too much either for you or me. I didn't quite grasp, for instance

'And I thought to *walk* into the sunlight & at once *be present on the crest of the foam.*'

I must now close as they say; I am just going up town to get a copy of today's *Écho de Paris* before it is sold out. A new volume of that remarkable concern, the *Journal* of the Brothers Goncourt, commences serial issue therein today, & I am anticipating some aesthetic fun.

This is not a letter.

Sincerely yours, Arnold Bennett

5. Sturt's essay is unknown, and the novel seems never to have been completed. Ken is W. W. Kennerley.

Frank Sturt (1859–1930) kept a bookshop in Farnham. During this period he and his brother, Bennett and his brother, Kennerley, and Joseph Hill all belonged to a literary and artistic circle that held some of its meetings in the home of Bennett's friend and landlord Frederick Marriott. Marriott was born in Stoke-on-Trent in 1861, and in his youth in Shropshire he was a tile painter. He was now art master at Goldsmiths' College.

'A Political Crisis' cannot be positively identified. During 1892 and 1893 Bennett was beginning to make his way as a writer of light fiction, some of it of a political cast. He published several such pieces, unsigned, in the *St. James's Gazette*, which Sir Sidney Low (d. 1932) edited from 1888 to 1897. The only unsigned story in the *Gazette* during these months that can at all be said to deal with a political crisis is 'Strange Story', which appeared on 7 April 1894 and which displays the frivolous and easy style of Bennett's other writing of this time. It tells of a secretary of a Harley Street physician who would rather marry a politician than a doctor. She rearranges his prescriptions for several members of Parliament, and as a result some leaders of the Government receive soporifics and fail to attend a vital division on the amount of silk to be used on the uniforms of the Lords of the Treasury. She tells her favourite beau, the Leader of the Opposition, what she has done. He is horrified, and she has to settle for the doctor.

'A First Night' appeared in the *Sun*, a London evening newspaper, on 10 April 1894. The newspaper was first published in June 1893, and during the next year Bennett had at least seven signed stories in it, and possibly some other work.

The *Journal* of Edmund and Jules de Goncourt (1822–96; 1830–70) was the immediate inspiration for Bennett's own journal, which he began two years later.

BERG / MS. / 6
(*To George Sturt*)

6 Victoria Grove
10 Oct 94

My dear Sturt,

I gather from obscure hints of Mitchell (have you enjoined silence upon him?) that you are producing masterpieces in the way of short stories.

If you have anything that you care to print, & that you think might suit the paper whose literary department I have the honour to misdirect, I wish you would produce it. We want good short stories just now, & the literary public is also dying for a new sensation.

When shall we see you in the flesh?

Sincerely yours, E. A. Bennett

limit 2,700 words

BERG / MS. / 7
(*To George Sturt*)

6 Victoria Grove
28 Oct 94

My dear Sturt,

My thanks for your two letters especially the first. Yes, I think the first is quite unanswerable. But I should like to have a whole day with you to myself, to discuss the question of writing fiction.

'More continuous attention to reality' would be a fine thing. But you must remember that in order that a man sit down deliberately to be artistic, & be damned to every other consideration—he must have some inward assurance that there is a brilliant or at least pleasant conclusion to the dark tunnel which he is entering. (Rather mixed this, but with study you will unravel it.)

6. Mitchell Kennerley (1878–1950) was W. W. Kennerley's brother. He was associated with the publisher John Lane until 1900, and then went to America to become a publisher himself.

Bennett became Assistant Editor of *Woman* on 1 January 1894, having bought his way into the position with the help of his father. After about a month he took over the literary column, using the name 'Barbara' for his reviews. See Vol. I, pp. 13–16, for further detail.

I may say that I have no inward assurance that I could ever do anything more than mediocre viewed strictly as art—very mediocre.

On the other hand, I have a clear idea that by cultivating that 'lightness of touch' to which you refer, & exercising it upon the topicalities of the hour, I could turn out things which would be read with zest, & about which the man in the street would say to his friends 'Have you read so & so in the What-is-it?' I would sooner succeed as a caricaturist of passing follies than fail as a producer of 'documents humains'. And you know if it came to an alternative between a semi-luxurious competence, & fidelity to Art, Art would have my undiminished affection—and my back. It is glorious to sell all that you have & give it to Art, but I want my books & my pictures, & my stall at the theatre; & I want to be successful, & to mix with the fellows whose names shine in the foreheads of the magazines. Disgusting, isn't it? I think so sometimes.

I get no encouragement to be deliberately & exclusively artistic—except perhaps from you & Ken sometimes. Undoubtedly the best thing I have yet done has been refused by half the Editors in London. One of them said 'Very pretty, but not quite what we want.' But take a thing like the last story I sent you. I do it easily, I like doing it, I like to think I have done it. I show it to my Editor. He is enchanted. It is printed, & people write to the office to express their pleasure on reading it. Two novelists who called in congratulated the Editor on it. Even the *Pall Mall Gazette* quoted it. Am I to give up that line of business? Ought I? Art is not everything—although I once nearly thought so.

Of course I want to 'observe', & get these things as true as I can.

I started a novel the beginning of this month—not a conscientious novel, now, but a glittering, topical, meretricious business. But happening to mention one day to my Editor that I thought 'Occult' stories would go down well just now, & that I had a lot of material for them in hand, I was a little surprised to see him jump at the suggestion, & offer to buy the serial rights of eight stories at once. So, deeming eight stories sold in advance to be better than a novel perhaps on my hands, I have shelved the latter for a time, & am to be seen daily reading a vast tome *Mystères des Sciences Occultes*. I tremble to consider the bad art which will be compressed into those stories!

It is very good of you to write to me as you do; & if I may, I should like to ask you about some verses I am writing for music. Ken says you are learned in that topic. Sharpe, our pianistic genius, commissioned me to write him words for an album of six songs. I have done three & he is very pleased with them. But I should like your ideas on them—as verses for music. I have no fair copies by me, but I will send them down shortly, unless you forbid.

Kindest regards to the indigestion. The doctor is battling with mine.

Sincerely yours, E. A. Bennett

7. Bennett's best story was 'A Letter Home', which he wrote in 1893. It was a piece of naturalism, and had very little in common with most of his other early work, and it was the only one of his early stories that he chose to reprint in his first collection of stories, *Tales of the Five Towns*, in 1905. The more favourably received story was probably 'My First Book', in which a female novelist tells of the difficulties that followed upon her drawing a society queen from life. It appeared in *Woman* on 3 October 1894 under the pseudonym 'Sarah Volatile'. Bennett's editor was Fitzroy Gardner (1856–1936), who later deserted journalism for the theatre.

The abortive novel preceded the writing of *A Man from the North*, Bennett's first completed novel, by six months. The 'Strange Stories of the Occult' appeared in *Woman* from 9 January to 10 April 1895.

Herbert Sharpe (1861–1925), a professor at the Royal Academy of Music, was the most accomplished musician among Bennett's friends in the nineties. He was born in Halifax, Yorkshire. He and Frederick Marriott (see p. 10 n.) became acquainted when they were both at school in London, and they together began the 'musical evenings', meeting alternately at their two homes. His album of songs was apparently not published. Bennett gave a good deal of time to writing poetry for the next twelve years, and with very little success. One of his lyrics of this time, intended to be set to music, was published in *Woman* on 30 December 1896:

The Son's Lament

How shall I mourn thee,
Mother of mine?
Never I knew thee
Till thou wert gone!
Frail figure sitting in the lamplight,
Black hair and grey,
Worn fingers knitting in the lamplight,
Kind eyes and gay.
Great heart, good night!

C

BERG / MS. / 8
(*To George Sturt*)

6 Victoria Grove
27 Nov 94

My dear Sturt,
    Sincere thanksgiving for your too forbearing criticism, with
which I find myself able to agree, except as to 'Shimmer'. I
am of those whose faces are set against the persistent attempt
to introduce a quantitative scansion—if that term will serve.
The fetters of rhyme, accent, caesura, feet &c are already
heavier than I can bear.
    Seriously, I ought not to show my verse to anyone. 'Hunding'
was only my third attempt at serious verse. I have done some

How shall I mourn thee,
Mother of mine?
Never I knew thee
Till thou wert gone!
Stern wert thou, spoiling not thy children,
Quick to reprove;
Bold wert thou, fighting for thy children,
Armoured with love!

Sleep shall enwrap thee,
Mother of mine?
Ah, but I know thee,
Now thou art gone!
Brave heart, sleep well!

This was an improvement over a prize poem that he composed in May 1881
when he was a student at the Burslem Endowed School:

Courage! It is a glorious thing
To all who do possess it,
It makes the faintest heart to sing
With hope, and then, to bless it.

Courage gives the soldier hope
As he stands on the battle-field,
Courage gives him power to cope
With every sword and shield.

Look at that helpless burning ship
Floating helplessly on the sea;
But courage keeps up the manly hearts,
As they struggle manfully.

The ancient bards in the olden days
Had always a song on courage,
And present poets in modern lays
Have always a word for courage.

light verse which has been well received of the elect—for its funniness. Only Calverley and Praed bothered about strict technique in light verse. Not me! Although my most successful effort in versified humour was a correctly constructed sonnet. Excuse this stuff, & remember that I am deeply obliged to you. I know no one else who would have done as much for me so well.

I see no reason why I should not take your story as it stands. But I will if you please, leave myself the refusal of it. With regard to purely literary matters I accept or reject everything that comes to our paper absolutely at my own discretion. But in the case of a story like yours, which is over the heads of the foolish, amiable readers of our 'bright little paper', but which I should like, for the good of literature & the credit of *Woman*, to have in the paper, I should prefer to throw the responsibility for the acceptance on my Editor's shoulders. I can doubtless, by watching my opportunity, do this in the early months of next year, and I request you to allow me to do so.

You may perhaps be glad to hear that I have already sold ten stories to appear in the first quarter of 1895, one in the *Yellow Book*. I should like you to see this one; the others have no importance whatever, except fiscal.

Kind regards to the frère aîné & his wife.

Sincerely yours, E. A. Bennett

At last I am studying conversational French. 2/6 for 2 hours.

E. A. B.

RICKARD / MS. / 9
(*To John Rickard*)

6 Victoria Grove
27 iii 95

My dear Rickard,

I am very sorry to hear from Ken about your child's death, & I am just writing to express my sympathy for you & Mrs.

---

8. Charles Stuart Calverly (1831–84) and Winthrop Mackworth Praed (1802–1839) distinguished themselves in the legal profession but are best remembered for their humorous verse.

Sturt's story, 'A Courting Umbrella', appeared in *Woman* on 1 May 1895.

Rickard. I hope the other children will get on all right. Ken seems to think you are afraid for them.

I hope we shall soon be seeing you.

Kind regards to Mrs. Rickard & yourself.

Sincerely yours, E. A. Bennett

BERG / MS. / 10
(*To George Sturt*)

6 Victoria Grove
30.iv.95

My dear Sturt,

I send you by book post a copy of our special literary number with your special literary story in it. Your fatherly eye will note one or two minute alterations in the tale. And further, sundry re-arrangements of the paragraphs. As to this latter, your production came out at 38½ inches, & I was obliged to get it down to 37, our extreme, unstretchable limit.

You might animadvert to me upon my book reviews & 'Fiction of the Future'.

Kindly regards to Frank & spouse.

Yours ever, E. A. Bennett

Cheque will come for the story in the slow course of a few weeks.

BERG / MS. / 11
(*To George Sturt*)

6 Victoria Grove
10.5.95

My dear Sturt,

Just at this moment I am annoyed because I want to be disgusted and can't. You may know that Mrs Humphry Ward is one of my literary bugbears. I have never really read any of

9. John Rickard (1863–1960) was another member of the Bennett–Marriott circle. He was a staff clerk in the old Board of Education, Whitehall, where W. W. Kennerley was also employed. His daughter, Dorothy Rickard, describes him as a great reader and an amateur botanist and archaeologist.

10. In 'Fiction of the Future, A Prophetic Fantasia', 1 May 1895, Sarah Volatile indulged in a facetious forecast of the ups and downs of novels of sex, scandal, and sociology over the next decades. Sturt's 'A Courting Umbrella' was a small example of the first sort of writing.

her much-lauded works, but from casual glances into one or two of them & the perusal of copious reviews, I have felt instinctively that she was No Good. A new book of hers, a short one, *The Story of Bessie Costrell*, will appear in three months time & I have been promising myself the pleasure of scalping the woman. The tale runs through *Cornhill* in three instalments & in order that my onslaught might appear immediately after publication of the book, contemporaneously with the fulsome flatteries which the daily press is certain to shake out, I determined to read the thing carefully in serial form, and prepare a reasoned exposé. I have just returned from the Free Library.

The mischief is, I find the first instalment damn well done. It is beautifully arranged and selected. The writing, without being great, is dignified and decent; & it is perfectly clear that she knows what she is talking about, to wit, village life. She makes a healthy sort of second to Hardy himself—the devil take her!—though of course there is an impassable gulf between them. I should like you just to read the opening chapters: they combine so well artistic workmanship with the essential qualities of a popular serial. No mistake, she is a real artist. At which fact, taken separately, I rejoice. But one does not part easily or painlessly with the conviction of half a lifetime. I have always said that Mrs Humphry Ward never had done, never could & never would do, anything decent.

Thanks for your idea, but more thanks for your two letters, which have given me the sort of pleasure one says nothing about. I had the germ of the idea, already, floating about my novel, but I think you may have enabled me to enlarge it. I imagine that you will be surprised to hear I have finished the sixth Chapter of that novel. I have (wisely) given up the idea of the 'cubits' (did I give you the outline of my original scheme?); it would have been too much for my unskilled hand; my principal figure is now shorn of his extra inches, & is much more manageable. So far as I can judge now, there will be about eighteen chapters altogether; but I find I can't tell beforehand how much I'm going to write about a particular scene. I want to write the seventh chapter, completing the first division of the book, tomorrow, but am doubtful whether I shall. After I've done it all—I am serenely certain, now, that I *shall* finish the thing—I feel sure I shall write it all over again. Has it ever struck you—of course it has—that often the difference between good work & merely feeble drivel, is simply a matter of elaboration, that & nothing else? I could give some interesting instances, but am too idle.

Every Day's News, the last Pseudonym, contains this passage:—

'Literature was to him a passion & a torment. He was miserable when he did not write . . . and *he was miserable when he did*. Of the two miseries he naturally & constantly preferred the latter; but he sometimes said that he envied the people—without quite believing in them, or at least in the quality of their work—who affirm that merely to write is a perennial joy, who *profess to be carried away by their imagination*, to lose themselves in their own conceits. He took care always to keep his imagination well in hand; he was a despot in such matter, *with little weakness for his own offspring*, but the *friction*, the *effort of the whole business* was great.'

Pardon my underlinings. The passage describes my condition very well indeed, & I am more thankful than I can say to find someone else like me. For the author of this book evidently knows his character intimately; & as he makes him do something decent in the writing line, I am more happy still. I shall give the book a damn good notice.

My book reviews find considerable favour. The eclectic Chapman has much encouraged me by the statement that he reads no criticism which he likes better. I myself, candidly, think they are good & distinguished by wide sympathy! Kennerley pooh poohs them *en bloc*. He will have none of them. But then Kennerley always does slate anything of mine that I fancy. I comfort myself with the thought that he despised Turgenev's *Rudin*. The man that will say, on being told that *On the Eve* is a better novel than *Rudin*,

'I should hope it was!'

will say anything.

(I am tempted, by the way, to say that *On the Eve* is the finest novel I have ever read. I must lend it you. Its subtlety and restraint prevent it from ever being really popular.)

I wrote a topical story for the *St. James's* last week, & got slated all round for it. Kennerley said it merely bored him; Chapman was 'disgusted', but he added his opinion that only

E. A. Bennett could have done it. And yet the *St. James's* put it on their placards, an honour not given to a story by the daily press once in a twelve month. What the devil is a fellow to do? Am I to sit still & see other fellows pocketing two guineas apiece for stories which I can do better myself? Not me! If anyone imagines my sole aim is art for art's sake, they are cruelly deceived. An income sufficient to satisfy my naturally extravagant tastes, first, and then as much art as I know how to produce, but not till then.

Well, here's luck to your novel!

Read *Bessie Costrell* and let me know what you think.

Sincerely yours, E. A. Bennett

BUTLER / MS. / 12
(*From George Sturt*)　　　　　Lower Bourne
　　　　　　　　　　　　　　　[Farnham, Surrey]
　　　　　　　　　　　　　　　Sunday afternoon. 16.vi.95

My dear Bennett,

　. . . I am filled with penitence, (not to mention tears) for sending with the suggestion that you were no artist, salves to heal the sore that it might have caused. Bravo! my Stoic! who will have his powders without jam. I will not forget. . . . But,

11. In his review of *The Story of Bessie Costrell* in *Woman*, 3 July 1895, Bennett said of Mrs. Humphry Ward (1851–1920): 'Mrs. Ward is not the greatest novelist we have—her reputation is still much in advance of her merits—but she is an artist who takes herself seriously, and who esteems the artist's dignity above all other considerations.' The subject of popular literature continued to interest Bennett, and in *Fame and Fiction* (1901) he gave the same serious attention to several popular novelists that he gave to Ivan Turgenev (1818–83) and George Gissing.

Bennett began writing *A Man from the North* in mid-April 1895. Some years later he let the hero of his comic novel *A Great Man* write a story called 'A Question of Cubits', in which a brilliant youth is denied a career on the stage and the love of women because he is six feet eight inches tall.

Every Day's News, by C. E. Francis, was one of a series of novels published under pseudonyms by the firm of T. Fisher Unwin. Bennett reviewed it on 22 May 1895.

Frederic Chapman was the first manager of the publisher John Lane. In *John Lane and the Nineties*, his associate, James Lewis May, says of him: 'He had an immense knowledge of books and he had a true scholar's mind.' He edited the works of Anatole France in an edition issued by Lane in 1908, and he also did some reviewing of books.

The *St. James's* story cannot be positively identified. Apart from the date of publication, the most likely candidate is 'A Little Deal in Kaffirs', which appeared in the issue of 27 April 1895.

truly, what a fatalist you are. 'I exist as I am: that is enough.' One might add; 'that is fortunate.' The first temptation, seeing you with your nose so high in air, was to answer you with one word (on a postcard):—a word containing three vowels, and, for consonants, two ss, an h; and an l.

Still, there are questions that might be asked. For instance; Have you always existed as you are; and do you always mean to? Have you never been guilty of *trying* for anything? or never encouraged by achieving what you seemed to try for? It is absurd of the fatalist to try; for however discontented he may be, endeavour to change the unchangeable is quite illogical. But perhaps the fatalist, existing as he is, is resigned to being absurd and illogical; and by dint of facing the fact, contrives to be contentedly discontented. You must (if you are made that way!) forgive my clumsy expression. To 'contrive' is a verb not likely to be found in the fatalist dictionary; implying, as it does, that effort may have some existence apart from fate.

I suppose that, by the fatalist doctrine, Artists are born, not made? 'If I am an Artist, well. If not, well.' Evidently you have no choice, and are to be congratulated! Yet this puzzles me; that Art, as I have heard you say, is a matter of selection, which, I believe, is a kind of Latin for choice. Perhaps you can unravel this difficulty?

I used to have some doting notion, that you exercised choice (and exercised it rather well) in phrasing and arranging your stories: and further, that there were in all the world only some two or three books claiming to have been written in any other way; the Bible being the chief of these. Pray let us know what deity inspires you; and further, pray consider whether you do well to take the guineas for his work. Yet of course you will answer, that you have no choice but to take them. . . . Lucky man!

To be plain: all that about 'existing as I am' strikes me as pure rot. It is mere tautology. You might as well link arms with Jehovah, boasting 'I am that I am'. Concerning which phrase, and the mis-reading of it in church, there is a story.

And the indifference which you assume, along with most modern men (I have tried for it myself; and I suppose Oscar tried it) begins to look to me like a false position. As training, and as a means to an end, its value is immense. It checks hysteria, and damns cheap sentiment. But as a final position, it isn't easy to see how any artist can maintain it. To exercise choice, an artist must chuck away indifference. Let the philistines keep it to themselves.

And now, to mend the meaning of my former letter: In the choice of words and sentences, you are an Artist. It is admitted gladly. But as yet, either you show (to my mind) too little discrimination in the choice of subject; or else, you limit yourself to a class of subjects so narrow as to leave you practically no choice at all. It is my own opinion—strengthening every day —that subjects demand as much care in selection as do the words and paragraphs with which they are set forth. And for this selection, you have to abandon indifference, and see to it that your likes and dislikes are in good order.

But it should be allowed that you have a facility by which I am never tempted. The mere physical act of writing is often a nuisance to me. I think I could hardly stand writing of things that I cared for not at all. In this category are the subjects you generally take. It is a standing puzzle to me that you are not bored to death with them, long before you get to the act of writing.

I fear that somewhere I shall have to write a book on this subject, which has much intermittent attraction for me. In that case, Heaven help me, and inspire me with the fated words! Otherwise, they will exist as they are—unwritten. There appears to be a large heap of stuff worth setting down. But before beginning to preach, I want to practise a bit.

There is that novel of mine. The subject is not so well chosen as at first appeared. In fact, at times it stinks in my nostrils. At other times, it seems very well; and always, good enough for practising on. Kennerley managed to convince me that much practice is still needed to make my work of any value. Do you not rejoice to hear that he has been jumping on me, as well as on yourself?

But now we are waiting for your novel. You make me envious, with accounts of so many more chapters done each time you write to me. I am wanting to talk of mine with someone, but yet dare not do it, for fear of taking away my interest in it once for all.

With other work there is no real success to be recorded. My next story for *Woman* has yet to be discovered; and then written! Verily, this does seem to depend upon Fate. So to some extent did that of the 'Umbrella'. My satisfaction in that is considerably damped by the consciousness that it was more of a fluke than a work of skill.

I shall be glad of a letter.

Yours, George Sturt

BERG / MS. / 13
(*To George Sturt*)

6 Victoria Grove
20 July 95

My dear Sturt,

I send you a page-proof copy of my story in the new *Yellow Book*, which Mitchell has kindly furnished me with for your convenience. I shall be glad to have your notions about it. The only people whose views on it really interest me artistically are yourself & Fred Chapman. I have had Chapman's.

I owe you a letter & I have plenty to say to you, but am not in the humour for writing.

Thine, E. A. B.

The novel is proceeding.

BERG / MS. / 14
(*To George Sturt*)

6 Victoria Grove
29 Oct 95

My dear Sturt,

I was sorry to hear last night from Ken that both you & Frank have been 'laid aside'. I hope you are better, & *I hope*

---

12. Sturt's novel was a new undertaking. It ultimately bore the title *A Year's Exile*. No new story of his for *Woman* is known.

13. 'A Letter Home' appeared in John Lane's *The Yellow Book* in July 1895. In his review of the volume in *Woman*, Bennett said that the collection was hardly brilliant. He singled out Henry James's story, 'The Next Time', for special praise, and said nothing of Enoch Arnold Bennett's contribution.

Sturt wrote to Bennett about the story: 'It *is* good. And its goodness is at least

you are getting on with that novel. I always ask Ken how that
lazy devil Sturt is getting on with his work & he always replies
with a wash-my-hands-of-it-air: 'Oh I don't know (here he
glances casually at the ceiling), he hasn't been doing much at
it lately.' I suppose I must have had these replies for four or
five months now. I grow sicker & sicker & more sick, thinking
upon your damned indifference—idleness is another word, a
word I use to Ken. I know you have unsatisfactory health, &
vaguely I know that your 'foreman', or some other legendary
griffin with claws worries you, but I fail to rid myself of the
idea that what you want is simple steam.

'Yes' says Ken. 'But he's not fond of work like you.' Now I
am not industrious. I am aware that some people regard me
as both industrious & methodical; in so doing they offer me
a deadly insult. I grind my teeth with rage at the notion that
individuals go through life regarding me as industrious &
methodical. It is a curious paradox: I try to be both, &
miserably fail, & feel disgusted, & yet if I succeeded I should
be just as disgusted.

Therefore (a non sequitur, I am afraid) it is no excuse that
you are not fond of work.

Anyone whose opinion demands respect, could tell from a
very few pages of your stuff that you are an artist—a man
that can *see* beautifully, & only wants practice to enable him
to say beautifully what he sees beautifully. Who knows that
better than yourself? Then why, in Stevenson's name, don't
you set about it, & either do something or kill yourself. I was
reading that 'Envoi' of Kipling's last night, that we read
together one day, & I began to think about you, & I concluded:
Either let him show me something long & good, or let him go
to the devil.

When I sat down to write I really had no intention of making
a row with you. Anyhow it's entirely your fault, & I don't
care. So there!

I was in a bad way last week; I suddenly came to an un-

a partial vindication of the stuff I have before found fault with—the potboilers
which up till now you have palmed off upon me as specimens of your work. They
have at any rate made your English fluent, and plastic in readiness for when you
had got something really worth saying.'

suspected wide ditch in my novel, & remained on the wrong side for several days, indeed till this afternoon, when the right plank suddenly offered itself. I shall shift something tonight, I think. Did I tell you that I had begun to write it entirely afresh. I was fully intending to finish it by Xmas, but can't possibly do so now. And if I don't, what does it matter. As it's my first, I may as well spend myself on it. I *know* that the main idea is good, & I *know* that certain scenes are good, but whether the whole will hang together & *be* a whole—you know—I am desperately uncertain.

I have been searching for titles; I've captured three. In doing so, I got others, quite apropos of no novel at all. The finest, intended for a novel pornographic, was *A Lifter of Petticoats*. Do you not think this lovely?

I was telling Marriott of it.

'Marriott,' I said, 'I've got a new title for *Don Juan* or something of that sort—'

'Oh!' he interrupted in a flash, '*The Pink Pintle*'!

He certainly is a ripe genius at devising comic, alliterative titles.

I have less time than ever now for my own work, as I have been offered & have accepted the post of dramatic critic on *Woman*. As often as not this means 2 nights a week, subsequent fatigue next days, & the labour of doing the criticisms. I'm sure a man that has to spend half his time at an office, & in addition to review some 25 novels a month, & all new plays of any West End importance, can't be expected to do as much as a man who gives an occasional 3 hours to business, & pleases himself as if he were an orficer.

Pinero's new play is really fine, indisputably better than the *2nd Mrs. T.* & *Mrs. Ebbsmith*. Even Shaw bent his knees before it. It suffers from bad, in some cases atrocious, acting. The great theatrical event of the season is the first night of *Trilby* tomorrow at the Haymarket. It is causing an immense stir, & the advance booking has wiped out all previous records. But it cannot fail to be awful rot, of course.

Enough of this,

Yours ever, E. A. Bennett

I have just read Marie Corelli's new book—my first of hers. I can now understand both her popularity & the critics' contempt.

BERG / MS. / 15
(*To George Sturt*)

                                        6 Victoria Grove
                                          11 Nov 95

My dear Sturt,
    Your letter came exactly at the moment when I wanted something. I have just returned from 'putting the paper to bed', & don't reckon to work seriously on Monday nights; I was trying to bring myself to write a col. of reviews in advance so as to leave the week clearer for the novel. After I have written this, I shall no doubt get through the col. smoothly enough; the atmosphere will have been created.
    My dear *Globe* contributor, I find a novel the damnedest, nerve shattering experience as ever was. Nothing but my strong aversion to being beaten by anything on God's earth that I set myself out to whip, prevents me from throwing up

14. The influence of Robert Louis Stevenson (1850–94) upon Bennett was fairly considerable, and elements of his style can be seen especially in *Leonora* (1903) and as late as *The Pretty Lady* (1918), particularly in the closing passage. Rudyard Kipling (1865–1936) was another surprising influence. The last stanza of his *Envoi* reads:

> The Lord knows what we may find, dear lass,
> And The Deuce knows what we may do—
> But we're back once more on the old trail,
>   our own trail, the out trail,
> We're down, hull down on the Long Trail
>   —the trail that is always new.

Bennett's working title for *A Man from the North* came down to *In the Shadow*. Frederick Marriott (see page 10 n.) was probably the person chiefly responsible for Bennett's deciding to write a serious novel. It was his friends, Bennett says in *The Truth About an Author*, who made him a writer.
    The Benefit of the Doubt, the new play by Sir Arthur Wing Pinero (1855–1934), opened at the Comedy Theatre on 16 October 1895. *The Notorious Mrs. Ebbsmith* was produced earlier in the year, and *The Second Mrs. Tanqueray* in 1893. George Bernard Shaw (1856–1950) said in the *Saturday Review* that *The Benefit of the Doubt* was worth more than the other two plays 'rolled into one and multiplied by ten'. *Trilby*, adapted from George Du Maurier's novel, ran for almost a year.
    Marie Corelli (1855–1924) published one of her most successful novels, *Sorrows of Satan*, in October 1895.

the present one. And this, mind you, in spite of the facts that I have all my material in hand, & the whole thing mapped out in detail, & that I am not short of inspiration—as I believe they call it! It is the *arrangement* that kills one, the mere arrangement of 'sensation & event' which—in a manner o' speaking, one knows by heart. Conversations are the very devil to me—at present; I eschew them all I can, & when I can't avoid jaw, Keep it short & *très select*. This is à la de Maupassant, who could, however, do conversations *à merveille*, when he felt that way. I have developed so strangely this last three years—my first attempt at fiction was made exactly 2½ years ago—that I don't know what may happen in the future, but at present I do 'sensations' best, leaving events alone. With regard to the impression abroad that pages undiversified by dialogue are apt to be dull, I am persuaded that the dullness, apparent dullness, can be done away with by a judicious arrangement of paragraphs. The effect of a separate line of 4 or 5 words in the middle of two longish paragraphs must be seen to be believed. The French know this—they taught it me. Probably you are aware of it, but unless you have consciously meditated upon it, I venture to think that you have not grasped (excuse my cheek) the tremendous effect, even on an educated & trained reader, of paragraph arrangement.

Of course a determined attempt to write for the eye (the eye which reads a whole page in one flash, as it were—am I clear?) influences materially the details of style which are meant to appeal to the intellect only. If you have a long paragraph, you can't offhandedly cut it in two, or shove a short line into the middle of it. You must deliberately, from the beginning of the par., work up to the short line, or the short par. (If as is probable, you have thought out all this for yourself, kindly excuse my exuberance, but I am interested in the little matter.)

In my new vol. of the Edinburgh Stevenson, there is a luminous essay, reprinted for the first time from a *Fortnightly Review* of 1881, on 'Some technical elements of style in literature'. You must read it when you come up; it is profoundly interesting to a craftsman. He deals chiefly with the sweet uses of alliteration—subtle, concealed alliteration of course—& he damn well knows what he is talking about. The essential 'stylistic' (his word) differences between prose & verse are also finely set out. I read the thing last night in bed—after an evening at Chapman's—& was made to think thereby.

(I don't know whether you have seen any of Chapman's verse, but he is an accomplished artist—unlikely to express himself through constant fiscal troubles connected with a father who has failed in some way & has to be kept.)

Curious: My style has altered (improved, I trust) so much during the progress of this bally novel, that one reason for writing the whole thing again, is the difference between the earlier & later portions. I feel more sure than ever I did in my life before, that I can *write* in time, & 'make people care', too, as Hy. James says—though praps only a few people. Still, to have made fellow artists care—that is the thing! That is what will give ultimate peace of mind. Do you ever suddenly stand still and ponder: 'Suppose, after all, I am an artist, rather a fine one! But it can't be true. What am *I* that *I* should be an artist? Every dabbler thinks he is, — till he learns better. And yet, and yet. . . .'

I have never been in love (wish to God I had, when I am struggling with a love scene!) but I imagine that the joy of the artist when he first *knows* that he is an artist, is similar to the joy of the lover when he first knows that he is in love & loved; & the thought of both, after the first scepticism has gone, is: 'What the hades have I done to deserve this ineffable happiness?'

I have boasted to at least one person (another of my indiscretions) that I know I am an artist. I know no such thing. When I have read my first novel in print, I think I shall know.

Yes, I am well aware that this farrago, coming from a youthful person who has nothing to show, nothing done, is absurdly self-conscious & egotistic. But my dear villager, one writes to please oneself, after all, not to please the correspondent addressed. Is not this a great truth?

Apropos des bottes, have you got Roget's *Thesaurus* of English words & phrases? It is the most wonderful machine for getting at words that you know but can't think of at the moment, that I have encountered. Even when you have only an adumbrated notion of the idea itself, this precious volume will help you to define it, & end up by giving you the word to describe the idea it has itself defined. I bought it about a year ago, & wonder now how I ever did without it. If I had to choose between Shakespeare & Roget, I would let Billy go, upon my word.

I would advise you not to read my dramatic criticisms—yet. I am feeling my feet, & incidentally coming to the conclusion that although I can tell a good play from a bad one with some certainty, I know nothing whatever about acting. Besides this work is not paid well enough, & I have too many distractions, to tempt me to let myself go on it. Further, my criticisms are not seldom disingenuous. For sufficiently weighty reasons I praised *Trilby* to the skies though privately I am convinced that it is a damn silly worthless namby pamby piece of putrid rot.

(By the way, the MS. of *Trilby* can now be viewed in Bond Street, in a glass case, on payment of 1/–!! Such is the force of the *Trilby* boom.)

Tree was so enchanted with my notice of *Trilby* that he asked me to write a couple of short articles describing *Trilby* as seen by a deaf man & as heard by a blind man, & I shared the royal box with my editor's wife, at a second witnessing of the play. I was surprised & deeply gratified, when I came to write the articles, at the ease with which I could produce in myself the illusion of being blind & being deaf. The actual articles were, however, rot; I had no time to do them for one thing, & deliberately did them badly, for another. My editor is very pleased with them. Behold then the temptations which beset my path!

You might, if you care, read my criticism of Hardy's new novel in Wednesday next's *Woman*—though it contains little actual criticism, I imagine it to give a sort of impression of the book.

I am very sorry about the bankrupt & your £100. That sort of thing dries up the fountains quicker than anything.

I haven't yet seen the *Globe*. The *W.G.* article was competent journalism—all you intended it to be, I guess. I am told that the *Globe* article is 'delicious'.

I must return to technics: I believe in short chapters, 2,000 to 3,000 words, & in making, as a rule, each chapter a complete scene, & detached—of course there are exceptions. I learnt this from the brothers de Goncourt. I must get you to read their *Renée Mauperin*. To study the principles of its construction is both 'entertaining & instructive'.

My favourite masters & models: 1. Turgenev, a royal first (you must read *On the Eve* — *flawless* I tell you. Bring back such books of mine as you have; I have others you *must* read). 2. de Maupassant. 3. de Goncourts. 4. George Moore—the great author who can neither write nor spell!

Stevenson only helps me in minute details of style.

Excuse prolixity,

Yours ever, Arnold Bennett

15. Contributions to the *Globe* and *Westminster Gazette* were usually anonymous and nothing of Sturt's could be found.

Guy de Maupassant (1850–93) was one of the 'sweet influences' under whom Bennett said he wrote *A Man from the North*. The others were the Goncourt brothers, Turgenev, and Flaubert. Of Henry James (1843–1916) Bennett remarked in his Journal a few months later: 'His mere ingenuity, not only in construction, but in expression, is becoming tedious, though one cannot but admire.' Bennett's first attempts at fiction preceded the writing of 'A Letter Home' in the summer of 1893. See Vol. I, pp. 10–12.

In his first review of *Trilby*, in which Sir Herbert Beerbohm Tree (1853–1917) played Svengali, Bennett wrote: 'He [the dramatist, Paul Potter] has reduced the story to its most simple form; every dramatic inessential has been gently but firmly removed, and the result is a concise and complete drama which begins at the beginning and runs on to a logical end without in any serious way interfering with the leading facts of Mr. Du Maurier's tale. And as for Mr. Du Maurier's long, loving descriptions of studio life, and his innumerable illustrations of Trilby, and Svengali, Taffy, The Laird, and Little Billee—why, my dear woman, you actually *see* the whole thing.' Two weeks later, on 13 November 1895, he reported for the deaf man: 'I see three men in a studio, one tall, one small, and one stout. And a fourth I see, invisible to all save me—Love. I see him in the eyes of the other three; in the eyes of the tall man as he tosses his dumb-bells, in the eyes of the little one as he nervously handles a paint brush, and in the eyes of the stout man with the red face as he stands apart and moves his lips to the measure of a song I cannot catch. I know that a Girl will come soon, and here she is; she rushes in with a bound, and a twinkling of bare feet. . . .'

Thomas Hardy (1840–1928) and George Moore (1852–1933) were the two major English influences upon Bennett. 'Never in English prose literature was such a seer of beauty as Thomas Hardy', he said. Moore was his acknowledged master among the English realists. In his review of *Jude the Obscure* he saw something of a falling off from the best of Hardy's earlier work.

BERG / MS. / 16
(*To George Sturt*)

6 Victoria Grove
11 Dec 95

My dear Sturt,
Your news fills me with deep joy, placid satisfaction—that sort of feeling. *Et moi aussi!* I was working all Saturday till 10.30; all Sunday till 6.30 (after which I rewrote an article on Art to which Marriott will put his name); all yesterday till 9.30: about 6,000 words in the three days, & pretty good so far as I can make out. In fact I *know* that it is good if only I have got it comprehensibly on the paper. I gave 3 hours yesterday morning (staying away from office, having pleaded a chill on the liver) to about 300 words, & though these 300 be perhaps open to the charge of fine writing, there is a marmoreal undeniable beauty about 'em which persuades me to suspend the rule of striking out every sentence that is 'fine'.
I am looking forward to another 3 hours tonight.
My complacency is the more filling at the price since I had been gloomily looking forward to nothing serious till after Xmas. Xmas is a gay time with me. This household entire moves down to my father's in Burslem. Already we are booked for social entertainments on Tuesday Wednesday Thursday & Friday nights of Xmas week. I go on Monday 23rd & return Saturday.
I didn't want to make out that the dialogue article was precisely Stevenson. But it seemed to me devilish clear & concise. I never saw anything as good on the subject before. And he *is* a stylist, at any rate in prose. Of that be assured. A reviewer, instead of lapsing gradually into a lethargic state from which only masterpieces can rouse him, grows instead more & more sensitive to the least indications of excellence. At least I do. I know that I can read good second rate books without fatigue that people* with less critical apparatus would bore themselves to death over; & this not because I am blind to the faults but because I have a microscope for the beauties. Think this over. I bet you what you like Sonley-Johnstone comes to something.

. . . .

D'you know, I think I am going to improve in dialogue. A

* people = the laity who have some insight.

conclusion not arrived at from anything actually done, but from intimations, premonitions. I am going to do something good in t'dialogue pairts of my *next* book.

It seems as if our books would be finished together. The next Easter as ever is, I imagine will finish mine. And be damned to it. Shall not John Lane have the refusal of two masterpieces simultaneously?

My reviewing has been mixing me up with literary folk lately. One 'George Paston' (niece of John Addington Symonds) whose 3 books I have consistently belauded wants to behold me in the flesh, & she is going to; I like her work much.

Then the secretary of the New Vagabonds Club, one Burgin, a capable workman author, with not a whit of the *real* thing in him, appeared to be quite unduly struck with my notice (not at all favourable) of his latest chef d'oeuvre, & wrote to me, & before I know where I am, I am elected a member of the New Vagabonds Club, a coterie chiefly of journalists & authors with immense power on the press; they dined Mrs. Frances Hodgson Burnett on Monday night. I am not keen on being a New Vagabond, but editors galore & other influential people (John Lane for example) are in the same box, & it may be useful. There are several really tip top fellows, too, beside the bounders—Zangwill for instance & his brother.

In the next ten days I have 35 books to review. When I began to be 'Barbara' 18 months ago the difficulty was to get publishers to send books; the difficulty now is to make them understand that *Woman* can't review every blessed book issued, in a 1,000 word weekly article. Excuse this despicable bombast.

You owe this letter to the fact that I didn't feel inclined for my customary slumbers this afternoon.

Oh! my good fellow, the last 5 chapters of my book are the very devil; I tremble at the thought of overhauling—I mean rewriting them; but it will have to be.

Make no mistake: You *are* coming to London. I have quite settled the point. So has Brown. What in hell has it got to do with you? It is your friends who are concerned. Write me again soon that you have done another 8,000 words.

Ever yours, E. A. B.

16. Sturt's news was that the end of his novel, *A Year's Exile*, was in view. The Marriott–Bennett article is unknown. In an account of Bennett published

BERG / MS. / 17
(*To George Sturt*)

6 Victoria Grove
28 Jany 96

Dearest Sturt,

Six weeks since I received your letter! If intention, the best, could hold a pen & write, what letters you would have had from me in that space! Your agile disquisitions upon fiction as an exercise for the intellect & fiction as the presentment of feeling for the appreciation of feeling, make clear to me one great and lovely fact: I have no real interest in the theory of our sacred art. I don't care a DAM for it. Guided by an instinct which I cannot explain & on which I rely without knowing why, I seek to write down a story which I have imagined with only fitfully clear vision. Why I select certain scenes, why I make a beginning of a chapter at this point, and end a chapter at the other point, why I go into minute detail here & slur over whole months there—God only knows. The only vital part of any art can never be learnt & certainly cannot be

---

by Keele University Library in 1967, *My Association with Arnold Bennett*, Marriott describes the Potteries Christmas celebration that he and his family shared with the Bennetts:

'First there was a generous distribution of festoons made of laurel and ivy leaves, with focus points of holly and mistletoe, combined with bright coloured Chinese lanterns arranged according to a scheme which had been previously discussed and carried into effect by the younger members of the household.

A huge Christmas tree, freely covered with sparkling decorations and loaded with gifts, was illuminated by small coloured candles in the approved fashion. Books and other presents too bulky to be attached to the tree were arranged on a side table.

The means for making music were not wanting, for there was an American organ in the dining room, and a piano in the drawing room, and every member of the family had been taught to play. Frank, the second son, played brilliantly, and took as keen an interest in music as did Arnold.

Sons and daughters alike were practised in Choral singing, and were all good readers of music. Tertia, the youngest of the three daughters, was the chief vocalist, and possessed a voice of exceptional quality and purity of tone, and I believe that if she had had the advantage of training with a good professor, and had taken up singing as a profession, she would have made a name.

A Christmas party at the Bennetts was a stupendous affair, and the room in which it was held was filled to overflowing with relatives and friends of the family. . . .

Arnold Bennett was the chief organiser, and his personal qualities of thoroughness and foresight were manifest. Nothing was left to chance where he was concerned in the management. He arranged the programme of entertainment which followed the distribution of presents from the Christmas tree, and as I

talked about with the slightest advantage. And yet one likes to talk about, & to hear it talked about. At an afternoon tea business on Sunday last at the house of a member of our staff with whom I have recently chummed up vastly (the same being a married woman) I met a girl (I believe we had been invited to meet each other) who has written three novels, two of which I know to be good & which I have praised in *Woman* not without enthusiasm. Her name is Symonds (niece of John Addington S.) & she calls herself George Paston. About my age. We fastened on to each other at once in spite of her extraordinary plainness of feature, & just jawed about ourselves for two hours. Well, she is just like you & me, has precisely the same difficulties, the same exaltations, depressions, full stops, frenzies of production. As she is by way of being a person of distinction, I thought you might like to know this. Except yourself, I never met anyone with whom I was in so complete (artistic) sympathy. She gave me one or two tips & I gave her one. I don't think she knows more of writing than you or me (certainly not than you)—another comforting fact!

had a budding reputation as a raconteur and mimic, I was included in the list of entertainers.

Bennett had repeatedly seen my mimicry "turns" and he knew the stories I had in my repertoire, so before the entertainment was timed to start, he handed me a slip of paper giving the titles, and the order in which they were to occur.'

W. H. Sonley Johnstone possibly came to an early death. His article 'Dialogue in Fiction' in the *Sunday Sun*, 1 December 1895, is the last thing known of him. In 1892 he published a pamphlet on the Cardiff Festival, a year or so later he edited the first of a projected series of translations of continental literature, and in 1895 he published with Chapell a cantata for children.

John Lane (1854–1925) was one of the two or three most enterprising publishers of his day, and for this reason and others a high proportion of his books were reviewed in *Woman*. Doubtless Bennett was not altogether pessimistic about the chances of *A Man from the North* with him.

George Paston (Emily Morse Symonds, d. 1936) was a cousin of John Addington Symonds. Her early feminist novels, *A Bread and Butter Miss*, *A Modern Amazon*, and *The Career of Candida*, had a considerable vogue.

George B. Burgin (1856–1924) was a prolific author whose most recent book Bennett had reviewed on 4 December 1895. He was on the staff of the *Bookseller* and seems to have run the New Vagabonds Club from his home in Middlesex.

Mrs. Frances Hodgson Burnett (1849–1924) and the Zangwill brothers (Israel, 1864–1926, and Louis, 1869–1938) doubtless compared notes with each other on *Little Lord Fauntleroy* and *Children of the Ghetto*.

James Brown (1863–1943), musician and amateur painter, had been a schoolboy friend of Sturt's in Farnham, and his sister Maud married Frank Sturt. He was now a member of the Bennett–Marriott circle. In the 1920s he was a leading figure in musical education in England.

If you were here I could tell you several notions I picked up, but damned if I am industrious enough to write them. Come up, man, & stay here a week end. One thing, she firmly believes in working only *2 hours* (think of it!) a day, but not shirking that whether she feels in exact trim or the reverse. I think I must give the 2 hours a trial. I couldn't get her to give George Moore a good word. But never mind, he is an artist. I have just been reading his first novel. It is magnificent in parts. I willingly own that next to Turgenev he has influenced my little methods more than anyone.

I should have got more out of her had we not frequently been interrupted by an abnormally clever woman who writes for the *Pall Mall Gazette*, but whose extraordinary range of conversation soon began to annoy me. However, I shall take particular care to encounter Miss Symonds again as soon as may be; I think she ought to be cultivated. My novel is progressing, though slowly. Two thirds of it are in the hands of the typewriter. I *may* finish at Easter. Let's hear about your recent experiences pretty soon.

Your letters, I find, run along with considerable grace & smoothness. Don't expect that sort of thing from me. Sometimes I seem to take a horrid delight in making a letter clumsy. What's the odds?

Ever yours, E. A. B.

BERG / MS. / 18
(*To George Sturt*)

6 Victoria Grove
18 Feby 96

My dear Sturt,

I was rarely startled (& not more startled than delighted) by the first sentence in your letter. It came to me just as I was going off to the theatre (Saty night) bowed down by inchoate influenza & by a week of more or less enforced idleness. It made me feel quite merry; I had a good time at the theatre (not with the play, but during the entre'actes with a kindred

---

17. The woman on *Woman* may have been Mrs. C. S. Peel (d. 1934), novelist and writer of books on household management. Some years later she became editor. For her description of Bennett as editor, see Vol. I, p. 15.

soul of the softer sex); & by midnight the influenzaic aches had departed utterly & instead of looking back at idleness I was looking forward towards furious creativeness, and quite happy! (The said furious creativeness has not yet begun to occur, by the way; reading of other people's novels has caused me to modify the treatment of some later episodes, & I am just now in the wilderness forty days; I expected to emerge upon the meadows today but didn't. However, I am tolerably cheerful. There is one short chapter intervening between me & a scene that I am much in love with & intend to write entirely anew, & I know I shall enjoy myself there. I have just extracted a 'rise' out of my chief to the tune of nearly £60 per annum with no extra labour involved, & I feel now that I can devote my ample spare time to art, with a water-tight fire proof A, somewhat more leisurely than aforetime. But I wasn't going to talk about myself in this letter.)

Your 'draft' of course means a fairly finished writing, judging by the fragment of a novel of yours which I once read. When I remember the essential realities of that fragment (though there was a certain inarticulateness about it, which has I believe since disappeared from your writing) I have excellent hopes of this new novel. If you have only kept it severely simple, & not tried to deal with too much, I am sure it will be all right. Of course you will send it to Lane; it will be submitted to G. S. Street, & you couldn't get in front of a saner, more sympathetic critic, or, I think, a more conscientious one. Despite Street's virtues, however, let me here urgently advise you to have it typewritten. The difference which typewriting makes to the effect during reading could not be credited by anyone who is not experienced, as I am, in the perusal of the two kinds of MSS. I know the best typewriter in London, & shall be happy to superintend the process of typing. I do not advise this, I absolutely order & command it.

I am not enchanted with either of your titles. *The Sixth Sense* I would damn at once, because it has no long vowel, & because it is too sibilant. The first objection is in my opinion fatal. *A Confirmed Bachelor* will pass muster vocally, but is not the phrase a little worn, debased? I seem to fancy so.

Kindly send me a sketch of the plot. My boy, I know the feeling you had in the parlour of the town surveyor's wife. The

town surveyor's wife it is, sir, & not we, who lives, actually
lives. Artists are so blasted self-conscious all the time, do what
they will. (One hears that Browning wasn't. But I dunner
believe all as I 'ears.) When I get into the company of the
town-surveyor's wife, I am invariably beatifically staggered by
the material for novels that is lying around, & for the very best
sort of novels too. By the way I know a good lot about my
second novel already—*mœurs de province* it will be, utterly un-
literary, & a damn sight finer than *In the Shadow*; I am looking
forward to it, & shall begin, D.V., next October.

I have just read Turgenev's *Smoke*. Man, we have more to
learn in mere technique from Turgenev than from any other
soul. He is simply unspeakable. I will ram this statement down
your throat when I see you, with the book in front of us.

Have you got my *Fathers & Children* (Turgenev). I only want
to know.

Write me a sketch of your plot, there's a good chap.

Yours ever, E. A. Bennett

BERG / MS. / 19   6 Victoria Grove
(*To George Sturt*)   8 March 96
                                        Sunday morning

My dear Sturt,

Of course I did not hope that the outline of your novel
which I demanded would give me any real conception of the
complete work. Therefore I was in no way disappointed. I
merely desired a peg on which to hang my fond fancies concerning it. But, though everything depends on the treatment,

18. Sturt reported completing a draft of *A Year's Exile*. George Street (1867–
1936) was an author himself (*The Autobiography of a Boy*). He read for Lane for
several years, and later became His Majesty's Examiner of Plays.

Sturt wrote to Bennett about the town surveyor: 'I went out to tea last night,
and beheld what would have made me humble, if I had needed:—a man about
my age (Town surveyor—a *practical* man) and his wife—a clean sweet sort of
English girl. I believe they supposed me "cultured" and fancied it very fine to
have me with 'em. Their talk! I *had* to talk down to 'em. And their singing—or
rather the man's singing (wife's not amiss to my taste) made me grin to myself.
Obviously they didn't know much about novel-writing: but about town-drains
and married love.'

Mœurs de province became *Anna of the Five Towns*, which Bennett began in
September 1896, four months after finishing *In the Shadow* (*A Man from the North*).

I have considerable expectations. The outline seems to me very round and satisfactory; it left me quietly pleased: which is best. The last bit you have not made clear to me, at least as regards the psychology—and the 'action', just at the end, seems to be chiefly psychological. I myself should have shrunk from the medicine incident (I mean that in which the murderous potion is dashed to the ground) as being both a melodramatic (compared with the rest of the story) and trite situation. But, again, all depends upon the treatment. All else has my dignified approval.

I shall not, under the circumstances, press you further about the typewriting. I have been thinking that your script is miraculously clear.

You may have guessed before now that I entertain a certain respect for your critical opinion upon things literary, & when that opinion differs from my own, my instinct is towards self-distrust. Believe, therefore, that when I say 'Pooh!' to your estimate of Turgenev, I am supported by an immense and abiding consciousness of being absolutely & entirely in the right of the matter.

On the Eve is more than a nice novel; it is a great novel. I think that if I could read it in Russian I should set it down as the greatest within my knowledge. It will repay the most minute study—that minute study which I hope some day to give it as some preliminary towards an article on 'Turgenev technically considered'.

I know exactly how you have been misled. The '*austerity of the technique*' has deceived you, sir, in the most cruel manner. What you need is a steeping in Flaubert, de Goncourts (especially de Goncourts) & de Maupassant. I am aware you have read a lot of French—but not enough & not in the right spirit, not with the iron determination to distinguish between matter and method. This done, like a schoolboy who has got through his Caesar, you may turn anew to the Supreme Turgenev with a better chance of appreciating.

He has not 'celarèd the artem', eh? With due respect to Horace, why in God's name should the artem be celarèd, by an artificial cloud of dialogue, digression & minor incident, such as our English novelists are accustomed to make? Turgenev *disdains*, simply disdains. There is no reason why art should be concealed, as there is no reason why it should be paraded. Art is art, & the artist need not be ashamed of it. What you implicitly demand is false modesty.

Turgenev, having conceived his story, deliberately strips it of every picturesque inessential, austerely turns aside from any *artfulness*, and seeks to present it in the simplest, most straightforward form. That is why he can tell in 60,000 words a history which George Eliot or Thomas Hardy would only have hinted at in 200,000. He is the Bach of fiction, whose severity & simplicity are mistaken (by those whose sensibilities have been cloyed by the Mendelssohns & Wagners of fiction) for lack of imagination & baldness. I used to think that Bach was a lofty creature without a heart; but I have been told by people who know that he is as emotional as any composer that ever lived, & I am now beginning to see as much for myself. This is rather beside the point, even as a parallel, but it may illustrate (vaguely) what I mean with regard to Turgenev.

I am just reading *Germinie Lacerteux,* the masterpiece (I fancy) of the de Goncourts. The austere simplicity of its presentment is—noble. Here are no pretty bits of dialogue, whose sole justification for existing is their prettiness; no purple patches of description dwelt on as a vain tenor dwells on his high C; no clevernesses in beginning or ending a chapter; no tortured symbolism of incident (a growing evil in these latter days)—none of these things; but the 'plain tale from the hills' of art, which depends for its effect on its unforced directness, and utterly scorns mere *device*.

It seems to me that this is what we in England ought to find profit and wisdom in. And I, for one, shall endeavour to imitate it—doubtless without much success, but the intention will be there.

I have not touched my novel this week past, the demands of *Woman* & of my new bicycle having been too imperious to be ignored, & I am afraid I shall not put in a full seven days next week, as I have a darn silly short story to concoct.

I feel now that I could do a remarkably good short story (5 or 6,000 words)—so much has the novel improved my ability, & when *In the Shadow* is in the shadow, I just will have a go at one, & see if it won't be ten times better than 'A Letter Home'. I assure you that though I am getting pretty weary of *In the Shadow*, I am positively anxious to begin the new novel, which will have some such title as *The Strange Woman* (being a study of a *femme incomprise* whom I know well).

(By the way how much of fact is there in the characterisation of your story? I thought I saw darkly certain piquant resemblances.)

This afternoon I go to discuss 'shop' with the girl 'George Paston' whom I mentioned to you. If my acquaintance with her progresses (as I imagine it will) I must take care that you meet her; you will enjoy the conversation of a *woman* who emphatically knows what is what.

Well, to your task, & God be with us all!

Yours ever, E. A. Bennett

P.S. Thanks. Don't send the book. I have discovered the one I thought you had, in the hands of Dr. Farrar.

BUTLER / MS. / 20
(*From George Sturt*)

Lower Bourne
Monday night. 16 March 1896

My dear Bennett,

Several times you've written nice and flattering about my judgment in matters literary. Well, sir! I've not written about yours, so far as I know: but let me tell you what I have *done*. I have read again, and solely on the strength of your reiterated recommendation, Turgenev's *On the Eve*. And I can't remember ever before reading a book the second time, before I had forgotten the first reading.

It paid. I climb down part way. *On the Eve is* better than a merely nice book. It is very magnanimous of me to say so. . . . I took it from the shelf, with the intention of being fair, but also with a conviction that justice would not hinder me from

---

19. The typewriting circumstance was that Sturt's income was likely to be minus £60 in the current year, not enough for him to be able to afford a typist.

The silly story was probably 'In the County Court', which appeared in *Woman* on 28 March 1896.

Dr. John Farrar was Bennett's physician at this time, and he remained a friend. He and Herbert Sharpe grew up together in Yorkshire, and he was a member of the musical-evenings group.

belittling it. And be sure that I was ready to pounce on those one or two passages which in memory seemed poorly done. . . . But—the book had the best of me, every time.

There was one part which, at first reading, seemed a poor and clumsy expedient: namely, the extracts from the girl's diary. Indeed, I still think that diary is dragged in by the heels rather mercilessly, rather barefacedly. Neither did I lose the feeling, that as a matter of fact the girl did *not* write it herself, but allowed Turgenev to write it for her, from imagination.

And yet—it is *well* done: a sweet bit of imagination: sweet enough to excuse its own presence.

The Venetian bit passed over my head. Turgenev seems to be trying to give some atmospheric impression which I've been unable to seize. I leave it to you to apportion blame for this,—to him or to me. Only, for my justification, be it understood that by the time that passage was reached, I was eager to find the book faultless.

I'm not with you, however, in calling it a 'great' book. And it would not be hard to tell you why: only, it is quite possible that we give the name 'great' to qualities that are quite different in kind. I should call this book 'accomplished', 'exquisite', 'beautiful'. The qualities that are meant by 'greatness' in my mind are not in favour now-a-days. We are shy of them: writers haven't the confidence in themselves—they lack the almighty cocksureness, that alone can produce great work: that is to say, sublime improbable exaggerated splendours that whirl you off your feet and knock you down and trample on you. Victor Hugo could do that: so (though not so gloriously) Dumas. Scott has done it for me, and will again, I hope. (Soon I'm going to read *Heart of Midlothian* again. Quite lately, *Guy Mannering* has given me more enjoyment than any other book for perhaps twelve months.)

And yet—there's something else, that constitutes 'greatness'. For instance, *Tom Jones* didn't overcome me at all. It bored me. But now, looking back to it, it seems gigantic, in a way that Turgenev's book does not yet seem. So also does *Wilhelm Meister*.

These, Sir, be statements of fact. Tonight I've neither the time nor the inclination to analyse them. In fact, I'm tired and bored, after being away from home all day. No novel writing for me today. I'm pining for other kinds—or else for none at all! Several notions for stories or dialogues have been attracting me; and yet more, the lovely possibility of finishing and perfecting short things, before they begin to fester in the flesh.

However—I'm going to see about some supper now. And then not write another word (yes—there's a letter must be written to Brown) before tomorrow. But I'll hope to send to you again soon. If in the meantime the spirit should move you to write, it will be a joy to me to hear from you.

Yours, George Sturt

I never procured that *Thesaurus* of Synonyms. Will you again send me particulars, so that I may order?

BERG / MS. / 21
(*To George Sturt*)

6 Victoria Grove
31 Mch 96

Sir,

You indubitably *are* magnanimous. You have a great mind. Else you could not have written the first page of your letter of the 16th. Only a great man with a great mind (& great men do not always have great minds) can change his views without for a moment losing his dignity. Your honoured communication gave me much joy. Not, sir, the mean delight of having scored, triumphed; but that large & extensive bliss which the angels are reported to experience over one sinner that repenteth.

I am with you about the Venetian part of *On the Eve*. It occurred to me that probably the fault was neither with the author nor the reader, but with the translator. I can quite conceive that a subtle effect of atmosphere might be marred by a translator. Is it not so?

I did not make myself clear on certain aspects of Turgenev's technique. Nor shall I trouble to do so now, because I know that viva voce I can explain myself without any fag. I will just mention that I didn't refer to an absence of symbols in his work, but to an absence of 'symbolic incident'. If you don't happen to know what I mean by 'symbolic incident', I will also explain that when I see you. It is a very interesting question, how far 'symbolic incident' may be legitimately used.

When I use the term 'great' in reference to a work of art, I mean (in a very high degree, of course) 'finely conceived and (practically) flawlessly worked out'. I call *Persuasion* & Keats's *Ode to a Nightingale* great works of art. Victor Hugo I should rather call 'big'. But these terms are loosely used, & carry different significations to different men.

Your remarks about your novel have a confident tone which much pleases me. I have mentioned to several people that I know a man who in the cloistered seclusion of a Surrey village is now finishing a novel which will make an indentation upon the smooth surface of the age. Notably to 'George Paston'; & when I saw that lady at the Writers Club on Friday, one of her first questions was about your respected self. The Writers Club, you must understand, is a club of women. I went thither upon her invitation & found myself in a long low room with many women (not *obviously* literary, I thank God) balancing cups of tea in their hands, & talking like the very devil. I had a comfortable & inspiring talk with 'George Paston' & certain others of the elect, & learned several things worth knowing. 'G.P.' has just finished her novel. Six months, 2 to 2½ hours per diem. Not excessive, is it?

I am progressing with my little thing, slowly but most surely. It is being typewritten something lovely. I wish I had written it in a book & not on sheets. Future novels will be drafted on sheets & rewritten in a book specially prepared for the purpose, with special paper. Of course high-minded Spartans like yourself are above such trifles, but as for me, I know that writing in a pretty volume on graceful paper will have a certain indirect effect on the work, because it will help to kindle my enthusiasm.

Bicycling is the rage now. I got my machine about 3 weeks ago & Marriott has had his a fortnight. Mrs. Marriott's has long been ordered but doth not yet appear. I find cycling a most excellent practice. Weather permitting, I spend the afternoons upon two wheels, & coming home in a disgusting state of healthiness, work like Hades from 6 to 10 or thereabouts. It is noble, I tell you. Distances entirely disappear. I ran over to

Richmond the other afternoon intending to have tea with James B. but the house was locked up & none answered my angry knocks, so I stuck a card in the keyhole, for a sign, & ran back home, 6 miles in half an hour. I have also to thank cycling for a certain intimacy with Brown's friend Alcock, who has very delightful rooms just off the Strand, where I have tea once or twice a week. Music is his love, but he is an all round chap (failing only in the graphic arts) & a most ingenious talker. Just now he is going through the Stevenson fever, a severe attack. (About the 15th April I shall be in your neighbourhood on a short bicycling tour with the Sharpes, Alcock & sundry others.) I am staying in London for Easter, in order to work. Think of that. Such a thing has never occurred before in the history of

Your obedient Servant, E. A. Bennett

What a lift for *The Golden Age* in today's *Chronicle*! A. B.

BERG / MS. / 22
(*To George Sturt*)

Marlborough House
14 Apl 96

Dear Sir,

His Royal Highness the Prince of Wales commands me to thank you very cordially for your most kind invitation, & to say that he regrets to be unable to accept it. H.R.H.'s arrangements with the sovereigns of Europe who will accompany him on his projected tour through Surrey & Hampshire make it impossible for him to leave his party for the period you name, but if he finds himself able to detach an hour or two from his programme, I shall have pleasure in appointing an audience within the next seventy hours.

21. George Paston's new novel was *The Career of Candida*, which was published in November 1896.

Fred Alcock was a London customs officer and an amateur oboist of considerable accomplishment. He played in concerts of the Richmond Philharmonic Society under the baton of James Brown. He left England for Bermuda during the Second World War, and apparently died there around 1942.

The Golden Age, by Kenneth Grahame (1859–1932), received a very flattering review from A. C. Swinburne.

H.R.H. commands me to say that he will have pleasure in reading the MS. of the book which you are good enough to state you have finished.

Accept, dear Sir, the assurance of my distinguished consideration.

Dyghton Probyn, Comptroller

BERG / MS. / 23   6 Victoria Grove
(*To George Sturt*)   Saty ming
                                             [2 May 1896]

My dear Sturt,

For exercise I have just ridden over to Ken's for your novel, though I am so busy I haven't time to read it today. I have, however, snatched 20 minutes for the first two chapters. The first, to me, at first reading, is somewhat shadowy, but the second, my pippin, is *positively masterly*. I say this very seriously. I was so enchanted with it that I had no alternative but to express myself on the subject at once. . . . And now to my own novel, which will be finished in a fortnight from this day as ever is.

Yours, E.A.B.

BERG / MS. / 24
(*To George Sturt*)

                                             6 Victoria Grove
                                             4 May 96
[no salutation]

Well, Sir, I have read your novel, & I am ready to bet a guinea to a gooseberry that, if read by Street, it will not be refused by John Lane for reasons artistic.

I have the honour to inform you that I wouldn't give a damn for your opinion about this novel. You have been telling me that you don't like it; that you wouldn't care to have your name associated with its printed title page, & so on, & so on. Sir, you are an abject nincompoop. You have dwelt with it too long, & know nothing about it.

It is, in most ways, a very fine novel. It is one of the most genuinely original novels that I have ever read; I don't mean original in design, but in the outlook of the author.

Certain chapters of it, e.g. cap 15, in which summer in the country is described, are to my mind quite unique, & cap 15 itself contains some of the most memorable nature-descriptions that I can call to mind.

(If your own opinions should happen to clash with these, as they probably will, have the goodness to remember that I am much more likely to be right than you.)

The characters of Mitchell & of Mrs. Thomson, especially the latter, are drawn superbly. Mrs. Thomson, indeed,—damned if she doesn't remind me of Turgenev's women. There were times during the perusal, when I giggled to myself from pure delight at the way you had nailed her down. Thomson himself is good. Edith, shadowy, & Hartmann (to me) a mere vague shadow. Both Wright & Mrs. Wright are excellent. Mrs. Clarke is much better, I doubt not, in your mind than on the paper, I can imagine the functions you intend her to fulfil in the story, & her first introduction (cap 8) is well-timed & right, but I don't think she is *quite* realised, except in the latter part of the book. The passing sketch of the old rustic (I forget his name—the man who says, 'They don't *want* us') is quite good & convincing.

———

The great fault of the book springs from the fact that you can't use a large brush, where men & women are concerned. That really sums up all I have to say of adverse criticism. Too much stipple. Also, a little too much conversation, though all the conversation is finely (delicately) wrought, & illustrative too. Still, too much! Also the (moral) action of the story hangs fire, or rather appears to hang fire, through several chapters (e.g. 9 & 10). I don't think it does really hang fire, but its progress is not appreciated till after the impression that it is standing still has had time to make an effect on the reader. Which is bad.

Cap I wants re-writing, I think. And cap 24 (great temptation scene) though *right* in substance, & effective, needs re-arrangement & modification (I don't know how). Caps 9 & 10 want justifying.

E

There are numerous (totally unimportant) crudities or mistakes of style or rather of English, which, however, need not be referred to in detail at this stage of the proceedings. Also, I observe with amusement, various downright blunders of spelling. I roared at some of them—wouldn't have suspected you of them.

———

Your point of view is the point of view of George Sturt & of none other. Your technique, in many ways, strongly reminds one of Henry James's. I don't think the book could ever be popular, but if published, I will swear it would be deeply respected by

'a little clan'

the little clan that knows what's what. But I don't disguise from myself the fact that many men, not without taste, might read it & miss much of its, to me, striking beauty. That would be the fault of your technique, or rather not the *fault*, but one of its drawbacks.

In conclusion, let me say that . . . (your new titles are preposterous) is much finer than I suspected you were immediately capable of. If you have the pluck & the endurance, my boy, you can be a better man than Henry James. And don't conjure up the notion that my judgment is obscured by partiality, has been warped by a desire to be pleased. Nothing of the kind. A more frigidly impartial man than me doesn't exist, though you mayn't know it. I know what I am talking about, & I know I am right, whatever anybody else says. If every publisher's reader in London said this novel was unworthy to be called fine literature, I should still serenely know that I was right. But yet I can quite understand that the book would merely enrage many excellent people. And I should be shocked (though I should be a little surprised) if Street advised Lane not to publish it because it couldn't hope to be popular.

After reading it, I will not advise you any more to come to live in London. Stay where you are, & write like hell. You *know* the country.

Yours, E. A. Bennett

24. *A Year's Exile* describes the unfortunate influence of the city upon a country-man. In the great temptation scene, the countryman, Dr. Mitchell, unconsciously

BUTLER / MS. / 25
(*From George Sturt*)

Lower Bourne
Monday eveng. 11 May 1896

My dear Bennett,

Many thanks for your too-too flattering letter. Mind you, though, I don't regard it as gospel—all that you say about my book. Not that I accuse you of intentional flattery. No, sir! One blessed thing about you is, that you're able to give a tolerably true and credible account of your impressions: and I quite willingly believe that you have done so in this case.

But one of the first and last things I learnt in philosophy was this: That impressions need not be assumed to bear any resemblance to the things which occasion them. Granting this, it must not be assumed that my novel has all or any of the good qualities which you attribute to it.

Of course, I hope (and believe) it has some of 'em. But—do you know the story of the little boy who went to a party? He was Crosse and Blackwell's son, and his parentage seems to be a mystery. 'But that's another story'. The jam seemed nice to the other boys; young C & B however refused to have any, because 'he knew what was in it'. . . . So of this precious book, I know the old rag-shop where all the heroes and heroines were put together.

For instance—when you approve so highly of Mrs L T, and how I'd 'nailed her down'. Bless you—'twas nothing of the sort. I'm rather fond of her myself—but, hang it, I built her up; not nailed her down at all. I never met her or heard of her. What happened was this: I thought of the situation (by accident), looked about for any woman whose face seemed as if she might fill it, and finally—mere good luck—saw the lady I wanted, on the stage at Aldershot theatre. . . . And I suspect

---

prepares a murderous prescription for the sick husband of the woman with whom he has fallen in love. When he realizes what he is doing, he dashes the potion to the floor.

The quotation from Keats and the reference to him in the letter of 31 March 1896 are some indication of Bennett's developing interest in the romantic poets. The theory of literature that he advanced a dozen years later in *The Author's Craft* owes as much to Keats and to Wordsworth as to the French realists. 'All literature', he says there, 'is the expression of feeling, of passion, of emotion, caused by a sensation of the interestingness of life. . . . The book is nothing but the man trying to talk to you.'

that where I got the face, there also I found the gestures, the voice-tones, and all the rest of it: and that in fact the whole thing is a picture not of life as it is lived, but as it is travestied on the stage.

The same, or worse, is true of the other people. *I* never met an old labourer who talked as old Peter in the book talks; nor yet such an 'ousekeeper: although I know the faces of these two. . . . Doctor Mitchell I swear I shouldn't recognise, if I met him in the street. . . .

And then, although, in going along, the people became better known to me; yet at the end I could only guess what they would do and say. I didn't know, and still don't know, whether the guess was a probable one: and it follows that the book's end is not so inevitable as it ought to have been. Fact is, I wrote the last 2 chapters four if not five times; at last pulling up in despair on those that you have read.

Wherefore, if you had said of this book, that it was as good as the best of Henry James's, I should have tried to think that you were not far wrong, and then—have come to the conclusion that Mr Henry James was something of an ingenious fraud. . . . I *don't* think so, by the way. He seems to me to photograph from life; not to work from photographs of stage-scenes. . . . My observing powers don't bear naming beside his, even if I can analyse fairly well the things that do come under my observation.

Well, well! I believe almost entirely what you say about the technique (including the arrangement) of the book. The chapters where, you say, the action drags struck me in that way, too. I shd have altered one of 'em, but was in such a state, that I couldn't trust my judgment at all. The one chapter, about the summer weather, is the only one that was an entire joy to write. As to Chap I—daresay it needs rewriting, but I shall avoid doing so, if they'll let me. I've had enough of it, and don't care now.

Bad spelling!—the accusation only doesn't astonish me because I know I 'cant spel'. Still—that damned MS must have been read through a dozen times at the least. Pray Gawd that you corrected the errors you found.

The bad Sentences worry me more, not so much as the fault of 'stippling'. That criticism frightens me. I feel that it is just;

and yet—in any given place I can't discern the stipple. . . . Never mind; practice will do much. The most helpful part of your letter was in the end. 'Write like hell', says you.

Yes sir.

Please, mindful of your commands, I've been trying to write like that. Spent about five solid hours—in addition to the time given to cogitation—writing like hell yesterday. Not one moment of real inspiration all the blessed time. Result,—a story, about 2,000 words, worthless. But I meant putting him through.

Today I'm in for a rest: having gone through the blessed night with tooth-ache. Then business in Farnham 'smorning: and in the afternoon, a pilgrimage to the dentist at Aldershot; with whom I left three teeth, and so came home—none the worse, but much the better; only quite indisposed for any laborious writing.

It's good to hear of your novel being so nearly done. I 'spose you'll send it to Lane straight away? . . . By the way, my titles are 'preposterous', I know. They were but dummy titles— shots at a venture. . . . If you have any notion of a decent title for the thing, I shall be much relieved to hear it.

Some time ago you told me that you already knew a good deal about your next novel. . . . My next has yet to be discovered. There seems to be plenty of material, but as yet no sign of its crystallising into artistic form. But there's no hurry. My leisure will be so knocked about until the cold weather comes again, that I can afford to wait for things to settle down in my mind.

Enough of this.

Yours, George Sturt

By the way—I'm appearing in print in the next *Studio*. You're sure to see it; or blest if I'd tell you, because I've made an ass of myself.

25. The *Studio* piece (Vol. 7, pp. 218–19) was a letter in defence of the Science and Art Department of South Kensington.

BERG / MS. / 26
(*To George Sturt*)

6 Victoria Grove
16 May 96

My dear Sturt,

We feel rather proud, Chapman & I, because we imagine that, through an idea brilliantly suggested by Chapman & brilliantly carried out by myself, your novel has been snatched as a brand from the burning.

I expect that Ken has told you the state of affairs up to yesterday. Chapman called here on Thursday night about 10 p.m. to say that Lane had decided, in spite of a warmly appreciative report on it from John Buchan, not to handle your work of genius, on the score that it was *seksy* & America didn't want no seks-problems & he was determined to please America. In discussing the book with Chapman, Lane asked how it had got to the Bodley Head. Now Chapman says that it fatally prejudices a book in Lane's eyes to know that it has come through one of his clerks, & so Chapman told him that it had come through me, & that I had praised it highly to him, Chapman. So behold me constituted your London agent & champion. By arrangement with Chapman I called on Lane just to enquire like yesterday afternoon, & pretending to know nothing about anything. He gave me a most garbled version of Buchan's report (not knowing that I had privately perused the same) & said he couldn't see his way to publishing it. I asked why. He said sex. I said it was a perfectly clean & healthy book, & contained nothing I should be afraid to publish in *Woman*. He turned off here to compliment *Woman* on her literary critic. I brought him back, & he said he would think it over, & let me know Saturday morning.

I called this morning by appointment, & he said at once he thought he should publish it. He said he would look at it himself, & if he found any of the 'sickly descriptions of sensu*ous* passion' to which Buchan had referred (he showed me the report), did I think you would be willing to reconsider them? *I said you had given me full powers to do what I thought fit,* & that you certainly would amend any such passages, if found. I, however, ventured to predict none would be found.

He then proceeded to the question of terms. He said he had

been having a profit & loss account prepared for the first time in the history of his business, & that it had perfectly appalled him. In future the terms he was going to offer to all *new* authors was a royalty of 5 per cent. on published price for first 1,000, 10 per cent. for 2nd 1,000, & 15 per cent. for 3rd 1,000. He asked whether you would be agreeable. I, on your behalf, knowing that there is only one publisher in London who would offer such terms as these to a new author, said that you would. He then said that it was almost certain that he should accept the book, but that he would let me know definitely in a few days.

Judging from his manner & from the fact that he took the trouble to discuss terms, I regard the thing as settled, but you understand that it is not formally settled.

Buchan's report was a most able and fair one, agreeing marvellously with mine own. He describes the analysis of character as masterly, & says the book would do credit to any publisher. On the other hand, he calls the style sometimes slipshod, enlarges on the lack of cumulative interest, & also uses the phrase quoted *supra*. As a whole, his criticism is most gratifying & cannot fail to bring the blush of pride to the cheek of modesty.

I trust to be excused for having taken the whole business into my own hands without a word from you, but there was no time to be lost, & I knew that if appealed to, you would exhibit your usual damnable namby-pamby, sleepy indifference, & so with Chapman's approval I went at it.

I have pledged you to modify or recast little bits here & there if Lane asks it. Put that in your pipe & smoke it.

But I told Lane that personally I found nothing in the book but what was clean & sane.

You had better send me a line.

I finished my novel at noon, Friday. Lane expresses a polite anxiety to see it. I shall feel in duty bound to allay that anxiety immediately.

Respex to Ken,
Yours, E. A. B.

P.S. In great haste.

26. John Buchan, later Lord Tweedsmuir (1875–1940), was just beginning a highly successful career as a novelist and political leader, eventually writing *The*

LANE / MS. / 27
(*To John Lane*)

6 Victoria Grove
19 May 96

Dear Mr. Lane,
With this is my novel, submitted with trembling for your consideration. The reader will scarcely need to be informed that it is a first book.

Believe me,
Very truly yours, E. A. Bennett

BERG / MS. / 28
(*To George Sturt*)

6 Victoria Grove
29 May 96

My dear Sturt,
I have nothing more definite to report as yet concerning your novel. Lane gave me an appointment last Thursday morning, which I kept. But he confessed that he had been in the country, & had not got Chapman to read aloud to him extracts from the said masterpiece, as he promised to me he would. He said he was transcendently busy, & that I should hear further in about ten days.

You may like to be made aware of the facts that your criticism of your novel is regarded in London with amused contempt, & that your criticism of my criticism of your novel is mere perversity. My dear sir, did you imagine that I, a heaven-born critic, I who merely tolerate other men's views upon fiction, supposed for an instant that you had met your characters in the flesh & just set them down? Did *I* need to be told that you had not nailed a certain woman down, but built her up, & that no old labourer had really ever crossed your path & said such & such a thing?

I used the phrase 'nailed her down' certainly, & a perfect & apposite phrase it was too! Granted that you built the woman up, did not the supreme art lie in nailing her down after the structural process was over? Don't you flatter yourself that

---

Thirty-Nine Steps and becoming Governor-General of Canada. He was the son of a Scottish Free Church minister.

because you can write a devilish fine book, you can distinguish a devilish fine book at sight. Look back, dear sir, & reflect upon the mistakes you have made, the blindnesses of which you have been guilty, & the shameful enthusiasms in which you have briefly gloried. If you will be good enough to content yourself with creative work, accepting my critical deliverances in meekness & faith, I shall think better of you. Also your taste, at present lamentably narrow & defective, will be more likely to improve. When I see you I will explain exactly the demerits of your book; by dint of meditation I have come to a proper grasp of their significance. The merits, in spite of your well-intentioned humility, are doubtless patent to you; but I wager, though, on second thoughts, that the largest of these merits is hidden.

Why the Hades call yourself George Bourne? Why not George Sturt? If my name was Ebenezer Spoopendyke, Ebenezer Spoopendyke I would call myself, & dare anyone to laugh. And the reality is that Sturt is distinguished, Bourne atrociously commonplace.

The history of my own novel, in its later stages, has been of the lowest. I took it to Lane. He said 'call again in a week'. I called again in a week, to the very hour. He said, handing me a document, 'Here is the report on your novel.' I read it. It was very laudatory on all counts, & quite free from fault-finding except as to one trifling & quite inessential point. There was a rider that in John Buchan's opinion it would not be popular. Lane said: 'I will publish your novel.' I said: 'That is very good of you', or words to that effect, & so it was settled & we passed on to less important matters. It is to come out in the new series, 'Lane's Library', & as only three books stand previously accepted for that series in front of it, & one of these is ready for issue, there should not be a long delay in publication. Such are the short & simple annals of my first book. I sort of feel that I ought to think myself a devilish lucky fellow; also that I owe you an apology for marching ahead with my book while permitting yours, which should have precedence, being finished first, to linger by the wayside.

Thine, E. A. Bennett

28. Sturt published *A Year's Exile* under the pseudonym of George Bourne. He wrote to Bennett: 'It's wholly because of the blasted business, that I want my book

BERG / MS. / 29
(*To George Sturt*)

6 Victoria Grove
23 June 96

My dear Sturt,

I had intended answering your letter earlier, since I was feverishly interested in your references to the Surrey Labourer book, but my youngest sister—a sane, shrewd, humorous girl, sir, with a fine though disconcerting faculty for stripping away affectations from men & things & seeing them nudely whole— has been staying with me for a month past, & festivities have occupied my time. She went this afternoon, conducted home by her affianced lover, & lo! this evening I write—with a new pen.

I happened to call on Lane this morning. For high political reasons I had no intention of worrying him about your book, but I thought I would 'just enquire like' today. He had done nothing further, & invented several neat excuses on the spot very cleverly. However, I am quite easy in my mind about that book. The longer he keeps it hung up, the greater the certainty of his taking it. He said he had been ill & overworked & what not, but he would perpend & decide at the very earliest opportunity. I answered sort of confidentially: 'Don't inconvenience yourself at all, Mr Lane. There is not the slightest hurry', & his eyes thanked me. With a man like that, a seeming utter indifference pays.

John Buchan, the 'reader' of your book & mine, happened to be on a visit to Lane, & Lane introduced us & left us alone together in his private room for five or ten minutes. A *very* young man, fair, with a horrid cicatrice across his left temple, charmingly shy. I should say, a thoroughly good fellow, & in spite of his bashfulness, as cute as God makes 'em in these

---

to go under a pseudonym. Consider, sir: in a little town like Farnham, a man's private affairs are regarded as public property. Now, my best customers are either non-conformists who read Henry Drummond, *or* mere bourgeois capitalists who despise art and dislike the artists. I can fancy 'em saying of me, "If he's writing novels, he isn't attending to his business." Quite true: but I don't wish it to be formulated. I'm already suspected of being an atheist and a socialist.'

Buchan reported of *A Man from the North* that it showed 'great knowledge and a good deal of insight', and that the characterization displayed 'a succession of rare and subtle touches'.

latter days. I at once asked him (only in different terms) what in hell he meant by calling your book, or any part of it, 'sickly'. He didn't square up to that question, but he freely stated that in his opinion it was both 'clean & wholesome'. This view will be retailed to Lane at the proper moment. I was particularly charmed with the man. He will do something. He was very polite to me about my book. Said it was 'right' (with an emphasis that nearly brought the blush of pride to the cheek of modesty) & the style 'excellent'. I pray God it may be so, but as to the style, I doubt it may be a little exotic. I have no uncertainty now that the plan of the book is right & the climax absolutely inevitable. Then we returned to yourself. He wished to know about you, & I told him—bits. He was most astonished to hear that you hadn't lived in London. He clearly regards your book as a tour de force of analysis & that sort of thing, of interest chiefly to the literary artist; his attitude towards it is—a little—one of awe. I wouldn't detail all this to you, were it not that he immediately impressed me as a man of strength, one who *knew*, one who has got to be taken into account.

And now as to that Surrey Labourer book. Sir, that is a thing you will be able to make a good job of. It certainly sounds inviting. Also it will be rather new—to English literature. Turgenev has forestalled you, & a bit to spare, in *A Sportsman's Sketches*, which you shall take home with you next time you come to London. These sketches are obviously records of things seen & heard by the author during his sporting tours, records devoid of literary artfulness, but chocked full of the art of observation. I know that you will be both delighted & edified by them. I read some of them a few years ago, & thought they were *tame* & lacked form. Now, I know better. They do lack form, intentionally; but they are miracles of *selection*. Unluckily not one reader in a 1,000 could possibly appreciate them at their artistic value.

You say you acquired material at Cambridge. Precisely how do you acquire material? I ask because I am curious on this point just now. Do you write it down immediately you see it, or do you let it soak in till it happens to be wanted. I am more & more interested in the literary life of the brothers de Goncourt, & I read their, to the author, entrancing *Journal* daily. The singleness of their aim was positively terrific. No one, I feel sure, was ever more exclusively literary. And yet they made a point of seeing life, & they wrote down everything they saw—indecency for them doesn't exist. They took their material wholesale. *Germinie Lacerteux* (sir, a masterpiece!), for instance, is almost exactly the history of their own nurse. . . . In spite of that contempt for notions of decency, they were most careful not to be too realistic. They saw through realism, at the very zenith of its popularity in Paris. Example: *Germinie Lacerteux*, as first written, contained a description of a Caesarian operation, adorably done; they cite this description in full in their journal, with the remark:—'Je retire ceci, *comme trop vrai*, de mon manuscrit de *Germinie Lacerteux*. (It is curious that most of the journal is written in the first person singular, without any indication as to which brother holds the pen at the moment.) That is fine, that *comme trop vrai*, is it not? They were right, too, in withdrawing the passage: it fairly made me shudder, though there is no attempt at 'piling on'.

I have been at the trouble to copy out for you a passage disclosing their sensations during the first conception, 'enfantement', of a book. You will appreciate it, with comment from me.

I understand the de Goncourts. I know how they felt; their ideals are mine; I don't think they are gods like Turgenev; they are more *accessible*; one can get nearer to them, watch their methods more minutely. The methods of Turgenev are beyond our ken, really. One can only admire, in respectful silence. With the de Goncourts, one can say, 'Look here, old chaps, you've had some hard knocks, scores of men have made more stir & more money; but never mind; *I* understand, I know *exactly* what you have been after. My hand on it.' And they would take it, answering only with their eyes. That simple idea of keeping a journal, too, they have magnificently carried out, on an absolutely new plan. It is so easy to keep a journal (not a blasted diary) & the journal cannot fail to be valuable when it has reached any considerable bulk. About six weeks ago, I felt that I must keep a journal, simply *must*; not to do so would be criminal. (In a newspaper office one hears & sees a lot, or hears *of* a lot.) So I made a blank book, with my own fair hands, so that it should be all my own, *personal*; & very lovely the book is; Kennerley was nearly enthusiastic about its outward appearance, & you know what that means. And I began to keep a journal. It contains nothing private; any of my friends are quite at liberty to read it at any time; nothing indiscreet, in the large sense of that term. I guess it is pretty crude at present, but one can't fall into the art of keeping a journal in a month. There is, of course, the possibility that I may tire of it, & chuck it up. I recognise this. But I don't think I shall. I can see already that it will have several kinds of value, if I can only stick to it. I should say that it is not intended to include mere literary studies, material pure & simple. The matter of it may turn out to be material, but it doesn't stand there qua material.

I wait for news that the Surrey Labourer is finished.

Yours ever, E. A. Bennett

29. The Surrey labourer book (eventually entitled *The Bettesworth Book, Talks with a Surrey Peasant*) consists of the recollections of a man who worked for Sturt. Sturt had already recorded many of the man's tales, and expected to have the manuscript suitably revised by August 1896.

Tertia Bennett (1872–1949) was Arnold's favourite sister. As a child she had her first lessons from him, and a few years later when she was ill, he was again her teacher. She visited him frequently in London. Her fiancé, Willie Boulton, died in an accident in 1897, and she eventually married W. W. Kennerley.

After a visit to Sturt at the Lower Bourne, Bennett wrote of him: 'I had not been with him an hour before I was compelled to readjust my estimate of the depth of his immersion in literature. Writing occupies all his thoughts in a way I had never suspected. With the most perfect naturalness, he regards everything as "material", and he assumed that I should do so too. A more literary temperament than his it would be difficult to conceive. He doesn't 'search' for stuff; his task probably is to cope with the masses of material which thrust themselves upon his attention. He sits down in his writing-chair and handles note-books and papers with an air of custom and familiarity which I have never seen in a writer before; it was like Sharpe at the piano.'

Bennett began his journal on 27 April 1896. The first entry is reproduced in the three-volume selection published by Cassell in 1932–3.

The passage from the Goncourt *Journal* was of the date 13 July 1862:

'La peine, le supplice, la torture de la vie littéraire: c'est l'enfantement. Concevoir, créer: il y a dans ces deux mots pour l'homme de lettres un monde d'efforts douloureux et d'angoisses. De ce rien, de cet embryon rudimentaire qui est la première idée d'un livre, faire sortir le *punctum saliens*, tirer un à un de sa tête les incidents d'une fabulation, les lignes des caractères l'intrigue, le dénouement: la vie de tout ce petit monde animé de vous-même, jailli de vos entrailles et qui fait un roman. Quel travail! C'est comme une feuille de papier blanc qu'on aurait dans le tête, et sur laquelle la pensée, non encore formée, griffonnerait de l'écriture vague et illisible. . . . Et les lassitudes mornes, et les désespoirs infinis, et les hontes soi-même de se sentir impuissant dans son ambition de création. On tourne, on retourne sa cervelle, elle sonne creux. On se

BERG / MS. / 30   1 Cecil Court,
(*To George Sturt*)   St. Martin's Lane, W.C.

                             29 June 96

My dear Sturt,
    I will assuredly come down on Saturday if fine on my bicycle. I can easily run down in 3½ hours, but will allow myself four. I should get into Farnham about 1. Will you send instructions how to find your place. I know your brother's shop & the Lion & Lamb so you can start your explanations from either of these points. I *must* return to town on Sunday. If I leave after a very early tea, I shall be all right for a supper at Chelsea. I am most anxious to use my bicycle for this trip as the exercise will do me great benefit, sir, & the roads are so adorable.
    Touching Alcock, I should be delighted to occupy a pew with Alcock at your place, but if he comes we shan't have to talk shop, you know! He wouldn't be able to come before the evening.

                                   Yours, E. A. B.

---

tâte, on passe la main sur quelque chose de mort qui est votre imagination. . . . On se dit qu'on ne peut rien faire, qu'on ne fera plus rien. Il semble qu'on soit *vidé.*
    'L'idée est pourtant là, attirante et insaisissable, comme une belle et méchante fée dans un nuage. On remet sa pensée à coups de fouet sur la piste; on recherche l'insomnie pour avoir les bonnes fortunes des fièvres de la nuit; on tend à les rompre sur une concentration unique toutes les cordes de son cerveau. Quelque chose vous apparaît un moment, puis s'enfuit, et vous retombez plus las que d'un assaut qui vous à brisé. . . . Oh! tâtonner ainsi, dans la nuit de l'imagination, l'âme d'un livre, et ne rien trouver, ronger ses heures à tourner autour, descendre en soi et n'en rien rapporter, se trouver entre le dernier livre qu'on a mis au monde, dont le cordon est coupé, qui ne vous est plus rien, et le livre auquel vous ne pouvez donner le sang et la chair, être en gestation du néant: ce sont les jours horribles de l'homme de pensée et d'imagination.
    'Tous ces jours-ci, nous étions dans cet état anxieux. Enfin les premiers contours, le vague *fusinage* de notre roman, la jeune Bourgeoisie (*Renée Mauperin*), nous est apparu ce soir.'
30. The address is that of the offices of *Woman.*

LANE / MS. / 31
(*To John Lane*)
6 Victoria Grove
10 July 96

Dear Mr. Lane,
Will you kindly send me the MS. of my novel, so that I may go through it & finish it off before my holidays?

I enclose a little article by George Sturt from this month's *Macmillan's*, which I should be glad if you could find time to read. I am sure that, short as it is, it will at once convince you that Sturt is an original & distinguished writer, with some sort of a future before him.

Believe me,
Sincerely yours, E. A. Bennett

P.S. Many thanks for Mrs. Charles Moulton's address. E. A. B.

BERG / MS. / 32
(*To George Sturt*)
6 Victoria Grove
11 July 96

My dear Sturt,
It was nothing more serious than a puncture, after all. I discovered the thing quite easily on Monday night by *stretching* the indiarubber in a basin of water.

Nevertheless it spoilt a ride home which might have been memorable. The first 10 miles were divine.

Whether owing to my visit to you or not I can't tell, but I have been in a most extraordinary humour for work this week; haven't been able to find enough to do; of course my novel is yet too inchoate for actual writing; besides, I don't want to start that till Oct. 1. So I 'went against' J.B.'s opera full tilt, & did the first scene in 2 days; posted it to him yesterday morning in fear & trembling, but was reassured this morning by a short but indubitably enthusiastic acknowledgment of

31. Sturt's article, 'The Slave of Summer', was a brief account of his Surrey labourer. Sturt complained to Bennett that the editor changed the article considerably.
Mrs. Moulton is unidentified.

receipt. I know now that I can hit his taste in the stomach with fine accuracy. The stuff ain't poetry, but it's unmistakably rousing & full of contrasts; it gives him a chawnst; & after all, in an opera, though the poetry *of the bare idea* must come from the librettist the poetry of the flesh & blood of the idea must come from the composer. Hein? Real poetry, besides being thrown away, only entangles the composer's movements.

By the end of next week I shall have finished half the first act.

Don't be afraid of making that Grover book extremely episodic; leave off *immediately* the interest of a chapter slackens. If one chapter extends only to half a page no matter! There is no reason why the book shouldn't be quite short, say 30,000 words.

Ever read Stendhal's *Physiologie de l'Amour*? If not, do. 1 franc is the price. It is vivacious, epigrammatic, & full of commonsense. I think he must be a great man. It was Miss Symonds mentioned the book to me, though she hadn't read it herself. I had tea with her at the Writers Club Wednesday. She knows *the differences between a man & a woman* better than anyone I know. I allow she has set me right more than once. She was extremely pleased with the 'Slave of Summer', which I set her on to read. I have sent a copy of the article to John Lane, & think it will knock him. 'Short as the article is,' I said to him, 'I feel sure that you will agree with me that it is the work of an original & distinguished writer, with some sort of a future before him.' Why, certainly! His discernment (of which he is proud) being thus put on its mettle, will show what it can do. Oh! Talk of Machiavelli—he ain't no clahss.

I understand I am to see you Saturday. Sharpe can't come, damn him, nor has he *any* free day during the next 3 weeks.

Yours, E. A. Bennett

This letter is merely to make you aware that my little visit was a delicious morsel.   A. B.

Kindest regards to Miss S & Miss Susie.

32. James Brown wrote his opera, *Rosalys*, for performance at the Welsh Girls' School in Ashford, Middlesex, where he taught. It was produced on 27 July 1898. One of Brown's brothers recalls that at the end of the performance there were

BERG / MS. / 33
(*To George Sturt*)

6 Victoria Grove
28 Sept 96

My dear Sturt,

Glad you wrote yesterday, & glad also to know that the book is finished. Tomorrow at 6 p.m. I begin my next novel: that is my news, & having fired it off, I may return to your letter.

---

calls for 'author', and brother James acknowledged them. Bennett, though, was so busy calling for the author that he made no response. The following lyric is the Prelude for a chorus of girls.

> All day and day long
> With dance and with song
> With foot and with tongue,
> We have frisked in the green of the wood;
> In the heat and the cool,
> By stream and by pool,
> Quite regardless of school,
> We have laughed and we've talked all we could.
>
> All day and day long,
> Day long and all day,
> We have each said our say
> As we rambled along
> In the shadiest green of the wood.
>
>   (very brief dance)
>
> And now it is night,
> And now will the sprite
> And the pigwidgeon white
> Make fearful the green of the wood.
> But we care not at all,
> We are asked to the ball
> In the countess' hall—
> Who cares for the shapes in the wood!
>
> For this day,
> Midsummer day,
> Is the birthday,
> And this night,
> Midsummer night,
> Is the birthnight
> Of the Lady Rosalys, Rosalys,
> Daughter of Dubric.

The whole of the libretto is reproduced in the Appendix of Margaret Locherbie-Goff's *La Jeunesse d'Arnold Bennett*.

Grover was the real name of the Surrey labourer, Frederick Bettesworth, of the *Bettesworth Book*.

Miss S. and Miss Susie are presumably Mary Sturt (d. 1922) and Susan Sturt (d. 1935), George's sisters.

F

Impressions, with regard to your book, it would be a mistake to let Jim's opinion influence you. During the last month I have made large additions to my appreciation of & respect for him, but literature ain't his forte. He can talk about it with an ingenuity almost devilish, but he *knows* nothing whatever about it. You & me'll settle what is good about that book & what isn't. We'll listen to J.'s views—& treat them as he, most properly, treats mine on music.

Touching your unbegun novel & your theories thereon, I repeat for the Nth time that for myself I 'don't do much to' theories. And as to 'body & soul'—I don't think I know what you mean. I sort of cotton to 'shape', & I feel a deep attachment to 'Art-manufacture'. Of *course* it must be an article of art-manufacture—a thing of gross & unashamed artificiality. No novel could possibly succeed that wasn't. You know this. Why, then, try to get round to the backside of a truism, & unsettle yourself? If you have got hold of a story, tell it as plainly as you can, & be damned to divagations upon 'combination of two processes'. . . . But of course you mustn't tell a story *plainly*— I didn't mean that. I meant, well, you know—you will see it set forth in my book on Turgenev, of which I dream. Time is what I want. Time to read his various 'lives', his correspondence with Aksakov, his early work & the work of his acknowledged masters Pushkin & Gogol, & of a few others. Having assimilated & thrice chewed so much, I might begin. I really want to do it, yet have no real hope of doing it. Consider my present programme:—

> Burslem novel
> Shorter novel, about a tall man.
> Brown's [?damnation] opera.
> A 5,000 word foreign story

for our Xmas number.

> Literary Criticism
> Dramatic   ,,
> Editorial work
> Occasional articles & stories

to boil the pot.

It's a dorg's life! What time have I to write to my friends? To be myself?

Yes, I emphatically had a time on the continent. I took a book 3 parts full of notes in the first 10 days, & then ceased to note. It was a wonderful experience. When I got home, I began to set in order, fill out, & translate my notes, but after a little while, found I hadn't the moral strength to continue. So they will have to remain in the raw.

I got what I take to be good stuff about my native heath during the week I was down there—sort of synthetised the entire place, imprisoned it in one comprehensive impression. There is going to be *some* good in my new book. What dost think, for name of heroine & of book, of

SIS MARIGOLD?

Marigold is a genuine surname, as no doubt you are aware. It has been used by a fellow named C. T. C. James in a low-down comic novelette. Immediately I saw it, I grabbed & said to Mr. C. T. C. James, 'Here, I'll relieve you of that. Hands up!'

Yours waiting for the book, E. A. B.

BUTLER / MS. / 34   Lower Bourne
(*From George Sturt*)   In 5 minutes by the clock, you'll be
                      starting your second novel. May all
                      the gods smile upon your labours!
                      [29 September 1896]

My dear Bennett,

Happy beggar, beginning your book! And—to digress— happy beggar also, to know so well what time you'll have 'tomorrow'. I never know what time I shall have free; but only what I shall have occupied otherwise than in writing. . . . And now to begin this letter (but I've only about ½ an hour).

33. Sturt reported finishing *The Bettesworth Book*. The new novel was eventually begun and ultimately bore the title *The Extinction of the Keens*.

Bennett duly began writing *Anna of the Five Towns*, whose heroine possesses and marries gold but whose name Bennett decided later should be Tellwright. The novel by C. T. C. James is not known. On Bennett's novel about a tall man see page 19. 'The Christmas Chimes of Malyprès' was published in *Woman* on 9 December 1896.

Turgenev's friend Sergei Aksakov (1791–1859) is perhaps best known for his *Chronicles of a Russian Family*.

Bennett visited Belgium in August with James Brown and one or two other friends.

Yes, for the Nth time you tell me that you 'don't do much to' theories. . . . Well, take care that you never let it come to the $(N+1)$th time. What the murrain have you to do with talk of that sort? Are you, then, that man you once spoke of (you used the 3rd person—for a blind, perhaps?) who, admiring a play (by Henry Arthur Jones) which a critic told him he ought not to admire, blurted out the engaging confession that if knowledge spoilt his pleasure in a play like that, then he thanked God for his ignorance?—or words to that effect. . . . The two things are on the same footing. I don't pretend that a book can be written by theories: but I *know* that knowledge of what you do want to do and what you want to avoid and why is of considerable advantage in writing a book. The more accurately you know this, the better chance there is for you. . . . No 'theories' indeed! You'll be telling me next that a knowledge of mechanics isn't much good to an engineer, and that a musician needn't 'do much to' harmony. Out upon you! Fact is, you didn't understand my meaning, and in the manner of a sucking Podsnap (see Dickens: *Mutual Friend*) waved it aside with a sneer: 'Theory'; says you, 'pooh! Theory!' . . . A very good trick, sir, when you can pull it off with éclat; but be careful lest it only expose your ignorance.

You don't think you know what I mean by body and soul. . . . Look here:—In my mind I'm aware of 2 or 3 characters for a book; I know something about their attitude towards one another—their love, hate, selfishness etc etc; the sort of things that one would approve or else damn, in them. This is what I spoke of as 'soul'. Unluckily, I don't yet know how these 'souls' will express themselves: what their characteristic speech, gesture & behaviour are. I could write an analytical essay upon their characters, but cannot set down pictorially their external show, from which the reader might infer the characters, without the bore of being told by me.

On the other hand, I could go on writing as long as you like, describing the personal appearance, movements etc of people in the street. This is the 'body'. But I've not the key to this personal appearance etc; don't understand it, don't (as a rule) *care* a damn about it. The Key being the Character hidden under all this show.

And, theoretically—note that word!—Soul in the Abstract

isn't interesting, at any rate in a novel; you must show the flesh & blood: while, on the other side, the flesh & blood without the soul is mere weariness. . . .

My time is up. I have to go again to Farnham—and shall enjoy it. A sort of decorous carnival—bicycles, trade-devices, fellows in masquerade, processioning in the light of Japanese Lanterns, etc etc. My work folk, having obtained from me half-a-guinea towards expenses, are preparing a van, much decorated, and finally set off with a blacksmith's movable forge, the fire blazing my coals away, the anvil ringing under sledges. I must go and hide my cynicism under a simulation of admiration & delight.

Hang it, I envy them their unconsciousness.

Thursday: close on dinner-time. I've been thinking about 'Sis Marigold'. . . . The name is a good name; *but* not for every heroine. It suggests to me a kind of middle-class *Di Vernon* (Do you know your Walter Scott properly?): a showery-eyed impulsive damsel with a lot of pluck and misfortune, all coming right in the end.

You are, I'm afraid, no nearer the mark than Jim about my labourer book. 'Tisn't 'literature': from that point of view, it doesn't exist as a 'book' at all. Damn it I know what it is: I only know that the compiling of it seemed to me a duty; inasmuch as my opportunity was unique, and the stuff might let in a little light upon a darkish place. It hasn't been bad fun; but I'm glad it's over, or within 2 hours of that. I shall keep it another week or so: then try to send it to you in what I mean to be its final shape.

I'm sorry for your eyes, reading this. Please pardon: I've no notepaper.

Yours, G. S.

BERG / MS. / 35
(*To George Sturt*)

6 Victoria Grove
21 Oct 96

Sir,

I have the honour to refer to certain portions of your last sheet as '**OO**'. I reckon to be myself in search of that 'knowledge of what I want to do, & what I want to avoid, & why'.

I languish for that wisdom. But all the same if you begin to talk about the 'body & soul' of a book, then I grows cussed, like William Morris when the modern stage was mentioned. You can't divide a book into body & soul. The body & soul of a character of course I can conceive, but that's different. I therefore repeat that I don't do much to such theories. You know perfectly well what I mean; I never could explain myself, on any subject, & it's a shame of you to tease me. God bless me, you & Jim would talk the 'erection' out of Cleopatra's needle.

I have been rather astonishingly well for the last 14 days. I wrote a story last week for our Christmas number, with a Flemish scene. When I began I thought it was going to be something rather good, but I'm not ecstatic about it now. Quite out of my usual run, & therefore artificial, a mere *tour de force*. But you shall see it; the writing will pass in a crowd, & the idea is not inane.

Certain events (which I will relate when I see you—may it be soon) at the office have given me an idea for another novel; a study of religious mania—à la *Madame Gervaisais*, which you should read if you don't know it already. This makes 3 novels on the stocks or in the air.

With the chief of these, though I am not depressed as yet, I am not quite swimming along. I can't catch the tone I want; & I can't decide whether it is to be told solely from the standpoint of a single individual (like my last) or not. Nor can I decide whether a certain household shall keep a domestic servant or not—a little point, but it bothers me. However, I have written 2 chapters once & one twice, & the third & fourth are forming themselves, & the 7th is quite formed. By the time I have got to 7 I shall be able to see the blasted thing 'steadily & see it whole'. And then I shall 'put a nigger on the safety valve & a ham in the furnace', & 'let her rip down the Mississippi a regular rustler, sir'.

I haven't got that 'sinking feeling' that took hold of me sometimes during the progress of my first novel. Have I told you that that same is to be called *A Man from the North*?

Touching my 'Journal', that volume I showed you is full, & I have employed this afternoon in making a successor to it, twice as thick. The first contains 15,000 words, & extends over six months. I think a lot of it is rot, but there is some beef mixed up in the mess. It contains most things—'impressions', memoirs & hoc genus, & some philosophy (soi-disant). When you are up I would like you to look at it. It probably won't interest you, but you can tell me what you think.

And when in the name of Nelson *are* you coming up? I had supper with Miss Symonds the other night (her new book comes forth this week); she enquires after you regularly. And when is that book going to reach me? I haven't heard anything further of mine yet.

Three theatres this week! One tonight & 2 on Saturday, & all 3 rot. God preserve us!

Kind regards to your sisters & Frank & his little lot.

Sincerely yours, E. A. B.

BERG / MS. / 36
(*To George Sturt*)

6 Victoria Grove
11 Nov 96

My dear George,
Two lines.

I was ill all last week with abscess in lower jaw which burst (inside) on Saturday night. It would have been better sooner, only I was forced to go out every day to the office. I made two attempts to see John Lane & failed. I expect to see him on Friday next. I saw Chapman & intended leaving the MS. with him for Lane. But he advised strongly that it should be kept back a bit, pending the fate of the other book. He thinks the

35. Sturt replied: 'My theories are ○○ are they? Sir, you flatter me. I had not thought them so fruitfully virile. But what fiendish malignity is yours in endeavouring to deprive me of them! Is it envy?'

'The Christmas Chimes of Malyprès' is narrated in the first person by a romantic and passionate Englishwoman who on a visit to the continent climbs a bell-tower to see the carillonneur perform. She faints, he carries her to the top of the tower, and their eyes speak love. But she is betrothed to another, and that other soon commits suicide, and she retires to Staffordshire. Her name is Rosalys. The plot, character, and method of narration are the first germ of *Sacred and Profane Love* (1905).

The novel about religious mania on the lines of the Goncourt novel was never written, though Bennett perhaps subsequently enlarged the religious element of *Anna of the Five Towns*.

Miss Symonds' forthcoming novel was *The Career of Candida*.

acceptance of the 2nd might be an excuse for refusing the 1st & doesn't want this to occur. I had, vaguely, the same sort of idea, & therefore concurred. At his request I left the MS. with him to read if & when he has time.

I hope to make your 'Journal' this week & will send it you. No more now from yours truly in great haste, E. A. Bennett.

BERG / MS. / 37
(*To George Sturt*)

6 Victoria Grove
18 Nov 96

My dear George,

Sympathies herewith. You will come round all right, as doubtless you are yourself aware. Your revelations incidentally disclose how different your methods are from mine, in starting a novel. You seem to leave the 'real central motive' till the last. I begin with the real central motive—in my new novel, a girl's marriage forced on her partly by mere habit of submission to a parental authority not at that particular juncture exercised, & partly by another cause needless to specify. Having got that, I look about for a general atmosphere. Having got the atmosphere, the incidents suggest themselves. But I don't go in for much incident.

I was with Lane yesterday for 1½ hours. He said he was ashamed of himself about your book. But he was too much wrapped up in his about-to-be-issued Xmas books to get excited about either your MS. or anybody else's. He said he must ask me to give him till the New Year. I non-committed myself. If it is left with him he will beyond the least doubt accept it. That I am certain of. Both Chapman & I think it well to leave things alone, but we can quite understand your impatience, & if you care to risk it, I will get the MS. back & offer it to Heinemann. With regard to the other book I have not had another chance of speaking to C about it. I shall sup with him on Saturday night, & we will then fix up a modus operandi. I do hope that you will so far as possible determine with yourself that the uncertain reception of these two books

36. Sturt's journals, recently re-edited by E. D. Mackerness, were begun in 1890 and largely abandoned in 1893. He took them up again this year.

shan't influence your present work. I am conscious of not
having shone very brightly as a literary agent, but I am more
sure than ever that the stuff will be all right—ultimately.

My own trifle is to appear, it is said, Feb. or March. I
interviewed Johnny Lane last night for *Woman*, & we are very
chummy & all that. He promised to give me some 'reading' to
do, & I will damn well see that he does, too.

Sis Tellwright is temporarily at a standstill, owing to worries
in connection with *Woman*. Since Gardner's departure for
Amérique, facts have transpired to the effect that he has through
sheer carelessness played hell financially with the paper. It is,
however, a fine property when he has done his worst. He has
been forced to offer his resignation, and the people who hold
a controlling interest in *Woman* & in two other women's papers
are going to make one big company which is going to be a big
success. They have offered me the editorship of *Woman* & I
have accepted it, but details are not yet arranged, & won't be
for a month. Unless miracles or earthquakes occur, however,
I shall be editor, both formally & virtually, by the end of the
year & the fact will be officially communicated to the press.
In the meantime I have full control. My mind is bursting with
schemes; the journalist half of me is rampant; but things will
settle down & then the novelist shall have a show.

Thine, E. A. B.

37. Sturt's letter of 13 November 1896 complained of an inability to get his
new novel moving. 'I keep seeing things and being aware of things beautiful and
interesting. Not exactly romantic, any of them: but good to dwell on. Things that
give the feeling that "all's well with the world"; and that it's good to be alive
and part of the circus. A kind of placid romance, if romance at all. But when I
come to make a story, somehow the romance doesn't get into it. There appears
only the narrative, which fails to interest me. . . . I can't write a book of that sort,
ust for the sake of writing; or if I can, 'twd be a worthless thing. I need to feel
he "romance" (a vile expres sion) as the life of the thing, the story being only its
expression.'

The interview with John Lane could not be found. It may finally have gone
into another journal than *Woman*.

Woman, Hearth & Home (self-described as a dainty weekly for gentlewomen),
and *Myra's Journal* (a monthly) were controlled by the Beeton Company, famous
for its cookery book.

BERG / MS. / 38
(*To George Sturt*)

6 Victoria Grove
22 Nov 96

My dear George,

I suppose the novel is half written by this time!

I was with Chapman last night. He advises urgently a policy of entire inactivity. He is quite positive about the safety of the first book.

Enclosed is the promised 'Journal'. No charge of any kind is made for this kind of bibelot to any author named George Sturt who undertakes to use it for a journal. New volumes will be supplied at any time on demand within three days.

Hoping, sir, to make our profits out of the 'volume of trade',

We are

Your obedient servants
Straker & Co.
Very cheap stationers & bookbinders
Ludgate Hill & Coventry St.

P.S. I also return the voyage diary. It is excellent, & I was very pleased with it.

BERG / MS. / 39
(*To George Sturt*)

6 Victoria Grove
Wednesday 2. xii—96

My dear George,

Enchanted to hear that you have floored that novel at last.

This is to tell you not to expect letters from me just now. I am so damnably busy. And as if I hadn't enough to do I have arranged to write a book on journalism for Lane, & have taken a pupil in the same craft—a damn fool he is, too.

Of course I am open to receive communications from you— daily.

Touching *Woman*, I *do* trust to make a much better thing of it. But I reckon that already there is no other woman's paper

38. Sturt made a boat trip from London to Glasgow, and kept a journal of his impressions.

to come near it. I wish I could get my friends to see that it isn't edited for fun, or to meet *their* tastes, but as a business venture, depending on the suffrages of perfectly ordinary women as they actually exist—not as they might be & will be.

Yours, E. A. B.

BECKER / TS. / 40
(*To Ida Meller*)

1 Cecil Court
4th Dec. 1896

Dear Miss Meller,

Are you open to consider the offer of a regular engagement here in the capacity of Sub-editor? I should require your services about two and a half days in the week. Perhaps you will let me have a reply at once, as I find it necessary to make an arrangement instantly.

I have, of course, had no personal experience of yourself, and I should like you to know that my offer is made solely on the strength of the small paragraphs that you send us from time to time. I have gathered from the way in which these are done, that you would be likely to suit me.

Believe me,

Yours sincerely, E. A. Bennett

39. The original idea for *Journalism for Women* was probably an article on journalism written by Sarah Volatile, published in *Woman* on 5 February 1896. It was one of a series on *How Women May Make Money*.

40. Ida Meller (1864–1934) became Bennett's sub-editor. Her niece describes her as a very capable woman whose shyness precluded any startling success as a journalist. In his Journal in 1926 Bennett describes meeting her for the first time in several years:

'I met Ida Meller, to whom I think I gave her first permanent job, on *Woman* about thirty or more years ago, this morning in Sloane Square. She seemed to have changed little. She must be sixty at least, and is still in full work. She asked me if I saw Mrs. Goddard at all. Mrs. Goddard was on my staff before she was married, and I remember her husband, a lawyer's clerk, standing me a lunch so as to get me to agree to a furlough for her while she had a baby. She was very young and very beautiful. "She's a grandmother now," said Ida Meller. "Twice a grandmother. And just the same sweet nature, and just as young." I was staggered, because I had always thought of her as a young girl.'

BERG / MS. / 41
(*To George Sturt*)

6 Victoria Grove
15 Dec 96

My dear George,

My liver is a bit 'on' today: therefore I am certain to sleep well; therefore I don't mind how late I write. See how all things work together for good! It is now 10.30. Been at work since 9.30 a.m. as ever is.

You needn't trouble *Chapmans* for another month. The fact that it wasn't typewritten won't affect the MS.'s safety. By the way I hope you always write on the MS. itself above your name & address, the words, 'Stamped envelope enclosed'. Very often stamped envelopes get separated from MS. & lost.

Yes, my story was Tommy; but there were one or two lilac patches of description, or I deceive myself. All fiction for the time is absolutely off. But my chief sadness is that I can't even keep my dear little Journal going. I see tons of things, but only dimly as I pass hurriedly by them; & at the end of the day, if perchance I have time then for a look at the green volume, damme if there is anything to put into it. . . . However, in January I hope to have got everything, including the female, regular square. (This is the darndest new 'J' pen I ever wrote with.)

Sir, the two full page tinted illustrations in our Xmas No— I blush for them. Only, Gardner bought them without arsting me. No more of Mr. Finberg. Kindly look out for the issue of the 6th January, the first formally under my editorship. But do not expect any raising of tone. Because it just isn't going to be riz.

I am now myself in cap III of *Sentimental Tommy*. So far, it strikes me, as it struck me before in *Scribner*, as a little too merely facetious. Seems as if the beggar didn't know when he was being humorous & when merely funny à la Jerome. Having instinctive doubts of the book, I shouldn't have started it only for Miss Symonds' urgent recommendation. I had a pretty evening with her, Thursday last—a hurried dinner & then *Cymbeline* at the Lyceum. Her book is going rather well, & she is half through her next (a tale of literary life) which she says will be her best. Invariably she enquires after 'that Mr. Sturt'. She remembers *Longman's*.

Barrie's *Margaret Ogilvy*, though a trifle loose in the mere writing, is a divine thing, my boy—sort of book that immediately you have finished it you begin again. No fear of his reputation deliquescing just yet, with that to solidify it.

My book on journalism is essays—not fiction, but rather a practical guide; with aesthetic reflections on the art which has, say, raised the *Daily Mail* to 250,000 circulation & the position of first *newspaper* pure & simple in this great country. I can do that a treat.

Kind regards to your sisters & Frank & Maud. I should have searched out the last at Jim's concert, but didn't know her bassoon was there till afterwards.

Thine, E. A. B.

Keep on writing to me. Your letters are just now at their best.

LANE / MS. / 42
(*To John Lane*)

1 Cecil Court
23 Dec 96

Dear Mr. Lane,

I must apologise for not returning *King Noanett*. But I have been so awfully busy lately that I have not had time to finish it. I propose to take it into the country with me & to let you have it *next week certain*.

---

41. Sturt sent a manuscript to *Chapman's Magazine* and had no response from them. Complete files of the magazine were not available to show whether they published anything of his at this time.

Sturt thought that Bennett's Christmas story was mechanical, and he objected to the illustrations of A. J. Finberg (1866–1939), who later had more success as a writer on the history of art.

J. M. Barrie (1860–1937) published both *Sentimental Tommy* and *Margaret Ogilvy* in 1896. Of the latter, a tribute to Barrie's mother, Bennett wrote in his Journal a few days before: 'This book is a picture of a grave, mighty, passionate family of men and women. Instinctively, and all the time, I was comparing it with my own, and in particular comparing Margaret Ogilvy and J. M. Barrie with my mother and myself. Again and again, I had to acknowledge inferiority— inferiority of essential "character", apart from inessential talent—a lack of bigness, and a presence of certain littlenesses. Yet at the same time, I found us sturdy enough not to be ashamed of shortcomings. What we are, we are! "I exist as I am, that is enough." ' Maud was Frank's wife; see page 33n.

You might, if you are still of the same mind, now get the *Academy* to insert that paragraph about me. I shall leave you to write it. I don't think it should contain any reference to Mr. Gardner—merely say that I have been appointed Editor, after having been assistant editor for three years, & 'Barbara' for two years. I would like it to appear in the first issue of 1897, not before.

Merry Xmas &c.

Sincerely yours, E. A. Bennett

P.S. You haven't sent me any MSS. to read yet!   E. A. B.

BERG / MS. / 43
(*To George Sturt*)

6 Victoria Grove
28 Jan 97

My dear George,

I saw John Lane this morning & he accepted your book. It is to be published at 3/6 in Lane's Library, in the autumn, & you are to have a 5% royalty on the first thousand & ten per cent. afterwards.

Lane had told Chapman to read the MS. with a view to judging of its unhealthiness. Chapman read it on Sunday, & reported that the charge of unhealthiness was preposterous. If I might suggest, you would do well to write direct to Chapman in reference to his endeavours on your behalf, as he is a man who looks for and appreciates these formal acknowledgments.

Also you had better write to Lane at once in the strain of the enclosed. He is going to America on Saturday, but you can write all the same exactly as if he wasn't.

I shall now turn my attention to *Bettesworth*.

The 'letter' which I owe you shall follow in due course.

Thine, E. A. B.

42. *King Noanett*, by Frederic Jessup Stimson, a writer of fiction and also of popular accounts of law, was published by Lane at about this time.

No *Academy* paragraph on Bennett could be found.

43. The accepted book was *A Year's Exile*. *The Bettesworth Book* was still being considered. Bennett wrote for Sturt as follows:

'Dear Sir,

I understand from my friend Bennett that he has seen you & that you have accepted my novel *A Year's Exile*, for publication in the autumn in 'Lane's

BERG / MS. / 44
(*To George Sturt*)

6 Victoria Grove
31 Jan. 97

My dear George,

All day, & a beastly day too, I have been wanting to begin again with my novel, but couldn't centre my wits on it at all. It hasn't yet been seriously touched this year. I wait only for one little incident to shape itself and then I can march on up to, & right through, my great revival scene in the Wesleyan Methodist chapel, which is to beat Harold Frederic in his own chosen field. When this is sketched in, I shall consider that the first part of the book is achieved—three parts altogether. . . . Yes, I have known all along that a novel must have a purpose; to look at the matter from another side, it must 'expose' some aspect of existence in which the author is deeply interested. But it mustn't be didactic—at least it must only teach in the same way as experience teaches. All which is platitude. My novels will all have purposes. The purpose of *A Man from the North* is to 'expose' a few of the hardships and evils of the life of the young celibate clerk in London. Of course I use 'expose' in the French sense. As for *Sis Tellwright* (henceforward to be known as *Anna Tellwright*—Anna being the Christian name which I had decided on a year ago, & which I gave up because it had the same vowel sound as its first surname, 'Marigold', now abandoned), if it is not a sermon against parental authority, then I say it is naught.

By the way, I don't, & never did, see the purpose of *Dr. Mitchell*. Seems to me that it rather wanted a purpose—to *integrate* it. I should inform you that that same novel is known in Lane's office as *A Year's Exile*, which really is not half a bad title. Anyhow that title will do to go on with, & when I have read it again, I will fetch up a title or expire in the attempt. I will get the MS. off Chapman, & page it myself. Marcel Prévost, the author of *Les Demi-Vierges*, has got a fine title

Library' at 3/6, my royalty to be 5% on the published price for the first thousand copies & 10% afterwards. Will you kindly confirm this, & send me your usual form of contract in due course.

Please accept my thanks for the careful attention you have given to the MS (or something of the sort).

Yours ——'

for his new book, a sort of study of a woman's inside soul, *Le Jardin Secret*. I think he must have got it from the Song of Solomon:

'A garden enclosed is my sister, my spouse.'

And talking of quotations, how will this do for the title page of *Bettesworth*

'Sir, I am a true labourer: I earn that I eat, get that I wear, owe no man hate, envy no man's happiness, glad of other men's good, content with my harm; and the greatest of my pride is to see my ewes graze and my lambs suck.' *As You Like It*, Act 3. Sc. 2.

Last night at Ken's my faculty of observation, such as it is, was kept busy. I found there the typical Clerk and his wife. Where Ken had picked them up I know not, but they were extremely interesting, diverting, and agreeable. After we had been talking of Lamb's essays, Mrs. Henry Wood, *The Cloister and the Hearth* etc, the typical Clerk said: 'What is *this Yellow Book*, Mr. Bennett?' as if he was enquiring into the nature of some dim mystery like the differential calculus or bimetallism. The *this*, too, was very characteristic. I tried to get the pair down on paper this morning, but without much success. By the way my description of the *Yellow Book* in answer to his question showed masterly tact, & would have made Ken roar in secret had he been in the room. I described it so that if the Clerk happened ever to see the *Yellow Book*, he would say to himself 'What that chap told me about it was quite right'.

My Journal was very much in abeyance till a fortnight ago, but is going strong now. 33 pages filled of the new volume. . . . In a few hours February begins, & February must see a great progress in my novel.

Toujours à toi, E. A. B.

44. Harold Frederic (1856–98) had recently published his most famous novel, *Illumination* (*The Damnation of Theron Ware*), whose hero is a young Methodist preacher who lapses into sin. One of the most vivid scenes is of a Methodist revival.

Marcel Prévost (1862–1940) was specially interested in feminine psychology in his novels, as was Bennett himself. Charles Lamb (1775–1834) remained an interest of Bennett's, and had several pages of *Literary Taste* (1909) devoted to him. Charles Reade (1814–84) appears with *The Cloister and the Hearth* in the 'Library of English Literature' in *Literary Taste*. Mrs. Henry Wood (1814–87) was the author of the notorious *East Lynne*.

Bennett described the typical clerk and his wife in his Journal:

'The Clerk: a short man, with a merry, half-boyish face, and a good

BERG / MS. / 45
(*To George Sturt*)

6 Victoria Grove
8 Feby 97

My dear George,

New bread for tea, followed by the sort of inflated, un-important indigestion that shows itself in lassitude & gripes. But I had settled to draft a chapter (viii) of my novel, & I drafted it—6 pm to 8.15 with intervals for poking around & squinting at the *Pall Mall Gazette*. I did it badly, but I did it. The draft exists, & will serve. It has been a fine frosty day, & Frank & I were to run round the town on our bicycles about 8.30. I departed to the studio to arouse him, & was greeted by the sound of heavy rain on the roof windows. Of all the darned climates. . . . Hence this letter.

In my last letter I missed out the interesting part, by some oversight. I forget the details now, but it was about Kipling. I think I had to say that Kipling was frequently 'conventional' in the worst sense. To my mind he makes too much of those fine qualities of endurance, fortitude, self-sacrifice, courage, self-command &c which undoubtedly do distinguish the English as a race. He makes too much of them. He ignores truth for the sake of tickling the reader's palate (*your* palette, George), & satisfying his own tastes . . . That is one of his faults. I could prove it from almost any page of his work. Perhaps I have put it too roughly. Perhaps all I mean is that (to use the terms of another art) he has conventionalised his ornament too much for the medium in which he works. Anyhow he is not a realist. He will be picturesque first & picturesque last. I like him, but it is not the artist in me that likes him. In spite of such phrases as 'the rain fell like ramrods on the earth'; 'the lightning bespattered the sky as a thrown egg spatters a barn

---

moustache; keen in looks, yet every feature disclosing a narrow habit of mind; at first good-naturedly *too* courteous and deferential, afterwards assuming his natural manner of unaffected pleasantness. His wife: a woman of about 35, apparently older than the clerk, dressed plainly in red and grey; a broad face of peculiar shape, with long, censorious lips that came together in a straight line, and remained so; a sensible, sober face, full of what is called character. . . . She was very restrained till late in the evening when at the sight of some comic drawings she laughed immoderately and long, repeating, "I do think that's funny". . . .'

G

door'—wonderfully descriptive—I assert that he is not consciously an artist, & therefore not an artist at all. And especially
he is not an artist in words. I have never (in his prose work)
found a trace of the artist's passion for words & loving care
over them; & in his poetry I am convinced that the extraordinarily vivid images & similes that he gets hold of ('the
thresh of the deep sea rain', for instance) are used in the rough
just as they come to him. Besides, vivid images &c don't imply
an artist in words at all. He takes very little, if any, care over
mere expression. I cannot say what I mean, but Guy de
Maupassant can. Extract from his masterly 'Étude sur Gustave
Flaubert'.

'Quand un homme, *quelque doué qu'il soit,* ne se préoccupe
que de la chose racontée, quand il ne se rend pas compte que
le véritable pouvoir littéraire n'est pas dans un fait, mais bien
dans la manière de le préparer, de le présenter, et de l'exprimer,
il n'a pas le sens de l'art. . . .

'Les mots ont une âme. La plupart des lecteurs, et même
des écrivains, ne leur demandent qu'un sens. Il faut trouver
cette âme qui apparaît au contact d'autres mots, qui éclate et
éclaire certains livres d'une lumière inconnue, bien difficile à
faire jaillir.'

(The whole of this essay is superb.)

Kipling has the ideas; he has the poetic insight, the large
synthetic view which enables him to see an Empire in one sweep,
the poet's sympathy which illuminates all the dark corners of
human experience; but having seen, felt, heard—as an artist
would see, feel, hear, he is content. Forgetting that after all the
art of literature consists in *writing,* he is content to do the supreme
labour of all in a haphazard, rapid, careless fashion. True, his
expression is nearly always vivid, but this is due to the triumphant
vividness of his *seeing,* rather than to any care he may exercise
as a writer. He succeeds not because of, but in spite of, his
mode of expression. I fancy he would rather scorn 'mere'
artistry, & when it was mentioned would begin to talk about
fighting or famine or fakirs. I willingly agree that he is a great
man, but this doesn't touch the question.

There is more literary art in this line or two of Charles Lamb's
than in all Kipling's tales put together:—'Stones of old
Mincing Lane which I have worn with my daily pilgrimage

for six-and-thirty years, to the footsteps of what toilworn clerk are your everlasting flints now vocal? I indent the gayer flags of Pall Mall. It is 'Change time, and I am strangely among the Elgin marbles.' Yes, in that *strangely* & its position in the sentence, there is more literary art than Kipling will ever compass though he write as long as Tennyson and as fast as Mrs. Oliphant.

Do you hate me?

. . . .

I rejoice to say that I had a good time last week. I drafted 5,500 words, & 1,500 tonight makes 7,000. When I say 'drafted', that is what I mean. The stuff is rough. I fancy you would benignly smile at my methods of production. But I know myself, & my absurd limitations, & I have to get results as best I may, by dodging &c. If I were to begin to write care-fully, straight away, weighing & arranging with proper nicety, I should get sick of my work in a week. I can't do much at once, & I can't keep on for long, even in spurts, without real or sham results for my encouragement. This is due to a lack of sustained determination in my composition. This needed dogged purposefulness is not there. I have found that out, & I know that I can't put it there (no more than by taking thought I can add a cubit &c). Consequently I have to reckon with it. And so I divide my task into little portions which look big. Any sort of a draft will do for me, provided it is of the proper length. And in the first draft, I am content to get down the facts. The facts being down, I have done something; there is a foundation to work upon. Strange that this foundation being laid, I seldom have any desire to alter or amend it. (But I believe I have a considerable natural gift for arrangement which makes changes of foundation supererogatory.) In the first draft I don't pretend to go deep or to arrange minor detail. I only make sure of my general outline as I go along. The mere writing is appallingly unfinished; indeed it can only claim to be grammatical—nothing more. But at the most I have got something to look at (last week, e.g., some 35 pages of close writing). I have lifted the thing up to a certain height, whence it can't possibly fall down. The rest of the mountain can be taken in easy stages. By the way that sketch of the opening which you were pleased to like, was a second draft, which I did because I was desperately enamoured of the ideas in it, & had a fever to get them clearer.

No, a novel needn't have such a defined & definable purpose as I go in for. I go in for unity of theme partly because I like it, & partly because it is easier to get effects with a simple single theme, than with a complicated one. A small man can make a largish sort of effect if he confines himself to one single character, with no relief & turns it inside out. That is what I hope to do. I know I haven't got the creative impulse necessary for a big theme, but I fancy I can, by sheer force of concentration & monotony do something effective in a small way.

　　　　　　　.　.　.　.　.　.　.　.

About the summer, are you open to visit the continent with me—on the cheap?

Yours, E. A. B.

T E X A S / M S. / 46
(*To Edward Garnett*)

6 Victoria Grove
14 Feby 97

Dear Sir,

May I ask you to be so good as to give me further particulars of the book *Souvenirs sur Tourguéneff* mentioned in your introduction to *On the Eve*. I cannot trace it at the British Museum or through a bookseller. Also would you direct me to any other reliable French authorities on Turgenev. I have Dupuy's *Les Grand Maîtres de la littérature russe*, which strikes me as being platitudinous & not very informing or critical; also de Vogüé's *Le Roman russe*. Is there any French biography of Turgenev, & has his correspondence been published?

My excuse for thus troubling you must be that I am making a study of Turgenev as a constructive artist in fiction, & that I fully share your admiration for his work. The oftener I read it, the more sure I am that *On the Eve* is out of sight the finest

45. Frank Bennett came to stay in London for a time.
Bennett's earlier letter on Kipling is lost.
Mrs. Oliphant (1828–97) was a prolific writer of fiction, history, and biography. She was a mainstay of *Blackwood's Magazine* for forty-five years.

novel ever written. Your prefaces to the different novels
contain some of the best criticism of fiction that I have come
across. Especially that to *Smoke*. Strictly technical criticism of
fiction (particularly on the point of construction) seems almost
a minus quantity in both England & France. It is one of my
ambitions to revive it—if indeed it was ever really alive.

I may mention that I have more than once had the pleasure
of appreciating your edition of Turgenev in the columns of
Woman, a little paper of which I am editor.

With thanks and anticipation.

Believe me, Dear Sir,
Yours very truly, E. A. Bennett

P.S. I should tell you that I cannot read either Russian or
German. E. A. B.

BERG / MS. / 47
(*To George Sturt*)

6 Victoria Grove
12 Mch 97

My dear George,
I saw Lane for a few brief moments last night. He showed
me a second report on *Bettesworth*, by G. S. Street. It was
distinctly favourable & appreciative. Street evidently sees your
intentions & likes them. He has nothing but praise for the book,
quiet praise, & though he does not think it will sell well, he
opines that a sufficient number of readers *may* be found to
make it worthwhile publishing it.

Lane, however, is afraid. He funks it. He has one book of
yours already which (he says) he does not think will pay him,
& he is chary of another of the same unpopular stamp. 'High

46. Edward Garnett (1868–1937) was at this time literary adviser to Duckworths.
Later he was informal adviser to Joseph Conrad, John Galsworthy, and many
other writers. His full-length study of Turgenev appeared several years later.
Souvenirs sur Tourguéneff (1887) was by Isaac Pavlovsky. The works by Ernest
Dupuy (b. 1849) and Eugène Melchior de Vogüé (b. 1850) appeared in 1885
and 1886 respectively. Bennett's own study of Turgenev became an essay published
in the *Academy* on 4 November 1899. It was reprinted in *Fame and Fiction* (1901).
Bennett was not entirely lacking in German. See page 259.

class work, you know,' I said. 'Yes, that may be,' he said 'but —,' He said he didn't think he should take it, but that he would not give a final answer then. I am not optimistic, but I have some hope (if I don't hurry things) of persuading him into a right course of conduct. I am undecided whether it would be a good plan to make him decide at once on the threat of taking it away & going elsewhere. You had better consider. He might, thus confronted, surrender; on the other hand he might say 'By all means, try elsewhere'.

I enclose a copy of the first report. It is a bit rough, but now that the other report (of which I can get a copy in due course, for your soothing) is favourable, you are in a position to accept its strictures philosophically.

Hastily,

Yours, E. A. B.

47. The first report on *The Bettesworth Book* was as follows:
   'This is a record of conversations with an old countryman, apparently a gardener—the mere notebook of his talk day by day.
   We are told that this is a disclosure of the folk-mind. Well what does it disclose? Frugality, a love of adventure & the open air, an honest admiration for work, common-sense, & the inevitable tinge of stupidity. Altogether a complete character, consistent, realisable.
   But I have to quarrel utterly & finally with the method. This haphazard jumbling of remarks aimless and (except at rare intervals) without interest, is the extreme of prosiness. A character certainly arises out of it all, but a character without subtlety, without difficulty, which might have been sketched as well in half a page. Character drawing is either done in a treatise or in fiction. In the first we demand rigorous & scientific psychology; in the second the psychology must bow to the dramatic interest which is the fictional *sine qua non*. This book is neither one nor the other. It is indiscriminate gossip, & not even entertaining at that. The material is doubtless good; now & then we have gleams of what might have been made charming. The author's own style is admirable—clear, equable, full of finesse and grace. But the method debars the book from high artistic success, & its dulness makes it fail even in the low plane of the gossiping diary. Had he but selected, made his character the centre of a chain of incidents, made it reveal itself clearly & dramatically in action, instead of leaving us to search for the dim outline that appears through the dreary talk, he might have done well. As it stands it seems impossible for publication.'
Bennett wrote, vertically, in the margin 'Lane accepts my written refutation of all this as satisfactory. E.A.B.' and, by the favourable comment on 'the author's own style', 'hooray'.

BUTLER / MS. / 48
(*From George Sturt*)

Lower Bourne
Sunday morning 14 March 97

My dear Arnold,

Many thanks for your letter just arrived.

To urge Lane against his will in the matter of *Bettesworth* seems to me not quite fair business. If 'twere a work of Art, which he couldn't appreciate, then for his own good it ought to be shoved down his throat. But it isn't; and his objections are deplorably reasonable. I should do the same myself, feeling that besides my money, the fame of my business was involved. The report you've sent me (and it's a fair report) justifies him.

And then, he's not the man I care to be under any obligation to. Neither do I want him to be doing you a favour, even in his own fancy. That would be putting you in a false position— an evil recompense for the pains you've been at for me.

So that my recommendation is, to give him a little longer rope; and then try some other man. Heinemann?

It seems likely enough that no-one will take it. As I think you said, it wants a name to make it go. And it should be the name of an artist. I'm prepared, therefore, to have the book back and keep it by me, in the chance of future reputation enough to float it: or of a time to come when documents in their raw state will find a publisher and a public. (I believe that there is now a public that would welcome *Bettesworth*: but, it isn't a book-buying public.)

We agreed that it *is* a 'document'. For that very reason I have a respect for it, and should hesitate long before trying to make it a work of art. Half its value is in its crudity. . . . On the other hand, I don't blame Lane's reader for failing to see that. His report doesn't hurt my feelings a bit: in fact, I appreciate the worth of it. If all reports were so just, one need not fear for the reception of a genuine work of art. Is that your sentiment?

The man's criticism is a fine object-lesson on the duties and aims of art. I wouldn't like to accuse him of dulness, because he found *Bettesworth* dull. The fault is doubtless neither in him nor in *Bettesworth*, but in the presentment of the evidence. I have obviously failed (didn't try to succeed) in selecting and arranging the real admirable and interesting qualities of my material; I haven't stripped them naked; haven't singled out the intangible essence of the business and made it tangible. What one likes in *Bettesworth* is something that Intellect can't detect, but that the Senses are well aware of. But I have shoved it all in: and so the reader's senses get hold of stuff only fit for his reason; and (to quote Miss Freethy), he finds it 'Apples of Sodom'. He comes to it as an artist, expecting to use his trained senses: and he finds something meant for a Philosopher's brain. Of course he's non-plussed. I can see it as plain as anything: and yet am resolved that the thing must stand unchanged.

Meanwhile, after pushing the novel on a little further, I have been trying to do an artistic presentment of one afternoon spent with the old man. At first it bade fair to be fit for separate publication, in *Macmillan's* perhaps: but it turns out otherwise. Can't explain now how it is so; for I want to leave off. Yesterday was a busy day, encumbered with indigestion & a headache that kept me awake and has left me sleepy and stupefied. Dumb-bell exercise presently may do good. I didn't do it yesterday (likewise I starved); otherwise I have been a good boy in that respect.

Commend me to the Marriotts.

Yours, George Sturt

BERG / MS. / 49
(*To George Sturt*)

6 Victoria Grove
7 May 97

My dear George,

The meeting of the Art Workers Guild to which you are bidden takes place on Friday 21st, & I shall expect you here on that day or the day before, to stay a few days. I now have a spare bedroom, my old study. It can't be said to be furnished, but there is a bed & a PO, & what satisfied Théophile Gautier ought to satisfy you.

I am not yet quite well, but I am better. All my literary work is upset, & will be for some time to come, what with the changes here, & the Jubilee Number of *Woman*, the arrangements for which my accident has thrown awfully out of gear.

48. Miss Freethy is unidentified.

Frank is now fixed in this abode. After wonderful experiences, we have obtained the very prince of manservants, who cooks like an angel & is a terror to thieving London tradesmen. My mode of life is quite changed, & I am employed in getting used to the change. I have forgotten how to write. Since early in March my journal has been neglected—as regards the last month, perforce, seeing that I couldn't dictate *that*. Shortly I hope to be moved to take it up again. Never in my life have I had such a thorough upset and turnover as that thrice-blasted bicycle accident has brought about. It upset my whole system; then I had influenza, and went to Brussels to reinvigorate myself; came back with an appalling cold; had another attack of influenza; and once more this week I have had a sort of semi-influenza; all work in the meantime going to the dogs and elsewhere.

My sole solaces have been Dumas, & Nolan's delightful companionship at Brussels. He is an ideal mate for travelling.

Jim comes for dinner tonight.

Yours, E. A. B.

P.S. I hear vaguely that you are cycling well, but not writing much!

I cannot yet straighten my right arm, & any long spell of writing makes my hand ache like hell, but I believe the ache is good for it.

A near shave that I did not go with your Frank & Young to the Publishers dinner tonight.   B.

49. Bennett's Journal for 20 May 1897 reads:
  'Bicycle accident. Sunday morning, 21 Mch.
  Dislocation of the elbow.
  Chloroform operation 22 Mch.
  I carried my arm in splints for a month, and in a sling for six weeks. For three weeks I dictated all articles and letters.
  The orderliness of my existence was never so deranged before. Since the middle of March neither of my books now in progress has been touched.'
Frederick Marriott has described Bennett's early experience with manservants:
  'He engaged as general servant an ex-sailor named Fish; a very appropriate name in view of after events.
  Fish made an admirable start, working well and efficiently for the first few days, and we were all satisfied that he was a treasure. However, on the Saturday morning, just before Bennett left for the office, he gave Fish a few instructions and a sovereign, for the purchase of the weekend provisions. After the lapse of an hour or so, during which he tidied up the rooms, Fish left the house, sovereign in hand, and was never seen again by any of us!

DOCUMENTS / MS. / 50
(*To Mrs. H. H. Penrose*)

6 Victoria Grove
16 May 97

Dear Mrs. Penrose,

I feel conscious of sin in regard to your manuscripts. With reference to *An Unequal Yoke* I knew that Young was bitten by it, & so I asked him to supper & whiskey just in order to finish the matter up. Unfortunately some other men took it into their heads also to call that night & we couldn't say a word together. Then this absurd war broke out & broke the back of the publishing business at the same time. It is absolutely impossible to get a publisher to publish a work by a new author just now. So I followed the ancient policy of 'slide' and did nothing till your letter arrived. Then, stricken with remorse I fled to Youngs the same morning, & I said, 'Look here, if you don't want that MS of Mrs. Penrose's, plenty of other people do, so you had better decide this instant. Heinemann, Macmillans and Methuen are fighting for it now.' Whereupon he explained that he himself liked it very much, & his readers liked it very much, but really he couldn't touch it then—what with Jubilee & war. 'But' he said 'if you will put it before me again in October I will seriously consider it.' He gave me to understand that there was a strong probability of his accepting it then.

It is for you to decide whether you will send it elsewhere. I don't see why you shouldn't try other publishers, & if they fail you, shove it on to Young again in the autumn as if nothing had happened.

It was a remarkable coincidence that the name of the next servant Bennett engaged was Pond, also an ex-sailor, who proved to be a thoroughly capable and trustworthy man.

He kept the rooms scrupulously clean and tidy, and was an excellent cook. He was not exposed to the severe temptation that brought about the downfall of Fish, for he was never given sovereigns to shop with. Pond was such a success, that one of Bennett's friends facetiously remarked that it would have been better if he had got his Pond before his Fish.'

James J. Nolan (1869–1939) was Assistant Editor of *Hearth & Home*, and later was editor for half a dozen years. He spent much of his later life in India and Burma.

Charles Young (1861–1940) was manager of Lamley & Co., booksellers, in South Kensington, beginning there in 1885 and buying out the business some years later. He was a friend and neighbour of the Kennerleys in Putney, and met Bennett and Sturt at James Brown's home in Richmond.

Touching *Toddles: A Nuisance* I have read this with great pleasure, & if Toddles is Claude, I want to know him instantly, forthwith, and immediately. I object in toto to the subtitle (hackneyed) & the 'forewarning' (quite unnecessary and too self-consciously maternally proud). I don't like the name Toddles, but quite see that it can't be altered now; besides, 'nuisance' improves it. I don't think Lady Margaret is at all good. In books one has met her, but not elsewhere. She is too unrelieved, crude. On the other hand Mrs. Curtis is most excellent. The concluding chapters are very effective, but the death of Peterson ought to have been 'prepared' earlier. How does a doctor, by merely looking at a man, divine that his heart is affected?

This book will sell all right: Constables; Hutchinsons; A. D. Innes; A. & C. Black; J. M. Dent & Co; might be tried. I should not try either John Lane or Lamley & Co. I imagine you will have no difficulty with this book. If you will decide as to the mss. I will forward them wherever they are to go.

Thank you for your invitation for Aldershot July 1. It is, however, almost quite certain that I shall not be able to ride before August. My arm is yet quite stiff. Please let me know when you are coming to London. There is nothing good on at the Lyceum—*Madame Sans-Gêne*, artistically quite worthless, & although Ellen Terry is very clever in it, the part is not her sort, really. Why should you be specially ambitious to see Ellen Terry? She is a distinguished but not a great actress. If I was coming to London for a brief visit, my ambition would be to see the really great people & hear the really great things— not those of a merely insular reputation. Few people realise how insular we are. I should want a Wagner opera with Jean de Reszke or Melba, or at least a Mottl concert. It is only during the season, when all the greatest people in the world swoop down on London, that the low quality of our highly-esteemed entertainments becomes clear to me. For example, look at Pinero's *Princess & Butterfly*, the best thing we have had since Oscar Wilde's *The Importance of Being Earnest*, & really very good & charming; and compare it even with *Tannhäuser*, quite a youthful work, with Van Dyck in it. You can't compare it; it simply fades out—as an artistic product. Then think of Jean de Reszke in the third act of *Tristan*, or Vogl in *Parsifal*—

the greatest art-achievements of all—well if you think the matter over, you will wonder that you go to an ordinary theatre at all.

Ellen Terry—Ellen Terry is a pretty little child paddling up to her dainty ankles in the sea which is art.

However, no one who does not either travel through Europe or come constantly to London, can get at the true perspective of these things. Only I thought I would just explain that Ellen Terry was nobody in particular. There is no art like music, and no one who has not heard, *with understanding*, the later works of Richard Wagner can appreciate the emotional effects of which art is capable. Even *The Tempest*, Keats' *Ode to a Nightingale*, Turgenev's *On the Eve*, the three greatest literary works that I have met with so far, are insignificant when confronted by these. I perceive that I wander.

I have got all the proofs of my book. But there is no hope of it being published yet.

Sincerely yours, E. A. Bennett

P.S. I suppose you & Claude have read *The Seven Seas*.

50. Mrs. H. H. Penrose (May Elizabeth Penrose, b. 1860), novelist and historian, was an intimate friend of Bennett's. She was an occasional contributor to *Woman*. An article by her, 'Are the Worst Books Written by Men or Women?', appeared therein on 28 October 1896. Her novel *The Unequal Yoke* was published in 1905 by Alston Rivers. *Toddles* became *Chubby: A Nuisance, A Study of Child-life*, published without its forewarning by Longmans, Green in 1902. Claude, Mrs. Penrose's son, had his photograph printed in *Woman* in 1898 when he was five years old and could write letters to that journal (see page 100). *The Seven Seas* was a popular volume of Kipling's poetry, first published in 1896.

As the crossed-out words on page 38 suggest, Bennett was in the midst of a recent infatuation with Wagner. Twenty-three years later he supposed that architecture, not music, was the greatest art. Jean de Reszke (1850–1925), Dame Nellie Melba (1859–1931), E. M. H. Van Dyck (1861–1923), and Heinrich Vogl (1845–1900) helped in varying degrees to sustain the Wagner boom in these years; de Reszke was often spoken of as the greatest Wagnerian tenor of his day. Felix Mottl (1856–1911) was conductor of the opera at Bayreuth.

On the drama and on Ellen Terry (1848–1928), Bennett seems to have changed his mind too. He remarked some years later that the drama was the greatest force for education in life, and he recalled Ellen Terry coming up to him in a theatre once and saying, 'You don't know me, Mr. Bennett, but I know you. I'm Ellen Terry.' 'I blushed,' says Bennett; 'I think that great legendary figures really ought not to make such remarks to their juniors.' *Madame Sans-Gêne* was an adaptation from the French by J. Comyns Carr.

LANE / MS. / 51
(*To John Lane*)
St. Dunstan's Chambers,
10 & 11, Fetter Lane, Fleet Street,
21 Sept 97

Dear Mr. Lane,

This is to inform you that I am now doing the literary column of *Hearth & Home* as well as of *Woman*. If therefore you would like your things reviewed in that influential paper, please send them.

Will you please let me know when my book is coming out. It is now eighteen months since you accepted it, & I am extremely tired of waiting. I want also to have news of Mr. Sturt's book *Bettesworth*, which is still under your consideration. I shall be glad to call & see you if you will give me a definite appointment.

Faithfully yours, E. A. Bennett

ILLINOIS / MS. / 52
(*To H. G. Wells*)
6 Victoria Grove
30 Sept 97

Dear Sir,

For a long time I have been intending to write to you, & express my appreciation of your work, & also to ask what is your connection with Burslem & the potteries. Burslem (where I come from) is mentioned at the beginning of *The Time Machine*, & one of your short stories runs over the entire pottery district—I forget the title of it.

I enclose my review of your last book.

Believe me, dear Sir,
Faithfully yours, E. A. Bennett
(editor of *Woman*)

51. *Hearth & Home* and *Woman* were now issued from St. Dunstan's Chambers, 10–11 Fetter Lane.

Bennett did his first reviewing in *Hearth & Home* under the name of Sarah Volatile, beginning with the issue of 23 September 1897.

52. H. G. Wells (1866–1946) was six months older than Bennett, but had a much earlier success. He and Bennett became friends and remained friends

ILLINOIS / MS. / 53
(*To H. G. Wells*)

6 Victoria Grove
10 Oct 97

My dear Sir,

I am very glad to have your letter, & very glad to find that the Potteries made such an impression on you. I lived there till I was 21, & have been away from it 9 years, & only during the last few years have I begun to see its possibilities. Particularly this year I have [been] deeply impressed by it. It seems to me that there are immense possibilities in the very romance of manufacture—not wonders of machinery & that sort of stuff—but in the tremendous altercation with nature that is continually going on—& in various other matters. Anyhow I am trying to shove the notions into my next novel. Only it wants doing on a Zolaesque scale. I would send you a rough sketch of my somewhat vague ideas in this direction, but fear to bore you. To my mind it is just your field. As for the people, I know 'em inside out, & if you are a Northern man you would grasp them instinctively.

I am quite sure there is an aspect of these industrial districts which is really *grandiose*, full of dark splendours, & which has been absolutely missed by all novelists up to date. Tirebuck in *Miss Grace of All Souls* was too much interested in his individual characters to note synthetically the general aspect, & Nevinson in *Valley of Tophet* also let it escape him.

I trouble you with all this because you are the first man I have come across whom the Potteries has impressed, emotionally. There are a number of good men in the Potteries,

---

throughout their lives. All the important correspondence between them has been edited by Harris Wilson in *Arnold Bennett and H. G. Wells, A Record of a Personal and a Literary Friendship*, Urbana, Illinois, 1960. A selection from Bennett's side of the correspondence is printed in the present collection. Considerable use has been made of Mr. Wilson's annotations.

Wells's *The Time Machine* was published in 1895. The Potteries story, 'The Cone', appeared in the collection *The Plattner Story and Others*, 1897. The most recent of Wells's books was *The Invisible Man*, which Bennett had praised in *Woman* on 29 September 1897 for its understanding of science and human character, and criticized for its carelessness of style. In answering Bennett's letter Wells said that he had spent a few months in the Potteries, 'and the district made an immense impression on me'.

but I have never yet met one who could be got to see what I saw; they were all inclined to scoff.

Sincerely yours, E. A. Bennett

BERG / MS. / 54
(*To George Sturt*)

6 Victoria Grove
17 Oct 97

My dear George,

Just 2½ words to emphasise your turpitude in not writing to me all these long lonely years.

Also to tell you that I have this morning read Kipling's new book *Captains Courageous*, & that it is

MAGNIFICENT.

'Look 'ere' he says 'You fellows talk about style & that sort of claptrap. A real strong man' he says, says he 'can do without style. What do I want with style?' he says. 'Take your dam style' he says '& stick it up your behind. I never bothered my head about style' he says 'or theories of style, but this is a *book*, & you jolly well know it.'

That is what I imagine him saying. The tingling vitality of the thing; the incredible detailed information; the big humour, the sheer poetry: they simply stagger you.

It is not a novel, after all, but just a short story, filled out with detail. It is this sort of book that almost inclines one to believe in God, Providence & Co. By the way *Captains Courageous*, in plot, and essential sentiment, is as arrant a Sunday School Prize as the S.P.C.K. ever published. Yet you don't seem to care.

As for me, I am working like 10,000 devils. On Tuesday evening I shall have finished the draft of my Journalism book, & I hope to clear the book right off before Christmas.

Next Saturday Rickards & I go to Paris for a week.

Thine, E. A. B.

53. William Edwards Tirebuck (d. 1900) published *Miss Grace of All Souls* in 1895; Henry Woodd Nevinson (1856–1941) published *The Valley of Tophet* in 1896. Both works concerned life in coal-mining districts.

54. S.P.C.K.—The Society for the Promotion of Christian Knowledge.
Edwin Alfred Rickards (1872–1920), an architect, was described by Bennett in

LANE / MS. / 55
(*To John Lane*)

St. Dunstan's Chambers
11 Nov 97

Dear Mr. Lane,

In reference to our interview the other day, at which you gave me a definite undertaking to publish my book on or before the 1st February next, I think it is quite time that a formal contract was signed. You promised a long time ago to send me a contract, but it has not yet arrived. I will call & see you if you will make an appointment.

Believe me,

Sincerely yours, E. A. Bennett

LANE / MS. / 56
(*To Frederic Chapman*)

St. Dunstan's Chambers
2 Dec 97

My dear Chapman,

I saw Mr. Lane on Tuesday night, & he promised to send me a contract for my book, including the date 1st Feby, at once. May I ask you to see to this. I told him I would take George Sturt's book away at once, whereupon he said he thought he might take it, & asked me to give him another week or two to think it over.

Sincerely yours, E. A. Bennett

5% up to 2,000
10% up to 5,000
15% after.

1920 as one of 'the two most interesting, provocative, and stimulating men I have yet encountered'. (The other was H.G. Wells.) He and Bennett met in the early nineties and were intimate friends for many years. See further pages 178–9 and 266.

56. On the royalty figures for both *A Man from the North* and *A Year's Exile* see also pages 51, 74–75, and 102.

BERG / MS. / 57
(*To George Sturt*)

6 Victoria Grove
8 Decr 97

My dear George,

Just two lines to inculcate the fact that I am alive & received your letter with joy. *His Grace of Osmonde*, I fear, would not afford your private self much satisfaction, if it is anything like *A Lady of Quality*, which had neither style nor delicacy. I look for your review. With regard to your article, though admiring of the ingenuity of it, I yearned to tear the argument to rags. There is scarcely a single statement in that article to which I do not take violent exception. By this time I forget it & all about it, save my strong desire at the time to write to the *Academy* & play hell with it. I hope to revive the matter when I see you. Webster was intensely pleased with it, dreamed of it I believe, & only his modesty stopped him from addressing you thereon a note of congratulation. Marriott read it with awe; possibly it opened his eye to the strange fact that other arts than painting have their absorbing mysteries of technique.

I have finished my book—finished it last Saturday, 48 hours ahead of contract time. Unluckily Lane the other day reminded me of the fact that I had offered it to him some months ago. Of my long interview with Lane on that occasion I will not offer you an account—too idle. But I said to him I would take *Bettesworth* away at once, as I could place it elsewhere. 'But I was thinking of taking it,' he said. 'I just want to think it over again.' 'You have had many months to decide,' I said coldly, inimically, proudly.

Hums & ha's.

'I think I should like it' he says.

More hums and ha's.

'My instructions are to take it away,' I says.

'Well, give me another fortnight,' he says 'to decide.'

'Very good,' I says.

That Conrad book is magnificent.

Thine, E. A. B.

57. *His Grace of Osmonde* (1897) and *A Lady of Quality* (1896) were by Frances Hodgson Burnett. Sturt's review of the former appeared in the *Academy* on 11 December 1897. He praised Mrs. Burnett for her idealistic conception, but he

H

ILLINOIS / MS. / 58
(*To H. G. Wells*)

6 Victoria Grove
8 Decr 97

My dear Wells,

I owe you a good turn for pointing out Conrad to me. I remember I got his first book, *Almayer's Folly*, to review with a batch of others from Unwin, & feeling at the time rather bored (*you* know the feeling—I get through 50 or 60 novels a month for two papers) I simply didn't read it at all—wrote a vague & discreet par. & left it.

I have just read his new book *The Nigger of the Narcissus*, which has moved me to enthusiasm. Where did the man pick up that style, & that *synthetic* way of gathering up a general impression & flinging it at you? Not only his style, but his attitude, affected me deeply. He is so consciously an artist. Now Kipling isn't an artist a bit. Kipling doesn't know what art is—I mean the art of words; *il ne se préoccupe que de la chose racontée*. He is a great writer but not an artist. There are only about six artists among our prominent novelists. George Moore is one, though he writes, on the surface, damnably. But he can *see* like a poet. I greatly admire George Moore. If George Moore had been a South Sea trader & had learned grammar etc, he would have treated the sea as Conrad has treated it. I dare say ~~this sounds odd, but it is profoundly true, and, for me, throws~~ light on both men.

Some pages of *The Nigger* are exquisite in the extraordinary management of colour they display. But Conrad needs to curb his voracity for adjectives.

Have you ever read de Maupassant's *Étude sur Gustave Flaubert*, preface to *Bouvard et Pécuchet*—from which I quote

---

thought the execution was lifeless and sentimental. His article, 'A Note on Fiction', appeared on 27 November. It argues that there is little point in novelists seeking new subjects in the business or labouring worlds, etc., for the essential interest in any novel must be the human being. On the other hand, novelists in the past have certainly relied too heavily on human stereotypes.

Alexander Webster (d. 1919) was another member of the Bennett–Marriott circle. He was in the Inland Revenue Office for many years, and married the sister of Pauline Smith the novelist, who was a close friend of Bennett's after 1908.

The book for Lane was still *Journalism for Women*.

The book by Joseph Conrad (1857–1924) was *The Nigger of the Narcissus*.

above? It is a most illuminating business, & one of the best bits
of general literary criticism that I know of.

Sincerely yours, E. A. Bennett

RICKARD / MS. / 59
(*To John Rickard*)

6 Victoria Grove
8 Decr 97

My dear Rickard,

For thirty seven days I have been on the eve of replying to
your letter. But DUTY prevented. And now I have finished my
book (that I swore to finish by the 6th & actually did finish
on the 4th.—how's that?) & my lovely unrivalled Xmas number
is out (which I hope you may see it), & I am for the time being
almost free from care—save for a rasping altercation with a
Board of Directors as to the pecuniary value of my services.

Protector of the Poor, it is true that your slave now possesses
a garden, in which roses but a few weeks since were blooming
alone, but he intends to take damn good care to have nothing
to do with it. No, Sir, he will pay a man to garden that garden
for him. Why garden when you can get others to garden for
you? I reckon I can bask in a garden with any man, & enjoy
the prospect thereof, . . . but work in it, dig, hoe, prune, cut,
manure—*No, Sir.*

When in God's name are you coming to live out Fulham
way? If that happiness happened to us, you might fill out your
evenings & Sabbaths by bullying my hired gardener. The
glory of my new establishment will not, however, be its garden,
but its two studies. Sir, two studies—one for poetry, the other
for prose! Try to grasp that. They wanted to seize one of the
studies as a place convenient to put a sewing machine in!
God! I said 'No' to that. I said no clean minded young fellow
could decently procreate prose in the same room as he pro-
created poetry in. I said the sewing machine would look nice
& homely in the spare bedroom, & as the house happens to be
mine, so it will be.

How is the fiction getting along? I do wish you would let us
see some. In fact, when I think of you writing & writin' &
writin', & showing the stuff to no one, I curse at the frailties of

human nature. It is now some five years since I was to have sight of your fiction. But it comes not yet. Protector of the Poor, how long?

Might we not lunch together one day at our old frugal haunts? My digestion is now perfect, & I have the health of a cowboy.

Kind regards to your wife.

Sincerely yours, E. A. Bennett

BERG / MS. / 60
(*To George Sturt*)

6 Victoria Grove
16 Decr 97

My dear George,

Your review of *His Grace* was very good indeed, & suitable, though no doubt too kind.

This day I saw Lane. He said he was publishing your book early in the spring, & told Chapman in my presence to send you a contract at once. If this does not arrive within 7–10 days please let me know.

He made me an offer for *Bettesworth*: namely that he would publish it on condition that you receive nothing unless 1,000 copies are sold. No doubt he offers this in order to keep you (I incidentally mentioned about *Academy* & other papers). I do not suppose for an instant that 1,000 copies will be sold, but both Chapman & I advise you to accept the proposal, which, as your literary agents, we consider a fair one. In all probability Lane will lose on the book, which, excellent as it is, does not contain the elements of popularity.

---

59. Dorothy Rickard says that her father 'was a bit of a botanist and loved his garden. I remember he grew some beautiful carnations which he had crossed and produced, one he called "blackcurrant & custard" and another "raspberry & custard".' He seems not to have done a great deal of writing, and the only published essay that Miss Rickard owns is an account of an archaeological walk that appeared in the Civil Service journal *Red Tape* some years later.

In 1897 Rickard was living in Kilburn. Bennett himself had recently bought a home at 9 Fulham Park Gardens, into which he moved in February. According to Frederick Marriott, Bennett moved from Victoria Grove because he needed room for his sister Tertia, who was studying singing in London, and for his youngest brother, Septimus, who had won a National Scholarship for sculpture and was studying at South Kensington.

Please let me know your decision at once.

Lane is now under written contract to publish my book by 1st Feby.

No time for more.

Yours, E. A. B.

Everyone in this house is damnably unwell with cold catarrh or influenza.

BERG / MS. / 61
(*To George Sturt*)

6 Victoria Grove
29 Decr 97

My dear George,

There is a disturbing note of despondency in your last three letters: I know not the cause. What I don't like is the 'don't-care' attitude. Have you made up your mind whether you want to make real headway (from the worldly point of view) as an author, or whether your desire is merely to write according to *moods*, & in the intervals of business? Because it seems as if you had not. If you want to progress as an author, you absolutely must pretend to yourself that your very bread depends on your literary exertions. I am moved to such remarks as the above by such statements as one in your letter of yesterday:—that you have been *slaving all week* over an article for the *Academy*. No *Academy* article ought to take you more than 3 hours. It is absurd to suppose that a skilled craftsman like yourself cannot make his work profitable—cannot meet a market & extract a profit from the market price. And at congenial work too! This slow rate of production is merely a habit. And if quicker production means, at first, a deterioration of quality, never mind. The quality will still be good enough. All week over an article! I wrote two articles of 1,000 words each this morning, one literary, the other dramatic, in 85 minutes, & I did it because I had to. In the same circumstances you would have done the same. Zola's dodge of writing a fixed quantity every day is rare. It may affect quality sometimes, but the total effect is blessed. I wonder whether you could accept my dictum that your comparative sterility is due, not to constitution (mental

& physical) but to bad habits—introspection, waiting for the mood, & so on. Such is my firm belief, & I asks to be excused for thus lecturing my elders.

What an ass Hind must be! (I wonder whether he or anyone else could explain the term 'nervous' as applied to style.) And a bad judge, too. Your review was admirable. You 'got the hang' of reviewing right away, & as for the 'precious style of the *National Observer*', there was not a trace of it in your stuff. From your description, I could imagine exactly the way Hind would talk, & the sort of kind, blunt, slightly fatuous & conceited person he is. It is almost incredible that a man avowedly not an author could, having appreciated your 'Note on Fiction', have presumed to instruct you in literary technique. No, not incredible, but very comical.

Nevertheless, roll up those articles to Hind as fast as you can. They may lead to other & better openings. Lane opened his beady watery eyes when I told him you were writing for the *Academy*. (By the way, write to Lane for a contract at once.)

And fancy Hind saying that anyone could do reviews, when almost nobody can do them!

Your remarks about my dialogue are beside the mark. I know well enough it was not serious. But, granted the convention & class of work, it was just about as clever & neat as it could be. Remember that. It was the work of a man who knew what he wanted to produce, & produced it exactly. To my own knowledge it made a number of excellent people wriggle with laughter. 'Worthy of me.' Rot! I, at any rate, cannot rely on wheelwrighting for a living, & moreover when my paper wants a certain sort of thing, & I happen to be able to supply that thing at a more reasonable rate than it could be got at elsewhere, it is my business to supply it. I do supply it, & I reckon that in doing a thing well, whatever it is, I am not being unworthy. I have no desire always to be an artist. As I have said in my book: 'Art is a very little thing.'

I am very glad you are on the novel again. Rip along with it, & let's get it published.

Just now I am reading a most excellent & very *English* novel, *Lying Prophets*, by Eden Phillpotts. I have lately got rather chummy with Phillpotts, & he is a grand chap, though suffering from a total ignorance of French literature. He is a *grand* chap, & you must know him next time you come. Also you must read the book.

During the next fortnight I shall decide what to do during the next few months, & in the meantime I must get on with my Nursery Rhymes, of which I have done nearly half.

Ask Frank if & when he wants those library books.

To all, good wishes for '98, & quick recovery for your sister.

Yours, E. A. B.

Your new journal shall arrive soon. Would you care to be at the trouble to look through mine (I mean the first two vols.) and write me generally thereon?

P.S. Shall see Lane in a day or two.

---

61. C. Lewis Hind (1862–1927) was editor of the *Academy*. Sturt had an interview with him in which Hind complained of various aspects of Sturt's review of *His Grace of Osmonde*.

Bennett's dialogue, entitled 'The Train', was published in *Woman* on 8 December 1897. It concerns a young engaged couple who have to wait a long time for a train at a country station. The level of dialogue reaches its highest mark early on:

'Arthur (*sighing*).—Ah! what a holiday it has been!

Rose (*sighing in unison*).—And tomorrow it is over.

Arthur.—Yes, tomorrow I shall be back in Gray's Inn.

Rose.—And tomorrow I shall be back in Leeds.

(They comfort each other.)

Arthur (*cheerfully kicking his feet against the stonework*).—But I shall see you again at Christmas; and by that time I shall be a real live barrister.

Rose.—But there are so many barristers.

Arthur.—Just so. That's what relieves my mind. One more or less—what does it matter? I shall be raking the dollars together in no time. Then there will be a certain wedding. . . .'

Sturt had written to Bennett of the dialogue: 'This is not worthy of you, Arnold. I expect I shall have to do a paper on Dialogue, if only for your enlightenment. But then, hang it, you'll think it ingenious and yet want to give the lie to every conclusion I come to.'

Eden Phillpotts (1862–1960) was at this time Assistant Editor of *Black & White*. Bennett met him in May 1897, and wrote in his Journal: 'At the Press Club yesterday I met Eden Phillpotts, a man of 35, quiet, restrained, with a kind face and voice and a peculiarly flattened yet sturdy nose.' On Bennett's friendship and quarrels with him, see Vol. I, *passim*.

With *Anna of the Five Towns* in abeyance, Bennett seems at this point to have been very uncertain of what he was going to do with his life. His first *Journal* entry for 1898 begins: 'During the period of unproductiveness which has followed the completion of my book on journalism for women, I have been thinking about a history of the English novel in the nineteenth century. I believe in the course of a few years I could write such a history as would cast a new light on English fiction considered strictly from the craftsman's standpoint.'

Bennett's Nursery Rhymes are unknown. They may have been intended for

LANE / TS. / 62
(*To John Lane*)

St. Dunstan's Chambers
5th January, 1898

Dear Mr. Lane,

I send with this the MS. of my book, *The Art of Journalism for Women*, which you said you would like to see. You will remember that, in accordance with what passed in our interview, it is submitted to you on the understanding that if you like it you undertake to publish it within three months of acceptance.

I have consulted Mr. Sturt as to his book *Bettesworth*, and he is prepared to accept your offer, namely, that you publish it at your risk, but do not pay him any royalties unless 1,000 copies are sold, provided you will fix an early date for the publication. Mr. Sturt would prefer not to publish the book at all if it cannot be issued within the next few months. Will you please send him a contract for publishing his *first* book at once. He is very anxious that there should be no further delay as to this.

I will call on you one day next week.

Faithfully yours, E. A. Bennett

'The Children's Page', a new feature of *Woman*, which began with the issue of 18 January 1898. The page was conducted by Aunt Pen, who may have been Bennett's sister Tertia, who was visiting him frequently in London following the death of her fiancé earlier in the year. She did some writing for him for *Woman*, and later she published some children's stories. But Aunt Pen's lively and direct style often suggests Bennett himself. Frederick Marriott remarks that Bennett was especially fond of children and that in these years he was 'Uncle Arnold' to numerous children in the neighbourhood to whom he was unrelated. And Bennett also wrote a children's story that appeared in the Christmas issue of *Woman* in 1898. In the first weeks of the new feature, Aunt Pen invited letters from children, and the initial response came mainly from the sons and daughters of Bennett's friends. One of these children was Cedric Sharpe, and in case Bennett was in fact Aunt Pen, this present edition of his letters ought to represent her efforts. Cedric wrote, after receiving honours in a competition conducted by Aunt Pen: 'Dear Aunt Pen,—Please forgive me for not writing to thank you for the lovely story book. I was so surprised to get it and mother was so pleased. I had my photo taken with my 'cello. I will send you one as soon as the man sends them to mother. Your loving Cedric.' Aunt Pen replied: 'My dear little Cedric,—I shall be very glad indeed to get that photo, and I don't think I have anything to forgive, considering you have written me such a nice letter. Thank you for all the kisses at the end of it. I am sorry I can't print them.' Cedric was seven years old at this time. Some of Uncle Arnold's letters to him of several years later are printed below.

BERG / MS. / 63
(*To George Sturt*)

6 Victoria Grove
13 Jany 98

My dear George,

I am sorry to say that Lane would not meet me as to a date for publication of *Bettesworth*. He absolutely declined to fix a date, & so I withdrew the book. I think this is best. You should have had the contract for *A Year's Exile* by this time.

I have talked a bit with Phillpotts about *Bettesworth*, & he is deeply interested in it. At his request I have promised to lend him the MS. at once to read. He is a chap of rich experience, a thorough artist, & he will give me his opinion as to the best place to send the MS. to. I assume that you will not object to his reading it. His desire is to meet you, & I hope that may be soon. If you can give me a week-end during the second half of March, that will suit me. I do not go into the new house till middle of February, & a week or two will be occupied in settling down & fixing up.

Doubtless my last letter did not err on the side of consideration. That is always my weakness. And no doubt also, with regard to your modus operandi, I arrive at conclusions through misconceptions. Nevertheless I am largely impenitent. When I put down this equation: *Talent + leisure = productiveness*, I perceive that it isn't an equation, even after putting minus bad health on the left hand side. It was heroic of you to attempt one article per day—too heroic, a counsel of perfection. Say two articles a week, *and* the novel; and toe the mark every Monday.

You shall have your new journal in a few days. It will entirely eclipse the old one. I find my journal goes at the rate of 30,000 words a year, which is much in excess of the de Goncourt published average.

Lane is desperately excited about my little journalism book, his readers report being positively panegyric. He is going to publish it in 3 weeks; gave me a 15% royalty; & made me sign the contract at once. This is biz. . . . I am not doing much, being busy on the damned paper.

Frank's books shortly.

Thine, E. A. B.

LANE / TS. / 64
(*To Frederic Chapman*)

> St. Dunstan's Chambers
> 13th Jan., 1898.

My dear Chapman,

I shall be glad if you will let me have here to-morrow without fail the MS. of Sturt's *Bettesworth* book. I have an opportunity of placing it before a man of influence, and if you do not mind I will give it to you to read afterwards.

> Believe me,
> Sincerely yours, E. A. Bennett

BERG / MS. / 65
(*To George Sturt*)

> 6 Victoria Grove
> 18 Jan 98

My dear George,

I drafted the letter, partly because it was a much simpler & shorter process than explaining the circumstances to you, & partly because, when once before I drafted a letter for you, you said that it was a beastly nuisance to you to write that sort of letter. . . . Yes, I must plead guilty to a sort of fatherliness in matters of worldly conduct & mere business—a fatherliness which sits ill on a youth of my scant years. Never mind, you are a philosophic chap, & can afford to smile at the self-sufficiency which (I know) reeks from my every pore.

About that dialogue in *Woman*, you never grasped my view. My estimate of it as literature is doubtless like yours. All I claim is that it was done to produce a certain effect on certain people, & that it produced that effect, & that it was a skilled & workmanlike production. I never said or thought that it was funny. I said many excellent people thought it funny. So they did, & so I intended they should. If anyone says I am not entitled to help my paper & to earn my living by writing such dialogues, I will punch their heads for them.

Your agreement for *A Year's Exile* is precisely the same as mine for my novel.

I should certainly stick to the *Academy*. These articles might some day make a book. I find the expert opinion of Hind is

not very high, but he is regarded as a decent ordinary cuss
with more assurance than brains.

Tonight I have elaborated what I take to be a good idea for
a 3,000 word short story, & I hope to finish it by the end of Jan.
If I like it, it will appear in *Black & White*.

Headache better. Cold very slowly improving.

Yours, E. A. B.

Been reading Turgenev's correspondence. Interesting. *Have I
lent you a French book of Turgenev's?* Will see Webster.

BERG / MS. / 66
(*To George Sturt*)

6 Victoria Grove
6th Feby 98

My dear George,

I am now in perfect health & tolerably cheerful spirits. Up
to Thursday I had been feeble and ill-at-ease. Then I suddenly
decided that I could not be expected to do any serious work
till after I was installed in the new house. From the moment
of that decision I began to improve; slept well, & made the
harmless joke at breakfast. I had gotten hung up by a *serious*
short story. Now I am going to leave it till I have done something else—namely a long article on George Moore novelist,
to coincide with the appearance of his new novel. I reckon I
can do something with Moore. To work in this house was
hopeless, as, through no-one's fault, this study had become
perforce a sort of drawing-room. So I occupy the time of
waiting in reading G. M. & making notes. The business has
given me vague flitting shapes of ideas for a book on modern
fiction. Anyhow, I propose to take up criticism on a larger
grander scale, & in proof [of] my earnest intention, I may
cite the fact that I have turned over to my brother Frank
critical work to the tune of £70 per annum reg'lar. If this is
not enterprise, what is? In future, after next week, if ever you
see *Woman*, 'Frances' will have taken the place of 'Barbara',
and 'F.C.B.' that of 'E.A.B.' Frank can write well enough, at any
rate on the drama. What he will do with books remains to be
seen, but he has sufficient general smartness to 'keep his end up'.

I am sorry about Hind, & disgusted with the fellow, too. By the way I see nothing of yours in this week's *Academy*. It was like Hind's damned cheek to alter an article into a letter, & I do not think it would have hurt your future to ask him what the hell he meant. The market for your sort of literary article is, so far as I know, very limited indeed. You might try the *Bookman*, the *Spectator*, &, if you could make them longer, *Blackwoods*, *Macmillans* or *Longmans*, or any of the half-crown reviews . . . say 4,000 words, with a good title. I have not much hope of the *Bookman*, as Robertson Nicoll, though a sound enough critic in a certain limited range, has the taint of the 'memoir-expert' (if you understand) & doesn't really know the meaning of the term *literature* at all. When I start my monthly book-magazine the field for your articles will be enlarged.

You may rely on me justifying my faith in Turgenev. At present I am waiting for certain authorities as to facts etc. It would be impossible to deal properly with his work without more documents than I have, as I might conceivably form theories of his work & development which would be contradicted by published letters, journals etc. There is no Life of Turgenev, & I am experiencing great difficulty in obtaining books whose titles & dates I know. Young has an agent in Paris, & that agent in Paris strikes me as a damned fool. If it were not that Young is sort of 'on his mettle' to get these books, I would tell him not to trouble & go to a man in Oxford St. who I am sure would succeed. Of course they are out of print. That is no excuse to a bookseller as is a bookseller. I said to Young: 'Look here, I must have these books; never mind price.'

Of Dickens, dear friend, I know nothing. About a year ago, from idle curiosity, I picked up *The Old Curiosity Shop*, & of all the rotten vulgar un-literary writing. . . ! Worse than George Eliot's. If a novelist can't *write*, where *is* the beggar?

By the way Phillpotts confirms me entirely about Turgenev. You must talk to Phillpotts about placing your fiction articles. He has been in the house a fortnight with influenza. Now with regard to your coming up, I should like you to come up earlier than I at first stated, if it suits you. We move to 9 Fulham Park Gardens S.W. on Saturday next. How would a fortnight after that suit? Say you come on Friday the 25th February? We shall, I fancy, be straight & neat at the new house in a twinkling,

& I believe my mother & a certain aunt have longings for the vicious metropolis before Easter.

Talking of kids, what about a kid aged $3\frac{1}{2}$ who, after a terrible journey from Tipperary to London, buried his face in his mother's breast & quoted Kipling (whom he knows by heart):—'There's worser things than marching from Umballa to Cawnpore'.

Fact!

Thine, E. A. B.

BERG / MS. / 67
(*To George Sturt*)

9, Fulham Park Gardens
S.W.
23 Feby 98

My dear George,

When you come up, do you mind bringing your journal with you?

Today I have had a long talk with Eden Phillpotts, who has just returned to work after a very long spell of influenza. He is very pleased with *Bettesworth*, & he happens to be one who can properly appreciate it. He thinks it should find a publisher. He mentioned Innes or Methuen. Would it be better for me to present it to these people, or you? Exactly as you like.

Today my novel is out. Such of my friends as have read it and whose view is worth a damn, like it heartily in a quiet way. Phillpotts is going to review it for *Black & White*. He has given me a lot of sound advice about things in general. I have told him you are coming up, & you & he are to meet at a lunch.

I am working at a serious & rather long critical article on George Moore, which I hope I may be able to sell. I am enjoying the thing greatly, & have already much more to say than there will be room for. It is rather a big job. I have a good short story in tow for *Black & White*, but it is lying by as the Moore article is rather urgent.

Journal rather slow, & not quite the right stuff in it.

66. Sturt's 'letter' appeared in the *Academy* on 29 January 1898, and concerned a point of grammar discussed in an article published earlier.

W. Robertson Nicoll (1851–1923) ran the *Bookman*. Bennett's mature opinion of him is recorded in Vol. I, p. 140.

If Frank should trouble himself to read my novel, please transmit to me his opinion thereon.

Ever, E. A. B.

BERG / MS. / 68
(*To George Sturt*)

9, Fulham Park Gardens
15 Mch 98

My dear George,

If you are sending the MS. first to A. D. Innes, I think it would be an excellent thing to mention Phillpotts' name. I am sure he will have no objection. Of course you can use my name also, but it will not be of service to you. With Methuen's I do not think that either name will help. I should like you, by the way, to read Phillpotts' review of my book *A Man from the North* in this week's *Black & White*. In the same number is an article of mine on the Potteries, of which I believe you saw the MS. Anyhow I would that you read it again, as I deem it the best prose I have done. I shall want to see your sketch of the supper here. That sort of thing is (to me) excessively difficult, but you seemed to do it easily in an early chapter of *A Year's Exile*.

This day or two I have had an idea of making a little book of essays to be elaborated from my journal, entitled *Ideas & Sensations*. Sounds rather attractive, eh? It would suit Lane, & no one else, so if I did it, I should have to offer him another book after all.

I did a great day's work yesterday on the George Moore article. Six hours writing, besides ½ day at the office. I hope to finish this on Sunday.

Yours, E. A. B.

67. On Bennett's new address see page 96 n.

A. D. Innes (d. 1938) was one of Phillpotts's publishers. A. M. S. Methuen (1856–1924) became Bennett's publisher for a spell; see Vol. I, *passim*.

Phillpotts said of *A Man from the North* in his review of it in *Black & White* on 12 March 1898: 'If . . . the author of this remarkable book can point to it as his first sustained effort, he and novel readers in general may be alike congratulated. There is freshness of thought and great distinction of style . . ., for the author is a conscientious artist with a nice appreciation of the force of words. . . . He possesses further that rarest of gifts: self-restraint and self-denial.' And Bennett wrote in his Journal: 'It seemed strange and unreal to be treated by this finely serious novelist as an artist of the same calibre with himself.'

68. The Potteries article, published anonymously in the issue of 12 March 1898, expressed Bennett's imaginative discovery of the region that he remarked

BERG / MS. / 69
(*To George Sturt*)

9, Fulham Park Gardens
28 Mch 98

My dear George,

I trembled when I read about putting the novel away for six months. I hope you won't. It is really awful. But of course I know the feeling. I want badly to start mine again, & hope to do so after Easter, though I can scarcely afford to do so, I must earn brass, and writing novels isn't the way to do it. Having turned over £70 per annum work to Frank, I ought in the first place to make up that £70 (& a bit over). My idea was to make it up by critical work of a more sustained nature than *Woman* requires; but, urged by Phillpotts & others who do not understand precisely how the land lies, I am tempted to go in solely for the novel. I finished my George Moore article on Saturday afternoon—8,000 words, dear Sir, and it suffers from being cramped at the end. I really needed 12,000 words. Yet it is too long as it is; and I fear its inordinate size may wreck its chances with the monthly reviews; & for the 'staid' quarterlies its tone is somewhat radical & iconoclastic. Its price is fifteen guineas, & if it is sold, I will give 8 weeks to the novel. If not sold, it will assuredly serve for a book, as it contains some rather classy writing & plenty of sound. Today I took up a short story for *Black & White*, started before the said article. I worked at it a bit, & then suddenly I stopped, put all the sheets & notes into an elastic band, labelled 'em & pigeon

---

upon in his letter to H. G. Wells of 10 October 1897. The opening is an abbreviated form of the opening of *The Old Wives' Tale* (1908): 'North of a line drawn from the Wash to the beak of Carnarvon, and due south of the Trent's source, lies a tract of country some seven miles long by four at its widest, bearing in shape a rough similarity to the contour of England, less Cornwall and Devon.' And the article goes on to say of the industrial district: 'Here, indeed, is Nature repaid for some of her notorious cruelties. She imperiously bids man sustain and reproduce himself, and this is one of the places where in the act itself of obedience he insults and horribly maltreats her. To go out beyond the municipal confines where, in the thick of the altercation, the subsidiary industries of coal and iron prosper amid a wreck of verdure, ought surely to raise one's estimate not only of man but of Nature: so thorough and ruthless is his havoc of her, and so indomitable her ceaseless recuperation. The struggle is grim, tremendous, heroic. . . .'

Nothing came of the notion of *Ideas and Sensations* until 1906 and 1907, when Bennett had a few extracts from his journal published privately to send as Christmas gifts to friends. See pages 202–4.

holed 'em. In a flash of pure insight, I had seen that the thing would not work. For one thing it is damnably difficult to fix out a short story in which a lot of preliminary events must be disclosed. I have decided that no short story that is worth a cuss should need anything in the way of a prologue. My limit was 3,000. But the motive is a fine one, & remains for me when I have, say 6,000 words space, & a lot more technique in my guts. I took up de Maupassant to inspire me into a new theme; got one in about 5 minutes, & in an hour had arrived at the details. But it is too new to work at tonight. However the story will be finished this day week at 10 p.m. Mark that.

My journalism book is being rarely reviewed. It has had no less than 4 articles of over a column each. Very laudatory; but one or two people seem wilfully to misunderstand my reference to the *Thesaurus*. Either that, or they are remarkable nincompoops. The reviews of *M from N* are distinctly kind, though the *Academy* on Saturday really amazed me (for the moment) by a blasted bit of trifling. Jim was here Saty, also Ken & Young; we had rather an ambrosial night; needed you there.

Thine, E. A. B.

BERG / MS. / 70   205 Waterloo Road

BERG / MS. / 70   205 Waterloo Road
(*To George Sturt*)   Burslem
                                               Staffs
                                               10th Apl 98

My dear George,

I was just about to write you concerning your novel when I received your letter (forwarded here) about mine. It is extremely comforting to me that those two of my friends who know most about writing (you & Phillpotts) think best of my novel. Yet, though I have naturally every wish to believe you both, I cannot dismiss the suspicion that you *may* be prejudiced by too much good nature—both of you. But I hope not. I have no intention, nor does Phillpotts advise me, to write novels for

69. The *Academy* review, on 26 March 1898, was mainly concerned with Bennett's style, and objected to it: 'A *Man from the North*, in fine, is the kind of worthlessly clever book which neither touches nor moves the reader, neither interests nor persuades.'

money. But he points out that a few really serious novels give a man a standing that nothing else can, & thus indirectly pay very well by making a good market for ephemeral stuff. Thus Phillpotts himself now gets 8 guineas (5 here & 3 in America) per thousand for his pot-boiling short stories, chiefly on the strength of his serious work. So that serious work does actually pay. I shall take [? up] my novel again immediately I return to London.

I read *A Year's Exile* during the three hours' journey down here on Thursday afternoon, & have passed it on to Frank to review in *Woman*. As for me, I shall review it in *Hearth & Home*. I have now read it twice, and come to a definite conclusion about it. It contains a lot of beautiful work; the appreciations of the country are the best things of that kind I have ever read, & austerely written, too. The theme is clearly presented, but I think it lacks both originality & distinction—*intrinsically*. It is *treated* with fine distinction. During the first third of the book, the development is misted over with a damn sight too much *talk*—even allowing for the fact that you are dealing with a talking & argumentative set of people. And the talk is of that elliptic, fragmentary kind so difficult to make coherent on paper. Certainly you nearly always succeed in getting your effect, but I should have preferred a stricter economy of means in this respect, especially as the main theme is not a bit intellectual, but emotional.

The two women, Edith & Mrs. L.T., are awfully well done. I realise both of them completely. I think Edith stands out clearest to me. During the illness of Mrs. L.T. she [is] absolutely lifelike. Lane Thomson is good, & very original in conception. As to Mitchell, though I understood him perfectly, I have not yet very much *seen* him. I can only see inside him. He is for me a sort of soul without a bodily frame. But I seem to know his dog rather well.

You may take it from me that *A Year's Exile* is a damn good, distinguished, quiet book—*infinitely* better than the early work of Henry James, whom you in various fine ways resemble. Everything about it is more sober & more distinguished than anything I could do. It makes me feel specious & theatrical. Its surpassing merits are of course the descriptions of the country in summer, & the analysis of the in-various-ways

I

corroding influence of London on a country man. The style is splendid, & this reminds me that there are sundry very trifling solecisms which escaped you in the proofs. The only two I think of at the moment are 'somewhen' (no such word), & 'by now', for 'by this time'—which is of course quite too impossible.

I shall expect something big from this novel now in progress.

A lot of people have just come in, making the continuance of this impossible.

Yours, E. A. B.

BERG / MS. / 71
(*To George Sturt*)

9, Fulham Park Gardens
11 May 98

My dear George,

I am very glad I may come at Whitsuntide. I imagine we shall have a rare time. Suppose I come down Friday night, & we ride over to see Mrs. Penrose on Saturday afternoon? This will leave us absolutely free for Ken & Young, who, I under-

70. 205 Waterloo Road, Burslem, was the family home of the Bennetts from 1880 onwards.

Sturt said of *A Man from the North* in his letter: 'I like it! No mistake, I like it well! And I'm proud to know the author of it. My first impression (yesterday, I mean) was pure delight: today it is admiration irritated by despair—despair for me, be it understood.'

Bennett's review of *A Year's Exile* in *Hearth & Home* on 28 April 1898 did not mention any of the points of the present letter, but described the book as 'a notable work by a writer who makes no concession to public taste. . . . *A Year's Exile* has imagination and style and truth and reticence.'

Sturt replied to Bennett's comments on his language:

'I wish you to drop on any solecisms of mine that you detect—not in this letter but hereafter. For actually I do not know. "Somewhen" I have discovered to be inadmissible; but I never should have suspected that "by now" was wrong. When I was a boy, I talked a weak provincial language tinged with dialect. "Literary" English is an acquired speech with me, and it hasn't displaced the other but has merely been added to it. Many—most, of my relatives are still ignorant of aspirates; and I can distinctly remember the time of learning that they might be sounded. It was years, too, before I understood that "duke" is not usually called "dook". Of my two grandfathers, one talked broad Hampshire, and the other a racy Surrey variant; and so here I am, with those solecisims still apt to appear and betray me. I like them, too; but in their place, which is *not* in a book.'

The novel 'now in progress' is still the novel first mentioned on page 62.

stand, are to cycle down on Saturday afternoon and evening.
Let me know about this.

Since the beginning of March I have done the following:—

1.	Article on George Moore	8,000 words
2.	Article, 'Our Illiterate Novelists'	4,000
3.	Serious short story	3,500
4.	Potboiling story	5,500
5.	*Academy* criticisms	2,800
6.	*Hearth & Home* criticisms	12,000
	total	35,800

No. 4 is not absolutely finished but I shall finish it tomorrow.
Having done that, I shall consider myself free to have a spell
at my novel, about which I am getting very keen. You should
get hold of Havelock Ellis' new book *Affirmations*. It is all good;
and there is an essay on Huysmans that I have found very
inspiring indeed. It made me want to begin writing at once,
so exactly did it chime with my own ideas, some of them scarcely
yet enunciated even to myself. The reading of this book discloses such a wide learning on the part of the author that I was
moved to consider my own intellectual etc. limitations, which
certainly are appalling. Yet I cannot look back & charge
myself with having missed my opportunities to an extent anything like commensurate with my ignorances. It occurred to
me that it would be a good & pleasant thing to write (before
I grew too old to remember the details) a plain account of my
intellectual & aesthetic development, showing what had helped
& what had hindered it. I think such an account would be not
only piquant but valuable. What say you to this? I certainly
am shameless & brutal enough to make it candid & therefore
a true human document.

Just now I seem to be encountering a lot of new material
which I can't possibly use, being already overstocked. I wish
you were here to see it as it goes by.

Yours, E. A. B.

My journal is alive, but with a very jerky vitality.

71. Bennett's article on George Moore seems not to have been published except
in the collection *Fame and Fiction* of 1901. The article 'Our Illiterate Novelists' is

RICKARD / MS. / 72
(*To John Rickard*)

9, Fulham Park Gardens
27 Nov 98

My dear Rickard,

This is more than kind of you; it is lavish; & our heart goes forth to you for such thoughtfulness & good nature. I wish I had enough horticultural lore to appreciate your box & its contents at the right value. But damned if I should have known differently had it contained but potato roots & turnip blossom. However, I shall be aware of the flowers when they sprout, & in the meantime Mrs. Hill will have these plants under her special care. She knoweth of gardens & loveth the same. With regard to my gardener, he is a worthy & dignified man, & I cannot order him to do this & this; I merely suggest. He has mulched & he has put up that wire which you named to me, with the most pleasing results. I get him when I can, for he is in much request by the neighbours of this neighbourhood. I believe he is a very nice old man, with a craft & a love for his craft.

I saw Kennerley last night at Marriotts, where we had a jovial evening, two Japanese mannikins being of the party & very good company too. Kennerley will tell you. I expect to see Young tonight. I want to arrange another of those dinners, at which may you be present. The first one lives brightly in my recollection, we being one of a small handful left sober at the end of the wassail. Young's bereavement, however, will I am afraid postpone the dinner for a while.

Yes, I am in fine health, & working like a Civil Service clerk when the inspector comes round. It is an uncompromising high coloured blood & thunder sensational serial that I am now doing. In a way, I enjoy it. There is a certain mechanical skill needed, the exercise of which affords a low sort of pleasure. When I began, it was hard work, but I have caught the knack,

---

not known, neither is the serious short story. The potboiling story may be 'The Marriage of Jane Hendra', which appeared in *Woman* on 26 October 1898. Bennett's first signed appearance in the *Academy* was a short interview with an American editor published in the issue of 18 June 1898. During the next four years he was a principal contributor to that magazine, and published therein the shameless and brutal account that he called *The Truth About an Author*, which began appearing 3 May 1902.

& so palpably improved that it will be necessary for me to rewrite the opening chapters again, in order to bring them to the artistic (!) level of the remainder. I can do it now at the rate of 700 words an hour, on my head, so to speak. Since you heard, the 17,000 words have increased to 22,000, & by Thursday next they will be 27,000: that will be half the tale done.

How are those philosophic labours of yours getting along? Whenever I read your letters, I have a wish to see stuff of yours in print, & it is a mystery to me how I have lived so long & *not* seen stuff of yours in print.

My brother has returned to his native home, & London sees him no more, except as a visitor. Did you see the *Ill. London News* this week:—

> I never loved a Bahr-Ghazel
> To glad me with its nice white Nile,
> But when I came to know it well,
> It proved a British crocodile.

Kind regards to your wife.

Ever yours, E. A. B.

I have certain volumes for you, which will reach you before Xmas. B.

MANCHESTER / MS. / 73
(*To A. N. Monkhouse*)

9, Fulham Park Gardens
23 Dec 98

Dear Sir,

As the writer of the recent article upon you in the *Academy* I venture upon the intrusion of telling you personally that I was much impressed by your remarkable novel. I didn't express myself in the article—(one never does)—& it was

72. Mrs. Hill was the wife of Joseph Hill (see page 6 n.). When Bennett moved to Fulham he asked Mrs. Hill if she would manage his house, and the Hill family moved from Blackheath there.

Bennett's serial was *Love and Life*, rewritten and retitled *The Ghost* for book publication. See Vol. I, p. 19, for further detail.

The verse appeared in L. F. Austin's weekly column on 26 November 1898.

written with a number of others amid all the helter-skelter of Christmas reviewing. I ought really to apologise to you for the inadequacy & haste of it.

But certain aspects of your novel touched me very sympathetically. I felt, if I may say so, that you had the same ideas & attitude as myself—at any rate in some matters. One gets this particular pleasure so seldom, that when it does arrive the giver ought to be made aware of the fact.

I made sure that you had read *On the Eve*—to my mind not only Turgenev's finest novel, but the finest novel ever written—one of the score or so absolutely perfect works of art in the whole world.

Might I ask whether you are going to write about Manchester & typical Manchester folk? I also belong to the Midlands (the Potteries), & every year I am more firmly convinced that there is a very real beauty underneath the squalor & ugliness of these industrial districts. Few people, so far as I am aware, have suspected the existence of this beauty. George Moore has touched the edge of it in *A Mummer's Wife*, but I have not seen it mentioned elsewhere in fiction.

As to the error of fact in my article, I sent up to Lane for some biographical details, & it was his manager who told me you were a solicitor.

Believe me, Dear Sir,

Very faithfully yours, E. A. Bennett

BERG / MS. / 74
(*To George Sturt*)

9, Fulham Park Gardens
5 Jan 99

My dear George,

It was a noble action to send me that last letter, for in the matter of correspondence I have notably fallen short. You

73. Allan Noble Monkhouse (1858–1936) spent most of his life on the staff of the *Manchester Guardian*. He was also a novelist and playwright. His novel, *A Deliverance*, deals plainly and realistically with Midland life, but avoids the industrial scene. Bennett wrote of it on 17 December 1898: '*A Deliverance* has been praised for many things; in our view its chief claim to distinction is the beauty of its building, the nice manner in which effects are accumulated towards a series of crises. It breathes the very spirit of Turgenev.' Monkhouse had written of Turgenev in an essay collection, *Books and Plays*, some time before.

wrote me on the 26th June last (observe, I remember the date) & ever since then I have been intending to reply. However, the most glowing accounts of your health & varied activities have reached me from time to time, & I have said to myself: He's all right without letters.

I am jolly glad to know you have got to the end of your novel. I have high expectations therefrom. Please finish it off sharp— don't dally—and let's see it. I venture to suggest you don't let Lane have it.

Now I have been working prodigiously. Since Sept 12 to the end of the year I did 96,000 words, grand total, & out of this period you must take a week in Brussels. It is well over 1,000 words a day, including Sundays. The lump includes several short stories, a huge mass of criticism, & 35,000 words of a sensational serial. I began this serial (it will comprise 12 instalments of 4,200 words each & will be finished on 7th Feby) partly because I had a notion that my position, commercially, was not founded on a rock as it should be, & partly because I didn't see why I shouldn't write as good exciting fiction as anyone else. With regard to my position, this house costs a hell of a lot to keep going in a generous way as I like, & although I am actually earning ample for all purposes, my desire is to earn enough apart from my editorial salary. I am sick of editing *Woman*, & of being bound to go to a blasted office every day. I want to work when I feel inclined, & to travel more. I saw only one way of freeing myself of official ties, namely fiction. If other people can hit the popular taste & live on magazine & newspaper fiction, why not me? You may say that writing popular fiction is poor work. It is, absolutely, but it is a damn sight better fun than going to an office & editing a ladies' paper & pays much better—as I think you will agree. Having decided to make a bid for popular fiction, I began—Sep 12. I wrote a damn silly story for my own Autumn number; people liked it. I did a better one, much better, & sent it to my agent to dispose of. I also did a humorous story, which I think good (I mean in the popular sense) & also sent that to my agent. He hasn't disposed of either of them. Between you & me, I think I can sell my stuff myself better than my agent can, & I shall shortly give him the chuck. His failure, or slowness, does not upset me in the least because I know the things will be sold sooner or later. Then I wrote a thoroughly sensational story for the Xmas Number of *Hearth & Home*. It is called *Dragons of the Night* (lovely title) & I regard it as a bit of very good sensationalism. I should like you to see it. It was much liked by the ruck, & I have seen it described as the best story in all the Xmas Numbers. I also wrote a Children's story for Xmas Number of *Woman*. It came to me all of a sudden, & I (quite literally) jammed it down as quick as I could shift the pen. Regarded not only from the popular but from the artistic standpoint, I think this a very good tale. Did you happen to see it? Tertia was enthusiastic about it, & she knows a thing or two.

I began the serial towards the end of October, & swore to do one instalment a week, which I did, though I nearly killed myself at first to keep my oath. (Recollect I was editing my paper, doing Books for *Hearth & Home*, Theatres for *Woman*, & six articles a month for the *Academy*. I certainly reviewed over a hundred books in Nov and Decr.) However, after the fourth instalment (17,000 words in a month) I seemed suddenly to conquer the trick of the thing. I have to report an immense increase of facility, not only for rotten but for decent stuff. I believe I could fart sensational fiction now. Anyhow, several times I have sat down at 4 p.m. & done 3,000 words complete (not a mere draft) that day. But I have loftier heights yet to conquer. I know a girl who has done her 12,000 in a day, & 40,000 in a week. Her average is 1,000,000 a year, & she makes Three thousand pounds per annum. I did say last September that I would stick to sensational stuff till the end of 1899, just to see what headway I could make in that time. But I doubt if I shall. I am dying to get on with my Staffs novel, which lately in my mind has assumed a larger & more epical aspect. I do believe it will be decent. With my newly acquired facility (of which I am so proud) I fancy I could write that novel in six months, & put my best work into it. It will certainly be immensely superior to *A Man from the North*.

I have another book all ready for writing—a Christmas book —which I think may turn out well, & which I could do in six weeks if I had a clear field.

The one dark blot on my autumnal activity is that my journal fell to pieces. It simply *had* to be left. I was working

myself to the very last ounce of energy. But I have now taken
it up again, with renewed zest. How is yours?

I have a lot of things to discuss with you, & will you please
say when it will suit you to come up for a week-end, the sooner
the better?

Webster being in a rotten state of idleness, I had him staying
here for a fortnight last Novr, and he *had* to work. It livened
him up pretty considerable, & he has worked ever since. *He
has a surprising & genuine talent for fiction, & will inevitably do
something fine.* I only discovered this a few weeks ago.

Respex to all.

Ever yours, E. A. B.

Have you read Phillpotts' *Children of the Mist*? It is a *great* book.

74. In the Journal on 12 September 1897 Bennett wrote: '. . . partly owing to
the influence of Phillpotts, I have decided very seriously to take up fiction for a
livelihood. A certain chronic poverty had forced upon me the fact that I was
giving no attention to money-making, beyond my editorship, and so the resolution
came about. Till the end of 1899 I propose to give myself absolutely to writing the
sort of fiction that sells itself. My serious novel *Anna Tellwright*, with which I had
made some progress, is put aside indefinitely. . . .' The autumn story for *Woman*
was 'The Marriage of Jane Hendra'; the Christmas story was 'The Great Fire at
Santa Claus House'. 'Dragons of the Night' is fast and furious melodrama in which
a lovely young girl falls into the clutches of a secret society, the Dragons, and is
saved by a member who has fallen into her clutches. He commits suicide, and she
can then fall in love with a handsome young man whom she was trying to save
from the clutches of the law when that one member of the society trapped her—
himself disguised as a member of Scotland Yard.

Bennett's first agent was William Morris Colles (d. 1926), some account of
whom is given in Vol. I, pp. 21–22. One of the two stories sent to him at this time
was 'Mr. Penfound's Two Burglars', serial publication of which is unknown.
Bennett allowed it to be published in an expanded edition of *The Loot of Cities*
(first published 1905) that Thomas Nelson issued in 1917. It is the only very early
example of his sensational writing to appear in book form. The other story with
Colles is unknown.

Bennett's work for the *Academy* was largely anonymous at this time. His first
appearance with his full name came with an article on 'Old Dumas' on 12
November 1898.

The Christmas book came to nothing. In July 1911 Bennett did write a Christmas
book, *The Feast of St. Friend*.

The only known writing of Alexander Webster is *Somerset House Past and Present*,
which he wrote with Raymond Needham.

Children of the Mist, published in September 1898, was dramatized by Phillpotts
and Bennett—mainly by Bennett—in 1900.

CHEESEMAN / MS. / 75
(*To Mrs. H. H. Penrose*)

St. Dunstan's Chambers,
24 Jan 99

Dear Mrs. Penrose,

I feel that you & other people need to be enlightened on the subject of E. A. Bennett & sensational serials. Several persons have cast missiles at me for troubling with such things. But why should I not write an exciting serial if I so desire? Exciting fiction is as much a form of art as any other sort of fiction. I finished my serial last night, & I may say, quite without prejudice, that it is very good—ingenious, full of trepidations, and eloquent; those who begin it will finish it. You enquire my reason for this pot-boiling. I have a very good reason. It is not my intention to sit here all my life editing a miserable female paper, or any other paper. In fact I have now had as much of editing as I want. My desire is to be moving on, & I shall not remain at *Woman* a moment longer than I can help. But if I leave journalism, I must find something else. That something else is fiction. It dawns upon me that fiction is my forte. But if I continued to turn out psychological treatises like *A Man from the North*, I might earn some sort of a reputation, but I should not, most emphatically, earn a livelihood. Therefore I must do, to begin with, the kind of fiction that will sell. When one has acquired a name for marketable stuff, one can plank down anything, however good, & it will sell. Witness Eden Phillpotts & others. That is my 'lay' just now. I don't see that sensational fiction is any worse 'pot-boiling' than editing a weekly paper. And I know that I would vastly sooner do the fiction than the editing. It is nearer to my special faculty, & I can get real fun out of it. But my great ambition at present is not to be tied to an office, & my efforts are directed to the breaking of these chains.

I think £1 a thousand is fair pay—not less.

I will see to *Woman* being sent regularly.

Kindest regards to all,

Sincerely yours, E. A. Bennett

BERG / MS. / 76
(*To George Sturt*)

9, Fulham Park Gardens
7 Feby 99

My dear George,

Well, I have finished my serial, & written two short stories of 4,000 & 5,000 words respectively since I saw you. I had resolved to accomplish these things before turning to serious things, & now I'm dashed if I feel any special inclination towards serious things. There are at least three matters to which I might turn. On Thursday I shall read through so much as is done of the draft of *Anna Tellwright*, & see if I feel drawn to it. But I am 'at a loose end', as we say in the Midlands, & I hope you know what the phrase means.

At the moment I am in the act of discovering 'W. B. Yeats', the Irish poet, whose prose, to my mind, is just about equal to anything going round. I have been fascinated by *The Celtic Twilight*, a little volume of essays about fairies & spirits. I wrote down to Frank, full of enthusiasm, & advised him to get the thing. He writes back: 'I bought *Celtic Twilight* when it came out, & have admired it for six years now.' Today I gave Young *carte blanche* to get me Yeats' complete works. It dawns upon me that he is one of the men of the century, so aloof, so intensely spiritual, & with a style which is the last word of simplicity & natural refinement.

Next week I am going down to Torquay for a weekend with Phillpotts, & expect to have some jolly good jaws beside the whiskey bottle. He is a man who can't really argue. I can't argue myself, but I can argue him off his legs; yet he is always in the right ultimately. He is like Sharpe, he feels, & what he feels he absolutely relies on, knowing that arguments are merely the refuge of the clever.

Most extraordinary coincidence. You remember telling me of a short story of Phillpotts' that you would like to dramatise. A new play by him was produced at the Court Theatre the other day. To my astonishment & delight it was that very thing. It is called *For love of Pim*. It was very well done indeed, simple, direct, & strong; & damn well acted, too.

In the principal piece at the Court was our adored Miriam Clements, as regally lovely as ever, & just as bad an actress.

She was playing the sister of Louis Quinze; you may bet it suited her appearance.

I should like to be informed when you are coming up to me. Tertia will be up towards the end of the month for a month. Could you not arrive during her stay?

Yours, E. A. B.

WALEY / MS. / 77
(*To Stanley Hazell*)

9 Fulham Park Gardens
13 Feby 99

My dear Hazell,

I had a notion for a duologue last night. I have written it this evening, & now enclose it. I hope you may be able to read it; this is the rough draft. I have never before done a duologue for acting, though I have done several for print, & therefore I offer you this with some diffidence. If you don't like it, you will say so. If you do, should you care to do it for my party on Mch 2?

Should this be so, I should like to witness a rehearsal. Perhaps you & Mrs Hazell & [? Miss] Draper could come here on the afternoon of the next musical evening, & we could go through it. But I do hope if you think it feeble you will say so.

Don't disclose the plot to Fred or anyone.

With kind regards to all.

Yours fatiguedly, E. A. Bennett

76. The two short stories are unidentified.

Bennett and the spiritual W. B. Yeats (1865–1939) attended a séance together many years later. See the Journal for 8 February 1917.

Miriam Clements apparently abandoned the stage for the home several years later. She was appearing in *A Court Scandal*, a comedy adapted from the French.

77. Stanley Hazell (d. 1946) and his wife Florence were members of the Bennett–Marriott circle. Hazell was an amateur actor, singer, and composer. Marriott says that he had an extensive repertoire of humorous songs and was one of the principal performers at the musical evenings. Professionally he was an insurance clerk. Bennett's duologue was called 'The Music Lesson'. After the performance Bennett wrote in his Journal: 'Intense and genuine enthusiasm and applause about it.'

Miss Draper is unidentified.

RICKARD / MS. / 78
(*To John Rickard*)   [9, Fulham Park Gardens]

E. A. Bennett

at Home
Thursday 2nd March, 7.30

to celebrate the 10th anniversary
of his advent in the metropolis
Music, porkpies & other attractions *R.S.V.P.*

I *do* want you to come to this. And if you come, can you arrange to stay later than usual?

E. A. B.

BERG / MS. / 79
(*To George Sturt*)

St. Dunstan's Chambers
29 Mch 99

My dear George,

I am charmed that the novel is finished. I should send it to Methuens first, & I should lose no time in doing so. I have finished the draft of my Staffordshire novel. The time between now & Whitsuntide I propose to spend in potboiling. Then I shall return to the novel, & try to write it from beginning to end in one spell of six months. I may say that I am pleased with the draft, which is, however, only a draft.

Can you not come up for the weekend after Easter, Apl 7th? This would suit me admirably. Phillpotts is coming up from Torquay later in the month. I am going home (205 Waterloo Rd, Burslem, Staffs) tomorrow, till Wednesday morning, & to-day I am very busy putting the paper to press. Let me hear from you. Charlie & a large crowd are spending Easter at Witley.

Yours, A.

79. Sturt's novel, called *The Extinction of the Keens*, was never published.

In September 1898 Bennett and Charles Young arranged to rent a weekend cottage at Witley, Surrey, for three years. Bennett had been thinking for some time of leaving London, and this was the first step. He installed a piano there, and he and his friends entertained themselves much as they did at the musical evenings in London. Marriott tells an amusing story of the place, which for two

RICKARD / MS. / 80
(*To John Rickard*)

9, Fulham Park Gardens
6th. July 99

My dear Rickard,

I have been desiring to write to you for some time just to tell you that the plants supplied by you to my garden are in excellent form. But I have never had time to write. As a matter of fact I haven't time now, being at my busiest. Fourteen hours per diem, Tuesday, Wednesday, & today (I hope): this cannot be called bad for a man whose natural state is

---

hundred years had borne the name 'The Fowl House', and then briefly 'Godspeace', and was rechristened 'The Fowl Hatch' by Bennett and his friends:

'The cottage had no bathroom, but there was a plentiful supply of water from a pump in the back yard, and courageous guests who wished to bathe, could do so by sitting under the pump, while someone else worked the handle. Those alfresco baths were very jolly and boisterous affairs, and added greatly to the gaiety of the week-end holidays.

At that time Stanley Hazell had a song entitled 'The Maiden with the Downcast Eye' of which the first verse ran as follows:—

> I know a little maiden who is very very shy
> (Be careful of the girl who's shy)
> She has a modest manner and a downcast eye
> (Be careful of the downcast eye)
> She wears upon her forehead a little baby curl,
> (Be careful of the little baby curl)
> And everyone will tell you she's a simple little girl
> (Be careful of the simple little girl)
> There are all sorts of girls, there are many kinds of girls,
> Some of them are frivolous and some of them are shy.
> You can trust them all no doubt, but you may as well look out
> For the simple little maiden with the downcast eye.

After Hazell had spent a weekend with Bennett at Witley he added the following verse:—

> If you're staying down at Witley and you want to have a bath,
> (Be careful if you want a bath)
> You saunter from your bedroom to the sunny garden path,
> (Be careful of the nobbly gravel path)
> The regulation costume is a blanket and your boots,
> (Be careful of the woolly rug and boots)
> You take your seat beneath the pump, and then the water shoots.
> (Be careful when the water shoots.)
> There are all kinds of baths, there are warm and swimming baths,
> But the shower bath à la Bennett is the one you all should try
> Though, as reckless of the weather,
> He affects the altogether,
> You had better pass the "Fowl Hatch" with a "Downcast Eye".'

idleness. Somehow I always fall to writing letters when I am at the full stretch. Well, as to those flowers, I don't know their names (nor does Mrs. Hill) but I detect certain blossoms in the pleasaunces unfamiliar to me, & the word goes round: 'These are what Rickard sent.' To my mind, the garden is a mass of blossom, but I daresay experts would style it differently. It is a wonderful garden; gets practically no attention, & yet comes up clothed in rainbows & smiles each year. The roses are now on the downgrade, but the lilies are just on the eve of their prime—fully opened except the topmost buds of each cluster.

My brain is a sort of labyrinth at this moment of the most dissimilar things; I am doing an appreciation of Ibsen, an appreciation of Charlotte M. Yonge (imagine the contrast) & a sensational serial all at once. In October I hope to return to my serious novel. *Can you yet fix an approximate date for coming to the cottage?*

Yours ever, E. A. B.

RICKARD / MS. / 81
(*To John Rickard*)

St. Dunstan's Chambers
11th. Sept 99

My dear Rickard,

I haven't acknowledged the plants earlier because they arrived just as I was off to Llandudno for a week, & I knew you would be away. They were planted instantly, under your instructions, & I am very much obliged for them. It is very nice for me to have my own private nurseryman. I adore a monopoly. Ken & Young are away at the cottage, & I am working like Hades. Young is going to publish a little book of plays by me next month—attempts to write farces which are funny. I find views differ as to what is funny in a farce. However I have my own. When are you coming to live in this

80. The piece on Ibsen is not known. The one on Charlotte M. Yonge (1823–1901), author of *The Heir of Redclyffe* and many other novels, appeared in the *Academy* on 22 July 1899. When Bennett took his house in Hockliffe, Bedfordshire, little more than a year later, he became known to his friends as the heir of Hockliffe. His new serial was *The Gates of Wrath*, which he published in *Myra's Journal*, beginning 1 October 1899. It was revised and published in book form in 1903.

(Fulham) district???? I hope you enjoyed Brighton. The only time I went there I was bilious.

It pains Young & myself to see Witley spelt with an H.

Yours ever, E. A. Bennett

CALIF / MS. / 82
(*To Mr. and Mrs. Stanley Hazell*)

9, Fulham Park Gardens
19 Sept 99

Dear friends both,

We are having a musical evening, or at any rate a party of some sort at No 9 on Sunday next, & trust you will honour us.

I hope soon to let you have a printed proof of 'A Good Woman'. I have since written another piece, longer, 4 characters, which Carlos Young says is *much* better. Usually dispassionate, he is really 'knocked' by my latest. His judgment is erratic; the piece is, however, a *little* better than anything previous. Title: 'The Stepmother'. In due course, I will ask you to do me the honour of perusing it. This completes the book, now at printers.

Yours, E. A. B.

ILLINOIS / MS. / 83
(*To H. G. Wells*)

9, Fulham Park Gardens
24 Sept 99

My dear Wells,

A year or two ago we exchanged a few letters, & since then I have heard nothing from you, though I often hear *of* you from common friends—Roche, Lewis Hind, Eden Phillpotts etc. I am writing now because I must—to congratulate you on the short stories in the *Pall Mall Magazine*, which seem to improve as they go on, & which certainly strike me as being fine & in a very special sense *original* work. In this 'prophetic'

82. Encouraged by the success of 'The Music Lesson', Bennett wrote three one-act plays over a period of six days—'A Good Woman', 'The Stepmother', and 'A Question of Sex'. Charles Young published them as *Polite Farces* in November. See further, Vol. I, pp. 59–60.

line of fiction, I will not say that I know nothing else so *strongly* imagined, but I will say that I know nothing else where the imagination is used with such virtuosity in the manipulation of material, or where the invention is so fresh, adroit & convincing. (And this despite the fact that I disagree (ferociously) with your general vision of the future of the race. Nor do I think that the changes you describe or any changes equally radical could occur in that fraction of time called a century.)

The September & October stories seem to me masterly. Do you not consider yourself fortunate, this time, in your illustrator? I gathered from a passage in *The War of the Worlds* that you were not exactly enchanted with Warwick Goble's efforts. Still, Goble is a very nice chap, with the most serious aspirations.

Among the 200 odd books that I have pretended to review this year *The Sleeper* has not found a place. But I shall be coming across it sooner or later, & shall expect it to be very excellent. If it is on the plane of the stories, I can't understand why it is only in its 8th thousand. (Or rather I *can* understand.)

I have heard of your illnesses in a vague way from time to time. I remember one lunch with J. N. Dunn when he was awfully depressed about your bodily condition. I hope this business is now all over, & that you are able to work fair & square, unhandicapped.

Believe me,
Sincerely yours, E. A. Bennett

BERG / MS. / 84
(*To George Sturt*)

9, Fulham Park Gardens
19 Nov 99

My dear George,

I can't say how much your postcard desolated me, & desolated the people to whom I showed it. I had been looking forward with avidity to this week-end. Today I wanted to have one long jaw. Besides our disappointment & yours, there

---

83. Walter Roche was a journalist. He is not otherwise known. James Nicol Dunn (1856–1919) was editor of the *Morning Post*.

From June to October the *Pall Mall Magazine* published a series of Wells's stories, each of them entitled 'A Story of the Days to Come'. They were gathered together into a single long story in *Tales of Space and Time*, 1899. *When the Sleeper Awakes* appeared earlier in the same year. Wells was seriously ill in August.

K

is of course the question of the bronchitis, which I reckon is quite disgusting enough by itself. But I seem to have heard so often of your having asthma & bronchitis, that it never strikes me as being anything special that you *should* have it. Such is use & custom. I hope you will soon be restored, & that you will come up here *the very first weekend you have*. There was a sort of fatality over that dinner. Should have been 20 there, but from one cause or another only 13 present in the flesh. Corrie was too ill to come. We drank to the absent, & had the devil's own time. I fancy we all kept sober. Sep & I got home at 12.45, & the bill was £4-11-4, & that is about all. There were some good speeches. Nolan uttered a masterpiece of eloquence in a full-blast denunciation of Rice. Don't know why, but he always does this. Nolan was in the chair: he always is, & fills it A.1, being Irish & Limerick at that. I felt perfectly well this morning—absolute *health*, mind you; & so set to work straight on my novel. That book has been playing yellow hell with me this last fortnight. It is now a question of the final writing, the draft having been finished last June or so. Well, I could not *begin* the thrice-damned thing. Couldn't get a start out of it. For 12 days daily I hovered round it & couldn't begin. Then on Thursday evening I suddenly came up against it, & wrote from 4.45 to 12.15 pm. (with an interval for supper). Only about 1,000 words in that time, but fine good stuff. I felt joyous after that. I had three hours on it again this morning, & shall have two more tonight. After which I shall probably go up to Charlie's. My book of plays is out. I advises you to get it, as it will amoose the comp'y. Perhaps you ain't aware that on the strength of it Harrison & Maude, lessees of the Haymarket Theatre, asked me to go & see 'em the other day & viva voce requested me to submit to 'em a three act comedy. This is serious, & a darned good beginning for any young drawmatist. Ten to one they won't like what I do for 'em, but you gather they must have been struck considerable by the playlets.

Well, Skoal (if that is the word).

Yours, E. A. B.

84. Frank Corrie and David Rice were members of the Bennett–Marriott circle. Corrie was a particular friend of W. W. Kennerley, and is remembered by Miss Mary Kennerley as being very Scotch in appearance, 'exactly like the old

TEXAS / MS. / 85
(*To Thomas Lloyd Humberstone*)

9, Fulham Park Gardens
17 Dec 99

Dear Humberstone,

Many thanks for your letter, & the songs. I haven't anything to impart to you, but I thought I would just write, fatigued as I am. I was up till 1.15 am playing duets with Dr. Farrar. We played four symphonies (Beethoven, Haydn, & Schubert (2)) two odd movements, & the overture to the *Meistersinger*. You call this a good evening's work, don't you?

I don't know anything at all about equal temperament, except that I can't keep my own temperament equal, & I ought to be able to. I have a theory (not precisely new) that a man can rise superior to anything, but I'm damned if I can work it out in practice. I am of the worrying sort. Just now I am consumed with a fever to chuck up women's journalism utterly, & go in for fiction & criticism only. I could do it if I had the pluck of a louse; but having got used to a comparatively expensive way of living I haven't the courage to make the necessary sacrifice. Nevertheless, I swear I will get out of that damned office inside two years or shoot myself. (I always keep my oaths.) Not that I object to editing a woman's paper & looking after nursery notes. It is not that. I am in editorial control of my paper, but it is only one of several belonging to a company, & I can't tolerate working for a company unless I am managing director or God almighty or something of that kind. Moreover, though I can get a diversion out of editing *Woman*, there are other things that I want to do much more, & I'm not doing them, or not enough of them. I shall publish a book of literary criticisms next year which I trust you may see, as, in its curious mixture of worldliness & passionate

---

advertisements for Monkey Brand cleaning soap, with a thin face and very pointed beard'. Nothing else is known of either man. Rice may have been employed with a publisher.

On Septimus Bennett (1866–1926), Arnold's youngest brother, see page 96 n. On James Nolan see page 86 n.

Frederick Harrison (d. 1926) began his long reign as manager of the Haymarket Theatre in 1896. Cyril Maude (1862–1951), both actor and manager, was associated with him for about ten years. Very little came of Bennett's encounter with them. See Vol. I, pp. 59–60, and also the Journal for 10 November 1899.

feeling for pure literary art, it is as exact an expression of myself as I am likely to arrive at. There is no reason why you should interest yourself in my productions, but I do wish you would read, in this week's *Academy*, my article on George Gissing. That article is a real bit of ME. See? There are sundry other articles by me in the same issue, to wit,

'The Chroniqueur'
'No Soul Above Money'
'Children of the Ghetto',

all very Bennetty. Excuse this unbridled egoism. Now I come to think, my object in writing was to know more of an idea you uttered by chance on the last night I saw you, about your removal to London. My deliberate impression about you is that you could keep your end up anywhere, & that therefore. . . .

Well, Merry Xmas—a damn silly wish—why not always merry?

Have you read Housman's poems *A Shropshire Lad*? They are only immortal, that's all. I take them as a tonic.

Yours sincerely, E. A. Bennett

CALIF / MS. / 86
(*To Emily Phillpotts*)

Trinity Hall Farm
22 Jan 1900

Dear Mrs. Phillpotts,

I have sent on your letter. The address is merely Victoria St. I hope if you are ordering potteries that you have asked for artistic potteries, as they sell the other sort, though art is their speciality. By now I suppose your new house is progressing towards its inevitable fate of being artistic. Why a house for

85. Thomas Lloyd Humberstone (d. 1957) was a would-be journalist and author. A few years later he began editing an education year-book for the publisher Swan Sonnenschein, and for a time he was on the administrative staff of the University of London. Over the course of many years he wrote or edited a dozen books and pamphlets mainly concerned with education.

On Dr. Farrar see page 39 n.

Bennett's collection of literary criticism, *Fame and Fiction*, was published in 1901 by Grant Richards, who also published some of the work of A. E. Housman (1859–1936). Bennett's article on George Gissing (1857–1903) (*Academy*, 16 December 1899) was one of the major pieces in *Fame and Fiction*.

years the abode of massive ugliness should by a mere change of owners be forced into an appearance which must be distasteful to it, I do not know. I beg you to think this over before you order that plain stair-carpet & annihilate all those pretty fans & bric-a-brac.

I am very sorry to hear that Eden has suffered a temporary reverse at the hands of his formidable & hereditary foe. No doubt he will ultimately conquer, & in the meantime he has my sympathies. I have perused his agreeable verse in February *Pall Mall Mag.* I think that while Halkett has done very well with the illustrations he has gone very much off in his fiction department. Q's article is to my mind much better than Q's work usually is. In fact I was rather struck by it.

The genuine anxiety of the farm labourers up here about the Queen is perfectly surprising to me.

Sincerely yours, E. A. Bennett

P.S. I am trying to get the garden respectable for Eden when he comes here. We have now proceeded as far as the gravel for the paths.

BERG / MS. / 87
(*To George Sturt*)

9, Fulham Park Gardens
13th Feby 1900

My dear George,

It is possible you may not be aware of it, but you are on my conscience. I owe you letters. You wrote; I replied not; and so again.

Providence ordained that you should not be able to come up before Xmas. Had you been in a position to come, I could not have accepted you. Since Novr. last I have been harbouring my parents & one of their servants, & so the house is crammed. All are still here, & may be till Easter. My father has had a very serious nervous breakdown, & he is up here for a complete

86. Emily Phillpotts (d. 1928) and her husband were preparing to move into their new home, Eltham, in Torquay. Eden was something of a hypochondriac. His poem was entitled 'Song of a Sad Heart'. The *Pall Mall Magazine* was edited by George Roland Halkett (1855–1928) from 1900 to 1905. No article by Q—Sir Arthur Quiller-Couch (1863–1944)—appears therein at this time.

change. He is better, but in my opinion (& his own) he will never be the same man again. Happily it is not of the first importance whether he works or not, as his business is of the sort that continues well in the hands of his partner & Frank of this ilk. The pater and mater being here has somewhat disarranged the atmosphere in which I work best, but not so much as I feared. I have indeed worked continuously hard for $13\frac{1}{2}$ months. My novel, I grieve to say, has been laid aside, but I am at it again now, & I am doing short stories of Staffordshire which I really believe will meet with your approval. Anyhow they meet with mine. Arthur Hooley & I have finished the first act (& the outline of the rest) of the four act romantic drama which we are doing for Cyril Maude. This first act will be submitted to him in a few days. I have but small hope of an acceptance, but the thing (on its plane) is damn good. Arthur Hooley says it is bloody good—extra bloody; & he may be right.

My articles in the *Academy* analytic of the psychology of readers of fiction are piling themselves up. This is what they really are—analytic of the psychology of various sorts of readers—but they are appearing under the guise of studies in popularity. They much please Lewis Hind, & they will be issued in a vol. under the title (I think) *Fame & Fiction—studies in the popularity of novelists*. I myself think these articles are very good, and distinctly original, too.

Such is my record to date. All I need say further is that the anxiety to have done with the office & editing grows on me daily. How is your new novel getting along? Phillpotts' is nearly finished; it is to be called *Out of the West*.

I spent this last weekend at Malden (Essex) with Pater & Sep; a quaint hill-town on an estuary, & any quantity of stuff in it. But I am absorbed in the Potteries just now: a great place, sir, & full of plots. My father's reminiscences have livened me up considerable.

Remember me to Frank.

Yours, E. A. Bennett

87. Enoch Bennett was a self-made man. In an article written only three years before his own death, Arnold described him thus: 'My father began, and failed, as a pottery manufacturer. Then he took to pawnbroking, and cared not for it. . . . At the age of nearly thirty, he did what to me has always seemed a marvellous thing—he decided to become a solicitor, and at the age of thirty-four he became

TEXAS / T.D. / 88
(*To Stanley Service*)

St. Dunstan's Chambers
March 23rd. 1900

Dear Mr. Service,

Thanks for your letter of the 22nd and the M.S. *Life's Counterpoint*. I will return the latter with my opinion in a few days.

I confirm your letter, except that I should prefer the limit of time during which I am to receive a percentage on royalties, to be two years instead of one year. The arrangement should I think be worded thus:—If during the next twelve months I should influence any author to bring a book to you, or should suggest the idea of any book to you, and the name of a suitable author to carry it out, or should suggest and recommend any author who partly or wholly through my influence should give you the refusal of his work, then, in the event of such influence, suggestion or negotiation leading at any future time to a publication by your firm, your firm shall pay me five per cent. on all royalties or sums falling due to such author within two years of such publication being made.

I have worded the arrangement thus because, unless it is defined closely, I might towards the end of our agreement have

---

one and set up in practice in the Potteries. This was something of a feat for a man of his age, poor and with a growing family. The three examinations must have put a terrible strain on him.' Of his mother, Sarah Ann (1840–1914) Bennett wrote in the same article: 'My mother during the lifetime of my father was my father's wife. But when he died we immediately discovered that she, too, had a most powerful individuality. She had also the great merit of being "interested in people". Her curiosity about them was inexhaustible, detached, and her judgment sound— if harsh. Nearly all her children were great humorists and teasers before the Lord, but she never in her life really saw a joke.' Brother Frank returned to Burslem from London to enter his father's law office and eventually to take over the firm.

Bennett's early story 'A Letter Home' touched upon the Five Towns, as did *A Man from the North* a few years later; but the stories he was now doing were his first completed work set entirely in the Potteries. Some of them were gathered into his first collection of short stories, *Tales of the Five Towns*, published in 1905.

Arthur Hooley (1874–1928) was a cousin of the Kennerleys. He was a teacher and, later in America, an editor and writer. He and Bennett wrote *The Chancellor* in 1900, which Maude did not take.

On Lewis Hind see page 99 n.

Out of the West seems to have been a provisional title for Phillpotts's Dartmoor novel *Sons of the Morning*, published in 1900.

Nothing is known of Sturt's new novel.

all the trouble of negotiation with no profit, owing to the fact that the publication was made after the agreement had expired. And other similar contingencies might arise.

I do not for a moment suggest that such a difficulty could occur between you and me personally, but a long experience in dealing with limited companies has taught me that absolute precision in expressing the terms of an agreement may save a great deal of trouble. A Board of Directors, acting for shareholders, must necessarily, if a contract is dubious, apply to it strictly the meaning most advantageous to their company.

If you would be good enough to send me copies of your publications as they appear, I should be able to get a better idea of the lines on which you are working. And will you send me your announcements, *and a list of your authors*.

Believe me,

Yours very truly, [Arnold Bennett]

BERG / MS. / 89
(*To George Sturt*)

9, Fulham Park Gardens
9th April 1900

My dear George,

Kindly cause the MS. of *Bettesworth* to be sent to me without delay, as I have a notion therefor, if you permit. Pearsons Ltd have recently sought me out & constituted me literary adviser to their book publishing department—(they being fascinated by my articles in the *Academy*—think of this!). They want to raise the tone of their publishing. I propose to put *Bettesworth* before them under the title:—

TALKS WITH MY GARDENER
a study of the English peasant.

And I want you to let me write my own preface for it. You must let me do this, as it is very important in getting the book accepted, & you couldn't write the sort of thing I want—not

88. F. Stanley Service managed the book publishing department of the C. Arthur Pearson organization. The firm was notable for its popular magazines, and had gone into book publishing only in 1897. Bennett became their principal reader for a year. *Life's Counterpoint*, by Lily Perks, was published by Pearson in 1903.

being a hack journalist. Once the book was accepted, we could calmly strike out my preface & substitute anything you wanted.

In my capacity of adviser I could say to them: 'This book is good: publish it.' But under the circumstances I don't want to do this. I want merely to use what I call my 'influence'. I am not sure that I can get it accepted by any means, but I should like to have a try. I should tell them at once it wouldn't sell quite 100,000 copies, & that therefore you would be very amenable about terms.

Que dites vous?

Yours, E. A. B.

If I could get *Bettesworth* published I should be a proud man the day.

Have you written to Lane?

BERG / MS. / 90
(*To Cranstoun Metcalfe*)

St Dunstan's Chambers
8 May 1900

Dear Metcalfe,

Tiddy-fol-lol

I have worked Mr Catling's will upon this story (except the word 'decade'—if he is faddish enough to alter 'decade' to 'ten years', God give him grace to do it. He has my permission.) *Qua* author, I curl the lip of disgust at the notion of altering this perfect & delicate trifle to suit the tastes of one million two hundred & fifty thousand coastguards & washerwomen. (But that *Lloyds* should even dream of accepting this story alters my views radically as to what it is they are after, & makes me almost believe Mr Colles' dictum that the great public can appreciate great literature.) *Qua* Editor, of course I can see what Mr Catling objects to in the story.

But why can't he merely say what he wants without trying to explain his wants by a theory that 'so simple a tale' ought to be written in words of one syllable? This is the first time I

89. Sturt at first declined Bennett's offer, then accepted.

have ever heard of a proportion being established between simplicity of tale & length of words.

Anyhow, I'm damned if I'll alter 'decade'.

Yours, E. A. Bennett

For volume-form, I promise myself these poor cast-outs shall be amply re-instated.

TEXAS / MS. / 91
(*To Thomas Lloyd Humberstone*)

9, Fulham Park Gardens
23 May 1900

My dear Humberstone,

I was glad to have your letter, & the absolute decision about coming to London. I am always prepared to buy old oak desks, provided they are of good design, & what I consider a bargain. I have no doubt we can do business if you want, but I hope this necessity won't arise. In fact I don't think it will. I expect by the end of the year to be fairly hard up myself.* I leave London & my income simultaneously on 29th Septr. Do not be cast down, dear Sir, at the closing of this house. Look at the sad affair in this light: that when you come to London you will certainly want to leave it for week ends, & our new house will then be open to you with its rural charms.

I can't stop to write now, I am so fiendishly busy I don't-know what to do; but I intend to go to Witley both this week-end & next week-end.

Excuse brevity.

Not at all surprised at Miss [? Colle]. No *decent* person *would* be interviewed.

Yours, E. A. B.

* Just looking into my banking account. It is absolutely appalling.

90. Cranstoun Metcalfe was assistant or partner to W. M. Colles in the Authors' Syndicate. He was a writer as well as a literary agent, and published a novel, *Peaceable Fruit*, in 1904. He also did some book reviewing for the *Pall Mall Gazette*. Douglas Catling (1830–1920) was editor of *Lloyd's Weekly Newspaper*, the title of which varied somewhat over the years, from 1884 to 1907. 'Tiddy-fol-lol' appeared therein on 30 December 1900, and was reprinted in *Tales of the Five Towns* in 1905 with 'ten years' intact.

91. Bennett took a lease on Trinity Hall Farm, Hockliffe, Bedfordshire.
Miss Colle is unidentified.

CALIF / MS. / 92
(*To Edith Evors*)

St. Dunstan's Chambers
15 June 1900

Dear Miss Evors,

You can do me quantities of interviews, but not musical ones or histrionic ones. I have had an undue percentage of these lately. Get some novelists, or any other sort of weirdness, outside the Fabian Society. Pearsons is a good firm to be in— no Saturday work, & decent treatment. I am their publisher's reader, or rather the great panjandrum & final appeal court of their various readers; in fact a great bug in the book publishing department there. Next time I call I will discourse on your charms & abilities to Stanley Service head of that department.

Yours sincerely, E. A. Bennett

Miss Meller is to be the new editor of this esteemed periodical.

ILLINOIS / MS. / 93
(*To H. G. Wells*)

9, Fulham Park Gardens
2nd Augt 1900

My dear Wells,

I should like immensely to come down & have a day or so with you. I oughtn't to, but I think I will. I think I could come on Saty 18th (if this is the week-end you mean) strictly for the week-end. I am extended just now over a Tillotson serial. I have been 'laid aside' for a month with an abscess, & am already late with delivery, but the benevolent syndicate has granted me an extension of 6 weeks, bless it.

I write this letter from Burslem, whence I depart tonight, & where I have been observing the effect of the Wesleyan Methodist Conference on the community. I came down specially to observe the same, & have been well rewarded. The

92. Edith Evors was Bennett's secretary for a while at *Woman*, beginning in November 1896. He describes her in his Journal as 'the first genuine middle-class bachelor woman, living alone in London lodgings, that I have been intimately familiar with. A tall woman, slightly under 30, with big limbs and a large, honest, red-cheeked face, and a quiet, *intense* voice. Transparently conscientious; with little self-reliance, but a capacity for admiring self-reliance in others.'

public examination of candidates for ordination, the other night at Longton, was one of the most genuinely *interesting* things that I have ever watched.

It is enough for me that you & Mrs. Wells were interested in *Man from the North*. There is much in it that is not authentic, merely fanciful, & quasi-sentimental—I can see now. But I seriously meant all of it at the time. It was the first work I did, and before I had finished it the technique thereof had advanced so much that I had to go back & write the first half again. So you may guess what it was to start with!

Well, I shall look forward to seeing you; & thanks very much for what in this district the élite call the 'invite'.

Sincerely yours, E. A. Bennett

BEDFORD / MS. / 94
(*To A. W. Merry*)

9, Fulham Park Gardens
24 August 1900

Dear Sir,

Trinity Hall

Thanks for your letter & the enclosure. I return the latter with a few alterations in pencil. The only alteration of any importance is the inserted proviso on p. 4. I think that Mr. Adams will admit the justice of this. If he for any reason wished me to leave at the end of two years, he would have had his house vastly improved partly at my expense, & I should have got no adequate return.

I have made a few additions to the schedule. Every item has been agreed between me & Mr. Adams personally.

With regard to the papering, it is understood that I am to be at liberty to spend 2/6 per piece for living-rooms & 1/6^d for everything else. It is absolutely essential that I should be at liberty to choose my own patterns from the firm of Essex & Co. in Victoria Street. *Please confirm this by letter*. I am extremely particular about the wall-papers that I have to live with, & only this firm sells the artistic patterns which I require. I should be glad if Mr. Adams could let me have soon the number of pieces required for each room, & for the stair-cases,

93. The serial for Tillotsons was *The Grand Babylon Hotel*.

landings, passages; of course I shall have these latter all uniform.

I shall be at

Two Bridges Hotel
near Princetown
Dartmoor

all next week, & shall be obliged if you will send your reply to this letter to that address.

Yours faithfully, E. A. Bennett

BECKER / MS. / 95
(*To Ida Meller*)

Trinity Hall Farm
Hockliffe Beds.
9th Oct 1900

My dear Miss Meller,

I have just been looking, with surprise & pleasure, at this week's *Woman*. It is really very good. I felt sure that you would impress yourself on the paper, but I didn't think you would make it quite as fresh & attractive as it is. If you can keep this up, there will be a future both for you & the paper. I also like Mr. Bayly's idea for the new cover.

This house is in a frightful mess with workmen, but I am enjoying myself immensely. It looks to me now as if I should do little else in the future except write plays & novels. I have actual commissions for plays from both Frohman & Julia Neilson, & am very busy on them. I shall be in town again soon & shall then hope to see you.

With kindest regards,
Sincerely yours, E. A. Bennett

94. A. W. Merry was a surveyor in Leighton Buzzard, Bedfordshire, and Bennett was negotiating through him a lease on Trinity Hall Farm, owned by John James Reynal Adams, a member of an old Bedfordshire family. Merry's firm is now Brown and Merry.

95. Langton George Bayly apparently managed *Woman* and *Hearth & Home*, and he was editor of the latter journal until 1903 or 1904. He is not otherwise known.

Bennett, his father and mother, and Tertia went to live at Trinity Hall Farm on about 1 October 1900.

Charles Frohman (1860–1915), the American producer and manager, owned several theatres in London. The play he commissioned was presumably *Children of the Mist*, which, though technically a collaboration between Bennett and

RICKARD / MS. / 96
(*To John Rickard*)

Trinity Hall Farm
9 Oct 1900

My dear Rickard,
   I had joy of your letter. Yes, it is back to the land & the livestock. There are at present:—

> 1 mare
> 30 hens & cocks
> 1 dog
> 2 cats
> many mice.
> Human relatives.

   I knew perfectly well that the country would suit me—winter or summer, & it does. I Haven't been so well for 20 years. What is more to the point, I feel that I shall be able to work here. Goodness knows I have got enough work to do.
   I perceive you know something about the geology of this district. I want to get hold of that (in a compressed tabloid form), because until I do, I can't grasp the scenery. The scenery, however, is very Great, & Great are the villages. Greatest of all is Watling Street, sweeping past my meadow (acreage of estate, $2\frac{1}{2}$a.) in a stupendous straight line. What I like about Watling Street is its sublime disregard of everything except direction. It 'goes for' Holyhead with its head down, & it gets there, either over hills or through 'em, doesn't matter which.
   I should mention that this place is set on a hill, with a clear view of miles of downs—amid Bunyan's 'Delectable Mountains'. The district is infested with millionaires, dukes, & historic sites. You never say Rothschild up here. You say 'Mr. Alfred' or 'Mr. Leopold'.
   My sister remembers you with vividness (why not?). She reciprocates your regards.
   I want you to come up soon.

Phillpotts, was largely Bennett's work. It was never produced. Frohman had commissioned another play from Phillpotts the previous year. Julia Neilson (1869–1957), the actress, had just gone into management with her husband, Fred Terry. She took Bennett and Hooley's play *The Chancellor* but did not produce it.

I suppose you are the same philosopher that you have ever been. Your philosophic attitude & mystic insight into Nature are the two chief things I envy you. I regret to say that my feeling is that I shall be just as damn *literary* up here as in town. I shall never be *interested* in gardens. I want a nice garden (& shall have one) & a horse that will go (and have got one), but I don't want to be troubled with the details. I am now reconciled to this. I have no *real* interest in anything except eating, writing, music, & the graphic arts. And never shall have. It is a sad fact, but it's a fact. I would sooner play a piano duet than understand about inflorescences, & I would sooner write about digging than dig. When the gardener (we have got a most agreeable & talented young man from Essex) begins to hold forth to me about the garden, I feel the *dis*-interest creep over me, & it makes me shudder. I answer him with a hollow show of polite interest. Let the garden *be* there, but I only want it to walk on, with my feet & eyes.

I expect all this will sadden or disgust you.

Yours, E. A. B.

Yet I am passionately in love with rusticity & the country. I gathered blackberries Sunday morn & ate 'em Sunday night.

96. Wilfred Whitten, the journalist, has described a visit to Bennett at Trinity Hall Farm about two years after Bennett moved there:

'He was grave, orderly, sure of himself, and industrious in grain. Physically he was already on the massive side; one might say that he walked "with the slow motion of a summer cloud". . . . He . . . came, in a dog-cart, to Dunstable Station, and drove me with supreme control of the reins and other knowingness to his home. This was a pleasant house standing in a sloping field, open to all the air and all the light. What I feel about that visit is that I saw Bennett in the very act of becoming the man he became. His women folk were simple, kindly, refined. The house might have been transported by magic from Hanley to a Bedfordshire knoll. It was an entirely middle-class home, without any inventions or sophistications of science falsely so called. Its water supply came from the roof, to which it had to be pumped up from a well in the garden, and how it was done, though I saw it done, I cannot now conceive. At Hockliffe Bennett was between two worlds, the one he had not quite left and the one he had not quite entered.'

BEDFORD / MS. / 97
(*To A. W. Merry*)

Trinity Hall Farm
12 Oct 1900

Dear Sir,

I am having some difficulty now with Mr. Adams as to the wall papers. The price of wall papers was agreed on, & I have kept *considerably within the price*; & it was also agreed that I should have the papers from Essex & Co. of London (see your letter of 28th Augt). Mr. Adams himself said Messrs. Essex. I chose the papers, & now it turns out that Mr. Adams wants more discount than Messrs. Essex will give. Mr. Adams says that if *I* choose to pay the difference I can have the papers. This is of course ridiculous. The difference is some 6/- odd. The delay is getting serious. I am extremely anxious that everything should proceed pleasantly, but I shall be glad if you will write to Mr. Adams & tell him that,

1. I insist on having the papers I have chosen.

2. That I give notice of my right to claim damages for his delay in repairing the house. More than half the house is uninhabitable & the delay in every department of the repairs is gross. I cannot be expected to pay full rent for a house of which only two or three rooms can be lived in.

I shall be personally much obliged to you if you will do what you can to hasten matters.

Yours very truly, E. A. Bennett

BERG / MS. / 98
(*To George Sturt*)

Trinity Hall Farm
30 Oct 1900

My dear George,

I feel I scarcely saw you on Saturday night—a great & fine night. Your remarks on J.B., though you mayn't have suspected it, were fine, & touched me deep. You seemed like a strong man, George, & you are. I have never been through such a night as Saturday, & haven't got over it yet.

Now regarding your letter of the 27th there is a great deal of truth in what you say as to parsons, & one particular parson.

The particular parson, I quite agree, gives himself away all through his report. The point is: Do you *really* want that book published or not. I have a sort of idea that, now, you don't care a damn for anyone or anything. You have got hold of Emerson's special variety of 'self-reliance', & there you are. This is quite right. Only I want to know whether you actually *do* want that book issued. If so, you will have to do one of two things:—

(1) alter it.
(2) write some other books & make a name first, & *then* issue it as it stands.

See?

Yours, E. A. B.

CALIF / MS. / 99
(*To Edith Evors*)

Trinity Hall Farm
30 Oct 1900

Dear Miss Evors,

I have a sort of feeling that I have ignored two letters of yours, so I indite this to apologise, & to express the hope that you are comfortable & prospering. I have now cut my connection with London, & received a really very nice silver inkstand for doing so. I must thank you very much for your share

98. The Pearson organization seem to have had *The Bettesworth Book* read for them by a parson. Sturt wrote to Bennett on 27 September of the parson's review:
'It may be that the parson has put my back up. His criticism seems fair: and I bear him no ill-will for pulling me up at one or two howlers. But when he talks about "the old fellow's quaint narratives" then I behold the country parson, in whose sight a man like Bettesworth has next to no virtues, and is either coarse or "quaint". If my book has enough of the real man in it to grate on a parson's nerves, then perhaps it should not be altered. When one thinks of it, the mere notion of submitting such a man as Bettesworth (even in a report of him) to the judgment of a parson is absurd. All which considerations don't excuse my book, for failing to be a work of art. Don't you think I'm under any delusions on that score. . . . This, however, isn't what the parson wants. You twig his idea of re-construction: it's to be *my* notes and appreciation of the "country life". He wants *me*, to come and entertain him in his study, with anecdotes of the quaint old fellows in the village, so that we may smile over 'em together, and then sigh, and be struck perhaps by a "thought" for tomorrow's sermon.'
The Pearson firm did not publish *The Bettesworth Book*, and it was taken finally by Sturt's friend, Charles Young, for Lamley's in 1901.

L

in that gift. Behold me in a whitish house surrounded by 3 acres of orchard, meadow & garden, fixed on the summit of high ridge, with a clear view of many square miles of England. As I lie in bed I can see the sun rise, & usually I do see it rise. I am very busy, partly with vast quantities of work, & partly with seeing to the repairs & decoration of this house (I have the d—dest landlord you ever saw, & I worry him twice per diem on principle). I have written half a play since I came here, & many articles. I shall never be happy, but here I shall come as near to it as possible. (See me driving my mare—a great sight.)

With kindest regards & best wishes.

Yours sincerely, E. A. Bennett

BERG / MS. / 100
(*To W. M. Colles*)

Trinity Hall Farm
14 Nov 1900

Dear Colles,

What a self-convicted & ingrained nincompoop Methuen is! How blind to the dazzling success which awaits him! However, he has been advising Phillpotts to imitate *Cranford*, & a man who would do that would do anything short of marrying Marie Corelli! I would prefer Grant Richards to George Allen. I am just making a few private enquiries in that direction, first, & will let you hear the result later. In the meantime, pursue a policy of masterly inactivity.

There is one word in your letter which the combined intelligence of Hockliffe has not yet succeeded in deciphering. When we get at it, we shall fire 101 guns & hoist the Cuneiform-Sanskrit flag, reversed.

Children of the Mist (play) is practically done, & you will have it typewritten by the end of the month.

You might ask *Cornhill* & *Lloyds* when the —— they are going to publish my stories.

Sincerely yours, E. A. Bennett

100. Colles was trying to find a publisher for *Fame and Fiction*. The *Cornhill Magazine* did not publish Bennett's story 'A Feud in the Five Towns' until July 1902. On the *Lloyd's* story see page 137 n.

CALIF / MS. / 101
(*To Emily Phillpotts*)

Trinity Hall Farm
22 Nov 1900

Dear Mrs. Phillpotts,

Teale's address is simply 'Leeds'. But they have a showroom in Berners St., Oxford Street, to which it would be better to write.

Mrs. Peel, however, tells me about a grate which (similar in principle to Teale's) she considers both better & cheaper. It is to be found at Wright & Sons, Queen Victoria St. EC. It burns but little coal, & that of an inferior kind, & gives out great heat. If you enquire about it, you had better say that you want the sort of grate which Mrs. Peel has recommended to so many people.

This morning is a red-letter morning. A fire has been lighted in our new range! I expect on Monday we can actually have baths again!

I suppose you are alone now, & Eden disporting himself on the Moor. I have this morning sent the final act of *Children of the Mist* to the typewriter.

Believe me,
With kindest regards,
Sincerely yours, E. A. Bennett

RICKARD / MS. / 102
(*To John Rickard*)

Trinity Hall Farm
23 Jan 1901

My dear Rickard,

I was very glad to hear from you. I don't know any house round here that would do for Boutwood. In fact the dearth of houses is quite a remarkable fact about the country. There is only one house to let in this village, & that has five or six rooms; it is £12 a year, & a 4 acre field can be had for £10 more, at the back thereof. Witley would be entirely unsuitable for a

---

101. Mrs. C. S. Peel (d. 1934) was on the staff of *Woman* and around 1904 became editor of it and *Hearth & Home.* She wrote books on household management. See Vol. I, p. 15, for her description of Bennett as editor.

young married pair. No woman would stand it. True there are [? grounds], but the place is entirely too old; all the bedrooms open into one another. If you could live on the exterior picturesqueness & on the fine quality of the internal oaken beams, you would be happy, but you can't. In summer the house is great; in winter it is hell, except you take it in short doses, & *as a joke.*

When do you propose to come up here? I want some of your lore. I have come to the conclusion that though I enjoy the country enormously, I shall never know anything about it. I regard it in the mass. I don't think about flowers & vegetables naturally; I have to *make* myself think about them. This is a bad sign. I daresay I may ultimately know something about horses; I find myself interested in them naturally. I have now got two. Not that I want two, but owing to my natural inability to resist a 'trade' when I see the chance of a bargain.

This place is simply magnificent. About 6 times per diem you find yourself appreciating, savouring, the excellence of being alive.

I am in the middle of a spell of idleness just now.

Give my kindest regards & best wishes to Boutwood, please.

Yours, E. A. B.

BERG / MS. / 103
(*To George Sturt*)

Trinity Hall Farm
10th Feby 1901

My dear George,

How are you getting on with your journal? I'm damned if I can keep mine going properly. Last year I was producing so much else that it would have been absurd for me to burden myself with the work of observation for a journal, especially as during the last 3 months (up here) I was horribly bored seeing after 6 workmen continually in the house, repairing & decorating it. But I meant to make a start this year, & I have done,

102. Arthur Boutwood was a close friend of Rickard's, and had been employed in the same office with him for a time. He wrote several books, mainly on religious subjects, some of them under the name of Hakluyt Egerton. He died in the late thirties.

but without much success. The fact is I am too ignorant of everything to observe the phenomena with any fineness. I thought that, coming fresh to it, I should be the more likely to get hold of stuff; but I can see now that exactly the contrary was bound to happen. I haven't got down a single thing of any importance, though naturally I have found some drolleries.

I fancy I have sort of settled down now to a literary life, pure & simple. My nearest approach to journalism is reviewing, & of this I do a great deal. My facility in it steadily increases, & so, I think, does the quality of my articles. I have a book of criticism all ready for printing, & it ought to make a bit of a stir; but Grant Richards has had it for months, & neither I nor my agent can get a definite answer out of him. I am on the point of getting angry at the swine.

I have cleared off all plays for the present. The Hooley-Bennett partnership has proved extraordinarily successful. I hoped much from it, but it has surprised me. Considering we raked in £275 solid cash in the first year, getting two plays accepted, I reckon we can please ourselves, for the theatrical ring is a very difficult one to enter, far more so than the purely literary. I should explain to you that though I happen to be sole author of the little Haymarket play, it belongs to the partnership, according to agreement. When Maude asked us for a 1 act play we each wrote one (in 3 days), & it was mine that was took. We think little of that piece however; it is the big play that is going to make the big splash. I need not tell you that, so far, we attach no artistic importance whatever to anything we have done, but we hope in the future to write an *artistic* farce. Money is our aim, solely; Arthur wants to write poetry, & me fiction. I have actually refused a commission for another play, because I had sworn to recommence *Anna Tellwright* this month, & I have done so. I am rather satisfied with it; it is going fairly smoothly, but I may get stuck in it. With luck I should finish it by the end of April. I shall then do another serial, unless the play is in the meantime produced, as I shall have to earn something, & I can do it so easily with a serial. My serial in the *Golden Penny* is going famously, & the proprietors are enchanted with it.

I have chucked very hard work now; I hope for good. About 4 hours daily writing is my limit. At this rate I have done nearly 30,000 words this year, of all sorts; but I did practically nothing in the first 3 weeks of January. Although I am working much fewer hours, the whole of my time seems to be fully occupied. I am getting so damned open-air. I am keeping two horses now, & learning to ride (I have made my will). The estate is gradually being got into order, but I find that an enormous job. If I hadn't happened to have made a lot of money last year, I should have been stone broke by this time, through sheer lawful expenditure. I am profoundly satisfied with this life up here. My father's health is the one blot on the show: & it will gradually get worse till he loses all his faculties & dies. The case is perfectly hopeless, & the outlook not at all cheering.

I have just written another short story of the 'Five Towns'. Time, the year 1825, rather a novelty for me. Come up & read it, George. I want about 3 days solid *jaw* with you; we get quantities of visitors from London here (there are 4 in the house now). When will you come? The views from my study will be agreeable even to your sated eyes. Also I want to read that art book of yours, of which I can get no authentic details, either from you or anyone else. What has occurred to it?

Give my best respex to all your people at the Bourne & at Farnham & believe me, sir,

Your obedient servant, Bettesworth

103. Bennett gave up his journal entirely from 10 April 1900 until the end of the year.

The second Bennett–Hooley play was *A Wayward Duchess*, which was never produced. The partnership seems to have ended here. The Haymarket play was 'The Post Mistress', which likewise was never produced.

The *Golden Penny* serialized *The Grand Babylon Hotel*, beginning 2 February 1901.

The Five Towns story was 'The Elixir of Youth', set in the year 1825. It appears in *Tales of the Five Towns*.

Sturt was writing a group of essays on art that he intended to gather into a book.

CALIF / MS. / 104
(*To Edith Evors*)

Trinity Hall Farm
21 Feby 1901

Dear Miss Evors,

In reply to your letter of the 31st Decr., I am glad to have the same. I heard of you the other day as being still with Lady Pearson of Henrietta Street. I hope this will continue, but it doesn't seem to me to be capable of leading to much. Are you still writing? I trust so. When you die (whenever & however) I trust you will consciously remember, realise, & derive satisfaction from the fact, that your individual influence upon the world has been good, stimulating, & progressive. In other words, that you have helped to forward the sublime principles involved in the admirable chapter on the Parrot-woman in *The Quintessence of Ibsenism*. By the way I have lately attacked G. B. Shaw (the literary artist) with my full ferocity in the *Academy*, & a young lady in Birmingham, who evidently is prejudiced by a very proper gratitude towards him, has got herself extremely angry with me. Note—I have not had any premonition of your decease; but that idea just happened to occur to me, apropos of your regrettable tendency to self-depreciation.

I shall venture to hope that your enthusiasm for the theatre will continue until two of my plays are produced, by Julia Neilson & Cyril Maude respectively. Why they are not already attracting all London I cannot imagine, since everything is duly signed sealed & delivered. But the theatrical world is not as other planets. I am only proud of these plays as being gorgeous examples of my ability to meet a literary demand in a workman-like & grandiose manner. In the same way I am charmed with a serial of mine now running with great éclat & Reginald Cleaver's illustrations, in a sheet entitled the *Golden Penny*. To read the instalments each week does me good, they are so exactly what they should be (& good English thrown in gratis). I have now attained to the lordly eminence of declining commissions for serials. I *hope* not to do any more, but unless Julia sharpens up, I shall have to.

I thank you: my health is far better now than it has been for many years. I go out riding one hour per diem, & this is my salvation. The reason why I happen to be writing this letter now is that I am very busy. I always have most spare time when I am at my busiest. After multitudinous delays, I am at last on my serious Staffordshire novel—doing nothing else, in fact, except my usual weekly articles. I began it 15 days ago, & have written 16,000 words—about a fifth of the whole. I am attacking it tooth & nail, & unless God pokes his nose in, it will be finished by April 30th at 7 p.m.

I rather fancy your friend Grant Richards is going to publish a volume of literary criticism by the author of *Journalism for Women*. At any rate he has got as far as expressing his delight in the book & asking the lowest terms. When this comes out I shall be embroiled all round, as I have expressed my candid views in it on about 15 living English writers & some foreign ones. The reviews will be great larks. I shall probably have to retire to Boulogne till the scandal blows over.

It is seldom that I come to London. I think I have been only twice since September. If London can dispense with me, I can dispense with *it*. I saw *the* funeral & Mr. Bayly. Things are sliding along as usual at Nos. 10 & 11.

If you have not read *The Believing Bishop* by Havergall Bates (whoever he may be) (George Allen) let me recommend it to you as a fine disturbing book.

Yours sincerely, E. A. Bennett

104. Bennett remarked of Miss Evors in the Journal in 1896: 'She lives in Bloomsbury, and at night goes to socialist and anarchist lectures. "It is dreadful", she said to me today, "to think how *little* one can do! . . ." Full of easily aroused pity and indignation.' Apparently in 1901 she was on the staff of the *Lady Magazine*, which was published from the same address in Henrietta Street as the offices of the Pearson organization.

Bennett's article on Shaw appeared anonymously in the *Academy* on 9 February 1901, and said among other things: 'He is the indefatigable champion of social justice, not because he has a passion for social justice, but because he has an intellectual perception of it. . . . One might still be hopeful for Mr. Shaw's future as a dramatist . . . if there was any hint in his plays of creative power. But there is no such hint.'

Reginald Cleaver (d. 1954) was on the *Graphic* staff and was a contributor to *Punch*.

The funeral was doubtless that of Queen Victoria, on 2 February.

The Believing Bishop was published by George Allen. Nothing else is known of Havergall Bates.

BERG / MS. / 105
(*To Cranstoun Metcalfe*)

Trinity Hall Farm
28 Feby 1901

My dear Metcalfe,

Thanks for your letter. You had better accept those terms. They are bad, but I have known worse. There is no money in the book, but there is a jolly good ad. in it for me, & that is all I was expecting to get out of it. I don't see that 10% or 15% makes much difference. Suppose the book sells 500 copies—at 10% I should make £12, & at 15% £18. Difference £6. I can earn £6 in a day when I am writing serials. I don't reckon much of Grant Richards as a Maecenas, but in this particular instance I rather sympathise with him, as that sort of book never *does* sell. Let me have the copy; I have sundry other articles to include in it now, beside the second batch which you had some months ago.

The book would not do for any series, especially Blackwoods. It will flutter the dovecotes & make some people very angry, & Blackwoods don't want that.

Yours sincerely, E. A. Bennett

Thanks for the *Lloyds*. You might waken *Cornhill* up.

BERG / MS. / 106
(*To George Sturt*)

Trinity Hall Farm
23rd Apl 1901

My dear George,

I survived that party, which may in truth be *called* a party, in first class style. I caught the 9 a.m. from King's Cross next morning, with our Frank & his Florence, & was presently in the most gorgeous summer weather—which still continues. Whenever I am away for even a few days, the estate seems to get out of hand, & it takes me best part of a day to resume proper control. I could easily spend all my time in seeing after this place. As things stand, I only exist over it vaguely like a god in a cloud. I only accomplish the outlines of management. You will perceive this when you come. And when *can* you come? I should like you to come soon. There are several jaws that I want to have with you, & which won't keep much longer. I think you may name your own date, & I will make it fit. See? Let me hear soon. Your surmise as to this landscape is perfectly correct. It is a big simple landscape, with noble hills; pretty only in the villages. The road is a great & fine feature of it. This road is truly a thoroughfare, a river of *life*. From this study window I can see 8 miles to the West, & about 6 to the east. I can see the steam of North Western expresses 6 miles away on the right & the steam of Midland expresses 4 miles away on the left. I shall never have a study more ideally placed than this—not even by the sea. In my opinion the landscape here is superior to the generality of Surrey; there is more behind it; it is something like Sharpe. How great that man was on Saturday night! He was never greater than in his speech. His speech, the trio, & the Sonata dwarfed everything else, though I must say that Hazell's song-cycle was a perfect masterpiece in its way. *He* at any rate has no superior in England in his line. And yet he's fiddling about as an insurance clerk. Why? A simple soul, when it comes to the point. To see those chaps—Alcock, Hazell, Homan & some others, I'm damned if I can help feeling infinitely superior. They seem to be satisfied with so little, & to make so much of so little. I believe I am getting up a bit of a prejudice against Alcock. He was up here some months ago, & constituted me his father confessor till 3 am.; detailed the history of a thousand errors, weaknesses, fatuities, resulting in a complete life-mess from which he then saw no means of extrication. And yet all the time in his voice there was an accent of patronage towards *me*. It was tragic. The tranquil impudence with which, while speaking enthusiastically of *The Chancellor*, he will offer the most footling sterile criticisms of it, with a 'Look here, old man, you ought to know better than to. . . .' It leaves me speechless, his inability to perceive that he is making a damned fool of himself in my eyes. Enough. This is a digression. All the same, the spectacle of Alcock's gradual declension, which I now see with fatal clearness, is rather on my mind.

I think my novel is now fairly smooth. Half of it is irrevocably complete. I began yesterday afternoon & did 1,000 words, & this morning I wrote without a break from 9 am to 1 pm— 2,500 words. I hope to finish in six weeks. I can always work better in hot weather, & best in the hottest weather. I can *not* work in East winds. I am constantly disgusted that I can't work like Balzac, who literally wore out four chairs, & died exhausted at 52, despite a superb constitution. That is how I want to work —to pour it out in vast quantities, pell-mell, vast, immense, various. But I can't, for the ridiculous reason that I get tired. Although I am 33 & I have not made a name, I infallibly know that I *shall* make a name, & that soon. But I should like to be a legend. I think I have settled in my own mind that my work will never be better than third rate, judged by the high standards, but I shall be cunning enough to make it impose on my contemporaries. And that is something. My plays will make a market for my novels; this is a very neat arrangement.

I look to two men in our set to do something intrinsically better than me: Arthur Hooley & Alexander Webster. In these two I have faith. They have ambition. That is what so few have. Our friends are too content, George, too soon satisfied. Look at—No. I will mention no more names. It is 10 p.m. I retire to bed, to write 2,000 more words tomorrow. I hope you will like that novel. *Art & Empire* is one of the very best conceivable titles. It is a great title, & should sell any book. You have more than once promised me that MS, but I have not yet seen it. I shouldn't be at all surprised if Grant Richards took it. He has taken my book of literary criticism, & is an enterprising person of sorts. Wake him up soon, if he doesn't decide. He is the devil's own procrastinator.

George, if you don't write another novel—not only begin it but finish it, there will be carnage.

Yours, E. A. B.

Kind regards to yours.
I say, I was rather pleased with Mrs. Jim. B.

My journal is stuck up. I rejoice that yours isn't.

106. Frank Bennett had married Florence Rachel Wooldridge. Edgar Homan is known only from a verse in one of Stanley Hazell's songs:

> Then Edgar Homan, cheerful lad,
> Will keep us all from feeling sad
> By playing something blithe and glad
> Upon his famous Kiddem Strad,
> With which he once was badly had,
>   Though not by Sharpe of Putney.

BUTLER / MS. / 107
(*From George Sturt*)

Lower Bourne
9 May 1901

My dear Arnold,

Perhaps I can write to you tonight. It will be a species of idling. This morn I deserted a new novel (which is already getting dull, and not 5,000 written) in favour of a short farce. I had to go to Farnham when I had done about a third of that: and now this evening the thing looks pretty rotten and seems stuck in the plot. Nor have I the grit to drive it through. Sort of a chill on me, with symptoms of bronchitis etc: and my pipe tastes—as if it might be old stable manure that I'm a-smoking of. I want to idle.

But a good many times I have been grinning over the damnable arrogance which you own in your last letter. Grinning at *it*; not you. I know you mean it; yet all the time I can see in it only an attitude—a pose. You mustn't think that I want to convert you. The spectacle is too engaging. But I am tempted to 'review' you—dispassionately: and even to analyse, and discriminate.

For an instance: that you shd feel 'superior' to the chaps you mention seems to me not a logical position. You are simply different. You harbour an ambition that they don't share. It is intensely true: and you owe something to your difference. Your ambition drives you. . . . It causes you to get work (of a certain quality) *done*. It will make you successful, in the struggle for existence.

And in this, I rank it (your ambition) almost as high as— say—the Jewish Religion and other such preposterous obsessions. As the Hebrew Race owes much of its persistence to its extraordinary and logically worthless creed, so you. In this respect (as denizens of this earth's surface) they are superior to—well, say to me and others.

The others, meanwhile, have a sort of fatal pride. No kind of objection to 'Making a Name'; but no kind of slavery to it. The ideal seems too cheap for their high-nosed souls.

About the time your letter reached me, my attention began

Art and Empire was the title of Sturt's collection of essays. Richards was looking at it, but did not take it.

to be drawn (languidly) to Mr. J. Pierpont Morgan of the American State Trust. He also was 'making a name'; and possibly 'a legend'. And the *Daily Mail* was busily engaged, in trying to raise a scare about his success.

It occurred to me, though, as something very singular that the scare hasn't really come off. Singular, that a people like the English (or the Americans) didn't simply arise and wipe off Mr. Pierpont Morgan and his crew of millionaires—always supposing that they (with their names) mattered a tuppenny damn to anybody save themselves. The conclusion reached was, that other people were like myself—took no real interest in them. They are singular; abnormal; a species that we do not care about. More—we wouldn't have their money, at the price. Poor Morgan: what a nuisance, to have to come over here and float all this big thing. Daresay he likes it. *I* wouldn't do it, though. And again—poor Balzac; and poor E.A.B.!

But you can afford to forgive my smile.

Being hard up for reading, I have lately browsed about in a volume of 'Christmas Stories' by Charles Dickens. And look here, Mister Bennett; you may say what you like but C.D. is a *very great man indeed*. I don't know *anybody* who can get it on to the paper all alive, like he does very often. He out-Kiplings Kipling. He is what Fielding would have been with Kipling's gifts. And a good deal more too than Fielding—if in some respects a good deal less. He's less of the philosophic man-of-the world: and too much of (or at least quite enough of) the sentimental radical-reformer. But . . . .

Supper!

Friday morning. To resume about Dickens (for my so-called bronchitis makes me quite a skulker this morning)—there's never the least possibility of mistaking one of his thousands of characters for some other of them. And his interest in things—damned vulgar plebeian radical-reformer interest—is as catholic as Walt Whitman's. Only, where W.W. catalogues, C.D. does sketches. Imagine Whitman, written by Jacobs, with occasional help from Stevenson and even Kenneth Grahame—for I have found distinct passages of him in this volume—and you get at the sort of chap this is. In all my life, I know that I shall never write anything worth any average 10 pages by Dickens. And if your systems of criticism haven't got room for him, then you had better throw down those systems and build bigger.

I am beginning to despair of getting to Hockliffe yet awhile. Why will not those several jaws keep?

With me it's like this: In about 5 or say 6 weeks from now, I begin to give practically *all* my time to shop at Farnham, until annual stock-taking etc etc is through. Which will be about end of July.

During intervening 5 or 6 weeks, I shd like to get something done to a novel. Also, one or two people will be coming here for various weekends. I can't write unless I have heaps of leisure (perhaps not then, for I am feeling perilously near to being a failure); and real leisure has been a scarcity *for this two years*.

I suddenly grow weary of trying to write this letter. Sorry.

Yours, G. S.

KANSAS / MS. / 108
(*To Thomas Lloyd Humberstone*)

Trinity Hall Farm
14th May 1901

My dear Humberstone,

I should have answered your letter before, but I am so preoccupied with the serious, melancholy, & fine novel of Staffordshire life which I am just finishing, that I have been letting all my correspondence slide. (I find that living in the country increases one's correspondence enormously.) I am now on the last 3 chapters, which will 'write themselves', & D.V. the damn thing will be done by Sunday. So I feel fairly free. This enclosed article is the third of yours that I have read. The first (about modelling) was about the most *im*personal thing I ever came across. The second (Spiders) was much better. And this third surprises me by its force & vitality. I don't follow all your reasoning, & I don't think that you could

107. In the *Daily Mail* on 26 April 1901 there was a report of the billion dollar steel trust of J. P. Morgan (1837–1913), who was developing a process of extracting iron from low-grade ore. On 1 May an editorial on 'The Billion Dollar Trust' expressed alarm that, because of protective tariffs, American trusts that had snuffed out competition at home could invade the English free trade market and squeeze out their English competitors by dishonest underselling.

explain, now, what you meant by every paragraph; but I attach little importance to this criticism. The article is more a lyric protest than anything else. Save for one or two trifling solecisms, it is very well written indeed. In fact I have been much pleased by the personality which it reveals. If you can usually write like that on special subjects, you will soon sell your stuff. I now see that you have a marked literary gift. I inform you of this *ex cathedra*. You doubtless knew it, but the opinion of one of the first experts in the country in the art of detecting the literary gift, will not perhaps positively annoy you.

It is very improbable that you will be able to keep yourself in London during August & September. The idea of getting a journalistic situation for those two months is one of those comic opera-bouffe ideas that only occur to men of large ideas. You may be able to write a few articles & sell them, but that will be all. I know nothing whatever of education, except that I have never found time to educate myself, & therefore I cannot advise you as to the next three years. If I knew what was your *ultimate* aim, I could discuss things. I should be very glad if you could come over here for a bit—at any time—so that we [could] talk about things in general, away from the influence of those two men so inimical to force and concentration-of-effort (the two ideas which chiefly dominate me) W. W. Kennerley & Charles Young. When do you think you could come? Either now, soon, or in August–September. We have heaps of room. This place is not heaven, but it is an appreciable step towards that country mansion which I am going to build (before I am forty) by the sea's margin. At the present moment, the estate is at its best, I think. What with horses, dogs, & a fine orchard duly supplied with hammocks, & an uninterrupted prospect East South & West disclosing many miles of the magnificence of England, & lastly a field or meadow for 'Isthmian' exercises, I could be happy here, were there such a thing as happiness. Which there isn't. My father was glad to hear of your interest in him. He is not better, but worse. Nor is there the slightest hope for him. He is in every way feebler. My father has been rather an extraordinary man. His father was a working potter, & he too went into the potting industry. For some time he was a pawnbroker. Then, at the age of 30, with four or five young infants, he set to work to matriculate (think of it!), did matriculate, & became a solicitor at 35. He lifted himself right above all his relatives (though his elder brother, an artist, was a much cleverer man & made a pot of money in the States); he collected a library of 2,000 books; the best thing he ever did was to make me work at nights as well as in the day-time. It is peculiarly melancholy to see a man like this (full of force, once, though antagonistic to all forms of art) reduced to a mere Observer-of-Force by an obscure nervous disease which the doctors can scarcely even give a name to.

Yours, E. A. Bennett

ILLINOIS / MS. / 109
(*To H. G. Wells*)

Trinity Hall Farm
3rd June 1901

My dear Wells,

You & Mrs. Wells have my best wishes for the future. I am sorry to hear of Gissing's illness. I was in town last week, & could have arranged to review his two books then, but never thought of it. Hind gives me everything I ask for provided early birds like Lucas haven't stepped in beforehand & skimmed the cream off the week's milk. Living out here, I am somewhat at a disadvantage in that respect. But I am sending to Hind to tell him Gissing is on my mind. There is a rhapsodic essay on him (Gissing—not Hind) in my new book. Truly I don't think that Hind's personal relations with you have affected criticism. When he choked me off you, he had recently done or caused to be done a screed on you 'as prophet', & I remember thinking at the time he was editorially right in declining an 'enquiry' into you at that moment. To err is human & Hind takes full advantage of his humanity—even to allowing himself to be imposed upon by that literary fraud,

---

108. Compare Bennett's account of his father with the description he wrote twenty-eight years later, quoted on pages 130–1 n. His father's actual age on admission as a solicitor was thirty-three; the date was November 1876. The elder brother was John Bennett (b. 1841), a pottery painter, who was first taken up by Sir Henry Doulton.

Charles Marriott, author of *The Column,*—but I have found him singularly & rather finely careless of anything except (what he considers) literary justice. Such is my testimony.

I perceive you couldn't keep your new house out of the *Fortnightly*! This third article is the best yet. I have never seen so good an illustration of the scientific use of imagination.

Touching Gissing, do you think he will ever get a real 'shout'? I think not. What matter? The consciousness of the man who has written *Demos* must be a fairly satisfactory possession. Show him the enclosed if you care to. Or rip it up; it is a spare proof. I don't know whether vanity or a desire to give him a small satisfaction makes me send it.

My kindest regards to your wife,

Yours, E. A. B.

BERG / MS. / 110
(*To George Sturt*)

Trinity Hall Farm
1 July 1901

My dear George,

Yours of the 9th May remains to be answered. As to arrogance, ambition, & so forth, I can see your point of view, & it is of course a legitimate one. There are two temperaments, the 'pushful' (like Joe's) & the other one. But the thing about the chaps I mentioned is that their ideals, unless they express themselves badly, are much the same as mine, only they won't work up to them steadily; they show no continuity, & in the intervals of their laziness, they try to exonerate themselves to themselves by girding loftily at me. This is what strikes me as comic. They want to get something for nothing, & they won't.

About my work, I only do un-serious work in sufficient quantities to enable me to do serious work, & the proportion

109. The Wellses were awaiting the birth of their first son, George Philip.

Bennett concludes his essay on Gissing with these words: 'those who can bear to reflect upon the large issues of life will be grateful that an artist of Mr. Gissing's calibre has used his art so finely for the inculcation of fortitude and serenity'.

E. V. Lucas (1868–1928), later head of Methuens, was on the staff of the *Academy* at this time. Charles Marriott (b. 1869) published his novel *The Column* in 1901.

Wells was the subject of an article in the *Academy* on 23 June 1900. He published Part III of *Anticipations* in the *Fortnightly* on 1 June 1901.

M

of my un-serious work is decreasing every year. This is enough about me. I wanted to get a particular mood off my chest to someone & I have got it off.

I have not even yet made up my mind about Dickens, & I am glad that so far I have never expressed an opinion about him, except playfully, in print. I got fairly stuck in *David Copperfield* & the same in *Pickwick*. I am forced to admit that I am out of sympathy with those big Victorians. I believe it is their absolute lack of feeling for verbal beauty that puts me off. Understand, please, that my views of Dickens are still fluid—not dogmatic. Lately I have been reading Wordsworth with joy, for almost the first time. *Michael* quite overcame me by its perfect simplicity & power. I have read it about ten times lately. I expect you know it, but if not, read it. It is one of the great English poems. I really read very little for my own pleasure, having no time. But I am getting more time now. I have got level with my work, & shall try not to be engulfed again in an ocean of labours. 1,500 words a day in future, & no more. I am finishing a serial now, & after that I shall do nothing but two plays this year, beyond my weekly articles. This will mean five hours a day; the rest for meditation & prayer. I think I am quite fixed now to a country life; but I can't make a hobby of the damn country. I can't follow a plan to increase my love of natural history. I can only walk around & enjoy it ignorantly. The thing that pleases me most here is the view of the Chiltern Hills, which is truly magnificent. My gardener does what he likes with the estate. To eat our own vegetables & fruit is the limit of my connection with the garden; certainly the said vegetables etc. are the best I ever ate. I never have any 'ideas' about the country. People said I should soon begin to be 'drawn' towards it. But I am not. Yet as I say, I wouldn't go back to London for thousands per annum. Is this right, or merely curious & bizarre? I shall never live in town again: that I know. Another point: my chronic indigestion is not better, but slightly worse,—another prophecy falsified.

Could you come up latter end of August? I am trying to get Jim & wife up about then. Could you join them. My love to Frank & his wife. (Now there is a man perfectly & admirably logical in his passivity.)

And look here, George, am I or am I not going to read *Art & Empire*. The way you ignore my requests for that is too damned casual.

Yours, E. A. B.

ILLINOIS / MS. / III
(*To H. G. Wells*)

Trinity Hall Farm
16th Oct 1901

My dear Wells,

I sent you my 'bright' and amusing book as a return—feeble, but the best I could do—for the copy of *Love and Mr. Lewisham* which you caused to be sent to me. I hesitated seven days & seven nights before sending it. I kept saying to myself: 'Now will the incurable & amazing modesty of this great man prevent him from guessing the true reason why I have left him out of this my book?' (which however does not pretend to be a 'review of the state of contemporary fiction'). I at last resolved to send it & hope for the best. Alas! The worst has happened. You will have to see a doctor about that modesty of yours. Can you not perceive that I left you out

a. Because I felt incompetent to assess you.
b. Because nothing less than a whole book could contain you.
c. Because your popularity needs no explaining, being the obvious reward of merit.
d. Because it was my ambition, after 25 years of study, meditation & prayer, to attempt an elaborate monograph on you, & let this be the climax of my career.

?

You *did* perceive these reasons, revered friend. But again your modesty, by a curious intensification of itself, refused to let you admit them.

110. Joe is unidentified.

Bennett's serial was *Teresa of Watling Street*, serial publication of which is unknown. Chatto and Windus published it in book form in 1904. The only known play that may have been written during the year was *Her Grace's Secret*, an adaptation of Violet Tweedale's novel, written with an unknown collaborator.

Art and Empire was not published until 1910, by Constable, under the title *The Ascending Effort*. Bennett said of it in a review in the *New Age*: 'I am incompetent to review the book. . . . All I will guarantee is that episodically it is very remarkable, and that it is admirably written.'

Your views about my views of Gissing, Moore, & Turgenev leave me cold, having regard to your own article on Gissing in the *Fortnightly*, and to the fact, universally recognised by press & public, that on Moore & Turgenev I am the first & only authority in this country. Nobody else knows anything about these two writers except me, & when I ope my lips I expect a hushed nation to listen and acclaim. Still, in the future, I shall probably surpass even myself on these writers.

'So on my heels a fresh perfection treads,' as Keats said, evidently with me in mind.

I note lately the evidence of an extraordinary activity on your part. Perhaps you have observed how difficult it is to pick up a decent magazine without You in it. I took in the *Fortnightly* and the *Strand* in order to run even with you. And now damned if you haven't let me in for *Pearson's*! And I hear rumour of a 'Dream of Armageddon' in something else. You make your readers work. What I hunger for is the successor to *L. and Mr. L.* I will make a meal off that, I promise you. I will rend it to pieces (and remember that I am not precisely Lieut. Col. Eustace Balfour), for sternness is the highest compliment one can pay to that work which its author regards most seriously. (Dr. Johnson.)

My kindest regards to your wife, and I trust you all flourish.

Yours in all art and culture, E. A. Bennett

111. Wells wrote to Bennett on receipt of *Fame and Fiction*: 'I take your book . . . as a landscape in which I ought to figure, and I *don't* figure! It is written altogether without reference to me. And so far as that goes it seems to me rather unintelligent and commonplace. I am an absolutely unique figure in contemporary literature.' Wells's article on Gissing appeared in the *Contemporary Review* (not the *Fortnightly*) in August 1897. It was entirely laudatory, but was concerned with Gissing's developing use of a social canvas as the structural base of his novel, not with Gissing's moral posture.

Serial publication of 'A Dream of Armageddon' is not known. It appears in the collection *Twelve Stories and a Dream* (1903).

Lieut.-Col. Eustace Balfour (d. 1911) was one of the authors of a government pamphlet, *Cyclist Drill*, which Wells attacked in the *Fortnightly* in December 1900. Balfour replied in the issue of February 1901.

FALES, NYU / MS. / 112
(*To Thomas Lloyd Humberstone*)

Trinity Hall Farm
18 Oct 1901

My dear Humberstone,

It always takes me about a month to answer a friendly letter. Any letter relating to business, anything that means money to me, I can answer with amazing promptitude. But mere friendship is naught to me. You now see me in my true colours.

I am profoundly glad to hear that you won your case. You are a pugnacious & pertinacious devil, which qualities will carry you far, especially if you can always contrive to be as much in the right as you were in that case.

I think the article on Sir John Gorst is able & shows a sufficient grasp of the subject; the tone of it also seems to me to be right. But like the famous article on Almighty God, it 'lacks actuality'. If these things are not sold in the very instant of the crisis that calls them forth, it is U.P. with them. The one thing you can do is to keep it by you till Sir John Gorst once again gets himself into the public eye.

As it stands, I think little of the chances of 'Coventry'. I never see the *Speaker*, which you say publishes similar articles, but I know that such articles are highly scarce in the periodicals. With pictures, it would or should suit the *Queen*, which does definitely go in for that sort of thing; also the *Ill. Sporting & Dramatic News*. But its chances are slender. People don't want to know about their own country. If Coventry was in Italy, it would be different. As the article is not finished it would not be proper for me to criticise it finally. As it stands it lacks distinction, for a good paper, & is much too good for a bad paper. I think you exaggerate the uniqueness of Coventry. Also the contrasts between the old & the new in Coventry are too 'facile', too prettily sentimental. You can see them in a hundred towns. The writing is good enough, except that your conventional & slightly sentimental attitude towards the town has led you into conventional & sentimental stock-phrases. Such locutions as

'veritable poem in stone'
'old world courtesy'
'flood of sound' &c. &c.

ought to damn it in the eyes of the editor of any high class weekly (*you asked me not to spare the rod*). 'As to how' is a form that I violently object to. You can't make a preposition or prepositional phrase govern a sentence.

Did you see any of Arthur Symons' articles on various cities? They have appeared in *Fortnightly* & other places, & are to be issued in a book called *Cities*. These seem to me to be the model of what such articles should be.

I don't know anything about *Academy* prizes. But this article wouldn't win one, as it stands. The reviews of my book have been amazingly appreciative. Glad you are happy. Damned if I *ever* was.

Yours, E. A. B.

ILLINOIS / MS. / 113
(*To H. G. Wells*)

Trinity Hall Farm
23 Nov 1901

My dear Wells,
    Neither of your books has come my way, reviewing. For one thing Hind always keeps these plums for himself, & my ladies'

paper is not interested in publicism. I have read in

Strand, & hasten to insult & annoy you by stating that the last two instalments are among the very best things you have done. I have read *Anticipations* in *Fortnightly*, & hasten to say that I have been absolutely overwhelmed by the breadth & the sheer intellectual vigour of them, not to mention the imaginative power. These articles really have made me a little afraid of you. Either you have in a supreme degree the journalistic trick of seeming omniscience, or you are one of the most remarkable men alive. And I say this plainly, without any undercurrent of fun. The only fault that I have found with these articles is

112. Sir John Gorst (b. 1835) was Vice-President of the Committee of the Council on Education, 1895–1902. Earlier in 1901 he was involved in a controversy over the use of public funds for school dances. Arthur Symons (1865–1945), poet and advocate of the French Symbolists, published his book of *Cities* in 1903. And Humberstone, after due thought, published a pamphlet on *Coventry of the Future* in 1947.

that *occasionally* there appeared to be a certain turgidity, or confusedness, which struck one as though it might have been avoided either by greater length of explanation, or by severe re-writing. It was as though you had tumbled some of the stuff out of a flowing bowl, like Dumas. I gather from a review that the conclusion of the book has not been printed in the *Fortnightly*—& this the most interesting part of the book. For this reason I should like the book. I had meant to buy it (sinning against my principle of never buying new books), but if I can get it for nothing I can put the price into the missionary box.

With my London-Matric knowledge of German I have struggled through the appreciation of you in *Die Zeit*. I see the writer lights on most of the things that I have singled out for you.

Have you read the first Realistic Scotch Novel—*The House with the Green Shutters*? It is not first-class, but it is glorious after Barrie, Maclaren, Crockett & Co. You see Scotland in it for the first time in your life.

Yours, E. A. B.

RICKARD / MS. / 114
(*To John Rickard*)

Trinity Hall Farm
26 Dec 1901

My dear Rickard,

I was very glad indeed to hear from you, & regret that a man who writes letters so perfectly in the classic English epistolary style of Cowper & Edward Fitzgerald does not write to me oftener.

I have nothing valuable or interesting to impart to you at this moment, or perhaps at any other. I am very busy, & have done more work this year than in any previous one. But *cui bono* I don't know. I suppose that I keep pumping it out for the same reason that you maintain an attitude of philosophic, meditative, observant calm. What I envy you for is the

113. *The First Men in the Moon* ran in the *Strand Magazine* from December 1900 to August 1901, and *Anticipations* in the *Fortnightly* from April to December 1901. Wells replied to Bennett: 'I am glad to tell you your modest surmise is correct. . . . I *am* great.' The article on Wells was by Fr. Graz, *Die Zeit* (Wien), No. 364.

The House with the Green Shutters was by George Douglas (G. D. Brown, 1869–1902). Ian Maclaren (John Watson, 1850–1907), Samuel Rutherford Crockett (1860–1914), and J. M. Barrie were his despised predecessors.

quietude & content which evidently pervades your existence. I think I am never happy, & I don't expect to be. I am continually kidding myself that I shall be happy when I have done a certain thing. I do it, & then begin over again to kid myself that I shall be happy when I have done something else. So it runs. I have written one good novel this year, not yet published or announced, which I shall expect my friends to enjoy. The man that doesn't enjoy that novel is no friend of mine. So this is a warning to you not to begin it without an immovable prejudice in its favour. My sole consolation in this world of unrest is that I do naively admire a lot of my own work. Is not that something to be thankful for ?

I ruptured myself partly with riding & partly with [? pumping] immediately afterwards. I am quite comfortable now in a truss. Kennerley is staying here, not very well in health. I hope you are satisfied in your new house as I in mine. My kind regards to your wife.

Yours sincerely, E. A. Bennett

P.S. Best wishes for the N.Y.

FALES, NYU / MS. / 115
(*To W. M. Colles*)

Trinity Hall Farm
5 Feby 1902

Dear Colles,

Thanks for your letters of yesterday, & cheque for £15.2.5. I shall be glad to have a final settlement as soon as conveniently possible.

With regard to plays, I have read the copy correspondence which you send me. It certainly contains no definite arrangement, and you have certainly done nothing for me in regard to *The Chancellor*. I should not, however, like you to think that I had treated you unfairly, and therefore, without prejudice to my legal position, which I need not tell you is unassailable, I am happy to undertake to pay you a commission of $2\frac{1}{2}$ per cent. on my share of the profits of *The Chancellor* accruing due to me up to the 23rd June 1903 when I have received them. (I see I

114. Bennett finished *Anna of the Five Towns* on 17 May 1901.

suggested two years in my letter of 23rd June 1901.) You may stamp this letter as my formal undertaking. I think you will admit that this meets the case fairly.

Yours very truly, E. A. Bennett

BERG / MS. / 116
(*To W. M. Colles*)

Trinity Hall Farm
10 Feby 1902

Dear Colles,

I fear I cannot agree to much in your letter. My letter is certainly stampable and produceable in Court. The 'without prejudice' does not apply to the undertaking in it generally; it only prevents you from accepting that offer & at the same time persisting in a legal claim.

I do not agree that you have done anything for me in the matter of plays, except of course in *Children of the Mist*, which you had from Phillpotts.

I cannot agree to you being my agent at all.

Yours very truly, E. A. Bennett

FALES, NYU / MS. / 117
(*To Thomas Lloyd Humberstone*)

Trinity Hall Farm
15 Feby 1902

My dear Humberstone,

Many thanks for your letter, which I can only acknowledge now. I am so busy with plays and ping-pong that I haven't a moment to spare. Tertia would lick you hollow at ping-pong, or my name is not Jesus Christ. You have a great knack of falling on your feet, & I am glad you are so well fixed up at the renowned 'Bradfield'. You are a frightful swell. I'd like to come over, but really can't. When will you come & see us, & be beaten at chess & ping pong?

Yours, E. A. B.

You will find that directory a hades of a job.

116. Bennett had put most of his affairs in the hands of J. B. Pinker in December 1901. See Vol. I, p. 22 ff.

Kennerley is all right, actually. . . . He is not engaged to be married so far as I know. He comes up here today.   B.

CALIF / MS. / 118
(*To Emily Phillpotts*)   [Trinity Hall Farm]
                                                     5 March 1902

> Why write *my* name 'midst songs & flowers,
>   To meet the eye of lady gay?
> *I* have no voice for Lady's bowers—
>   For page like this no filling lay.
>
> Yet though my heart may never bound
>   At witching call of sprightly joys,
> Mine is the brow that never frowned
>   On laughing lips or sparkling eyes.
>
> Take, then, fair girl, my blessing take!
>   Where'er on Devon's shores you roam;
> Or where, on further hill or lake
>   You brighten a serener home.
>
>   *originally composed by Lord Jeffrey*
>   *but very much improved* by
>   E. A. Bennett

TEXAS / MS. / 119
(*To Edward Garnett*)

                                          Trinity Hall Farm
                                          10th Mch 1902

Dear Mr. Garnett,

Many thanks for your further letter. You shake me. Yet I doubt if I *can* alter that ending. I quite see it is out of the picture, & of course its factual exactness is no excuse for it. But — Thanks also for the Gorki (Duckworths had sent me a copy before). Glancing at the preface I see with satisfaction

117. Bennett was contemplating writing a play with H. G. Wells. Only a scenario survives. Frederick Harrison invited Bennett to adapt an old English comedy for the Haymarket. That too came to nothing.

Humberstone's directory was *The Schoolmaster's Yearbook*, conceived by him, and edited by him for several years.

that you have jibed at Lucas Malet. *I* didn't review that novel
(*Calmady*) in the *Academy.*

I live in hopes of seeing you soon. I have told Lane to send
you *A Man from the North.*

Yours sincerely, E. A. Bennett

BECKER / MS. / 120
(*To Ida Meller*)

Trinity Hall Farm
12 Mch 1902

Dear Miss Meller,

Tillotsons are in want of a fashion writer to do their syndicate
column & arrange for drawings for it, & they asked me to
recommend someone to them. Naturally, I recommended you,
as the most reliable, capable, & business-like lady journalist
that it has been my fortune to meet. You will hear from them
immediately, & they have asked me also to write to you. I
needn't tell you that they are able to pay well, but won't pay
you any more than you force them to pay. I don't think I can
offer you any advice as to the negotiating. If you should see or
correspond with their Mr. Philip Gibbs, let me tell you that
he is an excessively smart & keen young man, but that a firm
tone will manage him all right. This is strictly confidential, &
you had better tear this letter up. I hope you are prospering
& in good health.

Believe me,
Yours very sincerely, E. A. Bennett

119. Edward Garnett read *Anna of the Five Towns* for Duckworths, and recommended that they should publish it. He wrote to Bennett that 'the novel has given great pleasure to my wife & to myself. I hope that its quiet strength will really reach the "public's" consciousness.' His major criticism was that the last chapter, which records Willie Price's suicide, ought to be eliminated as irrelevant and out of focus. Bennett asked for a higher royalty on the novel than Duckworths would pay, and the novel ultimately went to Chatto and Windus.

Garnett edited *Twenty-Six Men and a Girl*, by Maxim Gorki (1868–1936), for Duckworths in 1902. In his Introduction he jibes at 'novels of life de luxe for the Pulman car', novels 'in which the hero's emotions are laid less open to us than is the heroine's lingerie'. Lucas Malet (Mrs. Mary St. Leger Harrison, b. 1852), in her *History of Sir Richard Calmady: A Romance* (1901) was apparently the immediate target.

120. Miss Meller left *Woman* within a year or so of becoming editor. Sir Philip Gibbs (1877–1962) tells in his memoirs of how he took a firm tone with Bennett

AUTHOR HUNTING / 121
(*To Grant Richards*)

[Trinity Hall Farm]
15 April 1902

Dear Mr. Richards,

Many thanks for your letter. The result of *Fame and Fiction* is not absolutely dazzling, but another book ought to go better. It is impossible for me to disguise my admiration of you as an enterprising publisher. You are the one publisher in London that I know of, and I know a few, who has the courage of his convictions.

Yours sincerely, E. A. Bennett

TEXAS / MS. / 122
(*To Thomas Lloyd Humberstone*)

Trinity Hall Farm
4 June 1902

My dear Humberstone,

I rejoice you are going ahead with this thing. If you can tell me what you want me to write about, I shall be happy to do what I can for you. But personally I do not at the moment see how I can be of advantage to a Schoolmaster's Year Book. I think fancy articles are a mistake in a Year Book. You want nothing but serious informative or practically speculative stuff, all of it strictly topical & expert. In the *Literary Year Book* the Editor has made a grave error by introducing miscellaneous articles which are not informative & have nothing to do with the year. See the *Literary Year Book* & make yours as unlike it as possible & you will succeed. I think a 'real conversation' by Archer would be ill-advised. You don't want the diverting magazine-tone. You must be business-like, & have the air of

---

in negotiations over *The Grand Babylon Hotel* two years before, and paid only a pittance for that valuable property. Bennett tells the same story in *The Truth About an Author* (written around the same time as his letter to Miss Meller), and adds that he immediately realized his mistake.

121. Grant Richards (b. 1872) was one of the most enterprising and inefficient of English publishers in the first decades of the century. He was the first publisher of G. K. Chesterton, Alfred Noyes, and John Masefield, and also published Shaw, the Sitwells, Housman, and Joyce. He issued *Fame and Fiction* in September 1901. In his memoirs he expresses regret that he did not respond to Bennett's letter.

permanence. I think Wells would be an excellent man to get, as he is truly both an expert & very enthusiastic on education. I think that, *con amore,* he would write on education for less pounds per thousand than on any other subject. But of course you have got to pay well for his stuff. Even a short article by him would be of service to your venture. If you like, I will write to him & pave the way for you.

Don't make your book too article-y. About the best year book that there is, you know, is *Who's Who.* The *Statesman's Year Book* is a good thing, too. You will notice a complete absence of articles in both these.

Yours busily, E. A. B.

And let me know if I can do anything else for you. Are your week-ends free now?

RICKARD / MS. / 123
(*To John Rickard*)

Trinity Hall Farm
10th July 1902

My dear Rickard,

I seem to feel that I have been owing you a letter for three months. But as aforetime you have owed me letters for much longer than that, I will make no very genuflexionary apology for any tardiness in my own replies. I suppose you are still studying cuckoos. For several days, a month or so since, a cuckoo flew up the main road, every afternoon, in front of our carriage, alighting on every telegraph pole, & then flying off to the next one as we approached. Perhaps this, to me, singular fact may explain some of the mysteries of cuckooishness which make your life a pleasure to you. There is a partridge nest in my paddock, & as fine a Japanese lily in my study as you could wish to see, in my study; & that is about the extent of my news as to the flora & fauna of this district. Except that I have bought a grey mare to ride, & have a Dalmatian dog

---

122. Humberstone took Bennett's advice. William Archer (1856–1924), critic and dramatist, was a particular dislike of Bennett's. *The Literary Year-Book* began publication in 1897 and collapsed in the 1920s.

that speaks the final word of smartness. What is the origin of the superstitious objection to grey horses? Just now I am reading nightly in bed Boswell's *Life of Johnson*. I suppose you know it by heart. Without doubt it is the most agreeable & diverting thing in non-imaginative literature in English. I can never forget the Doctor's remark that since a man who buys & sells a penknife is not necessarily an ironmonger, the man who gets a wench with child is not necessarily a whoremonger. Not that I have either sold a penknife or got a wench with child, so far as I know. Your namesake with the additional S is staying here, & Kennerley enlightens us every week end regular. I trust you & yours are well. Being a philosopher you are always happy.

Yours, E. A. Bennett

ILLINOIS / MS. / 124
(*To H. G. Wells*)

Trinity Hall Farm
20 Sept 1902

My dear H.G.,

Knowing officially from you that for you 'no such thing as excellence exists', I will not conceal my satisfaction at your remarks about *Anna*. I reckon no one in this isle knows more about the *craft* of fiction than you, except possibly me, & I am always struck by the shrewdness of your criticisms of novels from that point of view. But I think your notions about verbal style are fundamentally wrong, & nevertheless it just happens in this instance that what you say about my style is, I think, mainly correct. There *is* a 'certain consciousness of good intentions' that has jolly well got to disappear. Also I am inclined to agree that I am not yet artistically adult (at 35!).

I don't think the book falls off *much* after the death of old Price, & I think the emotional quality of the end is as good as any. As to the under-developed photograph, this is largely a matter of taste. But I trust you understand that the degree of development to which I have brought the photograph, is what I think the proper degree. It is Turgenev's degree, & Flaubert's. It is *not* Balzac's. Anyhow it is the degree that comes natural to me. I note the possibility of your having second thoughts about the book.

I have had no reviews worth mentioning yet.

Theatre

What a pity you sent *The Sea Lady* to Maude! He is utterly without judgment.

All right. I will make the state of the case plain to Harrison myself. I scarcely fancy their enthusiasm will carry them up to £200. But if it does, I am 'on'.

If it doesn't, I am prepared to offer to pay you half of all I make out of *The Crime* up to £1,000, if you care to turn it over to me absolutely. I have, personally, no scruples about taking another man's ideas under the wing of my own name in a case of this kind. But you may object to such an arrangement. The suggestion is merely a suggestion, & you have my leave to ignore it.

Remembrances to Mrs.

Yours, E. A. B.

BUTLER / MS. / 125
(*From George Sturt*)

Lower Bourne
15 Septr. 1902.

My dear Arnold;

Well—I have read *Anna*. And behold it is good, and I strongly approve.

Bear this in mind, for I have some faults to find, and I don't want you to suppose that I think them damning. I only want you to consider . . . etc etc. . . .

My feeling is, that you haven't let yourself go sufficiently. The stuff is absolutely convincing, so far as it goes: only, it has partially failed to reach me, where I expect first-class art to reach. The *people* do not come close enough: I am not intimate with them. They are real—no doubt at all about that—yet only with the reality of people seen across the street, or overheard in a 'bus. You have studied them as though they were animals at the Zoo; and all you say about them is accurate,

124. Wells published his satiric fantasy *The Sea Lady* in August 1902. On *The Crime* see page 166 n.

but you have omitted to show the much more than that, which you obviously know and might have shown, if you had been so minded.

In other words, your people are not quite creations. Instead of writing about them like the God who made them, you write as if you were a recording angel. Consequently your book is a sort of document—a scientific treatise.

I wouldn't say this, if I hadn't an explanation to offer: or several explanations.

First: You refuse to be emotional yourself: you are unimpassioned, will not take sides, and all that—which is quite right. But, you seem unwilling to let the reader be emotional. You refuse to ask him to sympathise: you simply call upon him to observe. You ask him to say, Is this accurate? Is the drawing correct? Not, Are these living people, to like and dislike etc etc?

Consequently, you rob yourself of that help which you have a perfect right to demand from the reader—that sympathy with the subject, which would go out to your art and meet it half-way. You don't get at our imagination, but only at our intellectual judgment.

(If you say that this is the proper aim of Fiction, I reply that in that case Fiction is distinct from all other Fine Arts. For all the other Fine Arts exert the whole of their technique in an appeal not to intellectual judgment, but to *taste* and *feeling*. An appeal to the judgment of the intellect is an appeal to Science, not to Art.)

The second explanation of why *Anna* hasn't quite got at me is perhaps the same as this first, only that it touches more on the technique of the affair. I perceive a resemblance to the French methods—like Flaubert—or the Russian, like Tolstoy. Of course you intended this and, though I don't know much about these chaps, I fancy you have got the hang of the method extremely well. But it leads you (like them in my view) into an elaboration of the wrong things. You make an inventory of the furniture in Anna's kitchen: you even interrupt for that purpose an interview which obviously was of a most crucial nature. But while you give three pages to the inventory, you can spare less than a page to the interview, and when it is over, the reader feels dished, because something must have happened—some interchange of emotion between Mynors and Anna—which you have said nothing about. Were those trivial sentences which they exchanged really all? Or if not, was it worth while to spend so much time in describing the colour of the oak dresser that you had no space left even for the colour of Anna's face or whatever might manifest her feelings at the time?

I'm not complaining of details. They produce an 'atmosphere': but unless they produce the atmosphere required, they are out of place. In this case, the kitchen details produce an atmosphere of hum-drum domestic life, continuous through years—not an atmosphere of excitement and thrill and impending change.

I find this sort of thing all through the book, with the result (as already stated) that my acquaintance with the people is distant—more distant than with their possessions or environment. Towards the end of the revival meeting—a quarter way through the book—I didn't know Anna well enough to judge whether she was going to be converted or not.

Third Explanation. It may be that the tapping of a new and rich vein of material has tempted you to overdo the methods of Flaubert & Co. It seems to me that your plot was seductive, because of the chances it gave for describing things unknown to outsiders. Remember, I like these chapters—the Revival, the Pot-factory, the Guide to the Isle of Man, the Sewing Party, etc etc: they are extremely well done. Yet my feeling after one reading is, that you have too willingly allowed yourself to be dragged from your 'characters' to do these things, knowing how jolly vivid you could make 'em. You rather wanted to show off your 'properties'.

———

But when you do let yourself go, you can do it! In the chapter called 'The Downfall' there is some imaginative writing that I won't try to put an epithet to, but that I admire very greatly. So of course, in little bits, all over the book. Crisp and vivid and strong.

And that doesn't make me any the less eager to see you do, in the same way, the things that one wants: not the tables and chairs, but the men and women.

The Society (apart from its individuals)—the Sect—comes

N

out life-like. I recognise that the fate of a Society may be as enthralling a subject as that of a man or a woman. But then, will you not (using Flaubert's methods if you like) create the atmosphere of the Society by giving the members of it in elaborate detail?

Of course one knows that to you personally a display of sentiment may be a distasteful thing. At any rate if it amounts to *gush*. But, as a realist, you ought to remember that sentiment and passion and even gush are things quite as real as—say the talk at a sewing party, or the morning mist over a harbour.

Still—when all is said—your book is of the true genuine sort of Art. It's worthy of English Fiction, and will stand by the same tests that apply to Jane Austen and Thomas Hardy. For the real stuff is there.

Ever yours, George

I'm getting on, although not very rapidly, with my doings.

BERG / MS. / 126
(*To George Sturt*)

Trinity Hall Farm
4th Oct 1902

My dear George,

I am glad to be able to praise your article in this month's *Cornhill* with less reserve than you praise my novel. It is a fine, sound, & true thing, & the only faults that I find in it are purely superficial trifles—(a) an absurdly undue insistence on the fatuity of the Parish Magazine; not content with once breaking a butterfly on a wheel, you break it a dozen times, & then end by stamping on it. And (b) some solecisms & clumsinesses of style which neither you nor the editor of *Cornhill* ought to have passed. But these things are nothing, & less than nothing, compared with the genuine distinction & force of the stuff.

Your explanations of the partial failure of my novel are all wrong. The partial failure is not in the novel but in yourself. (Of course I can tell you exactly what I think.) If the characters do not seem real to you, not intimate to you, they seem real & intimate to every other person, expert or inexpert, who has taken the trouble to say anything at all to me about the book. Nay, they seem intensely real. I have been amazed at the extraordinary enthusiasm of people about the reality, the conviction, & the appeal of the book.

I have *not* studied the characters 'as though they were animals at the Zoo'; I have studied them as though they were human beings. When you say that I write about them not like 'the God who made them', but like a 'recording angel', I don't know what you mean, & I don't think you know yourself. And when you say the book is a 'scientific treatise', you are using an absolutely meaningless phrase worn out long ago in the futile attacks on naturalistic fiction. You must know that the book is not in the least a scientific treatise.

But what astounds me most is your remark that I refuse to be emotional, that I am unimpassioned. The book is impassioned & emotional from beginning to end. Every character (except perhaps a passing figure like the coroner) is handled with intense sympathy. But you have not perceived the emotion. Your note on the description of Anna's dresser is a clear proof of this. The whole thing, for some reason or other, has gone right past you. You are looking for something which you will never get in my fiction, or in any first-rate modern fiction— the Dickens or Thackeray grossness. I 'let myself go' to the full extent; but this does not mean that I shout and weep all over the place. I might have been seriously perturbed by your opinion on my novel (since I regard you as, potentially, one of the most distinguished writers now living), had I not remembered that you said just the same things about Turgenev when you first read him. It is a singular & surprising thing, but your taste in imaginative work is crude & unreliable. I don't believe you have any genuine critical standard.

Things have fallen out so that I may be able to visit your ancestral abode somewhat earlier than I expected: which I shall look forward to doing.

Remember me to all your people.

Yours, E. A. B.

126. Sturt's essay in the *Cornhill Magazine* was a descriptive piece entitled 'Some Peasant Women'.

BUTLER / MS. / 127
(*To Stanley Hazell*)

Trinity Hall Farm
12 Jan 1903

My dear Stanley,

I have perused your opus with my usual facility and effective-
ness. I know nothing whatever about music, but I know what
I like, & I like your opus. I also know what is good, & your
opus is good. If this information & my thanks are any use to
you, accept them.

I am arranging your work for piano duet, with obligati for
the dinner-gong, Tiger, & Freddy's critical faculty. These are
the three final bars:

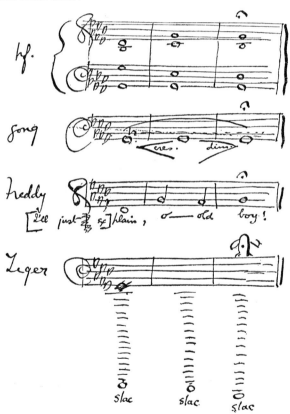

I leave here on Wednesday.
Kindest regards to all yours.

Yours, E. A. B.

STOKE / MS. / 128
(*To Lucie Simpson*)

Hôtel du quai Voltaire
[Paris]
18th June 1903

Dear Miss Simpson,

I was very glad to have your appreciative letter, & it was good of you to take the trouble to write it. I have been well satisfied with the general reception of the book, especially in America, but I dare say that you are aware that in the Potteries itself it has been gravely misunderstood by a lot of people. However, that can't be helped. My next novel which will be published by Chatto & Windus in the autumn, & will be called I think *Leonora* deals with high life in Wolstanton, [&] may therefore interest you. It is quite different from *Anna*, &, I hope, much better. I am just finishing it here, where I have been for the last four months. I return to London on July 1st & shall be there a week or two. Will you not come & have tea at my flat one afternoon (7 Halsey House, Red Lion Square)? I should like to talk to you about your work.

I don't comprehend your general objection to 'provincial novels', seeing that the majority of all the greatest novels in the world are provincial.

Believe me,

Yours sincerely, E. A. Bennett

It may interest you to know that *Anna* (written of course under French influence throughout) is being translated into French.

128. With the death of his father in January 1902 and the return of his mother to Burslem, Bennett decided to give up Trinity Hall Farm. He left it in January 1903 and went to Algeria for a month or more. On his return to London he passed through Paris and decided to make his home there. The Hôtel du quai Voltaire was his place of residence from 15 March 1903 until the following autumn. During the spring and summer he shared E. A. Rickards's flat at 7 Halsey House.

Lucie Simpson (d. 1954) was a literary woman from the Potteries. She met Bennett through Joseph Dawson, his printer friend in Burslem who printed three Christmas gift-books for Bennett in 1906–8 (see page 202 n.). In *Contacts, Literary and Political* (1952) she tells of her visit to Bennett in Red Lion Square: 'The afternoon

CALIF / MS. / 129   7 Halsey House
(*To Emily Phillpotts*)   Red Lion Square,
                                                   W.C.
                                                   8th August 1903

Dear Mrs. Phillpotts,

We have arrived with sorrow in London, & Rickards is asking Fate why he cannot live for ever in Torquay. You have done us both much good. I have seen the famous Town Hall & Law Courts at Cardiff, & really I have been profoundly impressed by them. We made a trip by steamer from Cardiff to Weston, & returned by moonlight & felt very sad and sentimental. It may interest you to know that I met the young Welsh singer aged 20 at Cardiff. She was driving with her sister behind as fine a pair of horses as I have seen for a long time. So we disposed of the sister, & sent Mr. Rickards to his Town Hall, & spent the afternoon together, & had tea in a classy Cardiff teashop. What do you think of this? I thought you ought to know. It appears to me that I have scarcely any secrets from you.

Gilchrist has 'come round', handsomely. He asks permission to dedicate his next book of stories to me. I shall be famous yet, it seems.

Kindest regards to you both.

Till the 28th,

Yours sincerely, E. A. Bennett

---

stands out vividly in memory. We talked, it seemed for hours, about things personal and impersonal, past and present. With the omniscience, not to say arrogance, incidental to youth, we did not hesitate to relegate to perdition this and the other unfortunate author who displeased us, or, to the same measure, exalt and appraise another. Between times I regarded, with not a little envy, the editions of French, Russian and English authors ranged in serried ranks on the low book-shelves round the room.'

On the French translation of *Anna of the Five Towns* see Vol. I, pp. 37–38, 46.

129. E. A. Rickards (see page 91 n.) was the designer of the Town Hall at Cardiff. In *Hugo*, begun in April 1904, Bennett makes use of his trip to Torquay and Cardiff. His hero, a department store owner and manager, decides to build a shop to end all shops. (It will be rather like Harrods.)

'Travelling home by an indirect route, he stopped at a busy English seaport, and saw a great town-hall majestically rising in the midst of a park. The beautiful building did not appeal to him in vain. At the gates of the park he encountered a youth, who was staring at the town-hall with a fixed and fascinated stare.

"A fine structure," Hugo commented to the youth.

"*I* think so," was the reply.

ILLINOIS / MS. / 130
(*To H. G. Wells*)

7 Halsey House
24 Augt 1903

My dear H.G.,

Your letter robbed me of my afternoon's sleep today (I only got it this morning). I think your criticisms are usually tonic & wholesome for me. And you impress me fearfully sometimes —it may be your matter or your manner—I don't know which. I really do think you have a power of finding fault with fiction which I have not seen equalled. And yet I also feel that you are incapable of learning what I *know*, critically, of fiction. Your outlook is too narrow, & you haven't read enough. You still cling to the Dickens–Thackeray standards, & judge by them. As when you say: 'How like Becky Sharp!' Would you say 'How like Eugénie Grandet, or Madame Bovary, or Maisie'? The strongly marked character, the eccentric, the sharply-defined type, is the easiest thing in the world to do (you wouldn't believe how I despise my Meshach Myatt as a creation) in such a manner that the reader can recognise all *his* acts for *his*. But the less typical can not, & ought not, to be done in this way, for the reason that they are not so in life. It is in remarks like that that I think you give yourself away, & impair the 'sanction' of what else you say. Far more important, have you grasped the fact that what I aim at is the expression of general moods, whether of a person or a whole scene, a constant 'synthetising' of emotion, before the elucidation of minor points of character? We should never be able to agree about the death of the husband. I take it you object to it because it is a *sort of coincidence* & because it solves (anyhow apparently) the difficulty of Leonora. I must talk to you some

---

"Can you tell me who is the architect?" asked Hugo.

"I am," said the youth. "And let me beg of you not to make any remark on my juvenile appearance. I am sick of that.". . .

"I want a shop putting up," said Hugo.

The youth showed no interest.

"And when I say a shop", Hugo pursued, "I mean a shop. . . . A *real* shop. Sloane Street. A hundred and eighty thousand superficial feet. Cost a quarter of a million. . . .'"

Murray Gilchrist (1868–1917), the novelist, was a neighbour of the Phillpottses. *Lords and Ladies* (1903) is 'affectionately inscribed' to E. A. Bennett. The Welsh singer is unidentified.

time about coincidences in fiction & in life. The fact that this death solves a difficulty is to me entirely beside the point. It is a part of the inmost scheme of my book. I seem to think that the novelists who would object to it that it was too timely, are too proud to take the genuine material of life as they find it. Or they are afraid to. Because life is simply crammed full of such timelinesses. Personally, I think the stuff after the husband's death the best part of the book.

Quite beyond argument, you are wrong about Rose. She is dead right all through. I know the type as well as you do. Whatever the 'dance' is, it is not fake. I have emphatically *been* there, & the thing is quite genuine, failure or not.

I fancy I shall make you a present of Twemlow, as I don't know whether I believe in him or not myself. When I began the book I didn't, but as I proceeded I gradually believed in him. The plot demanded an Anglo-American, & I simply invented him to meet the case exactly. I confess I have never met him. My brother (who is [a] good judge) said he was not convincing, but my sister (who is a better judge) is quite satisfied with him.

I feel in spite of my judgment that most of what you say is half true, in the annoying manner of half-truths. And I am much obliged to you for your candour (no one else will be so candid). I am conscious now of an intention to make you get down unconditionally on to your knees yet, in a future book. Of course I see you are dealing with the thing at an extremely high level, & that is all right. I do honestly wish, quite apart from this book, that I could fill you with a sense of your artistic limitations. No one, except Turgenev, ever had more technical skill than you have. But your perception of beauty is deficient; at least it isn't sufficiently practised & developed. However, go on & prosper—

'My confidence is unabated,' says Sir T. Lipton today. So is mine. (This is rather fine humour, eh?)

The Truth About an Author may be literature. But it isn't imaginative literature, & so cannot enter into the composition.

I hope this kidney trouble is nothing but what can be got over easily, & due merely to an imprudence. Let me know.

Yours ever, E. A. B.

130. Bennett's novel *Leonora* was formally published in October. Wells com-

ILLINOIS / MS. / 131
(*To H. G. Wells*)

4 rue de Calais
Paris
8 Oct 1903

My dear H. G.,

Many thanks for *Mankind in the Making*. Like *Anticipations* it
is very wonderful, and very uneven. Some of the things in it
are so excellent & so persuasive that they make one promise
one's self to forgive you all your sins, past, present, & to come.
All the criticism of the modern small home (p. 170 & thereabouts) is simply splendid. And I was very much struck
indeed by your suggested 3 'courses' of Higher Education
(p. 329 et seq.) & your general shelving of merely informa-
tional knowledge. Also by your schemes for, and defence of,
authors. Also by the close of the book. Much of the book is
really *human*. At the same time I will not conceal from you
that I often thought of your reference to 'jerry-building' on
p. vi as being decidedly to the point, & that to confess a sin is
not to excuse it. As with *Anticipations* I think the book might
have been much better if you had put more 'back' into it. You
replied, as to *Anticipations*, that if I only knew the amount of
'back' you *had* put into it, I should not etc. etc. Nevertheless,
I still think you might advantageously have martyrised yourself a little more. The sexual chapter was very disappointing
to me. It didn't seem to be thought out to a finish, & it seemed
to say either not nearly enough or too much. If you had other
things to say, not meant for England, I hope you will arrange
to put them in full in the French edition. That chapter was
full of unconvincingness for me. For example the suggestion
that 'adult' matter should, or could, be kept from the young
by means of a high price, struck me as singularly inept. I do
not see how it can stand up against criticism for a single instant.
And it is a crucial point. Also your remarks on literature as
such betray your fundamental inability to grasp what art is,

plained that the actions of the characters lacked inevitability—though John
Stanway's timely suicide, which enables Leonora to marry the Anglo-American
Twemlow, is preceded by an earlier suicide attempt that would have resulted in
the same end. Meshach Myatt is Stanway's uncle, and in his first appearance is
described by Bennett as a 'character'. Rose, one of Stanway's daughters, is an
unattractive, studious, and dull girl. Wells liked *The Truth About an Author*,
published anonymously in July 1902.

really. The literary sense can*not* be quickened in the manner suggested at the bottom of p. 372. If you could only see how you give the show away by such a remark as that about Plato on p. 334! As a mere matter of opinion, my opinion is absolutely the reverse of yours that 'every well-known living writer is or has been writing too much'. Quite the contrary.

And in view of your terrific indictment of the English peoples for mauling the English language, I think the mere writing of a lot of the book falls short of even a respectable average. In *Anticipations* the sentences were over-loaded, and the words badly arranged, & often the meaning had to be disentangled. The same here, only more so. You have just got to face the fact that I was continually, except in the best passages, irritated by the bad technique of the writing. How do you defend this: 'It is one of the most amazing aspects of contemporary life, to converse with some smart . . . woman etc' (p. 164)? There were sundry examples of bad grammar, scores of bad punctuation, hundreds of striking inelegance, & not a few of an obscurity that might easily have been avoided. You may say that these things are nothing, that you can't be bothered with them; in the spirit which asks me whether I can't see the humour of advising the literary aspirant to begin with spelling. But it won't do, my son. And I half believe you jolly well know it. I sit at your feet in many things, but when I ope my mouth on the art & craft of your trade, it behoves you to listen. There is a blind spot in your eye; either that or you are wayward. Now reread p. 1 of this present effusion.

I have got a 'charming little flat' here, & furnished it myself. When next you run over to Switzerland for half a day, you must look in.

Best respex to the Mrs.

Yours, E. A. B.

I hope this letter will get through on 2½d., but I have a sort of horrid doubt it will be overweight.

I am very happy to admit that that phrase 'the artist living angrily in a stuffy little corner of pure technique', is an example of brilliant witty writing & perfectly just criticism. It amused me for hours.

131. Bennett moved into his flat at 4 rue de Calais in September. His advice

STAFFORDSHIRE SENTINEL, 28 December 1903 / 132
(*To the editor*)

> 179 Waterloo Road
> Burslem
> [about 26 December 1903]

Sir,

Many years ago, a circumstantial and picturesque account of a man-and-dog fight in Hanley got itself into the papers, and the Potteries became known as the district where men and beasts fight together for the amusement of a public which had almost ceased to be human. To this day, natives of Hanley on their travels have sometimes to listen to the phrase: 'Hanley—oh yes, the man-and-dog fight!' No man-and-dog fight ever took place in Hanley. The entire account was a fabrication. But that is a detail.

At the present moment, the Potteries is undergoing a similar experience. When I landed at Newhaven a few days ago, the first printed thing that caught my eye was a newspaper placard: 'Vice in the Potteries: Shocking Details.' It was a London newspaper. Soon afterwards I learnt about the 'crusade' of the Honourable and Reverend Leonard Tyrwhitt. Upon this 'crusade' I should like, as a native of the man-and-dog fight district, to make a few remarks.

It is one of the easiest and one of the most dangerous things in the world to kick up the dust of what is called 'morals'. The mere word 'vice' will draw people together from afar as a dead dog will draw carrion crows. When I tried to buy the London newspaper which had placarded our 'vice', do you suppose I could get it? Not a bit. It was sold out. It was sold out all over London. And the fact is that for days past, half England has been feasting upon the panorama of our alleged enormities. I am told that Mr. Tyrwhitt preaches to a crowded congregation. Doubtless. And if the ministers of all the chapels and churches in the Potteries were to announce their intention to preach against 'vice', all the chapels and churches would have to put chairs in their aisles, or otherwise arrange for crammed audiences.

But one may be permitted to fear that the cause of virtue

---

to literary aspirants was in *How to Become an Author*, published by C. Arthur Pearson in September 1903.

will not be served by this amazing noise and chatter. And perhaps also one may be allowed to protest against the ignorant, foolish, and declamatory methods which have led to the noise and chatter, and to the vilification of the Potteries in the eyes of the country. I do not propose to examine Mr. Tyrwhitt's sermons in detail, though he lays himself open to ridicule and reproach in a hundred ways. I will only mention two points, to illustrate his tactics and his habit of mind. He compares the illegitimate birth-rate of the Potteries to that of the whole of England. What possible end can be attained by such a debating society trick? He ought to have known that the only fair comparison was with similar industrial districts where two sexes had to work together under similar conditions. Again, with a fine oratorial flourish, he states that where drink slays its thousands, immorality slays its tens of thousands. Much licence may be allowed to a man in the frenzy of galloping his hobby-horse, but he should contrive not to be absolutely silly.

It would be interesting to know whether any thinking man really believes at the bottom of his heart that human nature is worse in the Potteries than it is elsewhere. For my own part, I regard the theory that the Potteries is ultra-vicious as unworthy of discussion. I have lived in the Potteries, in London, in Paris, and in a pretty English village, and I have found that the most profound of our physical instincts produced much the same results everywhere. (I know that in the pretty English village a virgo intacta aged twenty was looked on as a decided curiosity.) I have found, further, that it produced much the same results in all ranks. It is about the morals of the working classes, I gather, that Mr. Tyrwhitt is so stridently solicitous. He urges the manufacturers to take this, that, and the other measures for the purification of their employees. But surely purification will have to begin where charity begins. What about the manufacturers, and all the other pillars of society? What about the men of means who come back boasting from London and Paris? And what about those who attend chapel or church regularly every Sunday in our town, while carrying on an intrigue, idyllic but highly immoral, in another town? Mr. Tyrwhitt should have begun, if he was to begin, at the summit of the social structure.

The truth is that Mr. Tyrwhitt is one of those well-meaning but ill-informed clumsy persons who blunders from time to time into the heart of the question which the wisdom of ages has failed to solve. Since man existed, 'vice' has existed, and there is no evidence to show that 'vice' is any less now than it was five thousand years ago. Some of the greatest philosophers known to history have thought well to hold their tongues about the question, but the Mr. Tyrwhitts of this world continue to step cheerfully and loudly into it. And, once well into it, they get so excited that the three qualities essentially demanded by the situation suddenly desert them. I mean, strict impartiality, infinite care in the handling of facts, and a thoroughly judicial frame of mind.

Up to now, what good has Mr. Tyrwhitt done? And what good is he likely to do in the future? Two years hence, will the gross quantity of 'vice' in the Potteries have been lessened by reason of his efforts? Every man who has reflected upon the past, and who is capable of looking a fact in the face, knows that it will not be lessened—not unless something very revolutionary occurs to human nature in the meantime. A temporary effect may be produced, but it will be only temporary. And Mr. Tyrwhitt might have achieved this effect much better if, instead of indulging in oratory, he had called a private meeting of manufacturers and other responsible persons and enlisted their private help. Mr. Tyrwhitt would have received less advertisement, but since all this advertisement must be painful to him, that would have been a loss.

On the other hand, Mr. Tyrwhitt has done a great deal of harm. In the first place he has aroused all that is unhealthy and prurient in the imagination of the youth of the Potteries and of England. And in the second place, by means of loose statements, perfervid exclamations, and a magnificent ignorance, he has put the Potteries to shame in the eyes of the country. Any hasty and hysterical individual can give a dog a bad name, but no conceivable amount of ingenuity can succeed in taking that name away again. Thanks to the misguided industry of Mr. Tyrwhitt, we are now ticketed before the world as 'The Immoral Potteries'. It matters not that the accusation is infamously unfair; we may as well resign ourselves to being 'The Immoral Potteries' for the next twenty years or so. And

Mr. Tyrwhitt has lived among us for 'eight and a half years' in order to accomplish this. I consider my words when I say that Mr. Tyrwhitt deserves, and will receive, the severest censure from the united commonsense of the district. People may hint that I ought to have respect for his motives and for his vocation. I have respect for both, but I am not dealing with them. When a man of Mr. Tyrwhitt's vocation uses it as he has done, with a sagacity so meagre and a result so scandalous, neither his motives nor his vocation should suffice to shield him. I say nothing of his imitators.

Yours, &c., Arnold Bennett

STOKE / MS. / 133
(*To Lucie Simpson*)

Hôtel d'Italie
Menton
30 Jan 1904

Dear Miss Simpson,

Many thanks for your letter. 'I am going to be candid.' You are quite wrong about *Leonora*. In every way it is a much better book than *Anna*. What women of forty *ought* to concern themselves with is not the point. What they *do* concern themselves with you will know, in your moments of self-candour, when you reach that interesting age. That women of forty, generally, do

132. 179 Waterloo Road was the address at which Bennett's mother lived during her widowhood.

The Reverend the Honourable Leonard Tyrwhitt (1863–1921), Vicar of Fenton and later Chaplain-in-Ordinary to the King at Windsor, preached two sermons on 'The Devil (and all his works) in the Potteries' on 14 and 20 December 1903. They were reported at length in the *Sentinel*, and evoked considerable response, including a merry sermon from another minister, whose congregation along with the *Sentinel* reporter cheered his every word. Tyrwhitt was not without a sense of humour himself, and the *Sentinel* took notice of his comments on Bennett's letter in a sermon delivered on January 3rd:

'In his humble opinion that letter was by far the lowest in tone and taste—and this was saying a good deal—of all that had yet appeared. . . . He had been making diligent inquiry as to who exactly the gentleman was, and there seemed, apparently, a good deal of doubt because the name in the district was little known. He was assured, for instance, in that end of the district that the gentleman was a commercial traveller, whilst out Burslem way people said he was a writer of fiction. He was still in doubt, though somehow he felt disposed to believe the latter, for as a fiction writer of second-rate type, the gentleman in question seemed eminently well qualified to pose.'

regret the past is an undoubted fact. That they long to be young again is an undoubted fact. That they are particularly, peculiarly, & specially passionate & prone to sexual excitement is an undoubted fact. It was the discovery of these piquant truths which led me to write *Leonora*. I didn't conceive the idea, & then search round for confirmation. The reverse. I don't think 'love' is 'woman's whole existence'. It was not Leonora's whole existence. She was extremely addicted to the higher walks of housewifery. But I think that 'love' is the major part of woman's existence. As it is of man's. I think there are only two things in this world really worth having—sexual love & the love of children. The next thing I expect to hear about you is that you are married. Over & over again, in a career intimately mixed up with many & diverse women, I have found that women with a tendency to 'sit on' love have ended suddenly & swiftly with marriage & become even more 'domesticated' than their sisters. (I had a striking & dramatic instance in Paris only two months ago. As you read this letter you will think that you know a great deal better than me, but there will come a time when you will perceive the limitations of the attitude towards life which abounds in the Writer's Club. How well I know it!) I'm very glad you think the style of *Leonora* more sympathetic than that of *Anna*. And I need not say that it ministers to my pride to have your appreciation.

Yes, I am *The Novelist's Log-Book* in *T.P.'s Weekly*. If you guessed it unaided, you showed the cleverness I should have expected from you.

Don't be angry with this letter. There are various forms of compliments & this letter is one.

I know not when I shall be in London again. I return to Paris at the end of February.

Believe me,

Yours sincerely, E. A. Bennett

133. Bennett spent a month at Menton with Eden Phillpotts. *A Novelist's Log-Book* ran in *T. P.'s Weekly* from 13 November 1903 to 11 May 1904.

ILLINOIS / MS. / 134
(*To H. G. and Jane Wells*)

Hôtel d'Italie
4 February 1904

Dear ones,

Your sweet note to hand. I have been here 20 days, & am writing a play with Phillpotts, which will be finished in a few days. For my views, ideas, & sensations, see *T.P. cum grano*. I do not expect to stay here after the end of next week, as my mother is disconcertingly ill & I am 2 days off London, where she is. I shall return to Paris. I only came to England for a few days at Xmas, & those few days I spent with her in the Five Towns, where I mingled in the great 'Vice' controversy with great pyrotechnic effect. Just before leaving Paris I read the first instalment of *F. of G.* in *Pearson's* & thought it extremely good, barring a few *minime* verbal infelicities. It cost me 2 francs to buy the number, but I couldn't resist it. I am now writing a humorous novel—I don't know why, except that I wanted to, & there was a humorous story of mine in January *Windsor* which the man who says is *not* humorous is a fool & no gentleman. Our play is marketable footle; hence I do not enlarge on it. Walking down Fleet Street the other day I was told you had yet another child. My felicitations. I hope all are doing well. I wish you would come to Paris for a few days. So easy for you. I've got a nice little flat there, right in the middle, & give afternoon teas there with immense effect. I don't know when I shall live in England again. Are you going anywhere in the summer? I had meant to stay here till middle of March but see *ante*. When I have finished this humorous novel, I have four other novels waiting their turn. I have instructed them to form a queue & wait quietly. I take it you are going to revert next to *Love and Mr. L.* vein. I hope so. I had an evening with your Parisian impresario Kozaciewicz, a few weeks ago, & found him decidedly intelligent, & interested sensibly in music too. These Parisian johnnies have a wonderfully just and clear-headed notion of you. You can't bounce them, you know. I suppose you *do* know. I do not think *Romance* is good. In fact it isn't, & I don't care who knows it. Ever read Dostoevsky's *Crime and Punishment*? English translation damnable; but it is a *novel*. I'm just reading it again. I'm very keen on Monte Carlo at present. I've seldom been more interested in anything than I am in M.C. Write & tell me you will come to Paris.

Yours ever, E. A. B.

ILLINOIS / MS. / 135
(*To H. G. Wells*)

4 rue de Calais
25 May 1904

My dear H.G.,

Much touched. My only surprise is you don't find more fault with it. As a matter of fact, I could have done it better, especially towards the end. But, having conceived it as a 'lark', I fell into the error of regarding it technically as a 'lark' also. One writing. No draft. Practically no erasures, & about two months' work at most. But then you always prefer the work which costs me the least trouble. Now *Leonora*,—but what is the use of talking about colours to the blind? And that reminds me that your last *Strand* story was really admirable. A little faint towards the end I thought, but fundamentally *damn good*. Strangely enough, though I never met anyone who perceived the satiric quality in *The First Men in the Moon*, I have met several who have spontaneously explained to me that the *Strand* story is a 'fine criticism of life'. After this handsome praise, if you should come across a story of mine in the May *Windsor* the least you can do is think it very good.

I must see you in the summer.

Yours ever, E. A. B.

134. Bennett misdated this letter January. He and Phillpotts left Paris on 14 January, and wrote *Christina* (*A Credit to Human Nature*) at Menton. The play was never produced.

Wells's *The Food of the Gods* ran in *Pearson's Magazine* from December 1903 to June 1904. Bennett's humorous novel was *A Great Man*, whose hero breaks the bank at Monte Carlo. His humorous story, 'His Worship the Goosedriver', appears in *Tales of the Five Towns*.

B. Kozaciewicz was translator, with Henry Davray, of *Anticipations* into French.

Romance, the novel by Joseph Conrad and Ford Madox (Hueffer) Ford, found more favour with Wells than with Bennett.

135. *A Great Man* was begun about 10 December 1903 and finished 13 March 1904, with an interruption of about five weeks. The *Windsor* story was 'Nocturne at the Majestic', reprinted later in *Tales of the Five Towns*. Wells's *Strand* story was 'The Country of the Blind', which appeared in April 1904.

o

BERG / MS. / 136
(*To George Sturt*)

4 rue de Calais
22 June 1904

My dear George,

The handwriting on your envelope gave me quite a start. 'Surely', I said, 'It cannot be that—' For you must know that I have often meant to write to you, & often postponed writing, saying to myself: 'Damn it, he's 4 years older than me, & he ought to set me a good example.' Well, you have done so. Needless to say I derive deep satisfaction from your remarks, some of which scratch my back enormously. It makes me uncomfortable, however, to reflect that I succeeded so well with a book which was a 'frolic' in every sense. On referring to my journal I see it took me exactly nine weeks to do. (By the way, how's your journal? I am just commencing Vol V.) I have not yet seen the faults of *Leonora*, at least not the faults which some people say are obvious. In my opinion it is easily my best book. My next book on the same lines is going [to] be bawdy, George. I am not a bawdy writer, God knows, but I have had a bawdy subject on my mind for some three years, & I am gradually perceiving that it will be rather fine. Just at the moment I am finishing a book on the lines of the *Grand Babylon Hotel*, from which I hope much lucre. I do *nothing* but fiction now, & have arrived at the stage when I can make £20 a week at it, minimum. Five years ago I would have looked on this as the ne plus ultra of paradisiacal bliss, but I am no more content than ever I was. In fact, life is a devilish odd thing. I think I have learnt more about it during the last 3 years than ever I knew before. I have books planned that will keep me employed till the end of 1906. But if I am any happier than when I used to cycle down to Farnham & Witley after a week of rottenness in Fleet Street, I do not know it. My belief is that some people are born happy & others aren't. I like Paris tremendously. Indeed I can't imagine myself living in any other city. It has spoilt me for London. What I secretly desire is a fine house in the seaside country near Folkestone for the summers, and this flat (which suits me excellently) for the rest of the year. And these things I must & will have. I shall revisit my Albion towards the end of next month. But shall I see you? I have read one or two articles of yours which filled me with joy. But you are quite right in not forcing yourself. I always envy you & always have done. Although you write little, you *can* write. And after all the world is divided into two classes, those who *can* write, and the rest. A man who *can* write, & who at 41 has the effrontery to say that he is 'pretty happy', cannot fairly ask for anything more. I am in a position to state that constant honest artistic production does not produce in the producer any particularly ecstatic sort of bliss. At best it is an anodyne.

It may interest you to know that what *I* consider the best thing in *A Great Man,* is Aunt Annie's request to the cabman after the accident: 'As quick as you can, but do drive slowly.' And I suppose I ought to know. I am issuing a volume of stories in the Autumn.

How is Frank? You will write to me again.

My kindest regards to all yours.

Yours, E. A. B.

CALIF / MS. / 137   *The* Hotel
(*To Edith Evors*)   Ardentinny
                                                         Loch Long,
                                                         Scotland.
                                                         18 Augt 1904.

Dear friend,

I have just got your letter. You ask for advice which cannot possibly be given. You already know all that I can tell you about journalism & how to get into it. Except by seeing editors & demanding situations at the pistol's point I know of no method of getting the said situations. As a matter of fact I thought you had left *H & H.* long ago. I certainly understood from some one, quite a year ago, that you meant to leave. I wish I could help you by pointing out to some 'royal road' for your feet, but I cannot. All the women I know seem to have joined the N. Lyceum Club, & they are all so proud of it

136. The bawdy book was presumably *Sacred and Profane Love*, which Bennett began in November 1904. The current novel was *Hugo.*

Sturt's most recent essay was perhaps 'Rival Techniques', which appeared in the *Cornhill Magazine* in September 1903.

that they are all asking me to lunch there. I don't know yet whether I can accept your invitation, but if I can I naturally shall take advantage of this kind suggestion. (Note: I have accepted no previous invitations.) I shall spend very little time in London this summer. It is a specially busy summer with me: this shall not occur again. I spent exactly 1 hour there on my way here, & that hour was in a cab. I am working up here in the midst of much rain, & the most superb scenery. I shall go to Staffordshire on the 31st & come to London about the 15th Sept & leave London for Paris about the 22nd Sept. I have now had a flat in Paris nearly a year. It is diminutive but it is exquisite, far surpassing our new London flat (No. 1 Vernon Place, Bloomsbury Sq.) in this latter quality. I trust you are well & calm.

Yours sincerely, E. A. Bennett

ILLINOIS / MS. / 138
(*To H. G. Wells*)

4 rue de Calais
27 Sept 1904

My dear H.G.,

I am disposed to agree with your own estimate of *Scepticism of the Instrument*. I don't, however, think that your third indictment of the instrument is quite new. At any rate it is one which I have often formulated (clumsily) to myself. I wish I was a 'scientific thinker', so that my praise of your brief but startling opusculum might carry more weight. I have had no opportunity till now of writing you, & I only write now because I want information from you. Outside the N.L.C., what Clubs do you belong to? I want to belong to a club (not the N.L.C.) where I can have a bedroom when I want it; I am going to chuck the flat. What do you suggest? Do you belong to the

137. Bennett visited Scotland for a few weeks to obtain treatment for his speech impediment.

Nothing is known of Miss Evors after this date except that in 1913 she edited *The Marie Corelli Calendar*.

Bennett and E. A. Rickards took a new flat together briefly in the same building that housed the offices of Rickards's firm—Lanchester, Stewart, and Rickards—for a few years.

Savile? I rather think Marriott-Watson is a pillar of that.
Kindly put your back into this club-question, as it is now important for me. I write to you because you look on clubs with
a fresh & unbiassed eye.

Respex to Madame.

                              Yours, E. A. B.

P.S. Ignore my next book. It is naught.

CALIF / MS. / 139
(*To Emily Phillpotts*)

                              4 rue de Calais
                              5th Dec 1904

My dear lady,

This is extremely nice of you. Not being a professional author
I cannot express the pleasurability of my anticipations of this
visit. It seems to me that I may be able to reach you by the
30th or 31st, but my movements depend on the caprices of
about 153 blood relatives, & I will write you later. If I can
arrive on the 29th I shall. This news of the closing of Eltham
distresses me. Bungalows are all very well, & I adore them,
but no bungalow is likely to match the most perfectly appointed
house I ever stayed in—& I have stayed in a few. However,
if you are going to wander, I shall see more of you, for you
cannot wander without touching Paris, & the next time you
pass through Paris, if you do not come to see me, I shall take
it as an unfriendly act.

The children, I trust, are well and good? But need I ask?
With what sort of feelings are they looking forward to your
prolonged absences abroad?

I have received the 2nd & 3rd acts of IT, but as I am in
the middle of the most 'dashing' chapter of Eden's book I have

138. 'Scepticism of the Instrument' makes an attack on logical thought. It was
originally a paper Wells read to the Oxford Philosophical Society. He published
it as an appendix to *A Modern Utopia*.

Bennett ultimately became a member of the Reform Club, which was political,
like the National Liberal Club, and also literary, like the Savile. H. B. Marriott
Watson (1863–1921), a prolific minor novelist, did belong to the Savile.

Teresa of Watling Street, the only one of Bennett's sensational novels that seems
to have embarrassed him, was published in October 1904.

refrained from reading his third act, lest I should get out of the key. I shall, however, deal with it almost at once. I am going to my forest of Fontainebleau tomorrow.

    Salutations cordiales et affectueuses, E. A. Bennett

By the way I can now *talk* French, really.

LEEDS / MS. / 140
(*To Edmund Gosse*)

            4 rue de Calais
            27 Feby 1905
My dear Sir,
  By this time you may have heard of the death, from pneumonia, of our mutual friend Marcel Schwob, which took place at noon on Sunday. I write to you, as I have been asked by M. Maurice Schwob, brother of Marcel, to communicate with Marcel's English friends. Madame Moréno Schwob is on tour in the south of France & cannot reach Paris before tomorrow. You may possibly think fit to write something about our dead friend. I know he would have liked a notice from you in the *Athenaeum*, of which he was a faithful reader.
        Believe me,
           Yours very truly, Arnold Bennett

  139. The Phillpottses apparently maintained both Eltham, in Torquay, and Duchy House, Princetown, Dartmoor, for some years after this date. *It* is presumably a working title for the play *An Angel Unawares* that Phillpotts and Bennett were writing together at this time. It was never produced. Eden's book is possibly *The Farm of the Dagger*, published in October 1904.

  140. Edmund Gosse (1849–1928), one of the more distinguished men of letters of the generation preceding Bennett's, had special literary connections with France (see page 213). He described Marcel Schwob (1867–1905), in his notice of him in the *Athenaeum* on 4 March, as 'perhaps the most learned man of his generation'. Only a few months earlier Bennett had dedicated *Tales of the Five Towns* to him, 'my literary Godfather in France'. No correspondence is known to have survived between the two men. Maurice Schwob (b. 1859) was an author, Madame Schwob a well-known actress.

ILLINOIS / MS. / 141
(*To H. G. Wells*)

4 rue de Calais
18 April 1905

My dear H.G.,

Many thanks for the book. If it was a novel I could say something useful about it, but as it isn't, I don't know that I can. The latter half of it is much more convincing & suggestive than the first half, & is also better done, but all of it is better than *Mankind in the Making*. The two things that strike me about the whole thing are the enormous difficulties you have had to face, & the continuous brainwork that there is in it. It is a book that deserves to be called 'gallant'. Of course what interests me most, & what will interest everyone most, is your development of the hierarchy idea. When I read your opening sentences about the Samurai I thought the notion was fanciful & impossible, but I was gradually convinced of its possibility. I see that some people are grumbling at you because such a caste would do a great deal of harm. But that is not the point. The point is whether such a caste will come into existence. It might. I think it would work first good & then harm, like most institutions. But anyhow you have handled it most fearfully well. It sticks in my mind. It is astonishing to me that a man of your imagination, so untrammelled as it is, my poor boy, should be capable of the attitude towards the Hampstead middle class disclosed on p. 56. This is one of your class-prejudices & you can't leave it alone. But you surely must see that what produces the Hampstead middle class will exist in no matter what Utopia. It is a relative matter. Relatively, the Hampstead middle class is a fine achievement of human progress; & relatively it is also the despicable thing you insist on rendering it. Your attitude to it is not that of a philosopher but that of a Chelsea painter who has not 'arrived' & sits drinking at the Six Bells while cursing all Philistines and plutocrats.

You are very good about women. I liked all that. Personally, my ideas are more oriental, but still there are times when I am not oriental. What you say about the ugliness of modern women's dress is absolutely wrong. Indeed your notions about material beauty are shockingly inferior to your other notions.

You would like to laugh me out of being a Cultivated Person, but you never will, & as a Cultivated Person I say that your remarks on architecture, for example, are painful. And yet you *have* a glimmering, sometimes, even about architecture. It is most extraordinary how, immediately you come to the region of moral ideas, your language becomes distinguished. 'The intricate, austere, and courageous imagination of our race' is admirably said. Your analysis of political parties in England fills me with awe. It is A1, & the indictment of Liberalism is excellent—though I *am* a Liberal, like yourself. There is something about the precocity of civilisation on p. 292 that also is worthy of you. But why should the Samurai have any religion? I hope you aren't going to defend that worn out platitude to the effect that religion is a necessity of man's nature. Because it isn't. Religion is done for—any sort of religion. Your notions of a religion for the Samurai startled me.

The botanist is bitterly & well done. You have got him & all his tribe perfectly on p. 232. And I think he serves his purpose very well in the book. I wouldn't like to pronounce offhand as to the success of the mere literary machinery of the book. But I rather fancy at present that you have succeeded in spite of it. I would respectfully point out that in the italicised prologue you have most definitely visualised the voice as a person on a platform at a cinematograph show, while in the italicised epilogue he is 'carried onward' through the streets. Arthur Balfour might dialectically defend this, but it is a little confusing. Sullivan's illustrations are not as good as the others he did for you. They show a notable falling-off—not in conception but in execution.

You understand, my attitude towards this book is very humble. I could only authoritatively find fault with its grammar. It has much impressed me, & some of its things stick brilliantly in my mind. Kindest regards to you both.

Yours, E. A. B.

141. Wells's *A Modern Utopia* was published in April 1905. Bennett was specially interested in architecture, and had once thought of becoming an architect.
Arthur Balfour (1848–1930), philosopher and statesman.
Edmund J. Sullivan (1869–1933), illustrator of many books.

ILLINOIS / MS. / 142
(*To H. G. Wells*)

4 rue de Calais
30 Sept 1905

My dear Wells,

Amid the chorus ('a great book, a great book') which that glittering novel has naturally called forth from most of my friends, your letter, with its thin small handwriting, is like a grandma announcing that I have been having too much sugar in my tea & must be content with half a lump. My dear H.G. you move me to explain myself to you. I have not yet decided whether I am a genius, but I shall probably decide, with that astounding quality of self-criticism that I have, that I am not. I am probably too clever, and, what is more important, too infernally well-balanced. I am ready to agree with you that no such woman as Carlotta ever existed. No character in any novel is more than a hint at the real thing, & it is right it should be so. You can't honestly say that Mr. Lewisham ever existed. You know, we all know, that after all our satisfaction with Mr. Lewisham, he never lived & couldn't have lived. He is an arrangement to suit the necessities of a convention; & here & there he bears a resemblance to a man. I choose Mr. Lewisham because he is one of the least unreal characters I can recall at the moment. All I would claim for Carlotta is that now & then she does what a real woman would do, & that her stiff lay-figure movements are sometimes really not so very stiff. Again, I must agree with you as to the style. But incidentally you must remember that this is not my style, but Carlotta's style, & that it cost me a Hades of a lot of trouble. I am inclined to think however that as regards style the best book I ever wrote was *A Man from the North*. The question of my style must really be looked into. I have never been in love. Sometimes the tears start to my eyes, but they never fall. These things are indubitable. I have no passion for Justice. That also is profoundly true. I recognise that progress is inevitable & that it can only be achieved by a passion for justice. But I reckon I am above a passion for justice. Here we come to 'the difference between our minds'. I look down from a height on the show & contemplate a passion for justice much as I contemplate the other ingredients. Whereas you are simply a passion for justice incarnate. You aren't an artist, except insofar as you disdainfully make use of art for your reforming ends; you are simply a reformer—with the classic qualities of the reformer. Hence your amazing judgments on Balzac, Milton, etc. Like all great reformers you are inhuman, and scornful of everything that doesn't interest you. Hence the complaint of the anti-Wellsites that in your 'scientific' novels, there is no individual interest, that the characters don't exist individually. A not unjust complaint. The pity is that these persons cannot perceive the 'concerted' interest of your 'scientific' novels. You are not really interested in individual humanity. And when you write a non-'scientific' novel, you always recur to a variation of the same type of hero, & you always will, because your curiosity about individualities won't lead you further. You are concerned in big crowd-movements. Art, really, you hate. It means to you what 'arty' means to me. You live in a nice house, but you know perfectly well you wouldn't care what sort of a house you lived in. When you say that a great pianist is not a marvellous person, you give the show away. For you he is not. The astounding human interest of a dramatic triumph is for you a 'silly uproar'. In these two instances you show clearly, as regards art & as regards life, where your interests stop. You won't have anything to do with 'surface values' at all. You don't merely put them in a minor place; you reject them. A couple of pages devoted to surface values will irritate you. You will never see it, but in rejecting 'surface values' you are wrong. As a fact they are just as important as other values. But reformers can't perceive this. They are capable of classing chefs, pianists and trains de luxe all together & saying: 'Go to, I am a serious person.' You are, you know. The same spirit animates you as animated George MacDonald's grandmother, who objected to the violin as a profane instrument. And the mischief is that, though you will undoubtedly do a vast amount of good in the world, you will get worse & worse, more & more specialised, more & more scornful. All this is not an explanation of you; but an explanation of me. It 'connotes' the difference between our minds. I proposed writing to you to offer Mrs. Wells & you the advantage of my presence for a night or so on my way to England early in December. If this suits, I can then respectfully listen to your defence. I am much too vain to mind being called 'not a poet', and 'not a genius'. But to be called a 'dear delightful person' rouses my worst instincts. It makes me feel as if I was like Marriott Watson or Pett Ridge, and I ain't, not really.

Hommages à Madame,
Thine, E. A. B.

ILLINOIS / MS. / 143
(*To H. G. Wells*)

4 rue de Calais
9th Nov 1905

My dear H.G.,

The only real seizable fault that I can find in *Kipps* is the engagement to Helen, which entirely failed to convince me. In fact it is useless to tell me they ever were engaged. I do not believe it. If you had made of Helen a less real and lifelike figure than she is, then I might have been persuadable. But she is extremely well done, and so she gives you the lie in the matter of the engagement. Ann is more than well-done, she is Very Fine, and the Ann scenes are the best in the book. After agreeing with myself that I read the thing all through with eagerness & joy, and after telling myself that I must not expect in your 'human interest' novels those aspects of life which you either can't see or disdain to see, I find myself asking what this book 'proves', & not getting any answer. As it is distinctly a fighting, 'tendencieux' book, I think I ought to have an answer. Why this immense animus against the 'nace' class of person, since we are all human together? Am I to understand that in your

142. Bennett had high hopes for *Sacred and Profane Love*, published in September 1905, but Wells did not like it, and few other people have liked it. The narration is in the first person, and the narrator is a passionately romantic woman whose love for a famous pianist is expressed thus (she has not met him, she has merely caught his eye at a concert): 'I blushed hotly, and I was conscious of a surpassing joy. My spirit was transfigured. I knew that such a man was above kings. I knew that the world and everything of loveliness that it contained was his. I knew that he moved like a beautiful god through the groves of delight, and that what he did was right, and whom he beckoned came, and whom he touched was blessed. And my eyes had held his eyes for a little space.' For the later American edition, Bennett wrote a preface in which he was at pains to dissociate himself from Carlotta's style.

Pett Ridge (d. 1930), was a popular novelist. See page 331 for another comment by Bennett on him.

opinion as a purposeful observer of life the 'nace' class is more ridiculous, or less worthy of sympathy, or less the outcome of natural & inevitable causes, than any other class? I ask for information. I don't think your ferocious hostility to about five sixths of the characters in the book makes for righteousness of any kind, & certainly not for artistic righteousness. Especially as you follow Kipps about on the stage with a rose-coloured lime light. What is the theory of this procedure? There is no doubt that you achieve the illusion of reality in spite of it, and not with its aid.

If you have set out to amuse & divert the B.P. you have richly succeeded in your aim. Ditto if you have tried to enlist their sympathies on behalf of the Kippses and the Anns. Ditto if you have tried to give impartial portraits of the Sids, the Mastermans and the Chitterlows. But if you have had any Larger aim, any aim of showing how & why one class of persons generally is superior or inferior to another, then I don't reckon you have succeeded—at any rate with thoughtful, judicious, and high-minded people like myself, Mr. Popple (if his name *is* Popple), and others.

You said last year, you even faithfully promised, that you were going to write with more care. God-a-mercy! After the sentence on p. 409 beginning: 'Next to starting a haberdasher's shop', I renounce the crusade. I respectfully give you up. Damn it, after all it doesn't matter how you write. But after your animadversions on the Head Master of Dulwich. . . ! By the way your *Westminster Gazette* article was magnificent, & filled me with holy joy.

I have a sort of idea that my objections to *Kipps* (except as to the engagement) are rather vague & 'theoretical'. But nevertheless I think they contain food for your thought. Such is my view. That there is 'a laugh on every page' is beside the point.

I trust to present my respects in person to Madame in about a month's time.

Yours ever, E. A. B.

143. The sentence on page 409 in *Kipps* that offended Bennett read: 'Next to starting a haberdasher's shop, I doubt if Kipps could have been more truly happy than during the weeks of preparation.' Wells's *Westminster Gazette* article, 'The Schoolmaster and the Empire', 21 October 1905, attacked an article by the Headmaster of Dulwich that had appeared in the *Independent Review*.

ILLINOIS / MS. / 144
(*To Jane Wells*)

31, Spencer Road
Putney SW
Saturday [16 December 1905]

Dear Mrs. Wells,

I suppose you knew all the time that that train didn't go near St. Paul's or Holborn. It went to Cannon St. and arrived in nice time for afternoon tea. Thanks to your admirable sandwiches, however, I suffered no discomfort, except from cold feet. What a line! In spite of the line being what it is, I would never, in your place, leave your house. In a word, you are misguiding yourselves in going to London. You will regret it, & what is more important, I shall. I shall have no place to call at, and be looked after, & be fed up with world-theories and the greatest music. In fact I shall take the cheap route, Southampton, & generally descend in the scale of things. Kindly think over this prospect, and remember me to Gyp, Frank, their author, & the pianola.

A merry Xmas,
Yours sincerely, E. A. Bennett

P.S. And a happy new year, but I hope you won't sell your house.

BERG / MS. / 145
(*To George Sturt*)

4 rue de Calais
Good Friday 1906

My dear George,

You never answered my letter over a year ago. I am thinking of printing privately, to distribute among my friends at Christmas instead of a Xmas card (not that I have ever distributed Xmas cards), a small volume of selections from my Journal which I started 10 years ago. Will you write a short

144. Mrs. Wells (Amy Catherine—Jane; d. 1927) and H. G. remained at their home in Sandgate until 1909, when they moved to Hampstead. Bennett spent December 1905 in England, and was visiting the home, at 31 Spencer Road, of W. W. Kennerley and his sister Tertia, who had married in 1903. On Gyp (George Philip) and Frank Wells, see pages 157 n., 188.

preface for it, of about a thousand words or so? Anything you like. Reminiscent, I should think. You remember the circumstances under which we formally began this journal business. I am convinced that a preface by you is just what the booklet will need to give it a final attractiveness. I shall put by way of a frontispiece a caricature of myself by Rickards. How are you, & yours?

I don't actually write this in Paris, but in the forest of Fontainebleau.

Ever yours, E. A. Bennett

BERG / MS. / 146
(*To George Sturt*)

179 Waterloo Road
Sunday [22 April 1906]

My dear George,

Many thanks for your two letters. I am in England for a day or two. It depends on what you write whether I write anything. You understand that it is impossible to print about 5/6ths of the journal. Either because it relates to friends, or too personally to me, or it isn't good enough, or it is indecent. If you can bring this fact into your remarks I shan't write anything. Of the remaining 6th there is of course plenty of interesting stuff. What I shall print will be a selection from the first two years of the journal. I am extremely glad that you have taken so kindly to the idea of the preface. I am here till Thursday, then I go to Kennerleys till Monday, & then I return to Paris.

Love to all yours, E. A. B.

P.S. The caricature is one of the Hockliffe ones. Not that with the dog.

---

145. *Things That Interested Me* was the first of three annual Christmas books that were printed privately for Bennett by his friend Joseph Dawson in Burslem. Sturt replied to Bennett's note: 'It's true, though I have not before realized it, that our correspondence was let fall at my end. I should have been sorry if it had made any difference; but I have never felt it a grievance that you didn't write.'

BUTLER / MS. / 147
(*From George Sturt*)

Lower Bourne
8 May 1906.

My dear Arnold,

I rather like this thing, and have a sort of hope that you may too.

But if you don't I'll not be stuffy about it. Chuck it entirely and ask me to do another—or ask somebody else if after all you wd prefer it; or make me alter parts of it that displease you. In short, do any mortal thing except tinker with it yourself to improve my work. I shall feel very proud of having any thing of mine in front of your book—too proud to let you have the credit of touching it. See?

As always yours, George Sturt

How wd you like me to sign the thing? I have merely put my initials.

Now, 9.30 pm, the third thunderstorm since 2.0 this afternoon is rattling up. . . . Really it has not left off all the time. How's a fellow to write or think, with that racket going on? And then, the lightning gets on my nerves. In other words, it frightens me.

No book in the house appeals to me. There is *Kipps*. I have read some of it, but don't think I can stand much more. I don't believe in it: the draper's assistant is not that sort of young man, I think, and the feeling will not be driven away, that this stuff is not anything that Mr. H. G. Wells really knows, but only something he would like us to think he knows.

Imagine the sound of one train in Putney Bridge Station letting off steam, and of another coming in—yourself lying in bed listening and wishing for quiet: such is the noise the rain is making now. G. S.

BERG / MS. / 148
(*To George Sturt*)

4 rue de Calais
10 May 1906

My dear George,

I am well satisfied with your preface, which, I regret to have to say, is a damn sight better written than anything in the Journal. I am also extremely obliged to you for doing it. The being flattered, dear Mr. Bourne, is on my side, not yours. And the preface itself is a proof of my skill in getting what I want. I will send you a proof of *it* soon, with a couple of brief footnotes I have made. Do you imagine me capable of tinkering at another person's work? Shame! There are two examples of Sturtian English in the preface, perfectly defensible grammatically & logically, but still not usual English. Do you suppose I would have them altered? Not me! I would not point them out to you even, for less than a sovereign (or near offer). I like them.

Here we are having nothing but storms of hail & thunder. But the weather is splendidly hot: which I like. The accounts in the English newspapers of May Day were grotesque.

Ever yours, E. A. B.

148. The first part of Sturt's preface to *Things That Interested Me* reads:

'Some ten years ago Arnold Bennett, taking me into his confidence not so much to obtain my advice as to offer me his own, informed me that he had begun to keep a journal. As yet he had published no books; the stream of his literature which now is being daily poured forth by the press had oozed but a few driblets into unimportant periodicals; but already he had decided to be a successful author, and, as he viewed it, the keeping of a journal was a most valuable part of the apprenticeship to that career. Accordingly he explained to me with what aims he was working, and by what methods.

On looking back, it is interesting to recognise the modesty which inspired him at that time. In the precautions he was taking to avoid the snares that beset young authors, one detects in him a suspicion that he was not without a share of our common weakness. The peril he most dreaded was idleness, and the sin of thinking without writing—a fault so heinous in his opinion that the opposite vice of writing without thought had few terrors for him. As for the feeble plea, that he had nothing to write about, nor nowhere to write it—the journal was to be the rejoinder to all such nonsense. Taking apparently *Words not Deeds* for his strenuous motto, he had bound himself, by horrid oaths for all I know, to write some huge number of counted words in his journal every day, wet or fine; and so he schooled himself to work, expecting when the effort should be transformed into a habit. Needless to say, the expectation was realised. The first volume of the Journal has been followed by many others. Compared with the great mass of the whole, the present little book is no more than the salad to a seven-course dinner.'

CALIF / MS. / 149
(*To Mr. and Mrs. Eden Phillpotts*)

4 rue de Calais
21st June 1906

My very dear friends,

Your letters gave me the keenest pleasure, & Eléonora also. And we shall hope to see you at the earliest opportunity. In the meantime, I may tell you that this courtship has been rather violent. Eléonora is recovering with her mother in the country, & I have been near collapse. One doesn't know what one has been through till afterwards. I cannot write letters now. I will write you later (I am so overwhelmed with correspondence that I have just chucked it all). I can't for the moment say a word as to my plans. But rest assured I shall stick to my original plans if I possibly can, so as to derange you as little as possible. I hope to marry in October. Well, your letters were adorable.

Ever yours affectionately, E. A. B.

BERG / MS. / 150
(*To Violet Hunt*)

4 rue de Calais
21st June 1906

Dear Miss Hunt,

The last words you said to me, in front of the Vanguard bus, désormais historique, were 'I shall write to you soon'. The reason why I did not write to you was that naturally, with proper modesty, I was waiting to hear from you first. I distinctly warned you not to read *Hugo*. Yet you go & read it, & not only that—you tell me you don't like it. You are not expected to like it, though it is a passably good book of its kind. It is astonishing that I cannot keep my friends from reading the *un*-literature which I write solely in order to be in a position to offer myself a few luxuries.

Mrs. Farley has possibly—nay probably—told you that I am about to offer myself the luxury of a wife. Without her

149. Eleanor Green was an older sister of the novelist Julian Green. She was twenty-four or twenty-five years old. The Green family were Americans, from Georgia, who settled in France in 1893, where the father served as European representative of an American oil company. She and Bennett became engaged on 15 June 1906 in the forest of Fontainebleau, after a courtship of a few months.

extremely good-natured aid I doubt if I should have succeeded. You know, Mrs. Farley & I are really great friends, and I owe you much for having introduced me to her.

It's a strange thing, existence, isn't it? Maugham runs after me on the boulevard & brings me to you, & in no time at all I am engaged to marry Eléonora Green. Since tasting the extremely mixed sensations of love, honestly for the first time in my life, I have re-read all that I had written on the subject. And I am astounded at the sheer insight I had. It has given me quite a new belief in myself (not that that was needed, by the way, as you must always have seen).

I hope you are not going to decorate your new novel with quotations. Someone ought really to speak to you seriously about that, & my sense of duty is such that I must. In the literary convention, it is *bad form*. You know that perfectly well. It is almost invariably a symptom of the third rate. And it annoys me dreadfully.

And now I wait to see what sort of a letter of congratulation a woman experienced in literature & life can write.

Yours sincerely, Arnold Bennett

ILLINOIS / MS. / 151
(*To H. G. Wells*)

Les Sablons
près Moret
S. & M.
Thursday [29 June 1906]

My dear Wells,

I meant to reply to your last letter, & then I waited for your return from U.S. & now I see the announcement of your articles in the *Tribune* & I sit down at once,—to tell you & your wife

150. Violet Hunt (1866–1942) and W. Somerset Maugham (1874–1965) were both living in Paris at this time. Bennett met Maugham early in 1905 and Miss Hunt in October 1905. Miss Hunt's new novel was *White Rose of Weary Leaf*, issued in 1907 undecorated.

Agnes Farley was the wife of an American dentist practising in Paris. She herself introduced Bennett to the Green family, presumably late in 1905. On 3 May 1906 Bennett wrote in his Journal: 'I went to have tea with Mrs. Green. She said that there were things in *Sacred and Profane Love* that she thought no man could possibly have known. She asked me how I knew these things, and whether women had told me. I said that women had not told me *those* things, and that I merely felt that those things must be so.'

that I am engaged to be married to a young woman of the name of Eléonora Green, a native of Savannah, Georgia, who has lived nearly all her life in Paris. Her age is 25. I can't tell you any more about her (except that she was destined for an operatic singer, & I stepped in just in time to stop her début), because I don't know any more. Let us see what kind of a letter of congratulation a publicist & a professional penman can write under these circumstances.

Love to you both, E. A. Bennett

P.S. How are you both?

BERG / MS. / 152
(*To George Sturt*)

Les Sablons
30 June 1906

My dear George,
  Your letter made a great impression on me, & also on her. We considered it distinguished & perfect. It is a great thing to be able to write, isn't it? I'm damned if I can write now. I am forced to finish a book just at the moment when the very foundations of that which is ME have been shaken, & I don't like it at all. I wish I could see you. But I can't. I am shirking *all* my correspondence. The book (on divorce) is to be finished in 3 weeks.
  Kindest regards to all yours.

Yours ever, E. A. B.

151. Les Sablons belonged to a gardener, and late in 1904 Bennett arranged to rent a first-floor suite there for occasional visits.

Wells went to America for a brief visit in April 1906. The *Tribune* published a series of articles on the trip, and they were gathered together later in the year into a book, *The Future in America*.

Miss Green's age is given as eighteen by Reginald Pound in his biography, and his account contrasts a naïve girl 'barely out of school' with a middle-aged writer. But although Miss Green's birth-date remains unknown, Bennett's figure is probably near the mark. The father and mother were married on 23 February 1880, and seem to have begun their family almost immediately. Eleanor was the eldest.

152. *Whom God Hath Joined*, commissioned by the publisher Alfred Nutt, was finished some time in July.

ILLINOIS / MS. / 153
(*To H. G. Wells*)

4 rue de Calais
Tuesday [July 1906]

My dear H.G.,

Your letter had an immense success with my girl. She has a passion for stern realism. I read her parts of it. Your Chicago article was very good. All that you say about marriage & Chicago is true. And as for your & your wife's good wishes, they give me joy.

I am—I mean we are—thinking of being married at a registry office in Folkestone, this being handiest. If you are summering in Sandgate, I wonder if you will let me accomplish a formal residence at your house. It means 2 days at the beginning of the legal term of 16 days, & then another two days at the end—four days in all. Continuous residence is not necessary. Will this worry you? It would occur in August *about* the 8th to 10th & 22nd to 24th. The marriage will not take place till October. Have no apprehension as to being worried in any way by the actual marriage. You will neither see nor hear anything of it. Eléonora will bring one friend over with her for a night, & the other witness I will get in the registry office.

I see you are turning the Fabians inside out?

Yours ever, E. A. B.

ILLINOIS / MS. / 154
(*To H. G. Wells*)

4 rue de Calais
Saturday [4 August 1906]

My dear H. G.,

I shall not come next Wednesday. My engagement exists no longer. Can't write to you about it now, but it's right bang off, anyhow. I shall hope to come later on, if you will have me for a day or two.

Yours ever, E. A. B.

153. Apparently neither Wells's nor Sturt's response to Bennett's announcement survives.

In February 1906 Wells delivered an attack on the Fabian Society as conducted by G. B. Shaw and the Webbs. He describes this 'storm in the Fabian teacup' in *Experiment in Autobiography*.

154. The engagement was broken off on 3 August.

BERG / MS. / 155
(*To Violet Hunt*)

Duchy House
Dartmoor
Princetown
Thursday [9 or 16 August 1906]

My dear Lady,
I have always been meaning to acknowledge your letter, but my life has been so rushed that I haven't had time till this moment. And now the only thing I have to tell you is that my engagement is broken off. Her feelings, violent enough at one time, did not ultimately justify marriage. Rather desolating, isn't it? However, such is life, & as you wrote me such a nice letter of congratulation, it is meet that you should know that such *is* life. I am up here on the Moor with Eden Phillpotts & his wife. I spent just enough time in London to get shaved.

Yours sincerely, Arnold Bennett

BERG / MS. / 156
(*To Violet Hunt*)

Duchy House
Saturday [11 or 18 August 1906]

My dear Lady,
I had your nice letter this morning. No, as regards your agency in my history. I may tell you that in spite of everything I wouldn't blot out the last six months even if I could. I knew a devil of a lot about women before. I know more now, & I have never yet bought knowledge too dearly. Besides that, I know more about myself, & can write infinitely better books. And I am a writer first; all the rest comes afterwards. I shall be here at least till the end of the month, so I shan't be able to look in on you, as you suggest. I hope you will be in Paris during the autumn as usual. I shall move in to a new flat in October, something more roomy & less altitudinous. But I shan't play you Chopin. I shall play you Bach, for whom I have developed a perfect passion.

Yes, I think Mrs. Farley & I understand each other pretty well.

Yours sincerely, Arnold Bennett

156. Eleanor Green (who two years later became Mrs. Kenneth Joll) eventually wrote an account of her youth, and some portion of it is preserved in a transcript made by Reginald Pound. None of the account, as preserved, touches

directly on the engagement, but it does suggest something of the character of the relationship between her and Bennett.

'. . . he had a small but beautifully furnished flat in the centre of Paris: Empire, verging on the Louis-Philippe. His taste struck me as being very good, but erring on the side of reticence. . . . In one angle of his sitting room was a small corner cupboard filled with several heavily gilt and painted pieces of china of the same period as his furniture. Fired with enthusiasm at the [? sight] of his skilfully arranged collection, I began at once to buy as many pieces as I could afford of the porcelain. . . .

Agnes and I frequently had tea with Bennett, in spite of its being China tea: "the delicate perfection of which I was incapable of appreciating", according to my host. . . . And after tea he played Mozart sonatas. . . . One day he read us a paraphrase he had just finished of a poem of Verlaine's. . . . Bennett's conversation was varied and amusing; he was a charming companion, never dull, and I like to remember the long happy afternoons we spent together, he, Agnes, and I. . . .

. . . every evening after dinner he read *Whom God Hath Joined* . . . to Agnes and me. I remember objecting to the daughter, in the book, giving her father away [betraying to her mother his liaison with a governess] and having a heated argument with the author in consequence.

One evening, in Paris, he took me to the Grand Guignol. I had never seen this celebrated theatre and expected to be thrilled, and agreeably frightened, but not absolutely appalled. We saw the supposed lynching of the owner of a "death" ship. . . . Feeling rather faint, I turned round and the sight of the faces of the people back of me proved to be rather more dreadful, if possible, than the play itself: sadistic cruelty in every stage of development was what I read in the tense lines round the mouths and in the glittering eyes of the audience. Bennett and I rose, without a word to each other, and left. . . .

I think that Bennett, in those days, looked very like Dickens without the beard. One day, to my everlasting joy when we went to see him he had on a red waistcoat and somebody's grandmother—maybe Agnes's—remarked that on the one occasion when she met Dickens he was wearing a similar garment. Bennett in my opinion was so much nicer than anything he ever wrote. Once he asked Agnes if I liked his books. "Not all of them," said Agnes tactfully. "I should not care for her to like them all," was his comment. At that time I did not really care for any of them but later, when Bennett had passed out of my life for ever (I never saw him after 1906) I read and admired *The Old Wives' Tale*. All through the years since I have wished we might have been friends again, he and I, and talked together. I do not flatter myself that he went on loathing me. Far worse, it is more than likely that he forgot my existence.'

Mrs. Joll gave these notes to Reginald Pound around 1950, and provided him with further details that appear in his biography. According to him:

'Although her family and friends knew that Bennett was in love with her, Miss Green never fully realised it herself, nor did she understand that he was completely serious when he proposed to her in the forest at Fontainebleau. She liked him, considered him "nice enough", and always had a sympathetic regard for him, but she says that she never at any time thought of him in terms of the affections. He seemed to her always middle-aged and avuncular. . . . Her family had protested because she continued to leave his numerous letters lying unopened about the house, and finally her mother, deploring what she insisted was a discourtesy, pressed a paper knife into her daughter's hand and made her slit open each envelope in a considerable pile even if she did not propose to read the contents. . . .

ILLINOIS / MS. / 157   Le Grand Hôtel-Bruxelles
(*To H. G. Wells*)   Boulevard Anspach
                                      [Brussels]
                                      Monday [16 September 1906]

My dear Wells,

I have been yachting with anti-socialists in Holland & had
no address for a week. Your two letters have just arrived at my
bedside. So I can't come the day before yesterday. But I mean
to come soon. You will find it impossible to make me a socialist,
as I already am one. See?

I will write you again soon.

What price Bart Kennedy on America in the *Daily Mail*?
You are simply nowhere compared with his grandiosity. Which
reminds me that the title I had chosen for my new book was
discovered, at the last moment, to have been used by Fergus
Hume in 1891. Fergus, on being applied to, as a matter of

Mrs. Joll . . . has clear recollections of the final scene but thinks it unfair to
Arnold Bennett's memory to recall them publicly in detail. It is sufficient to say
that his speech difficulty appeared at its worst, that every aspirate deserted him
in this extremity, and that he was reduced to uttering comically pathetic threats
of social excommunication for Miss Green. "You'll lose the respect of the 'ole
world—and Mr. and Mrs. Farley too."'

One other account exists of the affair, by Miss Green's younger sister Anne, in her
memoir *With Much Love*. Here the scene opens with Eleanor bringing a letter that
she has read to her mother and saying, 'I don't know what I'll do', and her mother
saying, 'Your father and I both warned you. We even begged you not to make
fools of us.' This letter is one of a series, and the mother doesn't want to read it,
but Eleanor insists, for she wants her mother to reply, and she advises her to make
the reply 'nice . . . but not affectionate, I can't bear insincerity'. The mother agrees
to 'write one more note to that wretched man. For my sake because you express
yourself like a cook and for his sake because your letter would be from an unfriendly
cook. . . . Can't I put a little love in it?' Eleanor has been pushed into the affair
because Bennett is charming, because Agnes Farley has pressed his suit, and
because she herself is weak. She may even go through with it: 'Let me try to get
used to him a little longer, Mamma. He'll be broken-hearted if I fail him just as
he's looking around for an apartment.' So things go, and Eleanor is secretly
interested in someone else, and eventually decides that she must make the break,
after her mother refuses to do it for her. Fortunately Bennett is suspicious of her
behaviour, and one day when they are holidaying together, she comes upon him
examining the contents of her handbag. 'Uneasy Eleanor pounced on this occasion
to be furious . . .; she . . . broke the engagement. I draw a veil over Bennett's
rage, Papa's irritation and Mamma's loud relief. Eleanor stayed on with Agnes,
"a disgrace in the eyes of the world and her parents", as Bennett said in his anger.'

Neither this account nor the one given in Pound's book has the ring of truth
about it, and they seem all the less believable if Eleanor Green was in fact twenty-
four or twenty-five instead of eighteen. Bennett's letters tell us little enough, but
they probably contain the most reliable evidence of what happened.

courtesy, for permission to re-use the title, replied pompously that he would have been delighted to accord the grace, had he not recently granted a similar application from William Le Queux!!

Wednesday I return to Paris.

Hommages à Madame,

Yours ever, Bennett

ILLINOIS / MS. / 158
(*To H. G. Wells*)

4 rue de Calais
Friday [20 or 27 September 1906]

My dear H. G.,

Many thanks for the book, which I found on my return from Holland yesterday. I have already given you my views at large on it. I was in the Paris office of the *Daily Express* last night, and was shown your slaughtering of them. These reviews, though ineffably stupid & somewhat dishonest, were inevitable. And I take it that, had it not been for your new socialistic prominence, you would have received them with silence. But now you feel that the Cause is involved. Well, in your place, I should still be inclined to pursue a policy of masterly silence. The people who matter perfectly understand. And you never will persuade the people who don't matter that the close of the *Comet* is not profoundly immoral. Such is my notion. And I think you honoured the *Express* far too much by slaughtering it.

See you soon,

Yours, E. A. B.

P.S. This is quite private, & I would not be fair to the Paris staff of the *Express* if it got about through me: They were charmed to see the smashing. I don't think anyone has a lower opinion of the *Express–Mail* type of paper than the staffs thereof.

157. Bart Kennedy (1861–1930), author and journalist, began a series of articles entitled 'America Revisited' in the *Daily Mail* on 10 September 1906. Fergus Hume (1859–1932), author of *The Mystery of a Hansom Cab* as well as *Whom God Hath Joined*, saw Bennett use the latter title in October 1906. William Le Queux (1864–1927) used several religious titles for his novels of international intrigue, but not this one.

158. The final pages of *In the Days of the Comet* (1906) offer advanced views on love, and the review in the *Daily Express* on 14 September 1906 remarked: 'Anti-

ILLINOIS / MS. / 159
(*To H. G. Wells*)

3 rue d'Aumale
14 Dec 1906

My dear H. G.,

I happened to meet Davray today. He told me you had declined an offer of a conférence & a banquet here. I had not time to discuss it with him, but I gathered the refusal is because you are too busy. I didn't tell Davray that I should write to you, but I instantly decided to permit myself to meddle in your affairs to that extent. In my opinion if you do definitely refuse this thing you will make a great mistake—that is, if you care 2d. for renown & influence in France. I know all about the enterprise. It is under the very finest auspices in France, and has the active support of the very cream of the French Academy. A greater honour couldn't be offered to an English author. It is true they did it for Gosse; but that was a quid pro quo, in return for [? laudations] rendered by him during many years in the English press. With you there can be no interested motive on their part. You cannot possibly be too busy to attend to a thing of this kind. If you don't accept it, it will be because you have not realised the genuineness of its importance. But you may take that from me, & most seriously. The thing is no affair of mine, but I should have something on my conscience if I didn't tell you that your refusal would amount to a crime against yourself.

Yours ever, E. A. B.

Socialists will be a little comforted by the reflection that only by the interposition of a comet can Socialism become possible, particularly as, according to Mr. Wells, it entails, among other things, a peculiarly unattractive rearrangement of sexual matters.' The *Express* was at this time running some violently anti-Socialist propaganda. Wells replied on the 19th, having already been stung by a review in *The Times*: 'To say that it is my dictum that the ultimate goal of Socialism is free love is an outrageous lie. . . . I cannot conceive how any respectable paper—even in the utmost rancour of anti-Socialist propaganda—can have brought itself to make so wanton and so mischievous a statement.'

159. Bennett moved into his new flat at 3 rue d'Aumale at the end of November or in early December.

Henry Davray (1873–1944) edited the Collection of Foreign Authors for *Le Mercure de France*. He and Bennett were good friends. Wells replied to Bennett's letter: 'Now you realize my Greatness. Blow the French Academy!'

STOKE / TR. / 160
(*To Lucie Simpson*)

3 rue d'Aumale
[December 1906]

Dear Miss Simpson,

Many thanks for your kind letter and good wishes. It is a pity you will not be in the Potteries this Xmas. I understand there is to be great doings. (There is no nonconformist strain in me whatever, unless you take the word in its literal sense, in which I am nothing but nonconformist strain.)

You must have guessed before this that I am one of the most serious-minded, truly moral beings that ever lived. Still I keep my opinions to myself as they are apt to get me a reputation for un-morality.

I hope you will find a publisher who is not a rascal; there are such. Kindest regards,

Believe me,

Yours sincerely, Arnold Bennett

STOKE / TR. / 161
(*To Lucie Simpson*)

Grand Hotel Royal
San Remo
[February–March 1907]

Dear Miss Simpson,

Many thanks for your letter. I quite expected to meet you at Xmas. People who knew my especial keenness on women's clothes told me that you were to be seen extremely chic; but I never even caught a glimpse of you. I did meet Nancy Price at a lunch. Do I understand you to use the word 'perversity'? I thought she was very innocent. The fact is I have known too many actresses. I don't *like* actresses, as a rule. It isn't their fault, but they are spoilt by male fools, and they expect what they will never get—from me, and they are to be excused for expecting it. It is a mistake for authors who know all about the stage to meet actresses. The actress expects to be admired and the author expects to be listened to. Indeed if the author knows his business he insists on being listened to. I always do. So the result is not always ideal. As regards Eden Phillpotts, I would respectfully ask you to read my article on him which is to appear in (I think) the April *Fortnightly*. By the way he is here with me. This is supposed to be the best hotel on the Italian Riviera— and you observe the quality of their ink!

I feel that I can struggle on without Madame de Staël; but *Adolphe* is an undiluted masterpiece. Women always slang Benjamin Constant. I suppose because he had no illusions. I would sooner have written *Adolphe* than *Diana of the Crossways*—forty times sooner!

I must apologise for this ink. I hope you are flourishing, and that you will appreciate *Whom God Hath Joined* at its true worth. It is a clumsy book, but not dull.

Believe me,
With kind regards,
Yours, Arnold Bennett

TEXAS / MS. / 162
(*To M. D. Calvocoressi*)

Grand Hotel Royal
Sunday
[February–March 1907]

My dear Calvo,

Many thanks for the card. I was much amused by your letter. I think that an erotic club is needed down here. I wonder what you would 'do' in this hotel. I am now writing poetry. It is my present form of idleness. I intersperse it with climbing mountains. I begin to look forward to Paris again. Three weeks tomorrow I shall *be* in Paris, but I don't know how long I shall stay there. I seem to want to travel more. If only I had people to travel with! I am sorry to hear of Viñes' grief. I have sent him a brief line. The weather is terrifically gorgeous, and next week I will write a really fine short story. What I can*not* do when I am away from home is to write coherent letters.

Kindest regards to your mother who I hope is now quite convalescent.

Ever yours, E. A. B.

161. Bennett was in San Remo for a holiday during February and most of March.

Nancy Price, the well-known actress (1880–   ), played the lead in the stage adaptation of Bennett's novel *Helen with the High Hand* some years later.

No article by Bennett on Phillpotts appeared in the *Fortnightly* in 1907.

162. Michel Dimitri Calvocoressi (1877–1944), critic and writer on music, was

ILLINOIS / MS. / 163
(*To H. G. Wells*)

3 rue d'Aumale
1st July 1907

My dear H. G.,

I had to come back to Paris by telegram, to arrange legal
formalities for the accursed union. No end of trouble. However, I expect to be ruined artistically within a week from now,
and all your warnings will have been in vain. I am extremely
glad that you class *The Grim Smile* so high, though it shows a
failure on your part to appreciate things like *Leonora*. Still, I am
content. I suppose I shall see you both some time.

Kindest regards to your wife.

Yours, E. A. B.

---

one of Bennett's early Parisian friends. His particular interest was Russian music.
Ricardo Viñes (1875–1943), the Spanish pianist, was particularly noted for his
interpretation of modern French music. Bennett recorded an evening with the two
men in his Journal in 1905: 'At night I went to Calvocoressi's, and met Viñes . . . ,
an exceedingly fine player. The two first played a duet, and then Viñes had the
piano to himself. What struck me was the fine pure quality of the pleasure we
obtained, all of us, the simplicity of the enthusiasm; and yet what years of cultiva-
tion had gone to provide it, in all of us. Calvocoressi's mother sat upright, on an
ordinary cane chair, half blind with cataract, and encouraged our enthusiasm.'

163. The most reliable account of Bennett's courtship of Marguerite Soulié
(d. 1960), whom he met on 16 January 1907, is that by Georges Lafourcade in his
study of Bennett:

'In January 1907 Arnold Bennett who was looking for a part-time secretary
to help him with his literary work and correspondence was introduced to
Marguerite Soulié by his friend Calvocoressi. He at once accepted her services.
Mademoiselle Soulié . . . had come to Paris from her home near Montauban to
live with an aunt who had offered her a responsible post in the "maison de
haute couture" which she superintended. But her interests were chiefly in the
direction of dramatic art and she availed herself of her residence in Paris to take
courses in elocution. She could recite French poetry with distinction and
originality and had appeared on several stages. When she met Arnold Bennett
she had just returned from a prolonged stay in England where her aunt had
advised her to go to learn the language. Her knowledge of English made her
services doubly acceptable. Bennett was attracted by her good presence and
striking personality. On his return from a two-months' stay in Italy in the spring,
she nursed him through a brief but violent illness which had overtaken him in
his bachelor's flat. He thus had occasions to note her remarkable qualities as
housewife and organizer of a home. After consulting several of his friends, he
asked her to marry him. In the course of May they were engaged and their
wedding took place on July 4, 1907, at the Mairie du IXe Arrondissement.'

The Grim Smile of the Five Towns, Bennett's second collection of short stories, was
issued in June 1907.

FALES, NYU / MS. / 164
(*To Eden Phillpotts*)

Les Sablons
[no salutation]   1907 Aug 27
  Many thanks.
  The latest. (Kindly scan the 1st line as blank verse.)

TOWN AND COUNTRY

God made the country and man made the town.
And so, man made the doctor, God the clown.
God made the mountain, and the ants their hill
Where grinding servitudes each day fulfil.
God doubtless made the flowers, while in the hive
Unnatural bees against their passions strive.
God made the jackass and the bounding flea—
I render thanks to God that man made me.

Let those who recognise God's shaping power
Here but not there, in tree but not in tower,
In lane and field but not in street and square,
And in man's work see nothing that is fair,
Bestir their feeble fancies to the odd
Conception of a 'country' ruled by God;
Where birds perceive the wickedness of strife
Against the winds, and lead the simple life
Nest-less on God's own twigs; and squirrels free
From carking care exist through February
On nuts that God has stored. Pray let them give
God a free hand in wheat for just a year
And then of God's own harvest make good cheer.

This cant of God and man would turn me sick,
Did I not deeply know the age was quick
With large conception of a prouder creed,
Wherein we shall not feel the craven need
To count ourselves less noble than a weed.

For me, a rural pond is not more pure
Nor more spontaneous than my city sewer.
                                        E. A. B.

218   *4 September 1907*

KEELE / MS. / 165
(*To Frederick Marriott*)

[4 September 1907]
Wednesday

[no salutation]

Many thanks for your letter. We set out on our tour yesterday morning, & lunched at Chérdy, & had the same lunch, with the same people, as you & I had last week. We got to Charney (70 kilometres altogether) at 6 p.m. & slept there. Very good for Marguerite. The poor thing had rheumatism in her knees this morning, so we have only done 50 kilometres today. We are now as on the other side. Fine roads, great scenery, &, except one shower, splendid weather. Not hot and no dust. Had it not been for the knees, we should have got to our destination Vézelay (150 kilometres) tonight. We get there tomorrow.

Love to you both from both. E. A. B.

---

164. 'Town and Country' was published in the *English Review* in October 1909 with the third and fourth stanzas omitted and with some minor changes in the first two. As late as 1912 Bennett was contemplating publishing a book of poems. In the Journal for 12 March 1908 is the following entry:

'I have tried for two days to find rhythms for two poems that I found ideas for—one elegiac and the other Aristophanic, and can't.

I have read through first part of *Old Wives' Tale*, and am deeply persuaded of its excellence.'

He was producing *The Old Wives' Tale* sometimes at the rate of 1,600 words an hour.

165. Frederick Marriott and his wife had arranged some time earlier to spend a month in the summer of 1907 with Bennett in France, but when they heard of his marriage, they wrote to suggest deferring the visit. Bennett replied on a postcard: 'Dear Frederick, I shall need you all the more. A.B.' Marriott describes Marguerite: 'When the cab drew up to the door of the house, Mrs. Bennett met us radiant and smiling, and with a short halt between each word, said, "How do you do, will you take tea with me?", an opening evidently previously rehearsed. Our subsequent interchange of broken English and broken French, supported by expressive gesticulations to cover our deficiencies, was productive of much merriment. . . . She was a tall, graceful, and strikingly handsome woman, and she had excellent taste in dress.' Bennett and the Marriotts of course saw less of each other in these and later years than formerly, but their friendship remained intimate. In 1904 Bennett dedicated *A Great Man* 'To my dear friend Frederick Marriott and to the imperishable memory of old times', and Marriott in his memoir spoke of Bennett as 'an unfailingly generous and staunch friend'.

George Sturt in 1909

BUTLER / MS. / 166
(*To A. R. Orage*)

Les Sablons
20th Oct 1907

Dear Mr. Orage,

Many thanks for your letter & the 2 numbers. I think the paper is very interesting. Could you not make a speciality of giving Socialist Party or propagandist *news* such as can't be got elsewhere? And insist on formulating a definition of socialism, & a programme? Not of course that socialism can be defined; but these things are useful in a party machine. And what you want is to be talked about & to be indispensable. Now what sort of an article do you want from me? There are about 40 articles that I could do. It appears to me that what would suit you best would be a semi-autobiographic affair showing 'why I became a socialist'. It would doubtless be rather disturbing in its frankness, but it ought to interest the interested public. Sometime I am going to do an article for somebody entitled 'Shall my domestic servants wear caps?' It is a problem full of deep issues.

                    Believe me,
                    Yours very truly, Arnold Bennett

BERG / MS. / 167
(*To George Sturt*)

Les Sablons
4th Nov 1907

My dear George,

I have been for writing to you nearly every day for several months past. It is the continual rumour of your new book in the advertisement columns of the papers that somehow now makes me sit down. Also my wife is away in Paris for the night, subjected to dentists. I feel sure your book is too classical to

166. A. R. Orage (1873–1934) trained in his youth as an art teacher but became a journalist, editor, and publisher. His major accomplishment was the *New Age*, which he and Holbrook Jackson (see page 276) took over in 1907 and made into a powerful organ of radical Socialist opinion. Bennett began publishing his 'Books and Persons' column in the *New Age* the following March, under the pseudonym of Jacob Tonson. See Vol. I, p. 130, for an example of Bennett's own radical politics as published in the *New Age*.

please the general public, but I am looking forward to a few very satisfactory reviews of it. I wish I was a reviewer again. I have been persuaded back into journalism again, but not as a reviewer. I see myself now as a sort of moralist for the people. It is a strange rôle, but I find I am a most serious man, at bottom. And though I can't for the life of me see what is the objection to sodomy (vide recent German trial), I seem to be getting more & more 'earnest' every day. At the end of this year I shall have jolly near written 365,000 words in the year —much of which is nothing but Marcus Aurelius & Christ assimilated & excreted by me in suitable form. My journal is still kept up (seventh volume is just being finished), but I doubt if it is really any good. Arthur Hooley has written the preface for this year's Xmas selection, & I have had it printed in Burslem in rather a classy style in black & red. His preface is a scintillating pyrotechnic display, naturally. This year I have written one humorous novel, one romance in collaboration with Phillpotts, one popular play and one serious play, five short stories, 50 or 60 articles, and a slice of my next serious novel. This novel will be as long as *A Man from the North, Anna,* and *Leonora* all added together. It is a prodigious canvas. All about the 5 towns. After a sort of an impulse to quit those Towns I have found myself going back to them. The most interesting thing I have done is the serious play. The Stage Society invited me to write a play in the style of my 5 Towns novels, & they said if it wouldn't pass the Censor they would produce it without a license. However, there will be no difficulty with the Censor, & I understand it is to be performed at the end of January. I think it is extraordinarily good—it's no use pretending I don't.

The most curious thing that has happened to me is that I have practically lost all my ambitions except the ambition to be allowed to work quietly. This remarkable phenomenon coincides with my marriage, but I do not honestly think the two things are connected, as it has been 'coming on' for a year. I can make all the money I want and need; and as for the other things that are necessary to philosophic calm, I have them. I have always said that I only lived in a capital because I couldn't stand the country alone by myself. Now that I am no longer alone, you don't catch me living any more in Paris. I am giving up my flat there, although it is only 9 months since I finished installing myself in it—at a considerable expense. I have had the first floor of this house for several years, & I have now taken the whole house (charming, honest, working, productive garden—with no damned nonsense about it—I'm sure it would have pleased Bettesworth). The problem now is to get the furniture of two flats into one house. I enjoy myself all the time in the country; it is a district of great forests & fine rivers. I don't know anything about the 'country' & I never shall, but I enjoy being in it, though I can't even name the trees.

I come with my wife to England early in December. Marriott announces that he is going to give a grandiose musical evening on Dec the 14th in our honour. Perhaps you will be there. As I'm not writing a novel I can't describe anything relating to my wife. Nothing is more difficult than to give an idea of an unseen person. Her English will certainly amuse England. I feel as if I had always been married. I can't imagine myself not married. It suits me profoundly, & I never before did so much work in the time as I have done since my marriage. I suppose you are still writing. I should like to have a good rummage among your manuscripts and notes. I began making notes about this village, but I couldn't keep it up; I was too busy. I am learning Italian. But I think it is the last language I ever will learn. Learning is an awful nuisance & bore. I may be said to have a facility in French now such as is given to few Englishmen—& yet each day I feel more & more that you can't *learn* a foreign language. You never come within ten miles of knowing it like a native. And yet I think in French habitually when I'm talking.

Remember me to your sisters, Frank, & his wife. It is a devil of a time since I saw you, & I really think you & Carlos ought to have come here while you were in France.

Yours ever, E. A. B.

167. Sturt's new book was *Memoirs of a Surrey Labourer, A Record of the Last Years of Frederick Bettesworth*, issued in 1907 by Duckworth.

Marcus Aurelius and Christ were first united in the *Savoir Vivre Papers*, which were published in *T. P.'s Weekly* in 1905–6 (revised and published as *The Reasonable Life*, 1907), and *How to Live on Twenty-Four Hours a Day*, which began appearing in the *Evening News* on 6 May 1907.

Bennett's record of work for 1907:
> Humorous novel (serial), *Helen with the High Hand*, published in book form 1910.
> Romance with Phillpotts, *The Statue*, published 1908.

MANCHESTER PL / MS. / 168
(*To Annie E. F. Horniman*)   3, Ilchester Gardens W.
                                   [London]
                                   29 Jan 1908

Dear Miss Horniman,

I am happy to send you the MS of *Cupid & Commonsense*. I was hearing about your enterprise at G. B. Shaw's the other day. It is extremely interesting, & if it succeeds anywhere, Manchester is assuredly the place. I have the greatest admiration for the spirit of Manchester, & also for its press (although the London correspondent of the *Guardian* was really excessively rude to my play). I wish you every success.

                          Believe me,
                          Yours sincerely, Arnold Bennett

BUTLER / MS. / 169
(*To Charles Young*)   Villa des Néfliers
                                   [Avon S/M]
                                   1st May 1908

My dear Charlie,

As to *Cupid & Commonsense*, I think it will be better to postpone publication of this for a bit, as there is a great likelihood of it being played again, & the moment of its reproduction would be the moment for publishing it. What say you?

I enclose you a small cheque for your damnation account, with my best love.

        My wife sends her kindest regards,
                          Yours ever, E. A. B.

Popular play with Phillpotts, *The Sole Survivors*, never published or produced.

Serious play, *Cupid and Commonsense*, based on *Anna of the Five Towns*, produced by the Stage Society 26–27 January 1908.

Short stories included 'The Death of Simon Fuge' and probably 'The Lion's Share', 'The Silent Brothers', and 'Beginning the New Year', all of which appeared in *The Grim Smile of the Five Towns*.

Serious novel, *The Old Wives' Tale*, the first of four books of which was completed at the end of November.

The first notes on village life appeared in the Journal on 20 August 1907. Bennett was in fact unable to negotiate a lease on Les Sablons, and he and his wife settled instead at the Villa des Néfliers near Fontainebleau the following April.

168. 3 Ilchester Gardens was the Bennett residence from January to early March 1908.

Annie E. F. Horniman (1806–1937) founded the Manchester Repertory Company.

And look here, Carlos, I was forgetting to say that we expect you & George to come here during your next visit to France. Or there will be a hell of a row, so you can tell George.

BUTLER / MS. / 170
(*To Charles Young*)

Villa des Néfliers
[postmarked 4 May 1908]

[no salutation]

re Churchill, I am entirely with Wells. As to the tone of the *N.A.* towards the government, it irks me sometimes as a practical man, but I have come to see that it is necessary if the *N.A.* is to be logically anti-capitalist, as it is. The *N.A.* is not advocating immediately practical ideas. It is preparing opinion for ideas which will in future be practical. I think it is a devilish good paper. Read the review of Rees book on India in this week's. Read my article on a Riviera charity meeting in a forthcoming issue.

I only know of Jacob Tonson that he was an 18th century publisher. Kindly send me prospectuses of C. & Windus's 'Florence' books & 'Mediaeval Library'.

Our kindest remembrances.

Yours ever, E. A. B.

FALES, NYU / MS. / 171
(*To Frederic Chapman*)

Villa des Néfliers
15 June '08

My dear Chapman,

Many thanks for your letter. You must have worked hard. If Lane is sending copies for review to the *New Age*, I will deal

169. On the Villa des Néfliers see page 222 n.

Cupid and Commonsense was published in 1909 by Frank Palmer, not by Young.

170. Winston Churchill (1874–1965) was at this time President of the Board of Trade, and standing for election to Parliament. He had not long since deserted the Conservative for the Liberal cause, and was arguing passionately in favour of free trade.

The Real India, by Sir John David Rees (d. 1922), a civil servant and defender of the Empire, was savagely attacked for its ignorance and misinformation. Bennett's 'Diversion on the Riviera' appeared on 16 May.

with them. By the way, one of the funniest things I have lately heard is the account of an eye-witness of the meeting between Anatole France & Mr. & Mrs. Lane. It must have been wildly comic. They asked him what he thought of various English authors, & at last what he thought of Conan Doyle, to which he replied: 'C'est le fléau de nos deux pays.'

I know nothing of Winifred Stephens, but I will not conceal from you my opinion that her book is absolutely and entirely rotten.

Roden Buxton wrote to me some months ago asking me to contribute to the *Albany*, but as he wouldn't commission a story I didn't do anything. However I wrote to him about twelve days ago offering him a most wonder[ful] article, rather urgent, but I have received no reply. Is he dead?

The Kennerleys arrive on Friday.

I trust you will find an opportunity to read *Buried Alive*, not because I surely hope you will like it; but because I regard it as very important that you should see what I conceive to be high-class humour. You had better not read my autumn novel, as it would make you furious.

My wife wishes to be kindly remembered to you.

Ever yours, Arnold Bennett

P.S. I have now begun to collect a French library.

T. P.'S WEEKLY, 31 July 1908 / 172
(*To the editor*)

[Villa des Néfliers]
[July 1908]

Sir,

I have just read Mr. Nevile Foster's first article on *The Universal Machine*, which is chiefly a criticism of some of my articles. I hope that I shall not be deemed lacking in courtesy if I refrain from replying to it in detail. Mr. Foster is

171. Chapman supervised an edition of the works of Anatole France (1844-1924) that John Lane published in 1908. Winifred Stephens (Winifred Stephens Whale, d. 1944), translator and writer on French literature, published a book with Lane in 1908. The *Albany Review* was a short-lived venture by Lane.

Buried Alive, written in January and February 1908, was published in June. The autumn novel was *The Old Wives' Tale*, not finished until 30 August.

simply discussing a question which for the purpose of my articles I assumed to be closed. That the question is not, and never can be, really closed, was beside my point. All human endeavour proceeds on the assumption that it is closed. My appeal was to the daily experience of every man, and no restatements of psychological theory can possibly weaken that appeal. This does not in any way diminish the interest and value of purely psychological discussion. Mr. Nevile Foster, however, should beware of commencing his arguments with the statement that I 'loosely used' one word when I meant another. There is no kind of excuse for such methods of controversy. With regard to that 'ridiculous situation' in which the brain, the soul, the instincts, and the will are all scrimmaging together for the upper hand, I quite agree that it is ridiculous. Indeed, I think I frequently said so.

My aim was not to find the clue to the origin of the ridiculous situation; my aim was to deal with the ridiculous situation in a practical manner. If Mr. Foster can show me the clue I shall be forever indebted to him. What most surprises me is his implied assumption that Libertarianism and Determinism are two mutually-exclusive doctrines. The tendency of the most modern thought is to reconcile them, impossible as the last may seem to people who have not familiarised themselves with the most modern thought. Mr. Foster's enthusiasm for Determinism will doubtless not prevent him from summarising the history of the great quarrel right down to date.

Yours truly, Arnold Bennett

FALES, NYU / MS. / 173
(*To Thomas Lloyd
    Humberstone*)

Hôtel du Portugal et de l'Univers
rue Croix des Petits-champs
25 Sept 1908

My dear Humberstone,

Many thanks for your letter. Apropos of going into journalism *T.P.s Weekly* are starting a Correspondence College for Mental,

172. Bennett's series of articles on *The Human Machine* began in *T. P.'s Weekly* on 20 March 1908, and ran through June. They had an immense success, and the editors capitalized on that success with *The Universal Machine*, which took a deterministic view of things. Nevile Foster is not otherwise known.

Literary, & Business Training. It is yet a secret. I only know of it because they have asked me to write some of the 'preliminary discourses'. (Doubtless they got the idea from my articles, to begin with!) I don't know whether they want anyone to organise or whether it would be in your line if they did. I know nothing. But it occurred to me that you might like to be aware of the matter. It might make an introduction to journalism, somehow; & possibly without you giving up your present post. Anyhow I can give you a letter to them that will have great weight, if you want it.

Possibly you would prefer to aim at once at something of a higher class. For of course correspondence colleges of this kind are really the most enormous bunkum. With your credentials as correspondent of *The Times*, editor of the *Year Book* (& its creator), & administrative staff of London Univ., you ought to be able to get something good. I don't know exactly what your post is at the Univ., but if it is chiefly bureaucratic, & gives you no scope, and offers no prospects, I should, in your place, chuck it unhesitatingly. If anybody can afford to take risks, you can. You are bound to make a living, one way or another. When you say that you have not the qualities necessary to success, I disagree with you. On the contrary I have always said, since I set eyes on you, that you were bound to succeed. You are extremely efficient, & extremely interested in yourself. What more do you want?

Ma femme vous envoie, à vous et à vos amis, ses meilleurs sentiments. Elle est très sensible à vos compliments si distingués.

Yours sincerely, Arnold Bennett

P.S. Note the address, which is for next week only. You addressed your letter 'Loire et Garonne', which, geographically, would be a devilish extensive department.   A. B.

173. On the beginnings of the Correspondence College, see Vol. I, pp. 74–75.

BERG / MS. / 174
(*To Ford Madox (Hueffer) Ford*)

Villa des Néfliers
9th Oct 1908

Dear Mr. Hueffer,

Many thanks for your letter of the 6th. The first word I had of your review was in last week's *Athenaeum*. This is not because I am not generally well informed as to English journalism, but because for a month past I have been travelling in the South and have read no paper, almost, except the *Dépêche de Toulouse*. Wells never writes except under obligation.

I shall be charmed to contribute to your review. I do not think I have any Five Towns stories unsold. I *had* one, which I took back from an editor who had commissioned it, on his ad misericordiam appeal to me that it was really too high-class! But I fancy that this is sold now. I will find out definitely. But are you in such a hurry? Why not give me a little time, and let me write you something in the vein of 'The Death of Simon Fuge', which possibly you have read?

The chief thing that I wish you in connection with the *English Review* is plenty of capital. You are certainly making a fine show to begin with.

I should much like to make your acquaintance. Are you ever in Paris? I do not expect to be in England before next March.

Believe me, with best wishes,

Sincerely yours, Arnold Bennett

174. Ford Madox (Hueffer) Ford (1873–1939) wrote to Bennett on the 6th, asking him if by any chance he had 'a Five Towns story that you think would do for me? If so, would you send it along? I know I am late in writing to you, but that is not from lack of admiration for your work, but simply because I have not the pleasure of your acquaintance.' He added that Wells had probably told Bennett about his new *English Review*, which was to begin publication in December 1908. The *Review* ran out of money within a year. Bennett's high-class story was 'The Glimpse', which was ultimately taken by the *New Age* (see Vol. I, pp. 102, 106).

TEXAS / MS. / 175
(*To Frank Harris*)

Villa des Néfliers
29 Oct 1908

Dear Frank Harris,

I was very glad to have your letter addressed to my pseudonym 'Jacob Tonson'. We have two intimate friends in common, Roy Devereux & Henry Davray, and we have certainly been on the very point of meeting for years past. I need not say that I shall be genuinely delighted to read *The Bomb*, & to do what I can for it—if in the meantime the *New Age* does not change hands! Nor need I say what I think of your work. *You* know as well as anyone what your work is, and you must be sure that anyone who can distinguish between literature and the other thing cannot fail to appreciate it very highly indeed. There is no author in England whom I should more like to meet than the author of *Montes*. You are often in France. When next you are over it would be a graceful act on your part to run down here. I myself live on literature, and as I spend over half my time producing work that will only be remunerative 50 years hence (if then), the task of living on literature is somewhat arduous, particularly for a man of expensive tastes! But I can do it down here, and maintain 'the dignity of letters'. Please come, therefore, and we will try that you shall not be disappointed.

I am expecting *The Bomb* by every post.

I expect that *Vanity Fair* has received a copy of my just published novel *The Old Wives' Tale*. It is extremely long. But I really should like to know what you think of it,—and its chances for 1958.

Yours sincerely, Arnold Bennett

175. Frank Harris (1856–1931) was at this time editor of *Vanity Fair*. His book *The Bomb*, published by John Long in 1908, was described by Bennett in a review in the *New Age* on 5 November as 'a book very courageous, impulsively generous, and of shining distinction'. Harris's collection of stories *Montes the Matador* was published in 1901, and when Bennett gave Harris his own collection entitled *The Matador of the Five Towns* (1912), he wrote in it: 'To Frank Harris, who has written better stories than any here.'

The *New Age* was in financial difficulty during most of Orage's tenure as editor.

On Henry Davray see page 213. Roy Devereux (Margaret Rose Roy Pember-Devereux, b. 1877) was a contributor to *Woman* and author of *The Ascent of Woman* and other books. She and Bennett were very close friends. *Whom God Hath Joined* is dedicated to her.

ILLINOIS / MS. / 176
(*To H. G. Wells*)

Villa des Néfliers
18 Nov 1908

My dear H. G.,

What am I to say in reply to your remarks? Considerable emotion caused in this breast thereby! Also no doubt a certain emotion in yours, as you cannot write such letters often!

We must strive to live up to this. That is all.

Orage has sent me your communication as to Frank Harris. Naturally, I was the reviewer. Harris was much moved by the review, & came down here to see me. He is certainly one of the most extraordinary men I ever met.

I am reading *1st & Last* which arrived a few days ago. As it isn't a novel I can't pontificate on it. However, when I have digested it I shall give you my ideas. There is no doubt whatever that it is a great deal too short, a very great deal. The *Westminster*'s objections to its tone are merely silly. Its tone, like that of *New W. fr. Old*, is perfect.

Yours ever, E. A. B.

I am getting rather tired of the *Westminster*.

BERG / MS. / 177
(*To Ford Madox (Hueffer) Ford*)

Villa des Néfliers
22 Nov 1908

Dear Ford Madox Hueffer,

I have been expecting that letter that you were going to write me, though I know you must be very busy. I send you this line to tell you that I am engaged upon a short ironic, humorous, but occasionally tragical sort of novel dealing with the mentality of the Yellow Press. It really ought to be called *What the Public Wants*. Have you read *A Great Man* or *Buried Alive*?

176. Wells wrote to Bennett about *The Old Wives' Tale*: 'It is all at such a high level that one does not know where to begin commending, but I think the high-light for me is the bakehouse glimpse of Sam Povey. But the knowledge, the detail, the spirit! from first to last it *never* fails. . . . Go on great man!'

First and Last Things was published in November 1908, *New Worlds for Old* in March.

This is in the same vein but of course far better! It would be useless for an ordinary serial, but to my mind it is the kind of thing that the *English Review* ought to pawn its soul for. I do not hope to place it as a serial. I merely, and hereby, give you formal notice that it will soon exist; so that you cannot say, as all editors *do* say: 'My dear fellow, if I had only known of that in time, I should have taken it like a shot!'

With best wishes,
Believe me,
Yours sincerely, Arnold Bennett

ILLINOIS / MS. / 178
(*To H. G. Wells*)

Villa des Néfliers
23 Nov 1908

My dear H. G.,

Those moments of 'worship' (p. 50). Of all the points in your book, this has most stuck in my mind. I wish you had enlarged on it, & not got out of it by referring to 'poverty of language'. I should like to have known what exactly you did mean—*do* mean. I regard this as the most important thing in the book, and it is not really handled. I myself have never, at any rate for 25 years, had the slightest movement towards worship or anything resembling worship. This is why I want to know what people do feel in that line.

p. 85 and p. 90—Against immortality & transmigration of souls. I think you are too summary here. Having regard to the enormous philosophic ingenuity of Buddhistic & kindred dogma, I don't see how you can dismiss transmigration of souls as imaginings of 'a race of children'. The memory difficulty has certainly been smoothed away for me. Here is another immensely important matter which I think you deal with too brusquely. By the way, I don't see the point of the references to Henley & Stevenson on p. 240. Personally (again) I am at present a believer in the transmigration of souls, as the theory which presents fewest difficulties. But if you can indicate to me any full attempt to make it seem impossible, I shall be glad to read the same.

177. The novel became the play of the same name.

After the above 2 matters, all others strike me as secondary.
There is an implied reference to 'Platonic' love on p. 211
which gives the reader to think that you think Plato brought
into prominence the notion of friendship between men &
women. I do not think this is so. My idea is that the phrase
'platonic love' has been quite changed in meaning, and that
Plato meant something quite different, and even more spiritual.
In other words I think you have carried on a popular error.
But I am not sure.

p. 169. 'Plane of the barrack yard higher' etc. This is enormously ingenious & effective. But it does not convince one. In
this military town I am a great watcher of soldiers, both in &
out of barrack yards, & although what you say is all right so
far as it goes, I would certainly put the plane of the barrack
yard *much* lower than the plane outside. Your remarks on the
future of war are A.1, and gave me light. The bit about cutting
an atom in two with a knife is extraordinarily illuminating.
This is what *I* call imagination.

Other matters that have stuck in my mind as being good,
fine, helpful, are

43. The ethics of controversy. I remember you once sat on
a Knight in the *Chronicle* for his crude notions of controversy.
79. The race walking in its sleep.
97. Gathering experience for the race.
(But you don't say where it's stored, anti-transmigra-
tionist.)
148. Ingenious reason for number of creeds in U.S.A.
192. Every theory has a finer offspring than itself.
245. *Thought has made me shameless.*
159. Against seceding.
195. All this against the popular notion of honour.
You will wake many sympathies here, I bet.
156. No 'beginning afresh'.
196. Against 'justice' and litigiousness. I like this much.
As you are undoubtedly a litigious person by nature,
this passage either speaks very well for your imaginative
power, or it is simply an ingenuous index of the change
going on in you. I think the latter. I think that *New W.
for Old* and this book show an immense development,

not in power, but in temper. They certainly increase one's *affection* for you.

It seems to me that you ought to make *1st & Last Things* a sort of annual, gradually enlarging it, & keeping it up to date. It must be of real value to anybody not absolutely crystallised into a hard, definite form. But either it contains too much, or it is too short.

For me, you scarcely justify your inclusion of 'metaphysics'. Nor do I consider that your metaphysics really *are* metaphysics. Metaphysics are inseparably connected with ontological specu-lation, the perfection of whose futility is unmatched by the futility of anything else in the universe. Whereas your remarks deal with phenomena. No. I will acquit you of metaphysics.

I shall read it all again. I can only criticise *novels*. I wish I hadn't read the first part of *Tono-Bungay* so *often*. I shall have to read it yet again in order to get the hang of the last part.

We are going to Switzerland (Mont Pélerin, above Vevey) for Xmas. We come to Britain in March. I am just finishing a Stage Society Play, about the Yellow Press.

Yours ever, A. B.

TEXAS / MS. / 179
(*To Edward Garnett*)

Villa des Néfliers
23 Nov 1908

Dear Edward Garnett,

(For I suppose it is you who have written the very masterly review of my novel in the *Nation*.) I just want to ask your opinion on one point. Have you read *A Great Man* and *Buried Alive*, two of my novels that do not deal with the Five Towns? If so, do you consider that in doing them I 'frittered myself away in pleasing the fourth-rate tastes of Philistia'? I do not seek to pin you to a phrase, but to have your opinion broadly, because I regard your opinion as a valuable one. Personally I

---

178. The letter mainly discusses *First and Last Things*. Bennett's interest in trans-migration was reflected in his novel *The Glimpse*, begun five months later, which is concerned with a man at the point of death.

Tono Bungay began appearing in the *English Review* in December 1908, and Bennett apparently had read proofs of the first part.

consider these two books just about as fine in the ironic vein as we are likely to meet with. I may tell you that I have no intention of sticking exclusively to the Five Towns. I often feel that I am short of room there. I do not think the third part (Paris) of *The Old Wives' Tale* is, on the whole, anything better than a first-class tour de force. Much of it is very good faking, but it is faking. You are wrong in assuming that Cyril's youth contains reminiscences, except as to stealing money. I was, however, never found out! Otherwise your review is a solid mass of rightness. I should be glad if you could spare a few minutes to reply to this.

Believe me,
Yours cordially, Arnold Bennett

BERG / MS. / 180
(*To Ford Madox (Hueffer) Ford*)

Villa des Néfliers
25 Nov 1908

My dear Ford Madox Hueffer,

In reply, I only asked you to write because your secretary had previously written: '*Mr. Hueffer will write to you himself in a few days.*'

I have only got one story in hand. I will not send it to you because I can place it elsewhere. I will only send to you something that is *too good* to be accepted by any other editor. I will do you something special by about the end of the year.

With regard to the serial, I will give you the opportunity of

179. In his review of *The Old Wives' Tale* in the *Nation* on 21 November 1908 Garnett singled out Book III as the weak spot, and thought the rest was superb. He noted that in a review of *The Grim Smile of the Five Towns* the previous year 'we pointed out that when the provincial [novelist] loses touch with his local types and local atmosphere and migrates to London, his artistic talent is usually frittered away in pleasing the fourth-rate tastes of Philistia'. He then goes on to say of *The Old Wives' Tale*: 'Most novelists are rarely quite one with their subject; a little above or below it. But Mr. Bennett really is his subject, the breath of it, intellectually, in a remarkable way.'

Garnett replied to Bennett's letter: 'If I overdid the "Philistia" business it is because I looked upon *The Grand Babylon Hotel* series as potboiling stuff absorbing so much of your development & energy. I read *A Great Man*, reviewed it, I believe, most favourably in *The Sphere*—but with all its justness & clever satire there is some element lacking in it: I think the detailed atmosphere is *generalized* instead of being particularized? *Buried Alive* I don't know.'

jumping at it for the August number. Like all my serious stuff it will be the best thing I have ever done!

A man like you is evidently too busy to read long letters. Hence I close.

Best wishes,

Yours sincerely, Arnold Bennett

P.S. I naturally count on you to keep the August opening open till you have seen my stuff. A. B.

BERG / MS. / 181
(*To Ford Madox (Hueffer) Ford*)

Villa des Néfliers
29 Nov 1908

Dear Ford Madox Hueffer,

I will try to arrange with the *Mercure de France*.

For the international political article, I think your best man would be Georges Villiers, of *Le Temps*. I don't know him. (Address *Le Temps*, Boul. des Italiens.) I could ascertain the names of other & less famous men, if you like. There are very few Frenchmen who have any international outlook that is worth a damn. They are comic in politics. I know Chéradame, who founded *L'Énergie Française* (the title of which review of course discloses his whole character). He knows all the facts, backwards, & is supposed to be a great authority on Austria. A lovable man, & taken seriously by everyone; but to me, politically, nothing but a vast joke. However, international politics is not my speciality; I am all for home politics, which are of course infinitely more important.

Why don't you ask Paul Adam to write about politics? He has a way of looking at them which is really quite *lyric*, and special.

Do you know the prose of Wilfred Whitten? If not read pp. 229–30 of Mrs. Laurence Binyon's *Nineteenth Century Prose* (Methuens, 1907). There is *none finer*. So there! And he ought to write for you.

I am much obliged to you for telling me that you have something in hand about 'The yellow press', as this fact changes my plans. My book on the Yellow Press has got to come out before anybody else's, and it will. Happily I have two novels on the stocks, and I think the other one will suit you better. Anyway I am counting on you for August. The book will not exceed 70,000 words.

By about the end of the year you will receive a long short story.

Yours ever, A. Bennett

TEXAS / MS. / 182
(*To Edward Garnett*)

Villa des Néfliers
29 Nov 1908

Dear Garnett,

Charmed with your letter. Your criticism of *A Great Man*—that it is too generalised—is a very good criticism. I quite agree with it. *Buried Alive* is better. I have no copies (except my own) of *Buried Alive* and *Whom God Hath Joined*. But next time I go to Paris I will get Tauchnitz's copies & send them to you.

I don't regard *Sacred & Profane Love* as anything more than a tour de force.

I don't regard *The Grand Babylon Hotel* etc, at all.

As to Jacob Tonson, you surprise me. Because really in criticism my fault is an impulsive generosity. Of course J.T. is 'agin the government'. That is what he exists for. He represents the creative artist, & he is the only representative in the press of that kind. I object to the general tone of the *New Age*, personally. But it is alive. Like all the contributors, I work for nothing; just for the fun & because I have an absolutely free hand. My stuff is not meant for seriously thought out criticism. It is far too hasty and facetious for that. But it *does* fairly indicate

181. Villiers is not known, unless he is Georges des Villiers, playwright and poet active at this time. André Chéradame (b. 1871) was a writer on social and political affairs. Paul Adam (1862–1920) was a novelist and essayist. Mrs. Laurence Binyon (née Cicely Margaret Powell), wife of the poet, was herself the author of several books. On Wilfred Whitten (*d.* 1942) see page 139 n.; he was currently on the staff of *T. P.'s Weekly*. In the event, the *English Review* did not publish a general international political article.

How far Bennett progressed with his serial novel version of *What the Public Wants* is unknown. Ford published the play itself as a Supplement to the *English Review* in July 1909. The other novel was presumably *The Card*, which Bennett began writing in January 1909.

a point of view, and it is a rare scorpion for the Robertson
Nicoll gang. Far from resenting your criticism of my criticism,
I am very much obliged to you for it.

The A's & the B's who tell you that you are a good critic are
immensely right. The only fault that I have to find with your
work is that sometimes you seem to be a little weary of literature,
& disillusioned. Or is it that the Aslaksen-like 'moderation' of
the *Nation* affects you? Mind you, I think the *Nation* out of sight
the ablest weekly. . . .

Your introductions to Turgenev's novels were an event in
my history—if that interests you.

Believe me,

Cordially yours, Arnold Bennett

FRANK HARRIS TO ARNOLD BENNETT / 183
(*From Frank Harris*)   *Vanity Fair*,
                                         33, Strand, [London] W.C.
                                         27th November, 1908

My dear Arnold Bennett,

I should have written before but have had two devilish law-
suits and have not only lost £500 but have had to find the sum
—not easy in these days!

And now, how am I to write to you? We represent the
extremes of two opposing theories of art. How you have been
able to do justice—and more than justice to me—I am unable
to imagine. I find it hard to do justice to you. I am indignant
with myself for want of generosity; but the truth will out, I am
angry with you. We owe each other frankness—you and I—
entire sincerity—that is the measure and proof of our mutual
esteem.

I've read your three books; but of course *The Old Wives' Tale*
is the one you would wish to be judged by. First of all, the
workmanship is astounding; finer far than George Moore's

---

182. Garnett wrote of Jacob Tonson: 'I think Jacob Tonson's tone in the
New Age is often *grudging*, even narrow! I don't mean in what he attacks, or because
he attacks; but because he doesn't often *define* fairly.' On Bennett's quarrel with
W. Robertson Nicoll (1851–1923) see Vol. I, pp. 140, 152, 155.

Aslaksen, a printer, is a character in Ibsen's play *The League of Youth*, said to be
based on N. F. Axelsen, who printed the periodical *Manden* with which Ibsen was
associated.

best; finer, I think, than Hardy's best. The style is always beyond reproach; thoughts, emotions, incidents, all perfectly clothed. The architecture too, as Goethe called the skeleton, superbly designed—no faults anywhere in design—no flaw. The storyteller's unique faculty everywhere apparent—then a masterpiece?

Half way through the book I thought so. I cried to my wife after reading Sophia's first adventure in Paris to her abandonment—'An amazing book! I must finish it'. Then the disappointment. You've made a fine creature, just when we are vitally interested in her and her tragic deception and the chances of her growth she falls to the ordinary! True to life, Yes perhaps—but not truer than the wild chance that she should pass the open portal into the future and become a symbol —magnificent. Half way through the book I envied you your amazing faculty for I thought you were going to do—what do I say? had done, a masterpiece—then—

If I am wrong you must forgive me. I thought you had painted the dull conventional English life of the home-staying, conventionally-correct sister at such length to give the contrast point, to make Sophia credible to us. I wanted her seduced and abandoned, and then I wanted her to take her life in her hand and go on making her body the servant of the spirit, determined to grow, to realize all that was in her, to get the knowledge she craved for, and to reach the heights! I saw, too, that such a woman would inevitably, sooner or later, come across some man big enough to appreciate her—a man who would have money, place, everything. The confession of such a woman to the man who loved her and whom she loved, seemed to me enormous. Then, the marriage, and the life in a foreign country, the great life she is born for, and then home yearnings and a visit to her stay-at-home sister and the contrast between the mangy tabby-cat and the superb wild animal.

And you could have done it all; your description of the execution and Sophia's rise above her ignoble husband—all show the true flame, and you preferred to bring her down to dulness and make her a lodging house drudge and quench her noble spirit in petty economies. You give her a muck-rake instead of a soul. It is all right but it depresses me, it disappoints me. This book seems to me but the pedestal of the statue. I want

R

the statue. Or is this merely a proof of my thirst for ideal things, for figures greater than life, carved out of some enormous cliff-side by a greater than Aeschylus. I should like to trace gigantic ebony figures out of the night itself with a flaming torch. I want the realism; but I want also to see the soul conquering its sur-roundings, putting the obstructions under its feet; heaping up the funeral pyre, if you will, from which the spirit may take flight.

You must not ask me for more than I can give. I am partly in sympathy with Ruskin's criticism when he talked about 'the weepings of a Pentonville omnibus'. If they live the usual Pentonville life and like-minded die the usual Pentonville death, then, I have no use for them. But Pentonville is as free to the night-winds and stars as any other part of this visible globe.

Now, my dear friend, I have done. I only wanted to write you this in my first free moment. Do you wish me to write it in the paper, *V. F.* if so, I will do it as well as ever I can. Send me a photograph of yourself to reproduce with it and I will do my best to make your popularity a little wider, as it should be, and your personality a little better known. In these matters I am now and always yours to command. . . .

But . . . [tell me] what you think of my Shakespeare book and Shakespeare play. Do not forget I must have both these back. Pray register them when you send them, and remember that I am longing to hear your judgment—make it absolutely sincere!

Yours ever, Frank Harris

TEXAS / MS. / 184
(*To Frank Harris*)

Villa des Néfliers
30th Nov 1908

My dear Harris,

I am not at the opposite pole to you. Because I am at both poles. I quite agree with your fundamental criticism of *The Old Wives' Tale*. That is to say, I quite agree with it in certain moods. I am capable of regretting that Sophia developed as she did. My original intention was to make her a magnificent courtesan. But I altered this, after due thought. I conceive that what she did in fact become was just as interesting & as good as anything else. What *you* want in life and in art is the *expensive* —I mean the spiritually expensive. I want it too. But not much of it (I did it in *Sacred & Profane Love*). At bottom I regard your attitude as flavoured with a youthful sentimentality. At bottom I am proudly content with the Pentonville omnibus. Why not? If I cannot take a Pentonville omnibus and show it to be fine, then I am not a fully equipped artist. (And I *am*.) Ruskin of course was a sublime sentimentalist. There is nothing better in my book than the return of Constance from the railway station after seeing Cyril off to London. Pure Pentonville! Not even sexual passion in it! If anyone says that such material & such an event are not proper for the very greatest possible art, I say that they are. (I never could argue!) People may talk about ideal art, heroic art. But let an artist get away from the *average* truth into an ideal of his own, & whatever he creates I will say to him: 'But I can imagine something more grand than that. Why the devil did you stop *there*?' What you wanted, in reading *The Old Wives' Tale*, was another book, but not a better one. To me the difference between one form of human life and another is insignificant. *It is all almost equally exciting.* That is my view. Someday I shall do another book in the expensive vein of *Sacred & Profane Love*. And then you will see. I shall be very much indebted to you if you will say in *Vanity Fair* exactly what you think of the novel. Go for it with all your fervour. If the article is as good as your letter it will be very good. But shove the article in at once or it will be commercially useless. I can't send you a photo, as I haven't one. I detest photos of myself.

I made the mistake of reading your Shakespeare play before your Shakespeare criticism. So I had to read the play again. I cannot expertly criticize the critical book, because I don't know enough. To me, as a piece of constructive criticism, it seems not the best piece of work of the kind that I ever read, but rather the *only* piece. It is merely and simply amazing. What of Coleridge I have ever had the patience to read is not to be compared to it. More damned nonsense has been talked about Shakespeare than on any subject on earth except metaphysics; and reading your book is like walking out of a lunatic asylum for Dowdens into an open field. What I should say of your portrait of Shakespeare is, in a very modified form, what Hume said of Berkeley's philosophy: 'It admitted of no answer, but produced no conviction.' The epigram is as false as epigrams usually are. What I mean is that you have to fight against a popular conception of Shakespeare which has been gradually growing up for over a century. To me, for example, your portrait was at first most disconcerting. I had an image of Shakespeare as a successful, hustling, jolly playwright of immense artistic power, *but somewhat disdaining that power*, and keen on material ends; always thinking of an easy old-age at Stratford. Of course I knew some of Hamlet was in him, but I thought it was quite lost for practical purposes in practical qualities. I thought there was a great deal of Falstaff in Shakespeare (as there was in Balzac). You smash my image to atoms, but it keeps reconstructing itself again in spite of you—from mere habit. I shall have to get used to it. (I express myself ill, because I am off my own line.) For the general public your book is at least 30 years before its time. And in 30 years (or so) people will be beginning to admit that in the way of constructive criticism it marked an era. (I assume that it is not finished. If it *is* finished, I consider it lacks at least a summing up. I think *I* could find a publisher for it.)

I thank God (except financially) that Tree never produced your play. What a hades of a mess the cabotin would have made of this character! My objections to the play are purely technical. I do not think that the subject emerges clearly. It is too episodic, and there is too much movement and too many characters. The whole thing (always in my opinion) needs an immense simplification—which would chiefly amount to an elaboration of the principal scenes and the cutting down or destruction of the others. Particularly, I do not think that Shakespeare himself emerges with sufficient weight; il ne s'impose pas assez, I mean. I perfectly admit that, realistically, he would be as you have made him. Where I venture (with diffidence & respect) to find fault with you is in the degree of realism that you have aimed at. Of course absolute realism is impossible in any art; but you have tried to write a play on the same plane of realism as a novel or a story. It cannot be done. The mechanism won't permit it, being far too clumsy. I do not think that, in a performance, you would get the effects which you have tried at. I think the girl Fritton is very wonderful, but I only think this by dint of allowing all the time for the constant error which I consider you commit. I wonder if you understand what I mean. What is more important than this—I think that, as regards the character of Shakespeare, you have slightly exaggerated in the play the special qualities which you have discovered in him by means of your critical method in the other book. And chiefly his intense sweetness and Christlike sympathetic understanding. In fact I think he resembles what an artist-Christ would be. He is idealised. I may as well obey you & be frank to the last word—I think he is a little sentimentalised. I know this will infuriate you. The play as a whole is too subtle; it is very beautiful, but its effect is one of over-subtlety, and this I count as a technical defect.

I have looked through *The Bomb* again. I can't really substantiate the sole charge I made against it. Such roughnesses as I had in mind are no doubt part of the narrator's character. But the sort of thing I mean (trivial enough) is this. On p. 1 for instance. Why do you make him say he is dying of consumption? We know these narrators who write from a consumptive's bed. They exist in thousands in fiction. I don't say you had not a right to have him dying of consumption; but I say it was a clumsiness to let him begin by saying so. He could have slipped the fact in later, with no sacrifice to truth. Then the second & 3rd paragraphs of the same page both begin with 'But'. It is nothing, of course. But these three things together produce a faint adverse effect on the highly sensitive reader to whom you appeal. And I call the producing of that effect a clumsiness on your part, and a proof that you do not write (highly finished stuff) enough. On reflection, this p. 1 is as good an example as I could find of what I mean. I attach only an infinitesimal importance to my criticism. And of course you may say that the effect was a calculated one.

I shall return the books by registered post in a day or two. And I am extremely obliged to you for letting me have them.

Yours ever, Arnold Bennett

P.S. I need not say that I am relying on you to write, *soon*, another of those 'dozen novels which you have in you'.   A. B.

P.S.2. Sorry about the £500.   A. B.

TEXAS / MS. / 185   Hôtel Belvédère
(*To Frank Harris*)   Mont Pélerin
                                         Sur Vevey, Switzerland
                                         13 Dec 1908
My dear Harris,
    I got your book & letter this morning, & another letter on
Friday. To my regret I have already swallowed the book, & as
we go to Switzerland tomorrow (address above till further
notice) I write at once. I think the book in the main wonderful,
& I read it greedily. If I was writing for the public about it I
should at once become lyrically enthusiastic, & point out all
its merits. I cannot do this to you. I don't know why, except
that it seems absurd for me to do so. I have an enormous

184. When he first conceived Sophia, Bennett wrote of her in the Journal, on
18 November 1903: 'The other [sister] should have become a whore and all that;
"guilty splendour". Both are overtaken by fat. And they live together again in
old age, not too rich, a nuisance to themselves and to others.' Not long before he
sat down to write the novel, he had other thoughts about her, which are recorded
in a portion of the journal published only in *Life and Letters*. The entry begins with
a description of a French peasant woman seen the previous evening.
    'She was an old woman harnessed to a cart containing merchandise whose
nature I could not distinguish. On either side of her was harnessed a dog about
as big as a pointer. An old man stalked majestically behind, at a distance of
several yards, carrying a very long staff and uttering at regular intervals a
mournful cry concerning his wares. The old woman was, in the accepted phrase,
"little more than a brute", and there was no doubt about it, no concealment
of it. . . .
    I knew that Sophie [sic], the second heroine of *The Old Wives' Tale*, was going
to live in France and be almost French, and I felt a tremendous naughty temptation to make the daughter of the most respectable Bursley draper sink in the
world and end her days as the companion of dogs in front of a cart. Why not?
What an outcry in the literary columns of the British press! What foamings at
the mouth of outraged critics! And how it would somehow serve them right and
do them good! However, I successfully fought and slew the temptation. Only
authors know the dazzling temptations of authorship.'
Harris reviewed *The Old Wives' Tale* in *Vanity Fair* on 9 December, and paraphrased
parts of his own letter and Bennett's.
Harris's play was *Shakespeare and His Love*, which was published in 1910; his
book was *The Man Shakespeare*, published 1909. Ernest Dowden (1843–1913),
professor of English at the University of Dublin, was author of several books on
Shakespeare.

opinion of myself, & you are the first man I have met in the flesh who I consider understands the craft of literature better than I do. Indeed I have never yet met anyone else whom I could regard even as an equal (because Conrad is so damned clumsy, constructively). As I cannot without forcing myself say to you direct my paeans of admiration, you must take all that for granted. Talking to an artist, it comes much more natural to me to criticize coldly, & to take for granted that the stuff is first-rate. When I say that I was disgusted at the shortness of the skimpy volume-let, that is about as good praise as I can offer. I have no comment to make on 'The Stigmata'. Which means that I don't see how it can be improved. I suppose the basis must have been used fairly often before. You have arranged it and embroidered it very subtly and honestly, and the effect is *got*. Has it ever occurred to you what a fine story, really, 'The Procurator of Judaea' might have been if Anatole France had possessed in any degree the gift of construction?

I think the raw material of 'The Irony of Chance' is finer. (This book ought to be called *Frank Harris's Book of Moral Tales*. For their 'morals' are appallingly impressive.) The idea of this particular story is 'great' (in the jolly, familiar sense). I want to criticize some details of the handling of it. A purely romantic story needs all the help it can possibly have from realistic treatment, & I think you have been too sparing in realistic details, & that some of your detail is scarcely well chosen. Mortimer's leading principle is thoroughly scientific—it is this kind of thing that is the highest flight of pure science. Why then this talk about mysterious numbers, 9's and 7's, and $7 \times 7 = 49$? This is not scientific. I do not believe that Mortimer believed in it. And even granting (for argument) that there is an occult quality in the number 7, that property, in a mathematical question, can only come out in the *relations* of numbers one to another. You might state, as a curious fact, that something was 7 times something else. But you say 7×7 *inches*. Why inches? Why not centimetres or centipedes? Then, as regards the casting of the hollow sphere. It is manifestly impossible to cast a hollow sphere in a mould, or to cast a hollow sphere entire in any way. A hollow sphere must be cast in at least two parts, & then joined. You say: 'I had made the mould hollow in order to get a skin of metal an inch thick.' How? My dear sir, it would not

convince your aunt, if you have one. You may say these details
are trifling. But when I read a story I see everything that happened, whether the author describes it or not. And I believe
intensely in the cumulative effect of details. A succession of
unconvincing details will wear away, or wear thin, the *sanction*
of a story, like water dropping on a stone. What I think is worse
is (p. 30) 'the laws that made the world had made my sphere'
(apropos of its oblate spheroidal form). No, sir! Nothing of the
kind. If your sphere had gone through the same process as the
earth, & been subjected to centrifugal & centripetal forces
caused by rotation, in a semi-fluid state, then it would have had
flattened ends. But that it should have had flattened ends after
being cast is to my mind a flat contradiction of 'the laws that
made the world', & it strikes a blow at the convincingness of
the tale. You may curse, but I regard the action of these world-
laws on your sphere not merely as quite unscientific, but as
sentimental. In regard to absence of detail, I think the circumstances attending the misapprehension as to the boy's departure
are insufficiently dealt with. Also the making of the hole. But
it is a thundering fine story. Now this amazing discovery of
Mortimer's and his exhibitions of it (whether credited or not)
would have made a terrific stir in the world. The public would
undoubtedly have been very excited, with the help of the *Daily
Mail*. There must have been a great effect on the public, and a
re-action from the public on to the characters of the story. Of
all this, in your story, scarcely a word. You have got the story
into a sort of water-tight compartment. Nevertheless the 'noise'
that the circumstances would have made is the first thing one
thinks of, & your almost ignoring of this gives the same effect
as the absence of landscape in novels previous to Walter Scott.

In 'Mr. Jacob's Philosophy', I suppose you had a reason for
making Mr. Jacob the conventional Jew (almost the Jew of
fiction), but I haven't hit on what the reason was. I know that
Jews with the outward characteristics of Jacob do exist. I have
several Jewish friends, quite intimate, & you could tell they
were Jews a mile off. But they are not greasy etc, though they
are fine judges of bric-a-brac. I seem to fancy that a less
obviously Jewish Jew would have suited your purpose equally
well. This is a mere fancy in the dark, & perhaps wrong.

I think 'The Magic Glasses' is the best thing in the book. It is noble. No spots on it. The narrative of Mr Penry himself, beginning on p. 13, is the best workmanship in the whole book, straightforward skill, and no frills. 'Solide facture' as we say here! The little girl at the end is immensely right, & she might so easily have 'mucked up the whole show'.

Here too, I suspect something of the water-tight compartment. The question is: how far these realistic allegories ought to *be* realistic. I cannot profess to be able to judge, as I can't do 'em, myself.

Every novelist (& dramatic poet) has his favourite character which he draws over and over again. You know how often Wells has drawn his Kipps. *My* character is Critchlow in *The Old Wives' Tale*. He keeps recurring (under different names, with slight changes) in my stuff. Yours is Shakespeare!! Have you noticed this? Joshua—Christ, Mortimer, & Penry,—they are all three the same man as the hero of your play—more or less, that is.

Your review of me was a most gorgeous affair, & gave great joy. But I don't know anybody else that could have successfully carried it off, at that pitch. What pleases me, of course, is that the article was bursting with the fact, between all its lines, that the writer of it was a man who knew what he was talking about. Nearly all the praise one gets is so infernally wrong, and out of shape. As though the critic had arranged a nice little piece of praise & then dropped it in the street & let a motor car run over it. Your choice of extracts did my heart good.

I violently disagree with you as to Élémir Bourges. I defy you to put your hand on your heart & say you have read the *Nef* all through. The only decently readable passage in all Bourges owes all its interest to John Ford. When I came to France I found in most literary circles a tremendous veneration for Bourges, & I flatter myself I have converted every Bourgesian I have met except Stuart Merrill. Bourges is 'la scie'. Men who have got something to say don't take 12 years to write a book and 2 years to correct the proofs. Bourges is without creative power, and no precisity of justesse in the use and balance of words can hide the fact. I will have none of him. I will have none of him, & I will have none of him!

Have you read Paul Claudel?

I have finished my play about the yellow press, & sent it to the Stage Society. It is entitled *What the Public Wants*. It is a joyful thing, and would please you. If the Stage Society fight shy of it, it will be because they don't want to tilt at the most powerful interests in Fleet St. But I think they don't care a damn for anybody, & that they will perform it.

By the way, as to your main criticism of *The Old Wives' Tale*, I fully recognise its force, & about half the time I agree with it.

I am just going to write a long short story for the new *English Review*. And then I shall do a shortish novel about the familiar theme of a man who is laid out for dead, but who comes back to life. I don't know why I should have been saddled with this notion, but I seem to see something rather fine at the other end of the tunnel. The thing will really be a short story which runs to the length of a novel.

I hope you will go on with the stories, & that we shall meet in March next. I want to have a whole series of yarns with you. I wish I had met you about 15 years ago.

I return the book by registered book post, & I shall hope to hear from you in Switzerland. Very many thanks, for everything.

> Yours ever, Arnold Bennett

BERG / MS. / 186
(*To Ford Madox (Hueffer) Ford*)

> Hôtel Belvédère
> 30th Dec 1908.

Dear Hueffer,

I send you by registered book post 'A Matador of the 5 Towns'. As a painter once said to me in handing over a sketch which I had bought from him, 'I think this will give you pleasure.' You asked for it to be long. It is a page or two shorter than Hy. James's story in the first number: between

185. The Bennetts stayed in Switzerland for three months.

Harris's collection of stories was *Unpath'd Waters*, apparently published privately. John Lane issued an edition of it in 1913.

Élémir Bourges (1852–1925) published his popular drama *La Nef* in 1904. The work of Paul Claudel (1868–1955) pleased Bennett a good deal more. Stuart Merrill (1863–1915) was an American–French poet.

What the Public Wants was produced by the Stage Society on 2 May 1909 at the Aldwych Theatre. A commercial production followed at the end of the month.

Bennett's novel *The Glimpse* was based upon his short story of the same name.

11 & 12,000 words. Kindly acknowledge receipt to me, and settle the price with Pinker & pay him in due course. I perceive from your contents page that you must have regular dealing with Pinker. I haven't yet seen your second number, but the first was a source of deep joy to me.

Best wishes,

Yours sincerely, Arnold Bennett

P.S. I couldn't get the stuff typewritten here—3,100 feet above civilisation. My apologies. A. B.

BERG / MS. / 187
(*To Violet Hunt*)

Hôtel Belvédère
7 Jan 1909

My dear Lady,

Well, this enthusiasm & ardour of yours for *The Old Wives' Tale* is highly creditable to both of us. I can't send you a copy of it. I have only one. I now make a practice of having only one copy of my books. But if you have read it, it is graven on your heart. I have sent you a little book which is a great bibliographical rarity. Of course if you are going to say that Balzac is superior to Stendhal, I will agree that he is, in his range. But Balzac never wrote anything so *fine* (in the true sense of the word) as *La Chartreuse de Parme*. That I am superior to de Morgan is of course true. I should be the last to deny it. What annoys me is occasional remarks, in reviews, that I am imitating de Morgan, of his 'school' etc. I had written a dozen books before de Morgan ever published anything at all, at least four of them far better than the clever old gent could possibly do.

We hope to see you in March. We shall be in London & in the 5 Towns for about a month.

Kindest regards from us to yourself & your mother, who remains vividly in my memory.

Yours sincerely, Arnold Bennett

186. 'The Matador of the Five Towns' appeared in the *English Review* in April 1909. Henry James's story was 'The Jolly Corner'. He shared the first issue with Hardy, Conrad, Galsworthy, Wells, W. H. Hudson, and Tolstoy. On J. B. Pinker (1863–1922) see Vol. I.

187. William de Morgan (1839–1917), a latter-day Dickensian, published his novels (*Joseph Vance, Alice-for-Short*) late in life.

ILLINOIS / MS. / 188
(*To H. G. Wells*)

Hôtel Belvédère
7 Jan 1909

My dear H. G.,

Many thanks. *Some*one has been doing some spadework for *The Old Wives' Tale*, so I put it down to you. I expected it to be an absolute frost, naturally, & it was at first. But after about a month it began to sell. It went into a modest second edition, & the last I hear is that it is selling regularly. Anyhow, I have had some really pleasing reviews. Of course any article from you would have been butter on my bread. I think enough has been said about Stephen Reynolds for some time to come. But I put him very much higher than Edwin Pugh, & I have a great admiration for him. I don't know yet about Hueffer, but I'm sure the *English Review* won't last unless he alters it considerably. I've written him an A1 short story, which he had the wit to commission, so that I will partly forgive him for not trumpeting the book. I am informed that my new play is 'simply terrific'. Why can't you come over to Switzerland now, and have a time?

Our loves to you both,

Yours ever, E. A. B.

TEXAS / MS. / 189
(*To Edward Garnett*)

Hôtel Belvédère
9 Jan 1909

My dear Garnett,

Many thanks for your letter, which is comforting. The only character in *W. G. Hath J.* that I consciously put some of myself into, is Mark Ridware, & in that I was 'assez rosse' towards A. B. I think there is a good bit of C. Fearns in most of us.

This letter is about another matter. No doubt you know all about Frank Harris; the high quality of his literary work & the

---

188. Wells tried unsuccessfully to get *The Old Wives' Tale* reviewed in the *English Review*. Stephen Reynolds (1881–1919) made a considerable name for himself in 1908 with *A Poor Man's House*. Edwin Pugh (1874–1930) wrote popular novels about lower-class life.

quality of his reputation in litigious cases. I have only met him once, but on the literary plane we have become very intimate. I never met in the flesh any man who comprehends literature as he does. He has written a book drawing the character of Shakespeare from the plays. Part of it has been privately printed, & it seems to me the most remarkable exegetical work of the kind ever done. As to its quality there can be no doubt whatever. It is in the first flight. Do you think, prima facie, that Duckworths would care to publish it? I should be indebted to you if you would write me a candid line, which I should regard as confidential. I need not say more.

With kind regards,

Yours sincerely, Arnold Bennett

P.S. I have never told you of my satisfaction at your publishing my friend George Sturt's book.   A. B.

TEXAS / MS. / 190
(*To Frank Harris*)

Hôtel Belvédère
29 Jan 1909

My dear Harris,
   Many thanks for yours of the 27th. I shall be extremely interested to read the book as a whole, but I shall certainly not attempt to offer you any effective advice about its final form. I am not competent to do this. With regard to publishers you will find that immediately they begin to make money out of you, they will lick your boots. And not till then! Yes, I will meet you in Geneva, with much pleasure. But I would sooner meet you at Lausanne or here. If you get to Geneva you are

189. Duckworth did not publish Harris. They published Sturt's *Memoirs of a Surrey Labourer* in 1907 and his *Change in the Village* in 1912. In 1909 in the *New Age*, Bennett wrote of the *Memoirs*, which was just going into a cheap edition: 'There have been a handful of persons who were determined to make this exceedingly fine book sell, or perish themselves in the attempt; and it has sold. But not with the help of the mandarins. It is too proud, too austere, too true, and too tonically cruel to appeal to mandarins. . . . Mr. George Bourne's description of his hero's death would no doubt put them right off. I give it in full: "July 25 (Thursday).—Bettesworth died this evening at six o'clock." Oh, Colonel Newcome, sugared tears, golden gates, glimmering panes, passing pilots, harbour bars —had Mr. George Bourne never heard of you?'

bound to go home through Lausanne, & it would be just as easy for you to debark at Lausanne as at Geneva. I don't know how you mean to get to Geneva from Nice without putting yourself to trouble. Much better go into Italy & come home by the Simplon. You will get a through carriage to Vevey. However I will meet you at any reasonable place. We leave here for Paris & London on Mch 1st.

Yours ever, A. B.

TEXAS / MS. / 191
(*To Ford Madox (Hueffer) Ford*)   37 Clarendon Road
Putney S.W.
26th Mch 1909

[no salutation]

The fact is, my dear Hueffer, that I should like to come and see you and have a chat, but the feeling that I have something against you would impair the naturalness of my demeanour.

I consider that either you or circumstances have got the better of me in regard to the story I wrote for you. In settling the price with Pinker you gave him to understand (wittingly or unwittingly) that the original overtures had come from me, that I had begun by offering you a serial and that on declining this you had by way of good nature suggested that you might like to see a short story. Accepting this as a basis Pinker agreed to an absurd price for the story.

There was no foundation whatever for all this. The overtures came from you & they were urgent and repeated, and quite spontaneously you said you would pay me a good price. I have all the correspondence: I made no mention of a serial until the story was arranged for. A man with your knowledge of the literary world must be aware that my ordinary serial price is at least four guineas a thousand, whereas you are paying me two and a half. Briefly I consider that I am nineteen pounds out of pocket on that story. And I should be surprised to hear that you consider $2\frac{1}{2}$ guineas a thousand a 'good price' for me.

Of course what Pinker arranges is final. I should never have referred to the matter if your note of the 10th had not seemed to me to make a little statement on my part desirable. And having regard to that note I am quite sure that **you** have no consciousness of having negotiated with Pinker on a wrong

basis and do not suspect that I have a grievance. So I tell you.
Believe me,
Yours cordially, Arnold Bennett
P.S. Many thanks for the extra proofs.

TEXAS / MS. / 192
(*To William Lee Mathews*)

Villa des Néfliers
24 June 1909

Dearest William,

Many thanks for your letters. I was very sorry to hear about
Hankin. I am writing something about him which you will see

191. 37 Clarendon Road was the new home of the Kennerleys. They moved
there in December 1906. Bennett was in England for the rehearsals of *What the
Public Wants*.
In *The Last Pre-Raphaelite* Douglas Goldring gives some additional details about
Bennett's quarrel with Ford. On 24 November 1908 Ford suggested the possibility
of a serial for the August number, and asked again for a Five Towns story before
then. A few days later he wrote again to say 'please remember that I want a short
story—of any length as long as it is long, and that I will pay a pretty good price
for it'. Bennett referred him to Pinker for settlement of the matter. Ford replied
to Bennett's present letter with an apology and an explanation (quoted in part in
Vol. I, p. 121), and eventually Bennett went to a party at Ford's, where Goldring
witnessed their reconciliation. The affair was not over, though. In 1913 in the
Outlook Ford made an amusing and slapdash attack on Bennett's lighter novels,
and then went on to say of 'The Matador of the Five Towns':
'I don't know a better piece of work in the English language, or a job better
executed. I had the honour of publishing it in the *English Review*. Naturally Mr.
Bennett quarrelled with me about the price I paid his agent for this piece of
work. He would. And in the midst of a rather grotesque correspondence I made
this distinguished author's acquaintance. (He persisted in saying that his work
was worth many, many hundreds of pounds, and I retorted that he had chosen
to send it me through an agent, and that the price was agreed. And, as I am
not really a business man, it seemed to me that I was in the right!)'
Bennett replied in a letter published on 11 October:
'Sir,—Mr. Ford Madox Hueffer's exactitude of reminiscence is so notorious
that a slip on his part becomes a remarkable phenomenon and ought to be
signalised. In his article on myself he states that I quarrelled with him about
the price of a short story for the *English Review*. This is not so. I accepted without
protest the sum which he paid to my agent. Soon afterwards he asked me to
dinner. I replied in sorrow that I could not come to dinner, as I considered
that he had done me in the eye over the price of the short story. He wrote to
ask me by how much I considered he had done me in the eye. I answered, by at
least ten pounds. He sent me a cheque for ten pounds. I attended his dinner. We
have been excellent friends ever since. Such are the facts of a singular episode,
and I possess documentary proofs of them.—Yours truly, Arnold Bennett.'
For other details of the relationship see Vol. I, *passim*.

under my pseudonym, 'Jacob Tonson', in next week's *New Age*. In this week's *New Age*, I have a few remarks about the theatre which may interest you.

Don Juan

I send the complete scenario by registered book post. I hope this will put you out of your misery. I hope also that Tree knows how to judge a scenario—how to see the play *in* it. If this scenario suits, I can deliver the play by the end of October. I may tell you it will be very good. Of course I shall do nothing whatever further without a definite commission and £100.

W. The P.W.

Does Hawtrey really mean to revive it? Or is he only saving his face?

Curious how capricious the receipts are! But they go up each week. And anyhow we cannot complain of a failure, as we have held all along that the piece would not succeed with the public, for whom by the way it was not written.

Trench. Haymarket

It must be remembered that I have *promised* to furnish a scenario to Trench, upon which, if it suits him, he will commission a play. I have the idea for this play. In case it doesn't suit him, the idea which I have would do for Marie Tempest. But I think it *will* suit him. Anyhow it is a great idea. I got it during influenza. A light comedy—continuous laughter. Title *The Honeymoon*. By the way, chumps have said that *W.T.P.W.* 'fell off' because the audience didn't laugh as much towards the end as at the beginning. My aim was not to make them laugh. The laughter in *W.T.P.W.* was purely incidental embroidery on a moral work. When I set out to make an audience laugh, I will guarantee to keep them laughing continuously, & more & more till the very end; till their sides ache as they go home. I know I can do this, & I shall do it in *The Honeymoon*. I take no credit for being able to do it. It is a mere trick that I was born with, of being able to make people giggle whenever I want.

Love, A. B.

192. William Lee Mathews (d. 1931) was Bennett's dramatic agent for several years. He was a businessman whose real interest was the theatre. He succeeded Shaw as Chairman of the Producing Committee of the Stage Society in 1905.

St. John Hankin (1869–1909), author of *The Cassilis Engagement* and other plays,

LANE / MS. / 193
(*To Frederic Chapman*)

Villa des Néfliers
10th July 1909

My dear Chapman,
To whom does the copyright belong of Le Gallienne's Háfiz lyric beginning

> Little Sleeper
> The Spring is here
> Tulip & rose are come again

?

If it belongs to R. Le G. do you suppose you could infinitely oblige me by writing to him & asking if he will consent to its publication to music by a young English composer named Havergal Brian—who has set it in the most exquisite fashion? Or are you not on such terms with R. Le G.

My wife's kind regards,
Yours sincerely, Arnold Bennett

P.S. Or could Lane grant permission?

---

had recently drowned himself, and Bennett wrote of him in the *New Age* on 1 July: 'I should scarcely care to say that he was a distinguished dramatist, though, of course, the least of his works is infinitely more important in the development of the English theatre than the biggest of the creaking contrivances for which Sir Arthur Wing Pinero has recently received honour from a grateful and cultured Government.' The previous week Bennett had written: 'Most decidedly there are not at present enough good dramatists to meet the demands of two artistic stages.'

The scenario of *Don Juan* was written expressly for Sir Herbert Beerbohm Tree, who is reported in the Journal as having decided that 'he hadn't enough dash to carry it off'. The completed play was written in a few weeks at the end of 1913 and the beginning of 1914. No one else was ever found with enough dash to carry it off. For further detail see Vol. I, *passim*.

What the Public Wants was produced commercially by Charles Hawtrey (1858–1923) at the Royalty Theatre on 27 May 1909 after two weeks of rehearsal. It ran for only a month.

Herbert Trench (1865–1923) was director of the Haymarket Theatre in 1909. He accepted *The Honeymoon*, which is certainly Bennett's most amusing play, but then did not produce it, and it was taken by Marie Tempest, who starred in it in 1911.

193. Havergal Brian (1876–), who has set many English lyrics to music, was struck by the Persian poem—as translated by Richard Le Gallienne (1866–1947)—one day while riding a tram in the Five Towns, and he set it to music, and it was performed for two or three years before he thought of the question of copyright. Arnold Bennett's aid was enlisted to find Le Gallienne, and the poet was finally located in a New York hospital, but not before Brian himself had given up and commissioned Gerald Cumberland to write new lyrics. Brian grew up in Staffordshire, and was a frequent guest in the Bennett household.

S

TEXAS / MS. / 194
(*To William Lee Mathews*)

Villa des Néfliers
14th Augt 1909

Dearest William,

We shall be delighted if you come. Had we known earlier we would have offered you a room etc. But we arrange our programme with a series of friends so that our space is always occupied. We have two spare rooms, but they can only be occupied by two people who are married or of the same sex, as there is a common cabinet de toilette for the two. And we shall have a young lady here during your stay. We can however shut one room off, & this room shall be your study and rest-room, it being fitted up for such. So that you won't need a sitting room at a hotel; a quite needless expense for you. The new Hotel Savoy is 2 minutes from this house. It is swagger & pretty good & large. Besides this there is only one other hotel near to, quite small, & near the station. We are on the other side the park from the town & the group of hotels. You will only want your bed & bath & petit déjeuner at the hotel. I think the Savoy will be your mark more than the other one, it being the ordinary hotel de luxe of commerce. But you can let me know. In other respects this house will be your home & you shall have a week (& as much more as you care for) in the life of a professional writer and painter (for he paints too).

I have told Iden Payne that he can't have *W.T.P.W.* until he has played *C. & C.*

I should like you to come as soon as possible—at any rate so as to have got in a good week before Sep. 7. About then I have my brother & sister-in-law coming, & they will occupy me so much as to make it difficult for me properly to savour your society. My brother is a first-class 22 carat pal; but my sister-in-law is merely an excellent woman who suits *him*. My wife's expressions of her desire for your presence, et salutations.

Alors, amuse-toi,
Yours, A. B.

194. During his adolescence Bennett was much more interested in painting than in writing, and when he was first in Paris he attended the Post-Impressionist Academy. He tells something of the latter experience in 'Graphic Art in Paris', in *Things That Have Interested Me* (1921). For examples of his sketching see the

KEELE / MS. / 195
(*To Margaret Marriott*)
                              [Chartres]
                              [postmarked 31 August 1909]
[no salutation]
    Chartres is the place you ought to have come to for a few days picturesqueness. The cathedral is the finest I ever saw. I came here yesterday & return home tomorrow morning. Today I have done two water colour sketches & one b. and w. I am really tired with working. The town is on a hill in the centre of the largest plain in France, and a river runs half way round it. The colour of the cathedral is marvellously beautiful. I trust you are now both in health.
                                          Love, A. B.

BIRMINGHAM / MS. / 196
(*To John Galsworthy*)
                              Villa des Néfliers
                              5th Sept 1909
My dear Galsworthy,
    Many thanks for yours of the 13th. I have been holidaying about. By this time you will have read *Montes the Matador*. Isn't it a great thing? I have got Marjoram's book and will refer to it. I have also been making a study of *The Country House*. You are one of the most cruel writers that ever wrote English. This statement I will die for. I don't know what made me read the book again, unless it was a curiosity to penetrate your future. Or perhaps to find material to say something malicious about you somewhere. I need not inform you that I tinglingly admire your stuff and that it enormously 'intrigues' me. But I do seriously object to your attitude towards your leading characters. And I have the effrontery to think that it will modify itself —is doing so. Of course, I could write reams about *The C.H.*
    I am now writing a play that Trench has commissioned. I shan't begin a new novel till 1st January.

Journal, Vol. II, and *Florentine Journal* (Chatto and Windus, 1967).
    Iden Payne (1881–) was Miss Horniman's producer in Manchester from 1907 to 1911.
    Bennett's brother Frank and his wife Florence were the family visitors.
    195. Margaret Hannah Marriott (d. 1938), Frederick Marriott's wife.

We are coming to London in Decr—at any rate passing through it.

Kindest regards to you both from us.

Yours sincerely, Arnold Bennett

BUTLER / MS. / 197
(*To Cedric Sharpe*)

Villa des Néfliers
30 Oct 1909

My dear Cedric,

The receipt of your song gave me very great pleasure. I cannot criticize it. In fact it took me all my time to read it, as I cannot easily decipher musical MS. But I was glad to observe that you have already acquired a distinct and rather distinguished style in musical MS. I reckon myself a bit of an authority on style in MS. I also liked your choice of words to set to music. I also liked the music, but more than this I can't say about it, as my impressions are so vague.

I want more. Indeed I want 8 and I won't W8. So go ahead. You will never arrive at the expression of your own personality unless you keep on composing & composing.

I have a water colour for you. I can't tell till after this letter goes whether the drawing can be sent by parcel post. But if it can I shall send it tomorrow or Monday. If it can't I shall bring it in December. If it gives you as much pleasure as the mere fact of having your song gives me, you are in velvet with it.

Our loves to you all.

Yours, A. B.

196. John Galsworthy (1867–1933) and Bennett met for the first time in April 1909 at Ford Madox Ford's home. Bennett wrote in the Journal: 'Slight *gêne* on my part . . ., seeing my recent articles on him.' The two men became good friends, but Bennett never cared very much for Galsworthy's work, and especially objected to his partisan attitude towards his characters.

J. Marjoram was the pseudonym of R. H. Mottram (1883–), author in more recent years of *Scenes That are Brightest* and many other novels.

The new novel was *Clayhanger*, begun on 5 January 1910.

197. Cedric Sharpe (1891–), distinguished cellist, was the son of Bennett's friend Herbert Sharpe. For Cedric's childhood correspondence, presumably with Bennett, see page 100 n.

Beginning with *The Old Wives' Tale*, Bennett's manuscripts were written in a fine calligraphic hand, with occasional decorations. See further, Vol. I, p. 363.

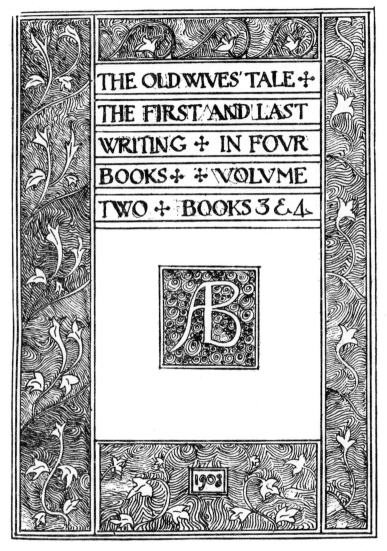

Facsimile of the title page of Volume II of the manuscript of *The Old Wives' Tale*, with Bennett's preliminary markings for the title showing

TEXAS / MS. / 198
(*To Frank Harris*)

Villa des Néfliers
30th Oct 1909

My dear F H,

Many thanks.

Snobbishness. In Shakespeare's time & much later an affection for courts and titles (combined with a corresponding antipathy to the common 'folk') was a perfectly proper affection, & did not involve the disdain of intelligent people. The course of evolution has changed this. The word 'snob' distinctly includes the idea of vulgarity and pretentiousness, and I consider it to be inapplicable to Shakespeare's case. Sycophancy is better, but even sycophancy is *much too strong*. Shakespeare was of his time in this matter: that is all.

Pembroke. There are several sonnets which seem to me (as a layman) to exclude the idea of innocence with Pembroke. All I say is that you have not absolutely convinced me that I am wrong. The fact is you do not say much in support of your contention of innocence. You rather assume innocence because he sent Pembroke to Mary. Why should he not have had a liaison with Pembroke during the earliest stages of his 'naissant' passion for Mary? If you say the idea is revolting, I say that I don't think it is. It wouldn't revolt me, & I think it would take a lot to revolt a man of Shakespeare's intelligence. High intelligence is seldom revolted. I admit, [? to my regret], that I am as an infant in the matter of homosexuality.

I hope you will speak with the greatest freedom in the *New Age*.

I also hope you won't sign your review of *The Glimpse* in *V.F.* But I am looking forward to it much.

I am too deep in my play to be able to talk about it. It is a very light comedy of a honeymoon, & it all takes place between the wedding & the consummation of the marriage! Though a light comedy, I deem it to be true to life.

Gosse is no creative good. But I think he tries to be broadminded, honestly. I have heard him speak. That was enough.

Gare à Kennerley.

I will not discuss *Nux Vomica* with you; when I come across anybody who seems likely to be able and willing to shout me

down, I maintain an august and impressive silence. Still, I like
your new title for the book.
Come, both of you.

> With choses de nous deux.
>
> Ever yours, A. B.

P.S. Your letter is dated 26th. I got it the 30th.
You are carrying influenza to inartistic extremes. We sympathise with you. But get up.

STOKE / MS. / 199
(*To R. W. Wright*)

> Villa des Néfliers,
> [postmarked ? 23 November 1909]

[no salutation]
In reply to your card, I had no 'career' at the Middle School.
And I cannot fix the dates. I must have left either late in 1883
or early in 1884. I think I was there 3 or 4 years. I came from
the Burslem Endowed School. I went into the Lower Sixth, &
rose to the Upper Sixth soon afterwards, & in due course I was
head boy. I passed no outside examinations while at the school.
I played left wing forward in the football team, but no matchcricket. I must have been less than mediocre at sports. Mr.
Hurley coached me afterwards in German for the London
Matric, which I passed almost immediately.

> Arnold Bennett

198. Bennett's letter takes a different tone towards *The Man Shakespeare* from that
in his review of the book on 21 October 1909, in which he said: 'I shall not attempt
here—I could only do it in the form of fiction—to express the emotion, the everincreasing emotion, which I experienced as I read steadily through his elaborate
book. I can only compare it with unforgettable sensations that have perturbed me
at moments when I stood between earth and sky on some high tor of Dartmoor. . . .'
This review itself was rather more restrained than an excessively long review that
was published in two issues of *Vanity Fair* itself, in which the reviewer expected
that *The Man Shakespeare* would last as long as Shakespeare's name.

Harris reviewed *The Glimpse* briefly and neutrally on 3 November.

Edmund Gosse (see page 194 n.) had not long since published his classic of autobiography, *Father and Son*.

Kennerley—the reference is to Mitchell, not W. W. See page 11 n. on Mitchell.
Harris was involved in publishing problems with him.

Nux Vomica was Harris's name for Wells's *Ann Veronica*, published October 1909.

199. R. W. Wright (b. 1882) was an assistant master on the staff of the Middle
School (now Wolstanton County Grammar School) in 1909–10. D. B. Hurley

BUTLER / MS. / 200
(*To Cedric Sharpe*)   Royal York Hotel
                                                        [Brighton]
                                                        16 Jan 1910
My dear Cedric,

I am glad to see that Halifax, birthplace of one great artist, and, I hope, of the father of another, has remained true to the only enlightened & patriotic cause in this country. This is beside the point.

I haven't been able to answer your letter before, as my eyes went wrong, & I have been obliged to consult oculists & stop work & so on—you know the racket.

Now in answer to the letter. I should not dream of being otherwise than perfectly honest with you. After all, this is the best compliment that one man [can] pay to another.

Are you asking me to give books to your library simply & solely as a friend, and are you asking your other friends, because the new library of the R.C.M. is really in need of outside subscriptions? If so, I shall send you some books with pleasure.

But if you are asking me because I am a friend *who happens to be an author*, I want to put a few considerations before you. Why should an author give books because he writes them? I am constantly receiving requests for gifts of my books to libraries & bazaars & things, & I always refuse them. There seems to be a general idea that an author *ought* to give his books, & that they cost him nothing. Beyond the first half dozen copies, an author has to pay for his books just like other people, except that he only pays wholesale price instead of retail. I paid the other day a bill of over £6 for copies of my books, to only one publisher! It seems to me that an author—especially one who makes great pecuniary sacrifices in order to produce only decent stuff (not that I take the least credit for that—I only do it because I can't help it)—ought to be the last person in the world to give books. He has written them. You might (in my opinion) as well ask a musical artist to give his services and also

(1844–1919), a linguist of international reputation, taught at the Middle School for more than thirty years, and became Headmaster. According to Thomas R. Roberts, in his pamphlet, *Arnold Bennett's Five Towns Origins* (Stoke-on-Trent, 1961), Bennett was at the Middle School from 9 May 1882 until the end of 1883, when he entered his father's law office. Thereafter he studied at night at the Wedgwood Institute. He entered the Burslem Endowed School in 1877.

pay for a seat at the concert. This is how it strikes me. And I tell you how it strikes me because I think that perhaps you haven't reflected on the matter. If, on reflection, you think that I ought to give the R.C.M. library some books because I am your friend *and* an author, I shall give some, as I would not 'go back on' your thoughts.

And as I said at the beginning, if you are asking me exclusively as a friend, with other friends, and not as an author at all, I am perfectly à la disposition.

Lastly I shall expect you to pay me the same compliment as I have paid you, & tell me exactly what you *do* think, and not to hide your real thoughts out of a mistaken sense of politeness.

Loves to all of you.

Yours ever, A. B.

TEXAS / MS. / 201
(*To Arthur Waugh*)

Royal York Hotel
8th Feby 1910

My dear Waugh,

Many thanks. There is only one trouble about the proofs. That is: the title is wrong. (This not your fault, but some copyist's.) It ought to be *Helen* with *the High Hand*. I really want this 'with'. I cannot imagine how the mistake arose. I shall put headings to the chapters, as I think these make a book more readable.

Buried Alive

I think you & Pinker must settle this. These people cannot settle it. I understand that you agreed to the cheap edition, as you did to the cheap edition of *The Old Wives' Tale*. And I was quite surprised to hear that you wished to withdraw the consent. I do not assent to the statement that I 'overdrew my account' with you. I got less for *Buried Alive* than I got for the novel immediately before it, & I am quite sure that my previous publishers were not precisely anxious to lose me. You were

---

200. Bennett stayed at the Royal York Hotel in Brighton for two and a half months from 1 January. He was writing *Clayhanger*.
R.C.M.—Royal College of Music.

good enough to express a high opinion of *Buried Alive* & I think
that the unsatisfactory sales ought not to be laid at my door.
We all take risks. Assuredly I do. And at your request I can-
celled an agreement & made a fresh one in order to lessen your
risks with *The Glimpse*. I will not fail to call on you when I
come to town.

Yours sincerely, Arnold Bennett

P.S. I will return the proofs as quickly as possible. A. B.

TEXAS / MS. / 202
(*To F. S. Flint*)

Royal York Hotel
10 Feby 1910

Dear F. S. Flint,

 I am sorry you paid for the production of that book. It is the
publisher who ought to lose on it. I have no editorial connection with *T.P.'s W.* & no influence whatever on their reviewing,
& their reviewing would not sell a single copy of your book.
Your volumes of verse will begin to sell a little when you have
published about ten of them: so keep at it.

 I don't see how poetry can be 'orchestral'. I have only read
a few things of René Ghil's. I am all for Verhaeren.

Best wishes,
Yours sincerely, Arnold Bennett

201. Arthur Waugh (1866–1943) was head of Chapman and Hall, who published Bennett's serious work beginning with *The Grim Smile of the Five Towns* in
1907 and ending with *Helen with the High Hand* in 1910. They took over from
Chatto and Windus. Bennett's quarrel with Waugh is recorded at several points
in Vol. I. The arrival of proofs of *Helen with the High Hand* with the running heads
reading 'Helen of the High Hand' was an incidental grievance. Bennett objected
violently to Waugh's view that when a novel did not earn back its advance on
royalties (as was the case with *Buried Alive*) the author had in effect overdrawn his
account. The Amalgamated Press issued sixpenny editions of both *Buried Alive*
and *The Old Wives' Tale*.

202. F. S. Flint (b. 1885), poet and translator, published *In the Net of the Stars*
in 1909. René Ghil (1862–1925) and Émile Verhaeren (1855–1916) were poets of
the Symbolist movement.

LILLY / MS. / 203
(*To E. F. Spence*)

Royal York Hotel
20 Feby 1910

Dear Mr. Spence,

Possibly you did not foresee that your letter would give me peculiar pleasure. I have been wanting for a long time to encounter you; but a playwright who seeks out a dramatic critic may put himself in a false position. I have gone about saying now for some years that E.F.S. is the best dramatic critic in London, and I have printed the same. In my historic diatribe against the *W.G.* in the *New Age* last year, I specially excepted E.F.S. and F.C.G. (what I object to in the *W.G.* is its growing Whiggism, and its accursed 'brightness' on Saturdays and its London Letter). When you were so amiable about *Cupid & Commonsense* but were unfortunate enough to say that there was no construction in one of the most brilliantly constructed pieces of modern times, I wanted to write and ask you what you meant by 'construction'. And when you produced your really adorable notice of *What the Public Wants*, I more than ever wanted to fall on your neck. But my discretion kept me quiet. I suppose I can now do what I want with impunity.

I well remember your criticism of Rostand; but when I wrote my article it slipped my memory, otherwise I should certainly have brought you in. I only said in the *Chronicle* that Henry James 'may be wrong', because the *Chronicle* is of such a 'hedging' disposition. I have no doubt whatever that you and Hy James are quite right. There is nothing whatever of serious or permanent value in anything that Rostand ever wrote.

I appreciate immensely (perhaps more than you think) what you say about *The Old Wives' Tale*. If you read any more of my vast & variegated output, please be guided by me. I know most about it. Let me suggest *Buried Alive, Whom God Hath Joined, A Great Man* or *Sacred & Profane Love*. All these books are short. All are entirely different from *The O.W. Tale*. But if you do not like at least *Buried Alive* I shall be desolated.

My wife & I are staying here for most of the winter. I wish you might be coming down. I should like to see you very much. And on the point of busy-ness I will not yield to you or anyone.

Believe me,

Yours sincerely, Arnold Bennett

MANCHESTER / MS. / 204
(*To A. N. Monkhouse*)

Royal York Hotel
22 Feby 1910

Dear Mr. Monkhouse,

Many thanks for your letter. It will give me the greatest pleasure to do 1,000 words or so on *A Hind Let Loose*. I expect I shall be a little self-conscious & costive, as I always am when fronting a new audience, but I shall do my best. I will let you know if I move from here.

With kind regards,

Yours sincerely, Arnold Bennett

P.S. I must say the various editions of the *M.G.* are a deep mystery. Yesterday in the 'London' edition, not a word (except the picture) about *Elektra*! And today not a word about *Justice*. Perhaps it was the Timbuctoo edition that they sent me. But it is rather trying to the faithful.   A. B.

MANCHESTER / MS. / 205
(*To A. N. Monkhouse*)

Royal York Hotel
4th March 1910

Dear Mr. Monkhouse,

I am very glad my article did not disappoint the editorial staff. It is ticklish work writing for the *M.G.* I should say that your remark about C.E.M. being afraid of damaging his ego by contact with others is very true. I don't mind telling you my first impression of him—probably as true & as untrue only as one's first impression of a strange country. I thought he was the

---

203. E. F. Spence (1860–1932) was dramatic critic of the *Westminster Gazette* for many years. F. C. G. was presumably Francis Grierson (1848–1927), musician and author, who did some writing for the *Gazette* in these years. Bennett attacked the *Gazette* on several occasions. Issues of the *Daily Chronicle* were not available to locate his article on Edmund Rostand (1864–1918). Some few years before, he saw *Cyrano* in France, and said: 'It amused me; I must say that for Rostand.'

204. On A. N. Monkhouse see pages 113–14. He was now on the editorial staff of the *Manchester Guardian*. *A Hind Let Loose*, a novel about journalism, was by C. E. Montague (1867–1928), chief leader writer on the *Guardian* and later a Director. Richard Strauss's *Elektra* had its first performance at Covent Garden on Saturday, 19 February. Galsworthy's *Justice* opened at the Duke of York's on the following Monday.

most extreme instance of constitutional timidity reassuring itself by intellectual pride (or arrogance) that I had ever met. The longer I live the more I am impressed by the importance of gestures as an infallible key to character. C.E.M. may be as cocky as he likes with a pen, but he gives the show away completely by that curious little feverish wistful cling of the hand at the end of a handshake. I could only judge this twice, but it was enough. Please don't regard this as an impertinent remark about a friend of yours, but as an observation made by one novelist to another.

I'm sorry I can't come to that dinner at Easter, but I shan't be in England. I should have come with the greatest eagerness.
Believe me,
Yours sincerely, Arnold Bennett

LILLY / MS. / 206
(*To Upton Sinclair*)

[Villa des Néfliers]
19 Sept 1910
Dear Mr. Upton Sinclair,
Many thanks for your letter & *Prince Hagen*. I found the latter awaiting me after a long absence from home. You have certainly got hold of a great theatrical idea. I am absolutely certain that its radicalism would not stand in the way of the play's production in England. The only criticism that I should venture to offer of the piece is that it is too summary, too short, & imperfectly realistic in detail. My notion is that, once the central idea [is] accepted, all the rest ought to be on exactly the same realistic plane, as, say, *The Jungle*. I should say that quite probably your agents will find a theatre for it in London. Or why don't they offer it to Manchester Repertory Theatre— which is a first class affair in every way?
Believe me, with best wishes,
Yours sincerely, Arnold Bennett

205. In his review of *A Hind Let Loose* on 3 March, Bennett remarked that Montague 'is essentially a cruel writer—nearly as cruel as Mr. Galsworthy'.

206. Upton Sinclair (1878–), the prolific American writer, was trying to interest an English producer in a dramatization of his novel *Prince Hagen*. He did not succeed, though Bennett did speak to one or two people about it. Bennett met Sinclair a year or so later and wrote in his Journal: 'Upton Sinclair. A brief chat. Not a bad sort of chap, I thought.'

ARNOLD BENNETT / 207
(*To E. A. Rickards*)

[? Villa des Néfliers]
[Autumn 1910]

[fragment]

. . . it is a pity that, having criticised it, you can't now read it. I mean for your sake. Because you make your first appearance in the last part of it, as an infant, and you may recognise one or two things. You will appear in the following two novels of the 'trilogy' (as the publishers and critics love to call it) and then you will be the hero of the fourth book, about London. You can't possibly understand yourself unless you begin at the beginning. . . .

[A. B.]

AUTHOR, 1 December 1910 / 208
(*To the editor*)

[59 rue de Grenelle, Paris]
[November 1910]

Sir,

The following instance of editorial delay may interest members. In June, 1902, I was commissioned by *Harper's Magazine* to write an article on 'The Future of the American Novel'. I wrote it in July, 1902, and delivered it immediately. It was then at once, with my consent, transferred to the *North American Review*, between which review and *Harper's Magazine* there was some managerial connection.

A few months ago (eight years after delivery) I received a letter from the editor of the *North American Review* stating that he had not yet printed the article and requesting me to revise it and bring it up to date! I declined.

207. This fragment of a letter is apparently all that survives of Bennett's correspondence with E. A. Rickards (see pages 91–92 n. and 178–9), who for several years was one of his most intimate friends. The two men met at one of the musical evenings at the Marriotts in the early nineties. Their friendship, and perhaps Bennett's letters, suffered from Rickards' excessive egotism. Bennett said of him after his death: 'Rickards always had a zest for life and for all manifestations of life, such as I have seldom seen equalled and never seen surpassed.' In the *Clayhanger* trilogy Rickards is Hilda's son, George Cannon. The fourth novel is *The Roll-Call* (1918).

It is true that I had taken the precaution of getting paid on delivery. But, supposing that I had desired, in the meantime, to republish the article, which was fairly elaborate, in a volume of literary essays?

Yours truly, Arnold Bennett

NATION, 10 December 1910 / 209
(*To the editor*)

59 rue de Grenelle
December 7th, 1910.

Sir,

In his singular letter Mr. Robert Morley says of these pictures: 'It is impossible to take them seriously.' What justification can he possibly offer for a statement so contrary to the fact? Hundreds of the most cultivated minds in Europe take them seriously. As an example of a cultivated mind taking them seriously, Mr. Morley may be referred to your distinguished contributor, Mr. Roger Fry. One also thinks at once of Mr. Bernard Berenson. Mr. Berenson has been nourished on the great masters, and his position as the greatest living art-critic is not often seriously challenged. Yet Mr. Berenson takes these pictures seriously. In particular, he has professed a profound admiration for Matisse. Mr. Morley may argue that all art critics are insane, and that only the plain profane man can be trusted. But numbers of plain profane men take these pictures seriously. I do, for instance.

Mr. Michael Sadler demands: 'Did Van Gogh burn with the same passion when he painted his boulevard as Cimabue when he painted his Madonna?' The answer is most emphatically, Yes! Let Mr. Sadler inquire into the details of Van Gogh's career.

The word 'daub' has been applied to nearly all great pictures at different periods by spirits like Sir W. B. Richmond and

208. The Bennetts moved into a flat at 59 rue de Grenelle at the end of October 1910.

Bennett's article was finally published in the *North American Review* in January 1912. In 1902 Bennett thought that Frank Norris, Theodore Dreiser, Edith Wharton, Gertrude Atherton, Hamlin Garland, and James Lane Allen were among the best American novelists.

Mr. Robert Morley; and both as a term of abuse and as an
argument it is worn somewhat thin.

Yours, &c., Arnold Bennett

MANCHESTER / MS. / 210
(*To A. N. Monkhouse*)

59 rue de Grenelle

9 Jan 1911

Dear Mr. Monkhouse,

Many thanks for your interesting letter. My memory is a sad
wreck & shadow of what it used to be. I most distinctly remember being struck by the realistic quality of a novel by you, &
when one is struck sufficiently hard one is apt to sit down &
write a letter; but the curious thing is that I have no recollection whatever of the letter! (Is not the mere fact that a novel
of yours has lived in the mind of a reader for 9 or 10 years a
reproach to you for having ceased to write novels?) I am very
glad you like *Clayhanger*. I have admirers who clearly *don't*.
And most reviewers have said that Hilda is quite *un*interesting.
(I am now dealing with this creature in No. 2 of the 'trilogy'.
I hate the word 'trilogy'.) I am certainly coming to Manchester
in the spring, and am looking forward to seeing you. Montague
has stood stoutly in the breach during the elections. Noble
warrior! I venture to think that sometimes he is perhaps a
shade, a trifle, a nothing, over-sarcastic at the expense of these
Lords, who after all are victims of historical evolution. I shall
peruse his book, but I expect I have read most of it already.

With kind regards & best wishes for the New Year of work.

Yours sincerely, Arnold Bennett

209. The pictures, by Cézanne, Van Gogh, Gauguin, Picasso, Matisse, and
others, were hung in an exhibition at the Grafton Gallery by Roger Fry (1866–
1934), and enraged numerous people. Fry wrote two articles on the exhibition for
the *Nation*, and the protests of Michael Sadler (1861–1943) and Robert Morley
(1857–1941) appeared alongside them. Sadler, who later was Master of University
College, Oxford, was content to argue in a fairly reasonable tone of voice that
art could not advance by retreating into primitive techniques. Morley, a painter
of landscapes and animals, thought the paintings reflected 'the debasement of the
lives of the painters living in the Gay City'. Sir William Blake Richmond (1842–
1921), painter and sometime Slade Professor at Oxford, wrote to the *Morning Post*
in a strain similar to Morley's. Bernard Berenson (1865–1959), the art historian,
was not a party to the immediate dispute.

TEXAS / MS. / 211
(*To John Lane*)

59 rue de Grenelle
17 Jan 1911

Dear Mr. John Lane,

You may have noticed that for some time I have been running an anti-censorship crusade in the *New Age*. I have now been asked to write an anti-censorship etc. article, as important as I can make it, for the *English Review*. I shall of course sign it. If you care to tell me anything about your adventures with *The Song of Songs* and *The New Machiavelli*, I shall be glad to make use of the information—with all the discretion, of course, that might be desirable. What I particularly want to know is—the reason that induced you to withdraw *The Song of Songs*, &, if the police came into the question, why they came in & what excuse they offered. Also, assuming there has been any difficulty as to *The New M* with either libraries or booksellers, how it was caused, & what were the reasons given by the objectors. Also any information as to your point of view as a publisher. Personally, I have had no trouble with libraries, and my sole aim in writing this article is the general welfare of English letters.

Yours sincerely, Arnold Bennett

LANE / MS. / 212
(*To John Lane*)

59 rue de Grenelle
23 Jan 1911

Dear Mr. John Lane,

Many thanks for your letter of the 23rd., [which told me] several things which I wanted to know. I have already [read] *The Song of Songs*, and commented on it, a long time ago. As [to the translation let me] tell you at once what I think. It is a bad translation [[(it seems to] be a clumsily shortened version of the original), [but I emphatically do not] consider that the badness of the translation is a reason for [attacking the book]

---

210. Bennett himself had not long since described the ancestors of members of the House of Lords as 'royal bastards'. See Vol. I, p. 130.

Clayhanger was published in September 1910.

T

on moral grounds, or for submitting to such an attack. I have heard [of no] objection to the translation from sundry literary people, but it [seems to me] insincere, & to be vitiated by literary pose. The question of [the badness of] the translation, and the question of the morals of the book, are [quite separate] and ought not to be confused. I read every word of the translation [and saw] nothing that could reasonably be censured on other than purely [aesthetic grounds].

I have seen the correspondence in the *Outlook*. [In this week's] *New Age* you will see some remarks of mine on the subject generally. I shall certainly refer to Boots' chemical casuistry.

I heartily agree with you that the matter is one for the Authors' Society rather than for publishers. Some time since I brought it before the Authors' Society as urgently as I could, and I roughly suggested a preliminary course of action, but the Committee did not see its way to anything useful, and I believe the matter, though not dropped, is in abeyance.

The New M is a magnificent work. The fact that Hubert Bland was commissioned to review for the *Daily Chronicle* fills me with a whole series of ideas upon literary London which I shall certainly never commit to writing.

Believe me,

Yours very truly, Arnold Bennett

212. Beginning on 23 December 1909 Bennett wrote a series of articles on library censorship in the *New Age*. He did not publish anything on the subject in the *English Review*. In one of the *New Age* articles he remarked: 'No one could guess . . . from the sweet Christian kindliness of my general tone towards Mr. Jesse Boot's library that Mr. Jesse Boot had been guilty of banning some of my work which I love most.' In October 1910 he corresponded with G. Herbert Thring of the Society of Authors on the subject, and expressed the opinion that the Society of Authors and the Publishers' Association could kill library censorship very easily, but that neither group cared to undertake the task.

John Lane came into the picture in 1910 when he published a bad American translation of *The Song of Songs*, by Hermann Sudermann (1857–1928). Scotland Yard informed Lane of a complaint alleging obscenity in the book—a complaint that the Yard did not yet associate itself with but felt that Lane ought to know about. Lane thereupon wrote to several authors to ask their opinions, and he also wrote to the Society of Authors. Eden Phillpotts expressed the general opinion of the authors when he said that 'the only things obscene therein were the Americanisms', and Thomas Hardy thought the book ought to be withdrawn because the translation was so poor. According to Lane, the Society of Authors did not respond at all. He then wrote to Sudermann and said that, all things considered, he felt he ought to withdraw the book and try to arrange for a better translation. Sudermann agreed, and a new translation was in fact published by Lane in 1913 (see pages 283–4). On 26 January 1911 Bennett discussed the matter in the *New*

NEW AGE, 2 February 1911 / 213
(*To the editor*)

[59 rue de Grenelle]
[end of January 1911]

[no salutation]

1. The most powerful argument for woman's suffrage is the fact that women want it. Undoubtedly a large majority of women who have studied the question feel a strong desire for woman's suffrage. There is and there can be no answer to this argument. To attempt to answer it is in my opinion to be guilty of fatuousness.

2. There is no reasonable prospect of obtaining woman's suffrage in the present Parliament. The Government has no mandate of any kind to deal with it, and its time will be fully occupied by subjects which the electorate considers far more important.

3. Militant methods have, in my opinion, succeeded so far. They would have succeeded more completely if the women who sought martyrdom had played the game when they found martyrdom. Not only their dignity, but their intellectual honesty too often gave way under the strain of martyrdom. At the same time it must be admitted that the organisers were frequently badly advised by their more zealous male supporters, who did not always escape the fatuity which masks their opponents. In particular the behaviour of certain husbands of martyrs did much to alienate the sympathies of the lukewarm. No hysterical male antics would in the slightest degree weaken my own convinced support of the cause of woman's suffrage; but then I am not lukewarm, while the electorate as a whole is either lukewarm or indifferent.

Age, saying: 'I do not in any way blame the publisher, whose hand was forced, apparently, by the police. But I should very much like to know who inspired the police, for I am not going to believe that Scotland Yard, in the intervals of its preoccupation with Sidney Street brigands, has found time to make a study of current fiction in the interests of London morals.'

Bennett dealt with some of the attacks on *The New Machiavelli* the following week. Hubert Bland (d. 1914), journalist and sometime Fabian, reviewed the novel on 17 January. He found it a clever book, but unpleasant and smug.

The tone of Bennett's two letters to Lane does not suggest that two months or so before he was calling him a 'damned rascal' in letters to J. B. Pinker. (See Vol. I, pp. 142, 144.) The second of the two letters here was badly damaged, apparently by water, and the words in brackets are conjectural.

4. I can suggest no alternative to militant methods. But I think that if the organisers of militancy were to make a closer and franker study of human nature as it notoriously is, with a view to avoiding in future the rather silly air of being constantly horrified by the spectacle of human nature in activity, the result might be a shortening of the war.

[Arnold Bennett]

BUTLER / MS. / 214
(*To A. St. John Adcock*)

59 rue de Grenelle
4 Feby 1911

Dear Mr St. John Adcock,

I am obliged for your letter of the 1st which reached me last night. With the best will in the world to help you, I'm afraid I can't do much. Owing to my objection to photographs, there are scarcely any existing of me. I enclose one, about 5 or 6 years old. You can get the latest from Mr. Frank Palmer, Publisher, Red Lion Court. I enclose also a photo of my study & my back; and also two caricatures (said to be admirably cruel) by my friend Mr E. A. Rickards, the well-known architect (designer of the Wesleyan Methodist building on the Aquarium site), and certainly one of the finest caricaturists in the world.

I enclose also some picture postcards of the Five Towns (with

213. Bennett's communications to journals took a variety of forms, and the distinction between letters, responses to queries, and articles is not always clear. In one case he changed a letter into an article, and got paid for it, by crossing out 'Dear Sir' and 'Yours truly'. Whether or not the editors of the *New Age* did the same with the present communication is unknown. It appeared in a special supplement devoted to women's suffrage, and was in answer to the following questions:

'What in your opinion is the most powerful argument—
    (a) For, or
    (b) Against woman's suffrage?
Is there any reasonable prospect of obtaining woman's suffrage in the present Parliament, and this immediately?
Have the militant methods in your opinion succeeded?
What alternative methods would you suggest?'
Hilaire Belloc made the briefest response:
'1. (a) Fun. (b) Sex.
  2. Yes.
  3. Yes.
  4. Bribery.'

my notes on the back). If you want more elaborate photos I dare say Mr. Bentley, Photographer, Hanley, Stoke on Trent, could supply you.

Photos were taken of all the scenes in *What the Public Wants*. But I never saw them. Mr. A. E. Drinkwater, Secretary of the Stage Society, Talbot House, Arundel St. Strand, could doubtless give you the name of the photographer. You could probably also get photos of the scenes in *Cupid & Commonsense* (an adaptation of *Anna of the Five Towns*) from the Gaiety Theatre, Manchester; and of both plays from the Royalty Theatre, Glasgow; but I am not sure.

I shall be much obliged if you will return to me in due course the photos & sketches, whether you use them or not.

And I shall also be much obliged if you can find room in your special number to point out that the name of 'The Five Towns', for the Staffordshire Potteries, was invented by me, & is not the proper name of the district. The district is constantly referred to by my fictional name for it, as though it were the real name, even in the district itself; and also by other novelists sometimes. For instance, H. G. Wells, in *The New Machiavelli*, lays a number of important scenes in the Potteries, which he calls the 'Five Towns'. The town of Burslem he sometimes calls by its proper name, & sometimes by my adaptation of it—Bursley. I do not want this statement, though, to come from me.

Yours faithfully, Arnold Bennett

HARVARD / MS. / 215
(*To William Dean Howells*)

Villa des Néfliers
1st March 1911

My dear Sir,

One does not usually acknowledge criticism, even when it is very generous or very just. But you are you; not merely the first essayist & the first novelist in America, but the beloved

214. St. John Adcock (1864–1930) was on the staff of the *Bookman*. The issue of March 1911 has an article 'Arnold Bennett: An Appreciation', by F. G. Bettany, and in the 'News Notes' readers are informed about Wells and the Five Towns.

Frank Palmer published *Cupid and Commonsense* (1909) and *The Arnold Bennett Calendar* (1911). A. E. Drinkwater (d. 1923), father of John, was an actor, and at this time general manager for Lillah McCarthy and Granville Barker.

'W. D. Howells', whose work has been enjoyed, almost as part of the planetary movement, ever since *Harper's Magazine* first came regularly into a certain house in the Five Towns (not far from Clayhanger's) 26 or 27 years ago. Hence I give myself the pleasure of writing to you in order to acknowledge your 'Easy Chair' article in this month's *Harper's*. I need not try to explain to you how much pleasure it has given me. You, being an imaginative writer, will know all about that. But I am charmed to have this excuse for communicating with one who gave me some of my first notions of what subtlety can be in literature. Do you remember 'The Mousetrap'? It is conceivable that you only half remember it. But I can well remember how my brother & I agreed, after reading it in *Harper's*, that it had set up a new standard of 'subtlety' for us. Also I feel it is my duty to reassure an observer so friendly as you are, on the subject of the pseudo-Arnold Bennett, author of unserious books. The need of money was the sole & sufficient explanation of those books. Although I flatter myself that I live to write, I should be ashamed if I did not write to live. The last of those books was written some years ago, & has just been published. *Denry the Audacious*. I must tell you, however, that I consider *Buried Alive*, though as you say a farce, as a quite serious 'criticism of life', & that I mean to continue at intervals in this vein. And further I want to rebut the charge of excessive length brought against *Clayhanger*. Everybody believes & says it is longer than *The Old Wives' Tale*. Far from being longer, it is 40,000 words (20 per cent) shorter. The optical illusion of excessive length is due to the typographical ingenuity of the publishers, who apparently desired to convince the American public that this book is the first third of 'a million word novel'. (See preliminary puffs.) As a fact, it is 160,000 words long (exactly)—that is to say, less than a third of the length of *Anna Karenina, La Chartreuse de Parme, Vanity Fair*, etc. It may *seem* long. For that I accept the blame. I did not begin fiction-writing by collaboration with our friend Phillpotts. I had written 15 or 20 books before he suggested to me the collaboration as a remunerative & colossal joke. Which it proved to be indeed. But we only did two books.

Well, I must try to live up to 'The Easy Chair'.

Believe me,

Your old, admiring & obliged reader, Arnold Bennett

GIDE / 216
(*To André Gide*)

59 rue de Grenelle
21 March 1911

My dear Sir,
I am particularly glad to have, from you, your new book, with its inscription. I thank you very much. For years I have known a number of your friends, and of course I have been reading your books for a long time; so that I feel that somehow we ought to have been acquainted before this. What pleases me particularly in a book like *The New Pretexts* (I had already read a great deal of it in reviews etc.) is the proof it offers that an artist is interesting himself in the daily *guerilla* of literature. Unfortunately few English artists do the same. I am sending you a copy of my last novel (pardon its extreme length!) and if you can contrive to like it half as much as I like your work, I shall be well satisfied. We are going to England early in April. Will you have the kindness to come in here some night *next* week, before we go; say, Tuesday, Thursday or Friday? I should really be very pleased to have a chat with you, either in English or French.

Believe me,
Cordially yours, Arnold Bennett

---

215. In his 'Easy Chair' column, William Dean Howells (1837–1920) said that Bennett's novels were divided into two groups, the good and the bad, and that the reader knew on the very first page what was facing him: 'the note of truth or the note of untruth is struck with the first word'. He lumped together *The Grand Babylon Hotel*, *The Gates of Wrath*, *The Ghost*, *Buried Alive*, and *The Glimpse* as bad work. Few of Bennett's critics have hesitated to make a similar pronouncement, and they have of course failed to agree as to which novels fall together. *Denry the Audacious* was the American title for *The Card*.

Howells' 'The Mouse-Trap', a dialogue, was published in the European edition of *Harper's* in December 1886.

216. The correspondence between André Gide (1869–1951) and Bennett has been edited by Linette F. Brugmans (*Correspondance André Gide–Arnold Bennett*, Genève, Librairie Droz, 1964). Only a selection of Bennett's letters are reproduced in the present collection. The annotation relies largely upon Mrs. Brugmans' edition.

Gide and Bennett had mutual acquaintances, particularly in Henry Davray and Valéry Larbaud (see pages 283–4 and 213), and one or the other showed Gide some favourable comments Bennett made about his work in the *New Age*. Gide then inscribed *Nouveaux Prétextes* (1911) to Bennett, and his first letter followed. Gide did not read English easily, and he gave up in the reading of *Clayhanger*, disappointed by 'ce long ruisseau au cours très lent'.

LILLY / MS. / 217   Authors' Club
(*To Upton Sinclair*)   2 Whitehall Court
                                                London
                                                30 Mch 1911
Dear Mr. Upton Sinclair,
    I have read your prodigious & all-embracing *Love's Pilgrimage.*
I should very strongly resent its being censored in England. It
deals candidly, here and there, with sundry aspects of life which
are not usually dealt with in English fiction, but which are
dealt with quite as a matter of course in the fiction of all other
countries except the United States. It deals with these matters
in an admirably poetic, lofty, and honest spirit. And no person
of real intelligence *and experienced in first-class imaginative literature*
could possibly object to the book on this score. Nor could the
perusal of it work anything but good in the mind of any person
whatever. That there should be any question about its reception
merely shows the wrong-headed hypocrisy & provinciality of
the English-speaking public's attitude towards art.
    Nevertheless I have no sort of doubt that when your novel
is published in England it will encounter very considerable
opposition, official or otherwise. I shall profoundly regret this
opposition, & I shall be ashamed of it, and I shall publicly
object, as I always do on similar occasions.
                                    Yours sincerely, Arnold Bennett

KEELE / MS. / 218
(*To Holbrook Jackson*)
                                                59 rue de Grenelle
                                                1st Apl 1911
Dear Mr. Holbrook Jackson,
    I am glad to hear of the success of your book, & sorry that I
can't contribute to your symposium. I haven't the faintest
notion what the fiction of the future is going to be like, & it is

    217. The address, the Authors' Club, may be an anticipated address, or the
dating of the letter in March may be wrong. The Bennetts came to England for
two months at the end of the first week in April. Conceivably Bennett was in
England very briefly at the end of March.
    Sinclair's novel was published in England in 1912, by Heinemann. Among
other things, it contains a description of childbirth.

exceedingly difficult not to write nonsense in these symposiums. Moreover I object to symposiums on principle.

Yours sincerely, Arnold Bennett

MANCHESTER GUARDIAN, 12 April 1911 / 219
(*To the editor*)   179 Waterloo Road
Burslem
[about 10 April 1911]

Sir,

I respect some of the ideals for which Dr. Moulton stands, and I respect his personality. And though I strongly dissent from it, I can respect his attitude in objecting to the unrestricted circulation of *The New Machiavelli*. But when he applies (as constructively he does apply) the adjectives 'dirty' and 'nasty' to *The New Machiavelli*, he gravely disserves his own cause and loses in esteem. *The New Machiavelli* is neither dirty nor nasty. It is an absolutely sincere and righteous work, the product of a brain which, in the opinion of highly qualified critics of all European nations, is one of the greatest forces for real progress in the world to-day. Dr. Moulton's phraseology about Mr. Wells's novel is unhappy; it is even unworthy of him. It is in any case extremely regrettable.

Dr. Moulton underestimates the number of people to whom the action of the Manchester City Council seems ridiculous. It undoubtedly includes a very large majority of those who have actually read *The New Machiavelli*, and these people alone are entitled to an opinion.

Lastly, one does not expect a controversialist of Dr. Moulton's calibre to employ that excessively futile word 'right-minded' without defining it.

Yours, &c., Arnold Bennett

218. Holbrook Jackson (1874–1948), joint editor of the *New Age* in 1907 with A. R. Orage, was now on the staff of *T. P.'s Weekly*. He published *Platitudes in the Making* in March 1911.

219. James Hope Moulton (d. 1917), professor of Greek philology at Manchester University, wrote a letter to the *Manchester Guardian* expressing approval of the censoring of *The New Machiavelli* and other works by the City Council. He saw 'nothing gained and a great deal lost by letting loose dubious dancers, problem plays, dirty novels, and unlimited drink'.

LEEDS / MS. / 220
(*To Clement Shorter*)

2, Whitehall Court
29 April 1911

Dear Mr. Shorter,

I see that you expect me 'to repudiate the picture of the Duchess of Sutherland' in *The Card*. I absolutely repudiate it. I have never seen the Duchess of Sutherland in my life. If I have seen her portrait in the *Sphere* I have forgotten the fact. My knowledge of the Duchess is that of the ordinary newspaper reader—rather less than more. There is only one portrait to be found in all my books—myself.

Your sincerely, Arnold Bennett

TEXAS / MS. / 221
(*To Lillah McCarthy*)

2, Whitehall Court
26 May 1911

Dear Mrs. Granville Barker,

So many thanks for your hospitality this afternoon. We did not worry you afterwards, as we heard the dread voice of the producer behind the curtain. *Nan* is the first play of Masefield's that I have seen. It is very beautiful indeed. It got hold of us little by little. I am very restive at the theatre, & it wasn't until the scene between the two girls in the first act that I began to feel the play. This is an admirable scene. I have never admired your acting more than in the love scene of the second act. You, & the scene, were simply exquisite. The last act is tremendously fine. The whole affair is startlingly noble, and an enormous credit to all the principals concerned. You have the

220. Clement Shorter (1857–1926), editor of the *Sphere* for many years, was a frequent subject of Bennett's critical barbs in the *New Age*. In *The Card*, the local representative of the aristocracy in the Potteries goes by the name of the Countess of Chell. 'Everybody in the Five Towns sneered at the Countess and called her a busybody; she was even dubbed "interfering Iris" (Iris being one of her eleven Christian names); the Five Towns was fiercely democratic—in theory. In practice the Countess was worshipped; her smile was worth at least five pounds, and her invitation to tea was priceless. She could not have been more sincerely adulated in the United States, the home of social equality.' In real life the local representative was Millicent Duchess of Sutherland (d. 1955), sometimes known as 'Meddlesome Millie'.

best part that I have ever seen you in. We were both also very struck by Miss Jerrold's acting.

We hope to see you in all your splendour on Wednesday night.

Our kindest regards, and gratitude, & congratulations.

Yours sincerely, Arnold Bennett

L'EFFORT, 5 June 1911 / 222
(*To the editor*)

[2, Whitehall Court]
[May 1911]

Cher Monsieur,

Il faudrait un long article pour répondre à votre question, et je n'ai pas le temps de l'écrire.

Je crois que l'influence de la pensée française en Angleterre est en régression. Les hommes politiques français sont très arriérés en comparaison des hommes politiques anglais. La philosophie française, exception faite d'un certain intérêt de snobisme et de dilettantisme pour Bergson, est à peine discutée en Angleterre.

D'un autre côté, la musique française exerce maintenant quelque influence nouvelle, et il en est de même pour la peinture.

Quoique le roman anglais paraisse avoir beaucoup plus de succès en France que le roman français n'en a en Angleterre, il est cependant indiscutable que l'oeuvre des réalistes français a eu une grande influence sur l'art anglais pour le bien. Moi-même, j'ai toujours suivi les maîtres français, et l'influence française qui se fait sentir dans mes ouvrages a été souvent remarquée par la critique.

Un des plus grands et des plus influents de tous nos romanciers, George Moore, était exclusivement influencé par des modèles et par l'idéal français, et il passe pour avoir introduit cet idéal dans notre littérature d'imagination.

Croyez-moi, etc., Arnold Bennett

221. Lillah McCarthy (Mrs. Granville Barker, 1875–1960) played the title role in *Nan*. H. Granville Barker (1877–1946) produced it. Mary Jerrold (1877–1955), who later played Rose in *Milestones*, played Jenny Pargetter. John Masefield (1878–1967) was not one of Bennett's favourite dramatists, and the comments here are doubtless on the polite side.

TEXAS / MS. / 223
(*To William Lee Mathews*)

2, Whitehall Court
10 June 1911

Dearest William,

Many thanks. Vernon came to see me yesterday. They are trying to get Gertie Millar, who would like to follow in the footsteps of Kate Cutler–Ethel Irving. Vernon believes in her possibilities. I told him I should rely on his judgment. Anyhow we can always veto when formally consulted. Gertie would be an immense draw. Vernon said they meant to produce [?early] in September.

Now, another thing. I told Lillah McCarthy I would let her see a play. (You know how you say these things to a young woman.) Drinkwater wrote for it. I temporised & said that it had no part for Lillah. I enclose his reply. I have now referred him to you, & told him that the play is 'out' for the moment, but that you will send it to him when it comes in. My idea is this: I don't want to do anything definite with *The Great Adventure* until *The Honeymoon* has been produced. If the latter succeeds, the value of the former would be increased. On the other hand I should like to help Lillah's venture if it can be done without too much sacrifice, & of course I should like to keep on good terms with her in case *The Honeymoon* for any reason fails. Will you therefore use your notorious diplomacy to keep the ball in the air through the summer? You needn't send the play at all for several weeks. And if they want to buy it you can always spend time over discussing terms. *If* she would do it properly, & reopen with it in state in the autumn, I would let her have it anyhow. We can well afford to go for artistic kudos & let the rhino wait. It is bound to come. I have just contracted for a short novel for which I shall receive £3,000 on account on or before the day of publication, & more to follow.

Thine, A. B.

223. Frank Vernon (1875–1940) was a friend of Bennett's. He had produced *Cupid and Commonsense*, and was now involved in negotiations over the production of *The Honeymoon*. At the end of June, Marie Tempest stepped into the picture, and the play was produced under her management and with her in the principal female role on 6 October 1911. It came off at the end of January 1912.

Gertie Millar (1879–1952), Kate Cutler (1870–1955), and Ethel Irving (d. 1963) shared a talent for singing as well as for acting. So did Marie Tempest.

The Great Adventure, based on *Buried Alive* and written in the autumn of 1910,

SPECTATOR, 17 June 1911 / 224
(*To the editor*)   2, Whitehall Court
                                    [about 12 June 1911]
Sir,
    I anticipate that you will permit me to say a very few
words about the article in your last issue criticizing the editorial
conduct of the *English Review*. By an ingenious device well
known in the craft of polemics you yourself state some of the
chief arguments which may be brought against the method and
matter of your attack. But you omit to answer them. In my
opinion, however, your article does not call for arguments. It
calls merely for protest. The fact that I am a contributor to the
English Review shall not prevent me from making the protest.
Indeed, if connection with the *English Review* were to be a bar
to speaking in its defence, not only myself, but most of the
leading writers in England would have to remain silent. The
crux of your charge seems to be that the policy of the *English
Review* resembles that of 'the shady second-hand booksellers'.
Mr. Thomas Hardy, Mr. Joseph Conrad, Mr. H. G. Wells, Mr.
Henry James, and Mr. Cunninghame Graham, to name some
names, will possibly receive with mild astonishment the news
that they have been lending their immense prestige to support
the lewd trickery of Holywell Street. Every reader of the *English
Review* will know what adjective to apply to the latest indictment. Whatever friends you may make in this singular crusade,
you have certainly, during the last year or two, aroused the deep
resentment of the literary artists of this country. Of this fact I
have personal knowledge. Happily it is the literary artists
alone who are responsible for our literature. Thanking you in
anticipation of the courtesy of insertion.–I am, Sir, &c.,
                                        Arnold Bennett

was not produced until 25 March 1913. Miss McCarthy was not in it, but Granville Barker produced it.
    The £3,000 was for serial rights to *The Price of Love*, offered by Harper's in New
York. Bennett wrote the novel in 1912–13.
    224. The *English Review* passed out of F. M. Ford's hands at the end of 1909,
and Austin Harrison, former correspondent on the *Daily Mail*, became editor. The
journal continued to publish some of the distinguished writers of the day. The
Spectator article took notice of some recent advertising in which the *English Review*
identified itself as 'The great adult review' on the grounds that 'the Editor does
not use the blue pencil on what the magazines call "naughty" words', 'authors

BERG / MS. / 225
(*To G. T. Bagguley*)

[2, Whitehall Court]
14 June 1911

Dear Sir,

I am obliged for the *Hortulus Anime*. I have not had time to examine it carefully, but so far as I have seen it is an admirable piece of work & I congratulate you on it.

I send by parcel post two other jobs: One is *Roget's Thesaurus*. This is a book that I use every day, fairly roughly. Please bind it how you like, *bearing this rough & constant usage in mind*. For the lettering on the back, please follow the cloth binding as closely as possible (but *not* putting the words 'Longmans & Co' at the bottom). Please use a square faced type, not tall & narrow: and keep the spacing between the letters as small as possible. I shall be glad to have this book very soon, as it is indispensable to me.

The other job is the two small notebooks, which are to be bound together in full calf, according to your own ideas. Please take out the blank pages at the end of the second book & put two of them at the beginning of the first. The black book is the first. No lettering on back, but lettering like this—NOTES FOR HILDA LESSWAYS—on the side. You will of course remove the present bindings & end papers.

Yours faithfully, Arnold Bennett

P.S. I shall be at 2 Whitehall Court till Friday morning, in case you wish to reply by return. A. B.

---

are not *requested* to write down to the mob public', etc. Said the *Spectator*: 'We all know what this means. We have all seen this kind of thing in the "leering", "knowing" cant purveyed by the catalogue-compilers of shady second-hand book-sellers when . . . they recommend some particularly nauseous work.' The *Spectator* cited a recent article by Frank Harris in the *English Review*, in which Harris suggested that sins of the flesh were not sins, and that if they were, they should be forgiven the more readily in women because women are more sensuous than men. To the *Spectator*, the propagation of such views was 'harmful to the State in the highest degree', and they intended to take no further notice of the existence of the *English Review*. As for Bennett's subsequent protest, 'we can only say that "the literary artists of this country" are welcome to their "deep resentment" '.

225. George Thomas Bagguley (1860–1950) of Newcastle-under-Lyme was a bookbinder of international reputation. He was educated at the Middle School a few years before Bennett, and in 1890 bought out a printing business in Newcastle where he had earlier been an apprentice. He bound books for Bennett for more than twenty years, including many manuscript volumes of Bennett's own works.

VICHY / MS. / 226
(*To Valéry Larbaud*)

2, Whitehall Court
14 June 1911

My dear Mr. Larbaud,

So that there may be no misapprehension, I will put in writing my ideas about selling the English and American rights of Madame Audoux's next book.

Marie Claire has sold as follows :

England	6,000	copies
English Colonial	6,000	,,
America (about)	20,000	,,
total	32,000	,,

The various publishers have paid royalties of *at least* £1,300 on these sales. I know the people who have received the royalties and made the profits, but I am not at liberty to name them.

My own agent, Mr. J. B. Pinker, Talbot House, Arundel Street, Strand, acted as agent for the sale in England and America of *Marie Claire*. I should strongly advise Madame Audoux to employ him, direct, as her agent for England and America. His charge is ten per cent. of all the money received. He is a thoroughly honest man, and I am sure that he can sell the next book better than any other man in England. If Madame Audoux does not employ him, she will certainly not make as much money as she might do.

If any person has told Madame Audoux that the English and American rights of her next book are only worth £50, and that it is necessary for her to make a contract at once, that person is an unscrupulous liar.

Madame Audoux ought to have a contract direct with English and American publishers, *and to receive a royalty herself on every copy sold.* I have not any hesitation in saying that, from England and America together, Madame Audoux might receive, on the day of publication, *on account* of royalties, at least £400. She ought on no pretext to sell the book outright in England and America.

As you know, I have no interest in the matter at all. My only desire is to see that Madame Audoux is properly paid. It would of course be advisable for her to finish the next book as soon as she possibly can.

To show you how strongly I think about the matter, I may tell you that I myself would be willing to pay Madame Audoux £200 on account of English and American royalties, on the day of publication of the translation (*if she left the whole matter to me, and delivered the manuscript this year*) and also to pay her every penny that I received in addition. Of course I should want no profit whatever.

Yours faithfully, Arnold Bennett

ARNOLD BENNETT / 227
(*To the Duchess of Sutherland*)

Villa des Néfliers
23 June, 1911

Dear Lady,

I am now safely at home again and can collect my thoughts. The only thing that I did not explain to you amid the romanticism of North Street was the somewhat subtle fact that if there is resemblance between you and the young woman in *The Card* it is simply because you are the sole representative of that particular class in the Five Towns. Obviously it would be absurd for an author with my material to omit from his work all the comedy that must inevitably spring from contact between the magnate class and the leaders of an industrial population. Obviously he cannot include that comedy without setting down the salient characteristics of each class, and obviously when one of the classes is represented by only one person, a certain amount of annoyance to that one person must result. I admit that it is a bit 'rough' on you. But then, as I told you, you are to consider yourself in the Five Towns not as a woman, but as an institution. This also is a bit rough on a beautiful woman.

226. Valéry Larbaud (1881–1957), novelist and critic, was at this time on the staff of the *Nouvelle Revue Française*. Marguerite Audoux (1863–1937), a Parisian seamstress, won acclaim with *Marie-Claire*, an account of her girlhood. She received £16 or £20 for English and American rights to the book, and her translator, John N. Raphael, apparently received most of the £1,300 paid in royalties. Bennett's original interest in the affair was that he wrote the introduction to the translation. Madame Audoux seems to have ignored Bennett's advice with regard to her next book. See further, Vol. I, p. 158.

I may say, by the way, that if I had had the advantage of meeting you before I wrote *The Card*, I should have insisted very much more on the Countess's beauty; indeed I should have tried to make some rather fine effect out of it (or I might have left the Countess out altogether; which would have been a pity!). Now I think you must admit that I am not the man to attempt the portrait of any person whatsoever in a novel, much less the portrait of one whom I had never seen. On the other hand, I willingly admit that certain characteristics of the Countess were suggested by public knowledge of you. But that is all. Considering that the whole book is written in a fiercely sarcastic vein, I think the Countess's portrait is a sympathetic one, don't you? Much more sympathetic than a caricature by Max Beerbohm! This is a clumsy letter, but I did not want to write you an article, and I hope you prefer it so. I hope too that you will be round here before the early days of August, as I have to spend August in London rehearsing a play, and then I am going to America.

Believe me, with a peculiar kind of glance that is at once admiring, apologetic and unrepentant,

Yours sincerely, Arnold Bennett

ILLINOIS / MS. / 228
(*To Jane Wells*)

Villa des Néfliers
Saturday [8 July 1911]

Dear Mrs. Wells,

My train ran off the lines at Mantes. First two coaches pitched over. Front part of my coach telescoped & the whole

227. Reginald Pound describes the dinner at which the Duchess of Sutherland and Bennett met, shortly after the publication of *The Card*.

'Bennett was one of Maurice Baring's guests . . ., with the Duchess, Anthony Hope, Austin Harrison . . ., and one or two others. Bennett had never met the Duchess and her name was wilfully mumbled when they were introduced by Anthony Hope, whose idea it was to place them together at table and watch events. After a little preliminary conversation, the Duchess faced Bennett with the question: "Why did you make fun of me in your book?" Bennett looked incredulously at her: the Duchess remembers his teeth sticking out of a nervous smile as the laughter of the others rose about him. She went on to make it clear that what she objected to about his representation of her was, above all, the insinuation that she was never punctual, whereas punctuality had always been as much a rule of her life as it was of his.'

U

coach smashed. For a few seconds I was in a storm of glass, flying doors, and hand-luggage. All over in ten seconds. A woman in front part of my coach had her leg broken. Having seen what there was to see, I hired an auto for 100 frs, & sold 3 places in it for 70 fr. & thus got to Paris for 30 frs. only a quarter of an hour late for dinner! Still I don't want to be in any more railway accidents. The only account that I have seen of the accident, in the *Figaro*, is inaccurate in every detail except the number of wounded.

I don't travel again on the Ouest-État for some years to come.

You will let us know which day you are coming here.

Kind regards to your mother & to Mrs. Bowkett.

Loves from us to the rest.

Yours sincerely, Arnold Bennett

GIDE / 229
(*To André Gide*)

Villa des Néfliers
21 July, 1911.

Dear Mr. André Gide,

Many thanks for your letter and the book. I read the book at once, d'un trait. This is praise, I think! It reminds me of *Dominique*. Do you regard this as an insult? Except that I should have liked Isabelle's character to be a little more fully explained at the end, I have no fault to find with this beautiful story, which for me has a classical air about it. I don't know that I am prepared to admit, in fiction, a difference between a 'récit'

228. On 6 July Bennett visited the Wellses at Pont de l'Arche. Returning to Fontainebleau on Friday he found himself in the railway accident, which he recorded in more detail in the Journal:

'I was in a sort of large Pullmanesque compartment at the back of a first-class coach, two or three coaches from the engine. The windows broke. The corridor door sailed into the compartment. My stick flew out of the rack. The table smashed itself. I clung hard to the arms of my seat, and fell against an arm-chair in front of me. There was a noise of splintering, and there were various other noises. An old woman lay on the floor crying. I wondered, "Shall I remain unharmed until the thing stops?" Immense tension of waiting for the final stoppage. Equilibrium at last, and I was unhurt.'

Bennett used the episode in his novel *Accident*, written in 1926–7. He also wrote an article about it that appears in the collection of *Things That Have Interested Me* (1921).

Mrs. Sidney Bowkett was the wife of a childhood friend of Wells.

and a 'roman'. Authors who want to save themselves the trouble of construction sometimes call a novel 'simple récit'. But your novel is charmingly constructed.

I am sorry I can't go to Pontigny. I should have liked to do so. But I am writing a play in collaboration during the month of August and je ne pourrai pas plaquer mon collaborateur. I have got the plaquette of St. Léger Léger's poems. Very interesting. The St. Catherine's Press is terrible for misprints! Even your limited edition of *Isabelle* is not free from them. There are a number in *L'Otage*. I shall hope to see you in the autumn somewhere. I left London on June 16th.

Yours always, sincerely, Arnold Bennett

Je relis *Tom Jones*. En effet, c'est épatant.

TEXAS / MS. / 230
(*To William Lee Mathews*)

Villa des Néfliers
4th August 1911

Dearest William,

Many thanks for your letter. Go ahead with Barker, and let us have the contract signed. But I shall be out of England in October & November, & don't want a play produced during those months. By the way, Marie writes me today that she will produce *The Honeymoon* about Oct. 10th. I have written her protesting against this further postponement, as it will quite upset my affairs in the States, & *I hope you also will do what you can to get the thing produced by the end of September*. Marie & I are on the very best terms.

With regard to a new play, I promised Knoblock at his request that I would say nothing of the affair till it was done,

229. *Isabelle*, described on its title page as a 'récit', was published in 1911. *Dominique*, by Eugène Fromentin (1820–76) was published in 1863. *Éloges*, by Alexis Saint-Léger Léger (Saint-John Perse, b. 1889), appeared in 1911. *L'Otage*, by Paul Claudel, appeared in 1911.

At Pontigny, both before and after the War, were held '*Entretiens d'été*', to which Bennett was often invited but did not go. They attracted Gide, Maurois, R. M. du Gard, and other well-known French writers.

Bennett and Edward Knoblock wrote *Milestones* between 1 and 24 August 1911. Knoblock (1874–1945), author of *Kismet* and many other plays, was an anglicized American.

but the fact is he & I are now writing a play in collaboration. A friend of his approached me on the matter, & Knoblock turned up with a ripping idea, just my sort. We share equally in the proceeds, but I am the senior partner, & my name comes first in the signature. He has come over to Fontainebleau to work with me, & the play will be finished at the end of the month. He thinks the Haymarket may like it. Anyhow we shall be fairly stiff on terms. You will of course have control of all my dramatic interests in this play. He also has an agent, I believe. Please say nothing of this till the end of the month.

About the middle of next year I propose to do the *Don Juan.*

Thine, A. B.

WESTMINSTER GAZETTE, 24 August 1911 / 231
(*To the editor*)

Villa des Néfliers
August 23 [1911]

Sir,

Your article accurately describes the manner in which M. Briand put an end to the French railway strike, but it omits to state the exceedingly important sequel: namely, the obstinate ill-will of the employees, resulting in bad services and enormous inconvenience and loss—and no inconsiderable bodily danger —to the public every day of every week. The condition of affairs on the Western (State) line is desperate, and the managers are notoriously at their wits end. The moral is obvious. I should hesitate to blame M. Briand for his action. He had to deal with a gang of adventurers, and he beat them. But he had also to deal with an immense multitude of genuinely aggrieved workmen, and with these he has been less successful. If the circumstances recurred the Government would certainly not use the same tactics again.

I heartily disagree with your remark: 'In no country in the world does luxury parade itself so openly as it does in Paris.' Not only is there far more wealth in London than in Paris, but its display is far more spectacular in London than in Paris. Paris must not be judged by a few hundred yards of boulevard. One can walk continuously for miles in London through streets and squares of houses not one of which is kept up on less than a thousand a year—and nearly all of them are occupied by the pleasing kind of person who contributes passionately to collections for railwaymen who have been faithless to their cause.

Yours faithfully, Arnold Bennett

TEXAS / MS. / 232
(*To William Lee Mathews*)

Villa des Néfliers
24 Augt 1911

My dearest William,

The least you can do now is to take offices in Arundel Street, I think.

The new play is finished. The first two acts are gone to the typewriter, & Knoblock is just looking through the third. I have the highest opinion of this play. I think it is extremely original, striking, dramatic, and true to life. I may tell you (as between ourselves) that I took the precaution of writing it myself. 98 per cent of the dialogue is mine, & I have kept the documentary proof of this. (But don't go & say so to Knoblock's agent!) The scheme of the play is wholly Knoblock's. I only slightly improved the construction of the second act. Knoblock is not much of an artist, in my opinion, but he is very highly skilled indeed in all matters of construction and of stage-effects, & he is one of the most agreeable, even-tempered men I ever met; delightful to work with. I enclose copy of a letter which we have agreed I should write to him.

It is understood between us that Eadie is to have the first offer of this play. But of course he must decide at once—say in ten days. It would not necessarily be for the Royalty. The play had better be sent to him by you. You will receive two copies in due course. Knoblock's agent is Golding Bright, whom doubtless you know. I suppose you will at once, as the agent of

231. Aristide Briand (1862–1932), Minister of the Interior at this time, put down a railway strike by mobilizing 200,000 men, most of them workers themselves, to guard the railway system. The strike had been threatening for several months, and bore revolutionary overtones. England herself was being crippled by railway strikes at the same time. The *Westminster Gazette*, in an editorial on the subject on 21 August, remarked that the real social issue had not been solved by M. Briand's actions, and had in some respects worsened. The gulf between classes had hardened, hatred of military service had deepened, and the just grievances that had brought on the strike were yet to be dealt with.

the senior partner, put yourself in communication with him, with a view to a joint plan of campaign.

My address will be 'The Authors' Club, 2 Whitehall Court S.W.' from Sept. 1st, but I shall not be in town any week-end.

Thine, A. B.

FALES, NYU / MS. / 233
(*To an unidentified person*)

Villa des Néfliers
[Summer 1911]
Dear Madam,

I quite perceive that this is only a ruse to get my autograph. I yield. If you have read the note at the end of *Clayhanger* (& you can't have read the book without reading the note) you must know that the second part is to be published in the autumn of this year. Clayhanger (so far as I know) is pronounced as spelt.

Yours faithfully, Arnold Bennett

BUTLER / MS. / 234
(*To Edward Knoblock*)

2, Whitehall Court
13th Sept 1911
My dear Knoblock,

Many thanks for your letter. I have had a letter of blank amazement from Lee Mathews about my interview with Vedrenne, & I'm dashed if I can understand it. I was not at all keen on Vedrenne & Eadie having the first refusal of our play, but you said you thought Eadie ought to have it, & I agreed, & this clause was put into our mutual letter. Eadie is in partnership with Vedrenne & can do nothing without Vedrenne, & the the play was sent first by our express instructions to Eadie. What for, if Vedrenne & Eadie were not to have the first refusal? Why put such a clause in our letter if it is to be a

232. Arundel Street was the address of the Pinker literary agency, and one or two other agencies. It is unlikely that Mathews acted as dramatic agent for anyone other than Bennett. Dennis Eadie (1875–1928), one of the lessees of the Royalty Theatre, took *Milestones* for that theatre, and played the role of John Rhead.

Bennett was in England from 31 August until he sailed for America on 7 October.

'dead letter'? In the face of the clause, why does Bright offer the play instantly to Harrison?

Vedrenne came to me about another matter (the date of production of *The Honeymoon*), & then asked me whether his firm had the first refusal of *Milestones*. In answering 'Yes', I imagined I was saying something that was notoriously understood. 'Yes' was all I answered. How could I have answered 'No'? I discussed nothing, & referred him to agents. What should you have done in my place? I told Lee Mathews that I hoped Vedrenne & Eadie would not get the play, that it would be made impossible for them to have it, by some means; but if they were not to have the first refusal, formally, our letter, & the sending of the play at once to Eadie, were merely ridiculous. Certainly, *I* hope they will not have the play; I hope that another management will be able somehow to engage Eadie for it. But if I was wrong, what does our letter mean? Supposing I had said 'No', what would Eadie have said? I hope you will send a copy of this part of my letter to Bright. And I hope that if you think some consideration has escaped my notice, you will let me know, as I am extremely anxious to behave correctly. I hate discussing business, but I can't prevent Vedrenne calling on me.

Nothing is easier than to make the terms impossible for Vedrenne.

With regard to the Cunard, my friend has no 'pull'. He only said he knew the johnnies on the boats & would write them or something like that. After your confession about snoring, I think I'd better have a cabin to myself. If I have a fancy to hear your snoring, I can always creep round from my own cabin & listen, can't I? Perhaps it will be best if I get my own berth and leave you to get yours; but I'll wait your reply to this.

I am going to Glasgow on Friday. Boucicault doesn't want me at rehearsals until he has got one act into some sort of order, & they only began on Monday, so I haven't been yet. I shall return from Glasgow on Tuesday. If you do not post your letter in good time on Thursday, you might address it to Royalty Theatre Glasgow.

Yours, A. B.

234. John E. Vedrenne (1867–1930) had formerly been Granville Barker's partner at the Court Theatre. Bennett met him in 1908. The two men seem always

w. morgan / ms. / 235   George H. Doran Company
(*To Margaret Marriott*)   Thirty-five West Thirty-second Street
                          New York
                          10 Nov 1911

Dear Mrs. Marriott,

I am very sorry that I was not in London to answer the question which you put to Marguerite & which she could not answer. Of course I should have been charmed to say Yes, but nevertheless Marguerite was quite right in not answering for me. I suppose it's too late now, but anyhow I will be a godfather in spirit. If Fred was here he would *really* be having the time of his life. He would be overwhelmed. I am.

Love to all,

Ever yours, A. B.

I return on Lusitania sailing 29th.

herzog / ms. / 236
(*To Elsie Herzog*)   [Indianapolis]
                                                 [Indiana]
                                                 20 Nov 1911

Dear Mrs. Herzog,

It was the person & not the personage to whom you were talking. It was the person and not the personage to whom you promised some very interesting written particulars; the which promise you have broken, & the which I beseech you to repair at once. How on earth do you expect the person to write true

---

to have been at odds.

Golding Bright (d. 1941) was a leading dramatic agent in England.

Dion Boucicault (1859–1929) produced and played the male lead in *The Honeymoon*.

235. George Doran (1869–1956) was Bennett's American publisher, and his host during most of the American trip. For details of the trip, see Vol. I, pp. 162–5.

The Marriotts invited Bennett to be godfather to their adopted daughter Minetta, born to one of Frederick Marriott's sisters. Of Minetta Marriott (now Mrs. Wainwright Morgan) there exists a limerick by Bennett, written when she was three or four years old. She was ill, and 'Aunt' Marguerite visited her:

> There was a young girl called Minetta
> Who was ill & wouldn't get betta
> She tried, it is said,
> To climb under the bed
> And wept when her Aunt wouldn't letta.

novels about women unless he can depend upon the friendly & frank collaboration of a woman now & then who isn't afraid of examining herself honestly? It was not nice of you to burn your communication. *I* would have burned it, à la rigueur! It was nice of you to write me, but not nice of you to omit the enclosure so positively promised. Now I shall really expect you to keep that promise.

It is the person & not the personage who writes my novels. The personage only appears on very formal occasions.

I had a most agreeable and inspiring evening at your house. Please give my very kindest regards to Mrs. Hellman, & to your husband, and believe me, expectant.

Yours sincerely, Arnold Bennett

P.S. I am writing this at Indianapolis. I shall reach N.Y. on Wednesday night.

BERG / MS. / 237
(*To Frederick Marriott*)   The Bellevue-Stratford
                                              Philadelphia
                                              22 Nov 1911
My dear Fred,
   I have had vague news of the auto from Marguerite. I don't see why it should wait while I choose the colour of green for the upholstery. You 2 ought to be able to do that between you. I want it to have all the necessary & best contrivances aboard, especially a speedometer, & also 2 methods of warning—a horn & also the horrid thing (whose name I forget but it is very menacing). Briefly I may as well have the best of everything on this crock. It may interest you to know that I could have got scores & scores of engagements to read extracts from *How to Live on 24 Hours a Day* at from £75 to £100 a night. In fact I could have paid for 3 Lanchester autos by showing my face to

236. Elsie Herzog (1877–1919) was the wife of Paul Herzog (1874–1925), who was solicitor to the George H. Doran Company, and a Director of the firm. Bennett visited the Herzogs on two occasions, and is remembered by their son, Paul M. Herzog, who was then five years old, as 'a man with prominent front teeth who was ill at ease with children, or at least with this particular child'.
On Mrs. Hellman see pages 295–6.

audiences. So I think I ought to be able to afford myself *one* good one.

Love to all yours, & many best thanks to all of you for looking so faithfully after Marguerite.

Thine, A. B.

Very glad Tommy liked the play.
Marguerite's version of his name is Thoma Glundy.

TEXAS / TS. / 238
(*To William Lee Mathews*)

George H. Doran Company
35 West 32nd Street
November 23, 1911

Dearest William:

Very many thanks for your letter of the 15th, and particularly for the postscript, which I entirely appreciate.

With regard to *The Great Adventure*, I do not see how there can possibly be any difficulty about the copyright, but I shall put this in the hands of Mr. Ames as soon as I see him. Certainly he ought to pay the full £400 in England.

With regard to the third act of *The Honeymoon*, I have no doubt that in the theatre it would be possible to do very much superior work, but I can assure you most seriously that it is quite out of the question for me to do the act afresh. It is a literal fact that if I were offered £2,000 to do this over again, I should respectfully decline. I am glad to see that Mr. Dion Boucicault thinks it would not be of much use to alter merely the end of the play. I quite agree with him. I should like you to understand exactly how I feel about this third act. The explanation given by 'Flora' just before the end is, I think, a little bit too abrupt; instead of being in one single speech, it ought to be broken up into a series of exchanges between her and 'Cedric'. Apart from this I have no serious fault to find, although I am inclined to think as regards the actual presentation on the stage that Mr. Vernon might have done something a little superior.

As to the returns, they seem to me to be quite satisfactory,

237. Tommy Gundry was a member of the Bennett–Marriott circle. He is not otherwise known.

but there is one question which I should like to ask; namely, how much the theatre actually holds in practice. For example, on Tuesday, November 7th, the return is £164.16. Yet on that evening my wife went to the theatre a few moments before the performance began with two friends, and there was literally only one single seat to spare in the house. I have no doubt that there is a perfectly proper explanation of this, but I am curious to know how it is.

I sail on Wednesday next by the *Lusitania*.

Yours ever, A. B.

HELLMAN / MS. / 239
(*To Hilda Hellman*)

Cunard
R.M.S. *Lusitania*
30th Nov 1911

Dear Mrs. Hellman,

It is appropriate for me to write this on Thanksgiving Day. Why are people so good-natured? Why are you so good-natured? Anyhow I am very much obliged, & indeed tickled by this gift from one who prefers women to men. The explanation of the phenomenon perhaps is that I am partly a woman, à mes heures. I hope you are by this time well into *Les Liaisons dangereuses*. And if you do not deeply admire & love *La Chartreuse de Parme*, please remember that the fault *is* yours. I have now sundry good reasons for coming back to New York, & not the least of them is to see you & George Sidney again. My kind regards to him. My best thanks & best wishes to you. And may you not lose that *nuance* of maliciousness!

Yours sincerely, Arnold Bennett

238. Winthrop Ames (1871–1937), American theatrical figure, was associated with the American production of *The Great Adventure*, which was first performed in New York on 16 October 1913.

239. Mrs. Hellman and her husband George Sidney Hellman (d. 1958), writer and dealer in rare books and manuscripts, were among the people whom Bennett met in New York. Of the gift, Bennett wrote in his Journal on the same day: 'It was an article for desk use, in silver, heavy and elaborate, engraved with my name, and the card on it bore the following words: "Thank you for all the delightful things you have written and are going to write during the coming year." George [Doran] will think he can guess the woman it came from at first guess. He couldn't. But he might guess it in three, perhaps. And I had five letters from other ladies, chiefly hating *Hilda Lessways*, but nevertheless all rustling with flattery.'

Along with his letter to Mrs. Hellman Bennett sent a list of French works for

HERZOG / MS. / 240
(*To Elsie Herzog*)

Lusitania
30 Nov 1911

Dear Mrs. Herzog,

Many thanks. Why offer excuses, when you simply wrote what I asked, & so put me under a great obligation? Nobody can offer useful personal advice. The only general advice is: to be honest with yourself, and, in being honest, to be discreet. I always keep my letters short. But I may tell you I am looking forward with great interest to my next visit to your home.

With best wishes & most cordial regards.

Believe me,

Yours sincerely, Arnold Bennett

YALE / MS. / 241
(*To Mrs. George Day*)

Hôtel Californie
Cannes
17 Dec 1911.

Dear Mrs. George Day,

Your protégé was duly invited to the author's lair in a Paris hotel, and had tea with him and his wife. He seemed to be quite at his ease, with a little touch of naivete now and then that had its charm. He talked quite frankly about everything, and made a very agreeable impression upon both the said author & his wife. He quite realises the difficulties he has to face. What with singing, piano, musical theory, & foreign languages, his days are certainly full. In fact he must be working very hard. However, he didn't look tired nor seem downhearted. On the contrary he was wearing a coquettishly quiet suit of clothes and a resolute neck tie, and was living most

---

her to read. The list was written on the back of a hotel bill; it included Gide's *La Porte étroite*, *Isabelle*, and *Prétextes*, Fromentin's *Dominique*, Constant's *Adolphe*, Stendhal's *L'Abbesse de Castro*, *Le Rouge et le noir*, *La Chartreuse de Parme*, and *Le Physiologie de l'amour*, and Laclos's *Les Liaisons dangereuses*.

Mrs. Hellman writes: 'There are two things that have remained in my memory about my conversation with A.B. that evening. He told me that he had never been in love until he was 39. He asked me whether I had ever thought of writing. When I said I did not feel I had the talent for it he said "Oh yes, anyone who sees the truth the way you do can write." '

cheerfully up to this apparel. I envied him his boots. He scarcely looks his age. His greatest difficulty, on the road to being a first-class artist, will probably be neither in voice training nor in learning to articulate foreign languages without an accent, it will be in acquiring an artistic education. He has of course practically no artistic education, either specially in music, or generally. He needs to hear vast quantities of music, and to consort with artists of all sorts. Undoubtedly as de Reszke is an old man (let us not forget), his general influence on his pupils' *taste* must be reactionary. Master Alexander has as yet heard practically *no new* music at all. Nevertheless I think he has made admirable progress in the time, for I can picture to myself what he was when you sent him over. I have put him on to a particular friend of mine who is one of the greatest musical experts in France, & I hope that something may come of this. I only wished that I could myself take him about to operas, concerts, picture-galleries and writers' studies, and hear all his impressions, and really explain the modern point of view to him at enormous length in all the arts. This would be a great lark for me. It might ruin him, but at any rate he would be inoculated.

We *liked* him.

So sorry I was so acutely indisposed when I visited you. (Because I was, you know!) And thank you again in particular for that tea. New Haven railroad station is the most awful I ever saw (I think). Strange that it should be so close to a house so nice and agreeable as yours! I enjoyed your university atmosphere, and was impressed by your youthful husband's air of responsibility. Lastly I regret you did not perform musically for me. But you are both very young, and so you must be allowed to refuse when you feel like it. My kindest regards, et meilleurs souvenirs, to both of you.

Cordially yours, Arnold Bennett

P.S. We expect to be here for the winter. When we go through Paris again, about April, I shall try to see the young man again.

A. B.

241. On leaving America on 30 November 1911, Bennett went first to England, and then he and Mrs. Bennett went to live at Cannes for four months.

Mrs. Day and her husband, George Parmly Day (d. 1959), entertained Bennett

STOKE / MS. / 242
(*To Lucie Simpson*)

Hôtel Californie
18th [January 1912]

Dear Miss Simpson,

Several times [?] I have to cut myself to the heart by refusing flattering invitations like yours. I am very sorry, but this kind of thing is entirely out of my line. I am merely a writer—not at all a speaker. In proof of my seriousness, let me tell you that while I was in the States I refused nearly a hundred invitations to lecture or read at a minimum of £100 a time. After this you will believe that I have a real objection to exposing myself.

Believe me,

Regretfully & cordially yours, Arnold Bennett

TEXAS / MS. / 243
(*To M. D. Calvocoressi*)

Hôtel Californie
23rd Jan 1912

My dear Calvo,

This is to wish you good speed on this formidable excursion. We shall anticipate with excitement & fever your accounts of 'l'amour en russie' when you return. We expect to be in Paris about—but not *at*—Easter. The weather here is everything that is damnable, & I am working very well. I don't know *what* Marguerite was writing to you about translations of my immortalities. But I should say that something might be arranged *if* you would tie yourself down to dates.

Behave yourself as much as you can. Our wishes for your welfare follow you like a sweet influence. Kindest regards from us both to yourself & your mother, who we hope is well & still making stylish hats!

Thine, A. B.

---

at lunch in New Haven. Day was treasurer of Yale University. Bennett noted in his Journal: 'Horrible railway station at New Haven. Drove up in a sort of funeral carriage. Nice wooden quaint house. G. Day a very quiet and patriotic sort of man.' Mrs. Day's protégé is unidentified. On Jean de Reszke see page 88 n.

242. The invitation was for Bennett to be guest of honour at a dinner of the Writers' Club.

243. Calvocoressi was a director of the Russian opera in Paris for a time, and

BUTLER / MS. / 244
(*To C. F. Cazenove*)

Hôtel Californie
27th Jan 1912

Dear Mr. Cazenove,
Many thanks for your letter dated the 26th. Heinemann's offer is very interesting & I am glad that so good a judge of literature should show some enthusiasm for my work. I cannot however consider his offer, as I have made a contract which works out very satisfactorily indeed. I may tell you that I am not very keen on a large advance, as it is so apt to lead to dissatisfaction. For the same reason, I have actually refused 30% royalty, because I thought the publisher would be over-reaching himself. My plan is to provide in the contract for a reasonable minimum advance in any event & to make the publisher actually pay in advance a sum equal to the amount earned to date by the previous book. This works very well. But anyhow the question of advance is for me a minor one. There are other clauses in my contracts which I regard as more important, & I don't think that any publisher would agree to a better contract than the one I am now working under. This letter is of course a purely friendly epistle, like yours.
Again thanks for your interest.

Yours sincerely, Arnold Bennett

---

the visit to Russia was presumably in this connection. Nothing is known of any translations by him of Bennett's works, though he did a good deal of other translating.

244. C. F. Cazenove (d. 1915) was one of the directors of the Literary Agency of London. Bennett was no more satisfied with his current publisher, Methuen, than he had been with Chapman and Hall or Chatto and Windus earlier; and William Heinemann (d. 1920) apparently made an approach to him through Cazenove, who of course was not Bennett's regular agent. On Bennett's relations with his publishers, see Vol. I, *passim*. Eventually he shifted most of his work from Methuen to Cassell.

FALES, NYU / MS. / 245
(*To Thomas B. Wells*)

Hôtel Californie
9th Feby 1912

My dear Wells,

I have seen your letter to Pinker of the 25th in which you say that the suggestion for extra articles came from me. This is quite contrary to the fact. It was not merely at your suggestion, but at your reiterated suggestion, that I began to consider the question of enlarging the series. The series is now enlarged, and definitely so. My mind is absolutely clear as to our interviews, and so far as I am concerned the point admits of no argument.

I do not and will not agree to the articles being published under separate titles. The series was commissioned, & has been written, as a series. I have chosen the general title & I insist on it, since the signature is mine. Also I utterly object to non-consecutive publication. When we discussed dates, you made no reference whatever to the possibility of non-consecutive publication, & agreed with me that the series could easily be finished in September.

I have no doubt that you perfectly understand the implications of this letter, my dear Wells, & that I have only to put the thing clearly in order to end any misconceptions.

Believe me,

Yours sincerely, Arnold Bennett

FALES, NYU / MS. / 246
(*To Thomas B. Wells*)

Hôtel Californie
11th Feby 1912

My dear Wells,

Many thanks for your letter of the 30th.

There will be no ninth article. Only eight.

The sixth article was finished a fortnight ago. About $\frac{1}{3}$rd of

---

245. Thomas B. Wells (1875–1941) was an editor of *Harper's*. The articles referred to were a series entitled *Your United States*. Six articles were originally commissioned, and eight were ultimately published in *Harper's*, consecutively, from April through November 1912.

it is devoted to the drama, & this will most assuredly have to stand. There is in it nothing libellous & nothing offensive. The reverse! If you Americans don't take an interest in your drama it is about time you did. As for me, I am always against popular 'correct' attitudes towards the arts, as they are always wrong. Anyhow you didn't engage me to write on America in any hope that I should reflect once more in your magazine the attitude of correct New York! At least I trust not. It may be a rude shock for you to find me praising things that you simply wouldn't touch with a pair of tongs, but you've just got to stand for it, my dear fellow. You will find that my all too brief remarks on the American stage will raise mountains of comment. In a word, both *Harpers* & I will 'get away with it'. How in the name of God can I write about the stage without mentioning names? And was I, a dramatist, to be expected not to write about the stage? Tut-tut!

Yours sincerely, Arnold Bennett

HARVARD / MS. / 247
(*To Colonel Harvey*)

Hôtel Californie
15th Feby 1912

My dear Colonel Harvey,

I hear with pain that you have taken advantage of my short temporary absence from the United States to arrange a dinner in honour of William Dean Howells. I suppose you were afraid that if he and I got together he might be found not disagreeing with those views on certain Victorian novelists which I have expressed once too often and which have procured my ruin in the esteem of all thoughtful Americans. I would have given much to be able to be present at this dinner; for there is no man of letters in the whole world whom I regard more highly

246. In his article Bennett remarked that 'the American drama is more closely related to sporting diversions than to dramatic art', and he added that he was ready to say the same of English and French drama. He did think that the money spent on theatres and theatre-going in America, coupled with the increase of mass education, indicated 'a more glorious hereafter for the American drama'. Printed comment on the whole series of articles seems to have been slight and favourable. Published in book form in 1912, the series bore the title *Your United States* in America and *Those United States* in England.

X

than I regard your guest. It may astonish you to learn that even thirty years ago—and more—*Harper's* used to penetrate monthly into the savage wilderness of the Five Towns, and that the first literary essays I ever read were those of W. D. Howells and Russell Lowell. (I preferred the former because they were more friendly, persuasive and human.) Thus I was at a tender age more American than some Americans. My delight in W. D. Howells has never lessened; it has indeed increased in proportion as I have learned to appreciate the subtlety of his wit, the sure fineness of his taste, the immense sweep of his culture, and the force of his creative gift. Criticism, travel, novels, plays— for I am not one to forget on this august occasion that W. D. Howells is an admirable playwright—I have feasted on his output, and stolen innumerable ideas therefrom, since the period when I could only smoke in secret; and I propose to continue feasting as long as Mr. Howells provides the fare. May that be a very long time! It is rumoured that the man is seventy-five years old. Incredible! Pick up almost any number of *Harper's* and you will find evidence that he is not seventy-five, but about forty-four—a nice youthful age,—and my own. I have never met Mr. Howells. When I go to America he retires to Spain, and when I come to France in search of him he has vanished to Timbuctoo. But I intend to meet him. And in the meantime I should like to express, through you, my profound admiration for him, and, if I may be permitted, my grateful affection. I cannot raise my glass. But I can raise my pen, and I do, to his health and long life and unabated activity. I feel very strongly about W. D. Howells. We of the Five Towns are always least articulate when we feel most strongly, and I realise that I have not said what I wanted to say. But W. D. Howells will forgive me.

Yours sincerely, Arnold Bennett

247. Colonel George Harvey (1864–1928) was President of Harper and Brothers from 1900 to 1915 and also owner and publisher of the *North American Review* (see pages 266–7). He arranged a party for Howell's seventy-fifth birthday, and had more success with an invitation to the President of the United States.

ILLINOIS / MS. / 248
(*To Jane Wells*)

Hôtel Californie
17 Feby 1912

Dear Mrs. Wells,
Many thanks for your letter.
Inflammation of the intestines.
Convalescent.
Strict régime.
But working.
Just began the further adventures of Edward Henry Machin, but my joy therein is clouded by the news that influenza has reduced you to shadows. Kindly become substantial once more.
I shall be charmed to have the proofs, & to know about how long I can keep them. Phillips of the *American Mag*, a most delightful man, stated with sad resignation to me that he had not been able to get any corrected proofs out of H. G. Or such is my recollection. However, I told him how great H. G. was, & he seemed comforted.

Nos sympathies les plus chaudes, Arnold Bennett

TEXAS / MS. / 249
(*To William Lee Mathews*)

Hôtel Californie
29th Feby 1912

Dearest William,
Mrs. C. N. Williamson, Maisonnettes Hotel, De Vere Gardens. Will you kindly see that two seats for *Milestones* are sent on my behalf to the above lady for one night towards the end of next week. Likewise two seats for *The Honeymoon*, which I believe is at Hammersmith next week. When you have done so, will you kindly drop a line to the above lady to say that you

248. Bennett suffered an attack of illness on 31 January 1912. It may in fact have been a light case of typhoid fever. The result was an interruption of serious work, notably the writing of the third Clayhanger volume. The sequel to *The Card*, *The Regent*, was written between February and April.
Bennett corrected proofs of Wells's new novel, *Marriage*. John S. Phillips (1861–1949) published the *American Magazine*, and serialized both *Marriage* and *The Regent* in it.

have done so, & that if the night doesn't suit it can be changed. And I shall be much obliged.

We ain't coming to the 1st of *Milestones*. You of course will be there. You will infinitely oblige us by, after the performance, strolling down to the telegraph office at Charing Cross, & spending about ten bob (which you will charge to my account) on telegraphing a truthful description of the first night. No flowers, by request. We shall have this telegram first thing on Wednesday morning, & we shall be glad to have it, as we feel a certain mild interest in the piece.

What is Iden Payne doing with *C. & C.* up & down the country? Has he got the rights?

I am now nearly well again & working in full blast.

Thine, A. B.

BUTLER / MS. / 250
(*To Cedric Sharpe*)

Hôtel Californie
3rd Mch 1912

My dear poor sweet Cedric,

Do you really suppose we keep such things lying about in our drawers? Although I have the greatest sympathy with young composers in search of a libretto, all I can practically do is to refer them to Wagner's example! When we come over I must see Mr. Goossens, & then I will try to suggest some way out of his difficulty. I am charmed to hear about the Borodine. I suppose it will be quite some time before you *really* see how great these quartets are! Your mother sent me a very nice letter the other day, & I have not replied to it, partly because it needed no instant reply, & partly because I'm too busy. But transmit to her my best thanks.

Thine, A. B.

249. Mrs. C. N. Williamson, the novelist (1859–1920), was a friend of Bennett's of several years' standing. *Milestones* opened at the Royalty Theatre on 5 March 1912. *The Honeymoon* had occasional productions in London and the provinces during 1912 and 1913. *Cupid and Commonsense* was produced in the provinces in 1911 and 1912. Iden Payne (see page 255 n.) produced it in Chicago in 1913.

250. Bennett eventually wrote two libretti for Eugene Goossens (d. 1962). See Vol. I, pp. 386–7, 409. He had already written one based on *Antony and Cleopatra* for a French composer, but it was never used.

CALIF / MS. / 251
(*To Eden Phillpotts*)

Hôtel Californie
7 Mch 1912

Dear Phillpotts,
Many thanks for your letter & the 'Pap'. I return the latter. It is a fact that though I mixed in every possible sort of society in U.S.A. I never came across any set that did not congratulate me, on entering it, upon having at last got to the real U.S.A. I've not lost sight of this in my articles, which for the rest pretend to be nothing but the superficialities of a 7 weeks stay. I don't think either you or your wife see enough theatrical productions to be able to judge how good *The S.W.* was compared to current standards. Anyhow I am quite sure that the affair did a great deal of good. Your kind vows for *Milestones* were richly realised on Tuesday. It now only remains for you to conjure away the strike, which is ruffling the theatres considerably.
I am practically cured, thanks.

Yours sincerely, Arnold Bennett

PALL MALL GAZETTE, 21 March 1912 / 252
(*To the editor*)

[Hôtel Californie]
March 17 [1912]

Sir,
In reply to Mr. Archer's letter, the authors' procedure, as regards the year 1860, was this. They practically read through the whole of *Punch* for that year, and chose a number of conversational phrases from its dialogues. They were much struck by the prevalence in 1850 of phrases which they had imagined to be quite modern. I cannot at the moment consult Mr.

251. The 'Pap' is unidentified.
Phillpotts's play *The Secret Woman* was granted a licence by the Lord Chamberlain on the condition that five short passages be deleted. The play was produced privately at the Kingsway in February 1912, and the Government took no action. A letter of protest against some would-be censors in Parliament was published in *The Times* on 14 February, signed by Barrie, Galsworthy, Masefield, Shaw, Wells, and others. By accident Bennett's name did not appear there.
Milestones was Bennett's greatest theatrical success. It ran for nearly two years. A general coal strike began on 26 February and lasted until 6 April.

Knoblock, but my strong impression is that 'faddist' was among the words discovered in *Punch* for 1860. 'I should love to' is certainly an old phrase. As for 'gone one better', I have been familiar with it all my life, and I can recall events in 1871.

The fact is that language changes more slowly than social conditions. We still say that a steamer sails. And even social conditions are very deliberate in their evolution. It was rather staggering to learn from a cartoon in *Punch* that the Albert Hall was being used for Suffragette meetings twenty-seven years ago.

Yours truly, Arnold Bennett

ILLINOIS / MS. / 253
(*To Jane Wells*)

Hôtel Californie
20 Mch 1912

Dear Mrs. Wells,

I return the proofs by registered bookpost. I have read them with care. I have of course confined my observations to misprints, punctuation, points of phraseology, & sentences of which I absolutely failed to grasp the meaning. I daresay H.G. may consider some of my criticisms as a proof-reader beneath notice; but having regard to his great onslaught, in the novel, on the general sloppiness of everything except pure research, I think it may be worth his while to consider them. I have had to disfigure the proofs with my remarks, as a mere question note would not have made my suggestion clear always. You can rub them out if the worst comes to the worst, as they are all in pencil.

I had great difficulty in correcting some parts as I was too interested in the narrative to fix my mind on H.G.'s shortcomings as a writer who knows the details of his business. The

252. A review of *Milestones* in the *Pall Mall Gazette* on 6 March 1912 commented on the clever use of change in language over the three generations that the play deals with, and noted parenthetically that the use of 'Shake!' instead of 'Shake hands' in the first act (set in 1860) must have been a slip. On the 11th Bennett wrote to say that it was not a slip. On the 15th William Archer asked whether Bennett could justify 'faddist', which, he said, the *Oxford English Dictionary* put no earlier than 1883. He also questioned 'he has gone one better' in the mouth of a young woman in 1860.

Labrador episode ought by all the theory of chances to have been a failure, but I don't think it is. It held me throughout. But then I am an *admirer* of H.G.—probably the best he has. Anyhow I am a thundering good proof reader!

Yours sincerely, Arnold Bennett

P.S. Where I have put in punctuation without a query, I think the question is beyond argument.

ILLINOIS / MS. / 254
(*To H. G. Wells*)

Hôtel Californie
21—3—12

Dear father,

No, they have not got me at all. Under no circumstances would I countenance this grotesque Institution. I suppose you never read my deathless article on it in the *New Age* 19 months ago. Go ahead & make a row.

Yours, E. A. B.

TEXAS / MS. / 255
(*To William Lee Mathews*)

Hôtel Californie
3rd April 1912

Dearest William,

Many thanks. I return Alice's statement. The position between you & me is perfectly clear. You are my agent for the world, & you are entitled on present & future plays to deduct ten per cent., & not more than ten per cent. nor less, from the sums paid by managers for my plays. You are entitled to make any arrangements you like with other agents & to decide your commission with them as you like. This is a matter which does not concern me. On the other hand you are not entitled to let

253. Wells replied: 'My dear Bennett, Your corrections are wonderful and precious. You have the best mind in Europe (in many respects) and I thank you very gratefully.'

254. The Academic Committee of the Royal Society of Literature elected Wells to membership, and Wells refused to accept. Bennett apparently did not have a similar pleasure.

another agent deduct 5% & then yourself to deduct 10% from what you actually receive. It appears to me (though the matter does not concern me) that Alice has done right, in the absence of a definite arrangement between you & her, to deduct one half of the usual commission, leaving the other half for you. But you alone are responsible to me for 90% of all moneys received. It may not have occurred to you that the responsibilities of an agent, legal & otherwise, are terrible and appalling! My agency work, it may interest you to know, costs me now nearly £1,500 a year—a sum for which I could keep a bally tame solicitor and an office staff going. No joke being a fashionable author!

The country is in a very interesting condition, & I agree with what you say. But as an example of a revolt of the poor against the rich, this strike has been a dazzling proof of the ineffectiveness of such a thing even when well managed under discipline. The poor have *suffered* all over the country. The rich have merely been infinitesimally inconvenienced.

Thine, A. B.

BUTLER / MS. / 256
(*To Cedric Sharpe*)

Hôtel du Rhin
11th Apl 1912

My dear Cedric,

I have just finished writing a novel in time to write you my congratulations on having reached your majority without sending your parents to an untimely grave—you must have had one or two near shaves, with your headstrong naughtiness. However, you have my best & most affectionate *good* wishes despite your misdeeds. We are all human—even your mother. Now I understand you have kept off alcohol to this date. I have the strongest feelings about alcohol, & am entirely convinced that it is a rotten bad thing for anybody with a spark of ambition in him, & that the men who lean up against bars & think themselves no end of dogs are miserable & complete chumps suitable

---

255. Alice Kauser (d. 1945) was Edward Knoblock's dramatic agent in America, and the present difficulty concerned arrangements for the production of *Milestones* there. It played in both New York and Chicago during the year.

only to be used as doormats. This letter, therefore, is officially to inform you that if you continue to keep off alcohol for another five years, it will be my pleasure & privilege to hand over to you at the end of that term, from my privy purse, the sum of fifty quid. This is all my message for the moment.

Thine, A. B.

My respectful greetings to papa & mamma, & hoping to see *them* soon. (You of course will be out.) A. B.
We leave here early on Monday.

TEXAS / MS. / 257
(*To William Lee Mathews*)

Hôtel du Rhin
14th April 1912

Dearest William,
Many thanks for your letter. I quite agree as to Selwyns. If they can't place it, let Alice have a try. But I don't for a moment believe that Alice can place it where they can't. I know too much about agents. The receipts of *Milestones* are really rather good, & I am glad to know that Australia is arranged for. I should like Loraine to do *W. The P.W.* And if Edgar Selwyn believes in it for America, let him darned well place it there! I shall see him next week in Paris. He never said to me in any definite way that he thought it could be done in America. But I know when he read the play he was rather knocked over by it—probably had previously looked on me as rather a gifted amateur for the stage. We have become extremely friendly, & I like him very much. But he has no taste & doesn't pretend to have any. Also he has little imagination, & didn't believe in the last act of *Milestones*. (He does now.) He doesn't believe in the last act of *Cupid & C.* Can't *see* it, unless he actually looks at it on the stage. Pardon my conceit, the last act of *W. The P.W.* is all right, & went quite according to my notions at the S.S. performance. What Hawtrey did with it I don't know. When Selwyn began to write a play here—a popular play— he asked me to criticize it *as* a popular play. He had done two acts. I did so. He never wrote another line of it! Nor could he

256. The Bennetts visited Paris briefly in April 1912.

answer a single criticism. But the way he took my destructive-
ness was a great tribute to his character. He hopes to have
recovered by the time he returns to America!

Thine, A. B.

HERZOG / MS. / 258
(*To Elsie Herzog*)

Hôtel Californie
14—4—12

Dear Mrs. Herzog,
    Your letter was very interesting & clever. No doubt you knew
that. But I am astonished that so careful an observer should
talk of my hair being plastered. It never is. And it is impossible
that it should be, as I never administer medicines to it.
MacDonald *made* me disorder it for the photo. It is always dis-
ordered at night, after I have been talking, or trying to talk;
so the portrait is not uncharacteristic in that detail. I could
have told you, without being told, that you *wrote*. I don't know
whether I care much for *A rebours* now. But I care for *Les Sœurs
Vatard*, though how anyone can understand its phraseology who
has not lived long in Paris, I do not see. Impossible for me to
divine what are the mysterious passages in *The Old Wives' Tale*
that puzzled you! I will however admit that no English novelist
ever suggested more unspeakable things, and got away without
being understood, than me in that book. I was inspired to make
the attempt by Wells's assurance to me once that one could say
what one liked even in an English novel, if one was ingenious
enough. By the way, Wells's new novel *Marriage*, of which I
have just read the proofs, contains more intimate conveyances
of the *atmosphere* of married life than anybody has ever achieved
before. I am rather annoyed, as I am about to try to get the
same intimacy in my Clayhanger–Hilda book, entitled *These
Twain*. These coincidences are distressing. I think you would
like *La Nouvelle Revue Française* (31 Rue Jacob, Paris. 1fr 50c.
monthly). The critical articles at the end are always quite first

257. Edgar Selwyn (1875–1944), actor and playwright, headed Selwyn and Co.,
theatrical producers. He supplanted Mathews as Bennett's American dramatic
agent. His brother Archibald was associated with him. 'Loraine' is unidentified.
No American production of *What the Public Wants* is known.

class, & much of the creative stuff is admirable. In fact, for literature pure & simple it is the finest review I ever saw. True, it is run by friends of mine! I have written two books while we have (change of pen) been at Cannes, but it will not be till July 1st that I attack that fearful Hilda Job. I have only been amusing myself here with reflections on U.S.A., & a piece of facetiousness for the *American Mag.* again about Denry Machin. We go to Paris tomorrow for a fortnight, & then to England, but where in England I don't yet know. Even God doesn't know.

I am getting more & more determined to write a book of verse.

Please remember me to the other Hilda.

Yours sincerely, Arnold Bennett

TEXAS / MS. / 259
(*To William Lee Mathews*)   Buckingham Palace Hotel
London, S.W.
6th May 1912

Dearest William,

I enclose a letter from Pinker as to copyrighting of *Great Adventure*, which explains itself. I also return a letter of Vedrenne's.

Last night's play was a most pleasing change. I thought it was very well translated *and* produced. I should somewhat object to the sham archaisms of the dialogue in the original, as I am convinced that this kind of play, with all its calculated unreality, will come off better with absolutely modern realistic phraseology. It showed me still more clearly the enormous possibilities of my *Don Juan* play, which by the way I still mean to write. The fault of the Spanish play, to my mind, is that the plot is not clear. I certainly did not follow it. But episodically the thing is charming, & it opens out new vistas. Wilkinson's *intentions* in the matter of scenery were on the right lines, but his sense of beauty is not sufficiently sure. I think his watercolours detestable. Nevertheless I applaud his effort here, & would see more of it on the stage. Such a night as last night I

---

258. The photograph by Pirie MacDonald (1867–1942) appears as the frontispiece of Vol. I. See also Vol. I, p. 163, on MacDonald. *A rebours* and *Les Sœurs Vatard* are both by J.-K. Huysman (1848–1907).

regard as really valuable, educationally, to the Society—in fact its educational value is superior to the actual value of the play itself. The notion of giving the hero's part to a woman is excellent; it helps immensely to keep the thing on the right plane of external unreality. She played it very satisfactorily, I thought, & looked admirable. And after all, speaking of the other principal female, what's the matter with Mrs. Benson? I have never disliked this actress. And she has the advantage of being able to act.

Many thanks for all the tickets. I'm expecting to hear from you with a rendezvous.

Eaton came out of her ordeal very creditably indeed.

Thine, A. B.

P.S. Have you sent prompt copy of *C. & C.* to Wareing?

MAYFIELD, SYRACUSE / A.D. / 260
(*To the editor of* The Times)

Buckingham Palace Hotel
[about 13 May 1912]

Sir,

A copy of the latest annual report of the Royal Literary Fund was recently forwarded to me from headquarters, and I have been studying its accounts. During the last twenty years the total annual grants have varied from £1,755 to £3,335. In 1910 £2,753.6.8d was the sum actually paid. To achieve this result £780.7.6 was spent, the principal disbursements being: —Secretary's salary £400, office rent £107, and Anniversary Expenses £189. I have no desire to criticize hastily the Royal Literary Fund; my attitude towards it is quite amicable; but at first sight its administration does certainly seem to fail in economy, and I think that the charitable public would be

259. The Bennetts came to England at the end of April 1912 to settle there permanently.

On 5 and 6 May 1912 the Stage Society produced Jacopo Benavento's puppet play, *Les Intereses Creados*, at the Prince's Theatre under the title *The Bias of the World*. Norman Wilkinson (1882–1934), the scene designer, was associated in these years with Lillah McCarthy and Granville Barker. Mrs. Benson may have been Mrs. Frank R. Benson (d. 1946). Miss Eaton is not otherwise known. Alfred Wareing (1876–1942), founder of the Glasgow Repertory Theatre, and managing director until 1913, produced *Cupid and Commonsense*, *What the Public Wants*, and *The Great Adventure* (first performance) there.

interested to know just why in the case of this renowned and old-established corporation the cost of collection & distribution should amount to over 28 per cent of the sum distributed. Surely all charities are not so expensively managed!

Yours obediently, [Arnold Bennett]

FALES, NYU / MS. / 261
(*To Lady St. Helier*)

Royal Albion Hotel,
Brighton.
22nd June 1912

Dear Lady St. Helier,

How charmingly you live up to your unique reputation! You are really very kind indeed, & I am exceedingly sorry that a series of mishaps make it quite impossible for me to take advantage of your kindness. I have been yachting about this coast without an address (hence the delay in this reply) in search of vigorous health but against the wishes of my doctor. I have now seen him again & been talked to like a child, & I have had to enter on a strict course of treatment which promises to endure indefinitely, so far as I can see. Tours, escapades, delights are forbidden to me; also work! Add to this that I have my aged mother here & that she is ill & cannot be left, and you will I hope condone my conduct in general & in particular. Both my wife & I are, as she instructs me to tell you, 'désolés'.

If you actually passed through the Five Towns, you have all my sympathies. They must have appalled you. One can only tolerate them by living in them. I shall only write two more books about them, as I have exhausted my material there, & besides I want to write about London—largely because so many people seem to be convinced that I can't write about London.

With renewed regrets, dear Lady St. Helier, & our united kind regards,

Believe me,
Sincerely yours, Arnold Bennett

260. Bennett's complaints about the Royal Literary Fund echoed those of other writers for many years. His letter appeared with negligible changes in *The Times* on 15 May 1912.

261. Lady (Mary) St. Helier (d. 1931) is described in *Who's Who* as 'indefatigable in service of the poor, and in Society is famed for her brilliant art of entertaining'. This particular occasion is not known.

TEXAS / TS. / 262
(*To Frank Harris*)

Royal Albion Hotel
July 2nd. 1912.

My dear Frank Harris,

You know that I think the play a very first class affair. But as I told you the last time I saw you, in Cannes, I should say that there would be considerable difficulty in getting it into an evening bill. To my mind the best plan would be to try to arrange for a series of matinée performances. There will be a series of quite interesting and serious matinées at the Royalty Theatre in the autumn, and if you care to read the play to Eadie and Vedrenne, I will see that they are made to understand the importance of the occasion.

My wife did see you here at the hotel, but as at that very moment there were certain paragraphs in the papers to the effect that you could not give your series of lectures in London because you were ill in France, she naturally assumed that you expected the utmost discretion from your friends. She received no message at all from you or your wife. By the way I was in Essex at the time.

Our kindest regards to you both,

Ever yours, Arnold Bennett

HERZOG / MS. / 263
(*To Elsie Herzog*)

14 St. Simon's Avenue
Putney
London S.W.
7th Augt 1912

My dear Lady,

I have not been able to reply to your letter before, & in fact I cannot reply to it now. I am still in a very enfeebled & unintellectual condition. I shirk all work & am idle on a really grandiose scale.

262. The play may be *Shakespeare and His Love*, written around 1904 and published in 1910, which Harris had not succeeded in getting produced.

This is the last known letter from Bennett to Harris. How soon the friendship between them cooled is not known. The real break came with the war, when Harris's anti-British sentiments clashed with Bennett's aroused patriotism. Marie Belloc Lowndes, a close friend, says that Bennett was deeply hurt by the episode, and would never discuss it.

The *A.B.C.* was very good indeed. But I had no idea that you wrote it. I knew that it must have been written by someone who knew the subject profoundly. You now see how justified I was in guessing that you wrote. I will now go further & say that I shall be rather surprised if you don't soon write a book —a novel of course, autobiographical of course. If you can get the construction right, it will be good. *Mais tout est là!* I note all that you say.

I am just going off in a yacht in search of my lost brain.

With best wishes,

Yours sincerely, Arnold Bennett

LEEDS / TS. / 264
(*To Clement Shorter*)

14 St. Simon's Avenue
5th October, 1912.

Dear Mr. Shorter,

I see that in your Literary Letter this week, you have been following the example of the United States newspapers, in assuming that I have confused the Sixth Commandment with another one. Of course, I made no answer to the accusation in the United States, but I think I may as well tell you that when I said the Sixth Commandment, I meant it. It is often surprising to me that my best jokes are unseen by anybody except their author.

Believe me,

Yours sincerely, Arnold Bennett

263. The Bennetts stayed at 14 St. Simon's Avenue for several months until their new home was ready. The house belonged to Herbert Sharpe.

The *A.B.C* is not known. Mrs. Herzog did publish privately a few commemorative volumes of poetry.

264. This letter was printed with negligible changes in the *Sphere* on 19 October 1912. In the issue of 5 October Shorter quoted a passage from *Your United States* that had to do with Bennett's visit to Philadelphia: 'I never was nearer breaking the Sixth Commandment than in one of its homes, where the Countess of Pembroke's own copy of Sir Philip Sidney's *Arcadia*—a unique and utterly unQuakerish treasure—was laid trustfully in my hands by the regretted and charming Harry Widener.' Shorter then chided Bennett, as he said others had too, for thinking that the Sixth Commandment concerned stealing rather than murder. Widener was a contributor to the collection of English books and manuscripts at Harvard University.

EDINBURGH / TS. / 265
(*To the editor of* Everyman,
  Charles Sarolea)

14 St. Simon's Avenue
October 18th, 1912

Dear Sir,

I enclose a letter for publication. I think it is lamentable that such clumsy and gross libels as those with which I deal should have been allowed to appear in the first issue of a paper with the high editorial ideals which you profess, and I hope that no contumacy on the part of your contributor will force me to take the further steps which the article undoubtedly deserves. I have sent a copy of the letter to Mr. Dent.

Yours faithfully, Arnold Bennett

EDINBURGH / TS. / 266
(*To the editor of* Everyman,
  Charles Sarolea)

14 St. Simon's Avenue
October 18th, 1912

Dear Sir,

I have been reading the singular article on myself, signed 'C. S.', in your first issue.

The writer states that I have 'deliberately chosen to suppress' my autobiography, and he gives the reason: 'Mr Bennett . . . naturally prefers to divert attention from the indiscretions of his youth.' 'C.S.' has no justification for such a statement. It is absolutely untrue. The book was remaindered years ago by the publishers, who now probably regret their rash act as much as I always did. If it has not been reissued in England the fault is not mine. I am and have been very anxious to restore it to the public. Unhappily I have not been able to inspire the publishers with my own enthusiasm for a very honest piece of work of which I shall never be ashamed. The publishers control this book. I have reissued it in America, and for years past I have

265. Charles Sarolea (1870–1953) was founder as well as editor of *Everyman*. He ran it for five years. Later he was Professor of French Literature at Edinburgh University. The publisher J. M. Dent (1849–1926) provided some degree of backing for the journal.

included it in the list of my works which appears at the beginning of all my books. By the way, 'C.S.' is wrong in supposing that it has 'almost entirely escaped the notice' of the critics. It has been utilized in scores of articles about me by scores of critics, English, American and French.

The writer further states:—'On the risky subject of *La Maison Tellier*, Maupassant only dares to give us a short story; Bennett has given us the longest of his novels.' If the first statement is absolutely untrue, this is a mere lie. The subject of *La Maison Tellier* is the licensed brothel and its inmates. Will any reader of *The Old Wives' Tale* come forward and assert that the subject of *The Old Wives' Tale* is the brothel? It is true that a couple of prostitutes appear in the novel as subsidiary characters, but the single episode in which they are concerned occupies forty pages out of nearly six hundred. If 'C.S.' has read *The Old Wives' Tale* he is guilty of a deliberate falsehood. If he has not he is guilty of something just as bad. Perhaps he has not read it. (He misquotes the very title twice.) In the face of it he says that the comic not the tragic 'aspect of humanity' appeals to me. Conceivably *The Old Wives' Tale* may gradually become known as a comic work! Indeed I should like to know what works of mine 'C.S.' really has read. He says that I am 'never conscious of a moral purpose', and that I have 'no exalted moral ideals', and no 'didactic purpose'. It does just happen that I have published four purely didactic books concerning the right conduct of life. One might almost suppose that 'C.S.' has read no book of mine except my autobiography. It is difficult to believe that he has read even his own article, which is full of absurd contradictions. For example, in one column I 'always maintain a high artistic ideal'. But in another column my 'scale of literary values is primarily so many pounds per thousand words'.

'C.S.' amplifies this insult thus:—'Those who, like the present writer, have the profoundest admiration for his magnificent gifts will be most sincere in their regret that he should have sold his birthright as a man of genius for a mess of pottage.' It appears that I helped to write *Milestones* 'mainly to make money'. 'C.S.' is here guilty of another serious libel. The basis of his accusation is that in 1901, when I was poor and needed an advertisement for my realistic novels, I spent, on my own confession printed at that time, a trifling portion of my leisure in

Y

writing plays for money and notoriety. (They were the best plays I could then write.) On the strength of this candour, he asserts that 'on my own admission', in 1911, when I had a great deal of money (for an artist) and more than enough notoriety, I wrote *Milestones* 'mainly to make money and to win the kind of fame which is convertible into hard cash'. This is the worst lie. 'C.S.' ought to be ashamed of himself.

Perhaps I may be allowed to remark, as pertinent to the subject, that though I have not suppressed my autobiography, I have suppressed my early plays, none of which has ever been performed. I have been told by pained experts in these markets that in suppressing them I have incidentally suppressed at a moderate computation some forty thousand pounds.

I make no comment on other gross offences in 'C.S.'s' article, and I should not have deigned to offer even this limited protest, did I not deem it my urgent if unpleasant duty to do so, and had I not a certain regard for the editorial ideals of *Everyman*.

Yours faithfully, Arnold Bennett

EDINBURGH / T.C. / 267
(*To J. M. Dent*)

14 St. Simon's Avenue
October 23rd 1912.

Dear Mr. Dent,

Many thanks for your letter of the 21st.

I am flattered by what you say, but would you not consider it rather odd to ask to contribute to your paper an author of whom the editor of the paper had said in his first issue that 'his scale of literary values is primarily so many pounds per thousand words'? I am not disposed to think that the article

266. *The Truth About an Author* appeared anonymously in the *Academy* in 1902, and was issued in book form anonymously by Constable in 1903. Not more than a year and a half later, in the end papers of the first edition of *Tales of the Five Towns*, it was listed among Bennett's publications. The first American edition, in 1911, bore Bennett's name. Early in 1911, when the Bennett boom in America was approaching its peak, various New York papers published lengthy extracts, to Bennett's considerable pleasure (see Vol. I, p. 153). Its original publication in England elicited very favourable reviews, especially in the *Author*, whose critic regarded it as a frank and trustworthy account useful to other authors. Bennett tried to arrange a new edition in England in 1910 if not before (see Vol. I, p. 134), and a new edition did appear in 1914.

was written with animosity, but I am quite sure that it was written with an absolutely inexcusable carelessness and clumsiness.

With my best wishes for the success of your enterprise.

Yours sincerely, [Arnold Bennett]

EDINBURGH / TS. / 268   14 St. Simon's Avenue
(*To J. M. Dent*)   October 25th, 1912

Dear Mr. Dent,
 Many thanks for yours of the 24th.

I am astounded that my letter does not appear in the second issue. The editor wrote me at the end of last week that he would publish it. And now on Friday you ask that it should be modified. An editor who prominently and without any excuse offers the gravest insult that can be offered to a responsible writer ought not to expect smooth words in reply. Neither you nor he seems to realise the enormity of the offence.

Apart from the question of libel, what is to be said of the taste of an editor of a serious paper who, believing that a responsible author has deliberately suppressed a certain book, deliberately rakes up that book and bases on it a scandalous article? Is this according to the canon of taste which you think proper to a paper with the pretensions of *Everyman*?

There is no word in my letter that is not richly justified. For example, a person who, having read *The Old Wives' Tale*, says that its subject is the same as the subject of *La Maison Tellier* is a liar, pure and simple. He is not merely mistaken, it is inconceivable that he should be mistaken. Carelessness really could not go so far; and if you have read the two works you know it as well as I do.

However, I do not wish to seem unreasonable. I have modified my letter. But I do so on the following express conditions:

1. The apology is to be unreserved and complete, without any attempt at justification.

2. The letter and the apology are to appear in the third number.

3. They are to have the same prominence and type as the

article. They are not to be tucked away with a lot of other letters under the heading 'Correspondence'.

I tell you frankly that, if either the apology or the prominence given to it is unsatisfactory to me, I shall not leave the matter where it stands.

Your editor's libels are already being copied in the provincial press, naturally. But do you suppose the provincial press will copy his apology? They will not. This is an example of harm done which cannot be repaired.

I am obliged for your suggestion as to republishing the book. My difficulty is not to find a new publisher. A dozen firms would be delighted to republish it. The trouble is that the original publishers will not let the book go.

Yours faithfully, Arnold Bennett

P.S. I enclose the modified letter.

268. Bennett's modified letter appeared in the issue of 1 November along with Sarolea's apology. Bennett's changes were of the following order. 'It is absolutely untrue' became 'It is untrue'. 'If the first statement is absolutely untrue, this is a mere lie' became 'This statement is scandalously untrue'. 'If "C.S." has read *The Old Wives' Tale* he is guilty of a deliberate falsehood. If he has not he is guilty of something just as bad' became 'If "C.S." has read *The Old Wives' Tale* he has a treasonable memory which unfits him for his task as a critic. If he has not, then how shall his conduct be described?'

The first part of Sarolea's apology read:

'Dear Sir,—I very much regret that my article should have inflicted pain and given offence to an eminent man of letters for whom I entertain, and for whom in that very article I have expressed, the most profound admiration. I also regret that my paper should contain one statement which, as Mr. Bennett proves, is not correct, and another which is misleading. These two statements I unreservedly withdraw, and for these I tender my most sincere apologies.

(1) I state in my article that Mr. Bennett, "after publishing his autobiography, has deliberately chosen to suppress it". I reasonably inferred that so fascinating a book by so famous an author could only have been withheld from the public for nine years because the author himself chose to withhold it. But my inference is obviously not correct. It is Mr. Bennett's publishers, and not Mr. Bennett himself, who for some mysterious reason have refused to republish a work of which Mr. Bennett himself anxiously desired a re-issue.'

The official reason given to Bennett for the failure to publish his letter in the second issue was that the editorial apology arrived at the printer's too late, and the issue was already run off. The real reason was that after hearing from Bennett, Sarolea wrote to his friend G. K. Chesterton for advice, and Chesterton's answer came tardily. In his letter to Chesterton Sarolea described Bennett's letter of complaint as grotesquely absurd. Chesterton replied that he was certain that Bennett would not sue, simply because the English law on libel was so capricious, and he thought that Sarolea's best course would be to make Bennett's protest and Bennett himself appear to be utterly foolish. How to do this? Suggest that no continental

TWENTY LETTERS TO JOSEPH CONRAD / 269
(*To Joseph Conrad*)

14 St. Simon's Avenue
22nd November, 1912

Dear Mr. Conrad,

I was very pleased and honoured by your letter this morning (I will not use any other word but 'honoured' to say what I feel). It gives me the excuse for writing one or two odd ideas in my head about your work. I have often had the impulse to write to you, but one refrains, from some silly notion about a conceivable impertinence. I read *Higuerota* again not long since. I always think of that book as *Higuerota*, the said mountain being the principal personage in the story. When I first read it I thought it the finest novel of this generation (bar none), and I am still thinking so. It is 'majestic and orbicular' and just peerless, and there's no more to be said. It's the Higuerota among novels. I was warned by an Ass that the latter half of *Under Western Eyes* was inferior to the beginning, and I have heard the opinion from others. It is not true. The whole book is superb. But people are so blind, and so infernally obstinate in complaining because a book is not something that the author never intended it to be. Only other creative artists can understand a creative artist. Which limits the public comprehension rather severely. But if one could but convey to you the *passionate* comprehension which some of us have of your work, I think the effect on your health would be good. I wish I could acquaint you with my state of mind—intense satisfaction in seeing a thing truly *done*, mixed with anger because I know I can never do it as well myself—when I recall the quiet domestic scenes behind the shop in *The Secret Agent*, here is rather the sort of thing I reckon to handle myself—but I respectfully retire from the comparison. What I chiefly like in your books of *Reminiscences* is the increasing sardonic quality of them—the rich veins of dark and glittering satire and sarcasm. We want a lot more of that in English literature. There was a lot of it, too, in the latter half

---

writer of any stature would think for a moment of attacking the larger liberties of the press. Suggest that no French writer worth his salt is less than candid about money matters. Imply, therefore, Bennett's provinciality. This will wound his vanity as nothing else can. You may be assured that he will not then dream of prosecuting the case.

of *Under Western Eyes*. I must tell you that I think the close of 'The Secret Sharer' about as fine as anything you've ever done. Overwhelmingly strong and beautiful.

I am one of your despised 'Yachtsmen'. This last summer I sailed in my craft (21 tons net) from Boulogne to Ostend in a storm one day. The rounding of Cape Gris Nez was the greatest sensation I have ever had in my life. Well, I thought of you all the time. Does not this amount to appreciative literary criticism and nothing else?

To me the idea of ardent young artistic people like R[etinger] carrying on a political campaign is chiefly comic. He has, so far as I know, no understanding whatever of politics. But these generous impulses must be humoured. He wanted to get you, and I could not refuse my small aid, seeing that he is one of those capable of real emotion before a work of art.

You would be magnificently welcome on any 'doorstep' of a house inhabited by me and my friends, and my wife and I *ne demanderions pas mieux* than to see you, at any time. But I must not leave you under the impression that I am at home here. We are simply living here for a few months with old friends, named Sharpe, while our house in Essex is being made habitable for us. We expect to be 'settling in' at the end of January. I am very sorry to hear about your health.

Believe me, with all heartiest good wishes and regard.

Yours sincerely, Arnold Bennett

P.S. I was forgetting to thank you for asking R[etinger] to come down.

269. This letter seems to be the only one of a dozen or so letters from Bennett to Conrad to have survived. Bennett wrote a few days earlier to introduce Joseph Retinger, a young Pole, to Conrad. Conrad replied, and mentioned incidentally that his health was poor and had been poor for years, and that he might one day turn up on Bennett's doorstep. To the present letter he replied that 'were it all as true as your intense sympathy will have it, its value would still be infinitely increased to me by the generosity of your recognition'. He denied that he despised yachting. For details on other correspondence see Vol. I, p. 317, and G. Jean-Aubry's edition of Conrad's letters.

Nostromo was published in 1904, *Under Western Eyes* in 1911, *The Secret Agent* in 1907, and 'The Secret Sharer' in 1912 in the collection *Twixt Land and Sea*.

BUTLER / TS. / 270
(*To Edward Knoblock*)

14 St. Simon's Avenue
27th November, 1912.

My dear Edward,

Many thanks for your letter of the 25th, which only reached me this morning.

I think I quite understand the situation with regard to *Milestones* and Lucien Guitry, and the terms proposed seem to me to be quite reasonable. I accept them, subject of course to any serious flaw in them Lee Mathews and Bright may discover in consultation. I am sending on your letter to Lee Mathews.

If you are thoroughly satisfied with Lemaître's work on your play, I should think that he might also be asked to translate *Milestones*. My only reason for agreeing to him is that his name would certainly carry a great deal of weight. I could put my hand on two or three men who would probably do the job much better than he could. But on account of their insignificance in the public eye, they would be unsuitable.

Of course no French adaptation can possibly be any real good unless it is thoroughly and constantly supervised by yourself. I must ask you to bear this clearly in mind. It is extremely wrong and unfair of me to refuse to take any share of the hard work of the French production. Nevertheless, I do refuse to take any share of the hard work of the French production. For myself, rather than be worried by it, I would infinitely prefer to have no French production at all. Happily we are not both built alike.

With regard to the United States, I myself am quite satisfied. Some people over there, however, seem to be a little dissatisfied, as they expected an absolutely record-breaking success. Among these people is my excellent friend Edgar Selwyn. In a recent letter he gave me to understand that there have been two factors against the triumph of the play. The first was that the theatre was too large; and the second was that the play was over-boomed at the start. He said nothing as to the bad elocution of the troupe, but there is no doubt that this has, in itself, caused a great deal of adverse remark.

We must now expect that the receipts at the Royalty will begin slowly to fall.

Marguerite and I will be in Paris at the end of the year. I am very anxious to see your flat and you.

Ever yours, Arnold Bennett

Good luck to *Kismet*.

U.C. / T.C.C. / 271
(*To William Lee Mathews*)   4th December, 1912.

Dearest William,

Many thanks for yours of the 3rd and the enclosures.

May I respectfully point out that the name of James Welch is spelt with a 'C'.

I fully appreciate the importance of what you say as to the manner of dealing with Granville Barker. Certainly the man who could write the first three acts of *The Voysey Inheritance* must be something of a genius, but the man who could write the fourth and fifth acts must be a fool. I should say that if we insisted on the condition that he must not both play the principal part and produce the piece, he will choose to produce, and for this I shall on the whole be glad.

Thine, [A. B.]

HERZOG / MS. / 272
(*To Elsie Herzog*)

14 St. Simon's Avenue
4th Dec 1912

Dear Mrs. Herzog,

I am well aware of the dates of your letters—Augt 27, & Nov. 5th. I have just read them again. They stand a second reading rather well. Perhaps what you ought to write is not a

---

270. No French production of *Milestones* is known. Lucien Guitry (1860–1925) was a leading actor on the French stage. Jules Lemaître (1853–1914), for many years dramatic critic for the *Journal des Débats*, translated Knoblock's great success, *Kismet*, in 1913.

271. James Welch (1865–1917) was an actor notable for his Shaw and Ibsen roles. Granville Barker's *The Voysey Inheritance* was first produced in 1905 and was revived earlier in 1912.

novel—at first, but some articles on social subjects. Most of the stuff written by women in American (& English) newspapers is simply dreadful piffle. You would at once take high rank over the scratching crowd—especially if you took the trouble to 'construct' your articles. An 'aimless winter' must be a mournful experience. You are now—according to your own prophecy— in the middle of it. If you decided to write an article a week, you would find yourself suddenly busy. Many thanks for the MS alphabet, which is filed. It is an excellent alphabet, full of skill. I have not written to you before because I couldn't. Many stars have to sing together in unison before I can sit down & write a letter which I am not bound by the code to write. Can you imagine—you can—what the daily correspondence of a notorious author is? I do not delay answering when I can dictate the answer. But many answers I cannot dictate. There are two quite different writers in me—one dictates, the other uses his own pen. The former is a dull, formal & pompous person, & sometimes a too facetious person. When I cannot dictate the answer, I usually let it go unwritten for ages, without a pang, & deliberately without imaginatively putting myself in the position of the correspondent unanswered. Moreover I have been reading Meredith's letters—undoubtedly one of the masterpieces of English literature—especially the 1st vol. When I contemplate the sheer brains that he frequently put into his letters I marvel but have no desire to imitate. I have merely a desire to write no letters whatever. When my letters are collected & published—& nothing that I can do will stop that happening—my posterity will certainly be disappointed & feel itself aggrieved. And I shall & do feel a malicious delight in its 'deception'. Posterity wants too much, & will pay nothing for it. My health is restored, I believe. Anyhow I am in full work —not on Edwin & Hilda, but on a novel for *Harpers*, which will bear no resemblance whatever to anything by Gilbert Parker or Mrs. Humph. W. The writing of it will be interrupted by our removal into the country. We now possess an early Queen Anne house near the Essex coast, & in February are going to instal ourselves there definitely for everlasting; our deaths will one day cause a sensation in the village which we shall dominate, & the English villagers & landed gentry will wonder, as they stroll through the deserted house, why the madman had 3 bathrooms in a home so small; they will not know that it was due solely to a visit to the U.S.A. My wife has succeeded in making me do less work. She may have succeeded too well. We shall see. We are to see George & his Maries just before Christmas, which we shall spend in Paris, where art and conversation are understood. Still, I amuse myself in London. It is the biggest place yet. Please remember me to yours, & our friends.

Yours sincerely, Arnold Bennett

ILLINOIS / MS. / 273
(*To H. G. Wells*)

14 St. Simon's Avenue
16th Dec 1912

My dear H.G.,

I return the proofs. As before, all suggestions are tentative. But where I have made a definite correction without querying it, I have assumed that you could not possibly contest its propriety. You may go on your way rejoicing about this book. It is all right, especially the difficult parts. I should judge it to be rather better than *Marriage*—certainly more homogeneous—& about as good as *The New M*; only it contains nothing so unconvincing as the hero's change of party in *The New M*. I think there are one or two short weak passages—such as the page or two in Paris, & a few pages towards the end, but naught to speak of. Mary is immense—& so are her letters. What is fine about the darned thing, & what is fine after your previous 2 or 3 darned things, is the generosity & reasonableness of its spirit,—especially the generosity. I have never seen this certainly outstanding quality praised in any review. Yet there it is plain enough.

We go to Paris in a few days for 10 days. We expect to be at Thorpe-le-Soken about Feby 15th. Let's know if you will be in London during January.

Yours, A. B.

272. Bennett began writing *The Price of Love* on 4 November 1912.

The new home was Comarques, Thorpe-le-Soken, Essex, just the sort of house Bennett had described to Thomas Lloyd Humberstone several years before (page 155).

George and his Maries are doubtless George Doran and his wife and daughter. See Vol. I, *passim*.

273. Wells's novel was *The Passionate Friends*, issued in 1913.

BOLL, PENNA / MS. / 274
(*To May Sinclair*)

14 St. Simon's Avenue
1 Feby 1913

My dear Miss Sinclair,
I have a most singular & unhappy faculty of leaving hostesses without thanking them for having entertained me & put me in the way of nice distraction. I always think of it in the street! Please pardon me. It is only my barbaric manners! Heart of gold etc., I assure you. I had a fine time.

Always yours sincerely, Arnold Bennett

TEXAS / MS. / 275
(*To William Lee Mathews*)

Comarques
[Thorpe-Le-Soken]
March 13th, 1913.

Dearest William,
Thanks for your telegram to which I replied at once. Here we have a fresh and a supreme example of the unbusiness-like methods of the Kingsway people. After the rehearsals had been in progress one week there was great excitement in the theatre because Allen had gone back on his verbal promise to release Miss Wish Wynne. Barker cursed 'these music-hall people' all over the place, and I naturally asked him why two men with the experience of himself and Drinkwater had not originally taken the precaution to obtain something from Allen in writing. His reply was the absurd one that it would have been rather a difficult thing to do. However, he admitted that the contre-temps had taught him a lesson. I was given to understand that Miss Wish Wynne was definitely released for a minimum period of nine weeks from the first night. The rehearsals have been going on for a further period of a week, and now I receive your pleasing telegram of this afternoon, which I take to be proof that for the second time in a fortnight Barker has failed to get

274. May Sinclair (1863–1946) and Bennett met perhaps in 1911. He recorded in his Journal after an evening spent with her: 'I rather liked this prim virgin. Great sense. She said she lived absolutely alone—not even a servant.' Miss Sinclair seems to have liked Bennett less. He was said to be the model for the unpleasant journalist who is the eponymous hero of her novel *Tasker Jevons: The Real Story*, published in 1916.

the affair put on a clear business footing. As I am entirely unacquainted with the details of the negotiations, I am only able to write Allen in general terms. Although I have been seeing Barker and Drinkwater almost every day they keep me in the dark as to their mysterious proceedings, and then when they have gradually slid into an awful muddle they suggest that I should help to drag them out by offering to do a sketch. I am quite prepared to do this if it will be of any help. But I must say that I do resent the Kingsway methods.

On the other hand my personal relations with both Drinkwater and Barker are extremely agreeable, so far as they go. And I am very deeply impressed indeed by Barker's absolute genius as a producer.

I am coming to town to-morrow and shall be at the Kingsway during the morning. You might let me know there whether you will have lunch with me, either at the Reform Club, or elsewhere if you prefer it. Perhaps I might get Barker to join the party.

Thine, A. B.

P.S. I have this moment received your telegram. If I do not hear from you at the Kingsway, I will expect you to call there and we will go out to lunch together.
Later. P.P.S. Allen has just replied to my telegram that he has given way. Good! But what a bloody nuisance these persons are! A. B.

SY / MS. / 276
(*To E. V. Lucas*)

Comarques
10 Apl 1913

Dear E.V.L.,

Grazia! It makes me want to be a bibliophile again. I have been such. More, I have been a bibliopole. And certainly one

275. The Bennetts moved into Comarques on 24 February 1913.
Allen may be Frank Allen (b. 1851), theatrical proprietor and manager, head of Moss, Stoll, and Allen Theatres. Wish Wynne (1882–1931) was a music hall and variety star. She made her début as a West End actress in *The Great Adventure*, as Janet Cannot, and had a great success. The play opened on 25 March 1913 at the Kingsway Theatre.

of the rarest pamphlets of modern times is my first catalogue
of rare books, issued when I was a lawyer's clerk. Come again
soon.

                                            Thine, A. B.

PROCEEDINGS A. L. A., June 1913 / 277
(*To the editor*)
                                            London
                                            April 15, 1913.

[no salutation]

In reply to your letter of April 1st, written on behalf of the
American Library Association, I do consider that to a certain
extent the fiction circulated in the public libraries of the United
States does help to enlighten the people on social and economic
problems. But I am bound to say that I think that we novelists
might do a very great deal more in this direction if we would
avoid sentimentalizing the truth in order to make it seem more
palatable, and also if we would adopt the habit of describing
more completely the general social background against which
our leading figures live and move.

                    Believe me,
                    Yours faithfully, Arnold Bennett

276. On E. V. Lucas see page 157 n.
Bennett tells something of his career as a bibliophile in *The Truth About an
Author*:
    'Another clerk in the office happened to be an ardent bibliophile. We became
friends, and I owe him much. He could chatter in idiomatic French like a house
on fire, and he knew the British Museum Reading Room from its centre to its
periphery. He first taught me to regard a book, not as an instrument for obtaining information or emotion, but as a *book*, printed at such a place in such a year
by so-and-so, bound by so-and-so, and carrying colophons, registers, water-
marks, and *fautes d'impression*. He was acquainted, I think, with every second-
hand bookstall in the metropolis; and on Saturday afternoons we visited most
of them. We lived for bargains and rarities. We made it a point of honour to
buy one book every day, and when bargains failed we used to send out the
messengers for a Camelot Classic or so—ninepence net; this series was just then
at the height of its vogue. We were for ever bringing into the office formidable
tomes—the choice productions of the presses of Robert and Henry Stephen,
Elzevir, Baskerville, Giunta, Foulis, and heaven knows whom. My discovery of
the Greek *editio princeps* of Plutarch, printed by Philip Giunta at Florence in
1517, which I bought in Whitechapel for two shillings, nearly placed me on a
level with my preceptor.'
Bennett issued two catalogues of rare books, in 1891 and (probably) 1892, both of
them entitled *A Century of Books for Bibliophiles*.

IDDESLEIGH / MS. / 278
(*To F. S. A. Lowndes*)

Comarques
13th May 1913

My dear Lowndes,

Lucas also went into the pit, & he said he heard a man say: 'This play is full of sly digs. I never saw a play with so many sly digs in it.' Hence Lucas has christened Comarques 'The Sly Diggings'. Sorry you didn't hear well. Lucas says he *did*, but I would sooner believe you. Anyhow it is a most striking success. No, Janet is intentionally younger in the play than in the book,—*and* slimmer! 28—& she looks it. We are enchanted with our house, but not yet reconciled to the clime; it is too *strong* in April & May & upsets my liver. However, I am taking measures. We are now settled, & I am trying to work, but the yacht is a great enemy of industry. We shall hope to see you here soon, both of you. Wells on agents is a chump. I have often told him so. He is down on agents *because* he knows he has made a chump of himself & dropped a lot of money by trying to manage his affairs himself.

The *New Statesman* is pretty bad, eh?

Our love to you both,

Ever yours, A. B.

STOKE / TS. / 279
(*To Hugh Walpole*)

Comarques
May 29th, 1913.

My dear Walpole,

I am glad to hear that you are back. June 21st is rather doubtful for the present, but July 5th is quite open.

In the meantime, I send you a book which I picked up as a bargain in the catalogue of a second-hand bookseller. You will

---

277. Bennett's letter was in response to a circular letter sent to eminent writers by officials of the American Library Association asking about the usefulness of the public library movement.

278. F. S. A. Lowndes (1868–1940) was on the staff of *The Times*. His wife, Marie Belloc Lowndes, had been a friend of Bennett's for many years.

On Wells and agents, see Vol. I, pp. 187–8.

The *New Statesman* began publication in April 1913.

see that under the headings of the different countries it gives on each double page a complete conspectus of all important events which happened during a given period. I consider it a work which is absolutely invaluable to the novelist who deals, however indirectly or briefly, with any past period. And I have used it constantly ever since I bought a copy of the original publication about twelve years ago. It is the basis of such works of erudition as *The Old Wives' Tale* and *Clayhanger*. For example, if you happen to have a character who was in the United States in the year 1893, you will see on pages 424 and 425, at a glance, everything of a spectacular nature which happened in the United States in that year. In fact, I can scarcely praise too highly the usefulness of this book.

My wife sends her kindest regards.

Yours ever, Arnold Bennett

s.a. / ms. / 280
(*To G. Herbert Thring*)

Comarques
5th June 1913

Dear Mr. Thring,

Mr. Pett Ridge is a friend of mine, & I should always be very happy to be of use to him, but on account of physical disability I have the strongest objection to going into the witness box, & moreover I make the worst sort of witness. Nothing else but this purely personal reason would prevent me from coming to the aid of Mr. Pett Ridge. I had heard generally of the case.

Believe me,

Cordially yours, Arnold Bennett

279. Hugh Walpole (1884–1941) published his first novel in 1909. Bennett met him the following year, and was instrumental in arranging for the publication of his books in America. The valuable work that Bennett refers to is not known.

280. G. Herbert Thring (1859–1941) was Secretary of the Society of Authors. Pett Ridge (see page 199 n.) was suing the *English Illustrated Magazine* for publishing a story that they implied was by him, and was not.

The origin of Bennett's stammer has been traced variously by interested persons. His mother (as reported to one of his biographers, Margaret Locherbie-Goff, via brother Frank) attributed it to a fall from a high chair when he was an infant. Marguerite Bennett said that it followed upon his catching his hand in a mangle at the age of 12, and Geoffrey West, who wrote an unpleasant book on Bennett, used her story but changed Bennett's age to 7. H. G. Wells sniffed a sexual-psychological origin. And another critic, more serious, went to Isador Coriat's

ROSS / TR. / 281
(*To Robert Ross*)

                                                            Comarques
                                                         June 27th, 1913
My dear Ross,
    Having now come face to face with the facts, and especially
the fact of my mother's health and great age, I am obliged to
decline your most kind invitation for the 3rd July. It would
really be quite impossible for either my wife or myself to come
down to London for the purposes of pleasure while my mother
is here. Our best thanks all the same.

                                   Yours sincerely, Arnold Bennett

P.S. Do you know Lady Speyer, or do you know anybody
whom I know who is on pretty friendly terms with her? I have
no desire to make her acquaintance myself, but a friend of
mine, a Hungarian pianist, with a considerable reputation on
the Continent, is anxious to meet her in the autumn.   A. B.

Stammering: A Psychological Interpretation and deduced therefrom that the stammer
was an attempt on Bennett's part to protract early oral pleasure.
    Frank Swinnerton, Bennett's closest friend of later years, said that with him
Bennett stammered only on occasions of emotional stress, and that with children
he could speak easily. Marguerite Bennett said that he rarely stammered in French.
Bennett's own most interesting, if indirect, comment on the subject comes in *The
Ghost*. The hero relates that he lost his speech when he was 3 years old. Seven years
later he regained it:
    ' "Mother!" I cried, in a hoarse, uncouth, horrible voice, and, casting myself
    against her bosom, I clung convulsively to her. From a hook in the ceiling beam
    my father's corpse dangled. He had hanged himself in the frenzy of his remorse
    for a murder. So my speech came again.'
    281. Robert Ross (1869–1918) was the great defender of Oscar Wilde, and also
an authority on art.
    Bennett's mother returned shortly afterwards to Burslem, where she died in
November 1914, aged 74.
    Lady Speyer is presumably Lady (Leonora) Speyer, wife of Sir Edgar Speyer
(1862–1932), one of the founders of the Whitechapel Art Gallery. The Hungarian
pianist is probably Theodor Szántó (1877–1934).

ROSS / TR. / 282
(*To Robert Ross*)

Comarques
July 4th, 1913

Dear Robert Ross,

Many thanks for your letter. You are a nice kind man, and I am extremely obliged to you. I am looking forward to the arrival of the books.

My Hungarian friend, Szántó, is coming over to play at some concerts in London early in the autumn I believe, and when the time approaches I will communicate with you again on this important affair.

Sprigge wrote to me about six months ago asking me whether I would accept if I were nominated for the managing committee of the Authors' Society, but I asked to be excused. I have been a member of the Authors' Society for some time, and I thoroughly believe in its usefulness. I am not, however, a man formed by nature to serve on a committee. I take a lively interest in the doings of the Society, and I pass a certain proportion of my time in being of practical use to young authors, and also old ones. I am considered rather good at this, and I am certainly more useful privately than I should be on a committee.

Yours sincerely, Arnold Bennett

LANE / TS. / 283
(*To John Lane*)

Comarques
July 5th, 1913

Dear John Lane,

Many thanks for your letter of the 4th, and the copy of *The Song of Songs*, which I am glad to have. I observe, however, that in the Preface you do not quote my letter, and the implication to the reader is that I ignored your request for my moral support in a matter which gravely affects the interests of literature in England. I think that either my letter ought to

---

282. Sir Squire Sprigge (1860–1937) edited the *Lancet* for some years, and was active on behalf of the Society of Authors from the time of its inception in the 1880s.

z

have been printed or that my name ought to have been left out of the list of authors on the first page of the introduction. Perhaps you would not mind writing to Herr Sudermann and explaining that I had in fact sent you an answer.

With kind regards,

Yours sincerely, Arnold Bennett

BROWN / TS. / 284
(*To Wayland Williams*)

Comarques
July 16th, 1913.

Dear Sir,

I am obliged for your letter and the enclosure.

I regret to say that I am on the point of leaving England for my holiday, and shall therefore be unable to give myself the pleasure of seeing you. In any case I should not be able to see you in your quality of a journalist in search of material for articles. I have been obliged to make this rule absolute. I find it infinitely more satisfactory that any communications which I may have to offer to the public should be made in precisely my own words over my own signature.

Believe me,

Cordially yours, Arnold Bennett

MANCHESTER / TS. / 285
(*To A. N. Monkhouse*)

Comarques
August 30th, 1913.

Dear Monkhouse,

I am very sorry that circumstances made it impossible for me to review Montague's book for the *Guardian*. I should much like

283. See page 269 for the beginning of this episode. In his Introduction to the new edition of Sudermann's *The Song of Songs*, Lane listed the authors to whom he had written for opinions about the earlier edition. Bennett was in the list. Lane also printed the letters of response by these authors. Bennett's was not among them.

284. Wayland Williams (b. 1888) was an American, with connections at Yale and Brown Universities. Little more than a year later an interview with Bennett was published in the *Daily News*, on 30 July 1914. 'I wrote this myself', Bennett remarked in some private notes, 'so as to get it right. However I did not much care for it.' The interview was primarily concerned with *The Price of Love*.

to have done so, as I am beginning to consider myself in a way as the official reviewer in the *Guardian* of books by members of the staff. When, however, one is in a small yacht cruising about the more or less uncharted waters of the Baltic Sea, it is quite out of the question to think of composing articles for the greatest daily the world has ever seen. The review copy of the book has at last reached me, and my firm intention is to keep it.

Please remember me to my friends in Manchester. I hope that you are at work on a fresh novel.

Yours sincerely, Arnold Bennett

BUTLER / MS. / 286
(*To Cedric Sharpe*)

Comarques
13th Sept 1913

Dear brother in Strauss & Stravinsky,

Marriotts are full of you & Evelyn. It appears you are to be married at Christmas, the point being absolutely decided. I therefore pour forth my fraternal blessing upon you both. Every marriage is a toss-up. You & Evelyn & all of us can only pray & hope for the best. It would be the same if you married at 32 or 42. I hear, however, that you are thinking of buying a house on the Building Society method at some place not on the map.

  Don't

 I say again:

  Don't.

You are bound to regret it if you do. It is the most expensive method of buying a house known to civilisation. Marriage is a trifle, but a bought house is apt to be a serious nuisance. Take my advice, which you will admit I seldom offer to you unsolicited, and don't buy any house on any system for a long time to come. You would be absolutely bound to regret it. You have a lovely tone on the cello, but you are not an expert in real estate transactions. My tone on the cello is appalling (I believe), but I *am* an expert on real estate transactions. If I bought a cello, or married a cellist for her tone, in the face of

285. C. E. Montague's new book was *The Morning's War*, published in August 1913.

your advice to the contrary, I should be a damned fool. If you go buying houses in the face of my advice you will be of course the wisest of created beings, as ever.

Look here, we should like you & Evelyn to come up here for a week-end before the day of doom & maternal tears. Est-ce possible?

Thine, A. B.

Hommages respectueux à Evelyn.
Marriott has brought 'The Rosary' to sing. But he can't sing it & he ain't going to.

STOKE / TS. / 287
(*To Alfred Wareing*)

Comarques
September 25th, 1913.

My dear Wareing,

Do not believe all you hear. I also have been told that there is a caricature of you in *The Regent*. It is news to me. But I am always being told this kind of thing. For example, I am informed that there is in the same book an exact caricature of Tree. Now, I have never spoken to Tree in my life, and I have never seen him except in public. Again, I have been told many times that the artist in *Buried Alive* is exactly like Sargent, and that he is exactly like Brangwyn. I have never seen either of these artists. Most strange of all, I was told a few weeks ago that the Jew picture-dealer in *Buried Alive* is exactly, in all his details, like Agnew; a person as to whom my ignorance is complete.

I shall be in town for one night next week, and if you could call and see me at the Berkeley Hotel at about ten o'clock on Thursday morning I should be delighted to have another look at you in order to see whether really I have caricatured you or not.

Our kindest regards,
Yours sincerely, Arnold Bennett

287. On Alfred Wareing and Sir Herbert Beerbohm Tree see pages 312 n. and 29 n.

John Singer Sargent (1856–1925), Sir Frank Brangwyn (1867–1956), and

GIDE / 288   Hôtel du Rhin
(*To André Gide*)   4 et 6 place Vendôme
                                   Lundi [27 October 1913]
[no salutation]

Or, mon cher ami, je ne veux pas vous embêter, je ne veux pas trop insister, je ne veux surtout pas manquer de sympathie, mais, il faut que je vous dise que vous êtes en train de me faire de la peine.

Ma femme et moi nous tenons réellement beaucoup à vous avoir à dîner. Nous aimerions mieux voir votre visage morose et entendre votre 'esprit fripé', que de ne pas vous voir du tout.

Pour le veston, on aurait été très vexé si vous étiez (fussiez?) venu en habit ou même en smoking. Le veston est de rigueur. Du reste, n'étiez-vous pas en veston l'autre soir à une des solennités les plus solennelles et les plus parisiennes?

Du reste, pour bien tailler une bavette, les après-midis sont inexistantes. L'esprit n'est pas encore chauffé. On ne vit pas.

Venez donc à l'heure qui vous conviendra le mieux. On s'arrangera. On vous soignera.

                        Bien affectueusement, Arnold Bennett

BERG / MS. / 289
(*To John Squire*)
                                   Comarques
                                   12 Nov 1913
My dear Squire,

I was glad to see your hand, as it forced me to write to you. About 5 or 6 weeks ago I had the impulse to write to you about the high satisfaction I had from your last book, but with the base indifference that sometimes paralyses the most ardent souls, I simply did not write. Your poetry gives me real pleasure. It is what I reckon modern poetry ought chiefly to be. It is what I should write myself if I could. The translations (which I had not seen before) are remarkable. I wish you would do more of these when you have time. I recommend to you

---

William Lockett Agnew (1858–1918), head of Thomas Agnew.

The Regent, which describes Denry Machin's adventures in the theatrical world, was published in September 1913.

Laurent Tailhade. (Such trifles as 'Place des Victoires', which I would give my head to have written originally in English.)

Yes, I think the paper has improved, & is still doing so. The last time it really annoyed me was quite some months ago, when it printed a gibe at Lloyd George about as clever as the *Daily Mail* could have invented, & finished the par with a mistake in grammar! Having said this, I went away for a holiday.

If I had time I would write you something. I have material for about ten million 'sketches' in my journals, but I never have time to read them. (They accumulate for my senility, when they will be extremely useful.) The fact is that the economic pressure upon me to write what I like at fantastic prices for periodicals with large circulations makes it very difficult to write for small circulations at no price, even though I don't want the money. Is there any reason why I should, unless I owned the paper I wrote in? *Brainy* people are always assuming that I write for money; whereas I only write what I want to write. It seems impossible for brainy people to conceive that I like writing *The Regent* and *The Plain Man and His Wife*. They mistake me perhaps for someone else of the same name.

I mean to look through my journals & see if I can find you something, but not for December.

I should be only too glad to have a yarn. But when? How?

Yours sincerely, Arnold Bennett

HERZOG / MS. / 290
(*To Elsie Herzog*)

Comarques
14 Nov 1913

My dear lady,

This is the first day that circumstances have combined to permit me to write & thank you for your various missives &

---

289. (Sir) John Squire (1884–1958), poet and editor, was at this time literary editor of the *New Statesman*. His recent book was *The Three Hills*, published in July 1913, with translations from Baudelaire.

Laurent Tailhade (1854–1919), poet and man of letters, published his poem 'Place des Victoires' in the collection *Poèmes aristophanesques*, 1904.

The Plain Man and His Wife, one of Bennett's pocket philosophies, was issued in October 1913.

messages, & to assure you that we still exist. I suppose you don't realise how difficult it is for me to get off a letter unless I have something positive and definite to say. It is even more difficult for my wife, but in a quite different way. Since I received your letter I have been as far as Sweden in the yacht, finished my Harper novel, written a long-short story, & spent a week in Belgium & a fortnight in Paris. And now I have begun my new play. As I shall start the actual writing tomorrow, I take the precaution of transmitting to you first our best wishes for your better health & your continued satisfaction in your son, & so on & so on. Also part of my object is to prevent you from asserting that I never write.

Our kindest regards to you both.

Yours sincerely, Arnold Bennett

YALE / TS. / 291
(*To Frank Vernon*)

Comarques
November 28th, 1913.

My dear Vernon,

Enclosed is a copy of a cablegram which I received yesterday from Ames. You will see that there is some considerable difference of opinion between Ames and Harding as to the success of the piece.

Miss Agnes Hill has approached me through an intimate friend of mine as to playing in my plays. I have suggested that she should put herself in communication with you. I do not know anything about her at all.

'Don Juan' is an extremely aristocratic man. In fact he is so aristocratic and so instinctively convinced of the social superiority of the rank to which he belongs, that in a sense he scarcely shows it He is extremely polite to his inferiors until he loses control of himself. He is a rather melancholy man, having been long occupied, without success, in the search for ideal love. He is not a sensualist as the word is usually applied to Don Juan. On the contrary he is extremely refined and rather

---

290. *The Price of Love* began appearing in *Harper's* in December 1913.
Bennett began some preliminary writing of *Don Juan* on 17 November. The actual writing of the play began on 12 December.

spiritual. His attitude towards women is tender, with a touch of the cynic. His age is between thirty and thirty five. He is a profound conservative, and is convinced that Spain is in a decline, and that the decline is entirely due to the unjust treatment given to the Order of Hidalgos, whose prosperity and continuance in all their ancient rights is, he is convinced, necessary to the prosperity of Spain.

If you want to get, in quite a short space of time, a general idea of what my Don Juan's environment was, you might read the first chapter of book VI of Prescott's *History of the Reign of Philip II*, and especially from p. 651 to the end of the chapter. The book (Routledge's edition) can be obtained at any library or booksellers.

Yours sincerely, A. B.

P.S. Shiel Barry is a remarkable Ilam Carve. Coached, he could be made to do a Don Juan. I should not have thought so until I saw him in the *Great Adv.*

WESTMINSTER GAZETTE, 8 December 1913 / 292
(*To the editor*)

Comarques
December 7 [1913]

Dear Sir,

Your contributor 'E.F.S.' accuses Miss Jean Aylwyn, who said *double entendre*, of a mistake in French. It seems to me that the question is: Was she making a mistake in English? Assuming that *double entendre* is bad French, can it not be argued that the phrase has become English, and rendered righteous by use, like *blanc mange* and *connoisseur*—words incorrect in French, but which 'E.F.S.' would probably permit himself to employ? I suppose that most languages enrich themselves by these transfers from other languages. Thus *smoking* (a dinner-jacket) and *footing* (foot-racing, or walking exercise) are absurd English, but perfectly correct French. Custom, and not logic, is the main

291. On Winthrop Ames see page 295 n. Lyn Harding (1867–1952) was in America to play Ilam Carve in *The Great Adventure* at the Booth Theatre in New York. Agnes Hill is not otherwise known. Shiel Barry (d. 1916) was the son of the well-known actor of the same name. He was killed in the war.

factor in the growth of a language. On this ground alone I think it could be maintained that Miss Jean Aylwyn was justified in saying *double entendre*.

But there is another and a much stronger point in her favour. *Double entendre* was correct French at the time when we took the phrase over. It became obsolete in France in the seventeenth century. The French used to employ the infinitive as a substantive more frequently than they do now. *Double entendre* in English is not a neologism, the fruit of 'the modern tendency to smattering'. It is to be found in Dryden. From time to time 'E.F.S.' shows in his articles that he is by no means a stranger to the more recondite subtleties of the French language. I therefore offer these remarks with deference.

Yours faithfully, Arnold Bennett

KEDDIE / MS. / 293
(*To E. V. Lucas*)

Comarques
27th Dec 1913

My dear Lucas,

It is impossible for me to write anything by February. This is serious. I can't throw off caprices, fables, fancies, like you. Not my line. And I am behind with my work, & acutely worried by my Spanish play. I send you two privately printed volumes of my Journal. If you can pick out a few items from these volumes you are welcome to them. This is the best I can do. Who will get the profit out of this Annual? If it is a commercial enterprise, and Methuen's rake in the profit they must pay for the clatter of my signature. On this distressing subject I must tell you that I am now at 33 cents a word in New York & that I have lately refused 1/- a word from the *Daily Mail*. I do not defend. I state a commercial fact. Methuen is a much cleverer

---

292. On E. F. Spence see pages 263-4. Jean Aylwyn (1885–1964) was having one of her great theatrical successes playing the cocotte in the French farce *Who's the Lady* at the Garrick, and the Lord Chamberlain or one of his men had observed her undress with some dismay. Spence did not think the play obscene, but he thought that the arguments brought forward in its defence were not very strong. In passing he remarked that when Miss Aylwyn said publicly that there are people who 'are ready to see a double-entendre in everything', she presumably meant 'double-entente'.

man than you think he is, because you don't see how he uses you. If the Annual is your affair commercially I am (truly) delighted to give you the morally-unimportant stuff, but on principle I never give to a publisher or editor—whose aim is money. Thus if you take the stuff, and the affair is Methuen's, I shall trouble you to allot to me the very tallest sum that you conceivably can, as I won't have the nosey Methuen walking up [&] down his garden & saying happily to himself that he has used you to rope in the golden calves. Will you please return me the book printed in 2 colours. The other you can keep (if you care to); it is a misfit, owing to a printer's error of margins.

One of your chief wishes is mine. But if you want to *sail* with me you will either have to come to Monte Carlo in spring or to Venice in September. The yacht will probably be in the Mediterranean all the summer. She starts in 10 days time. Come then. As for coming up here, you know you will be welcomed & petted whenever you show your darned beak in the place. You know you are a most difficult man to get hold of. And that even the proudest have to run after you & cajole in order to have you. So don't pretend. Say when you are coming. This is all for the moment.

Thine, A. B.

P.S. I shall be in London circa the 10th (10th 11th) Jan. We (M. & I.) are going to a concert—a good one. We want Mrs. Lucas to go with us. I know you won't. Still we might meet circa the 10th—all or any of us.

Marguerite is writing a novel. A. B.

293. *Methuen's Annual* appeared only in 1914, with a short extract from Bennett's privately published journal (see page 202 n.). Lucas paid £20 for the material. See also Vol. I, p. 204.

During the spring of 1914 Bennett was sailing in his yacht off the French and Italian coasts. For Lucas's account of him on one trip, see Vol. I, pp. 172–3.

BUTLER / MS. / 294
(*To Cedric Sharpe*)

Comarques
17 Jan 1914

My dear Cedric,
 This music is very graceful & comforting. I have already played both parts of the *Siegfried I,* & much of the Brahms. It is tragic that I have no one to play with me. The *Afternoon of the Faun* will I fear be more of an ornament than a utility. The

Siegfried is immense for 4 〔♫〕 s

Many thanks,
Thine, A. B.

BUTLER / MS. / 295
(*To Cedric Sharpe*)

Comarques
2nd Mch 1914

My dear Cedric,
 Both the people who consented to the original arrangement are somewhat to blame—I mean you & your mother. I made a bet with your mother that it wouldn't last, & the one bright spot in the affair seems to me to be that I have won that bet. The arrangement was impossible. When a man & a woman marry they have quite enough to do in attending to themselves without the additional strain of another generation always on the spot & at the table. It argues an astounding lack either of imagination or of knowledge of human nature even to hope that such an arrangement *could* last. However, seeing that it *couldn't,* & it *hasn't,* there is no permanent harm done. Do not attach importance to the situation. It will soon clear itself. It is not a question of ill-will, etc.; it is simply a question of complete incompatability of two generations at a critical period. I think you are right to go; but I hope this doesn't mean that you are throwing up the Oxford Rd. flat scheme without full reflection. It has drawbacks, but I think its advantages are greater. In any case, whatever you decide, don't talk more than is necessary to be polite. It is so easy to say things that are unforgettable. My sympathies are almost always with the

younger generation, but there are 2 sides to every question after all. Your mother has an absolute passion for you, & you have to accept it as a whole; you can't reject the parts that are inconvenient. Between parents & children the word 'ingratitude' has no meaning, though parents invariably use it with the most honest conviction. It is simply an expression of disappointment or annoyance—like 'damn'.

Let me know if I can be of any use to you.

We leave here Wednesday for the Berkeley Hotel, & shall be at Tertia's on Wednesday night. We go to Paris Friday.

Yours (& hers), A. B.

HERZOG / MS. / 296
(*To Elsie Herzog*)

Yacht Velsa
Monte Carlo
16 Mch 1914

My dear lady,

You shock me. Not by not liking *The Way of all Flesh*, but by liking *The Devil's Garden* and *Fortitude*. It is excusable not to appreciate at the first attempt a book which has the severity & austerity of a classic, but it is not excusable to lose your head about badness or mediocrity. About *The Devil's Garden* there is nothing to be said. It simply does not exist. *Fortitude* is by a man who has written one real book (*Mr. Perrin & Mr. Traill*), but *Fortitude* is undoubtedly a failure. In this view Walpole's three best literary friends—Henry James, E. V. Lucas & I—are quite agreed. I could, but won't, use a harsher word than 'failure'. You had better read both these books again in three years time. You will then blush—I hope. You have been looking for the wrong things in *The Passionate Friends*, & failing to see the right things. I like *The Dark Flower* very much, & wrote to tell Galsworthy so—a thing I have never done before about a book of his, though he is a friend of mine. It seems to me you had better read some *good* novels in which there is no slush nor tush. You might read *Bubu de Montparnasse*, by C. L. Philippe (if you haven't already done so), and *Dans les rues*, by J. H. Rosny aîné. I have been mistaken in you. With a couple of lines you have undone the impressions of a couple of years. You cannot be relied upon to distinguish a book from the other thing. The fact is, few can. Further, if you are idle, it is because you want to be idle. In a place like New York a woman as clever as you could find something rational to do if she really desired to find it. Now I have a young friend of the name of Pierre de Lanux, who writes for *La Nouvelle Revue Française*, which is assuredly the finest literary review at present anywhere in existence. He writes also short things of a fanciful nature which he much wishes to place on the American market. They would want, not only translating, but adapting & amplifying according to the idiosyncrasy of the American public. He asked me the other day when I was in Paris whether I could recommend anyone to him. I said it would obviously have to be a woman. No man could or would do it satisfactorily. Upon reflection I told him that I *did* know such a woman, & that I would mention the matter to her. I am now mentioning it to her. The terms would be 50% of the receipts, which seemed to me to be just. Of course the woman would have to occupy herself with getting the stuff on the market. If this idea appeals to you, you might let me know & I will put you in communication with de Lanux. He is young, personable, and of high talent (I think). If on the other hand the idea affrights your idleness, you have only to say so. My wife charges me with the expression of her grief that she has produced nothing sendable with your nice kind camera. She saith also that to send a postcard in thanks for the grapefruit which kept her Xmas houseparty in a good humour for three days was the act of a brute. Perhaps it was. The truth is she ought to have written herself also. You have doubtless noticed a certain frigidity of tone in this letter. It is because I have not yet recovered from the shock of your opinions about *The Devil's Garden* etc. You should be more careful. The [?revised] poem is ingenious. I wish you as much birthday happiness as you desire. I don't know how much that is,—I shall see. Of all qualities commonsense is the greatest. Accept this as an infallible dogma. I have dealt with your letter (of whose terrifying ingenuity nothing escaped me) as you wished.

Remember us to husband.

Yours sincerely, Arnold Bennett

P.S. We shall return home about the end of April. We hope to get to Rome in this craft. No fixed address, except Comarques.

A. B.

BUTLER / MS. / 297
(*To Cedric Sharpe*)

Comarques
6 May 1914

My dear Cedric,
  I foresee difficulties about that concert taking place at Comarques in June or July. Marguerite is almost filling the house for the summer with other people's children & a governess. Note that I do not object to this, & even if I did I could not very reasonably stop it because I wanted to fill the house with other sorts of persons for one night. Could the solemnity take place say in October without deranging the B.C.M.P. too much? Send me a line on the situation.
  All countries are alike. A French author, a friend of mine, describing a musical evening at his club with Ravel, Casella, etc. playing, & how nice it was, said: 'Enfin, il y avait juste assez de musique *pour ne pas s'embêter, et puis après, vous savez, il y avait le buffet*—c'était vraiment très bien.'
  Our loves.

Yours, A. B.

HERZOG / MS. / 298
(*To Elsie Herzog*)

Comarques
28 May 1914

Dear Mrs. Herzog,
  Two letters, and a scented necktie-carrier now lie before me. I appreciate your good will and good thought. I shall use the carrier at the next chance. The parcel arrived the day before my birthday. My birthday itself was full of minor disasters, and I did not work at all. We are certainly not coming to N.Y.

296. *The Way of All Flesh*, by Samuel Butler, appeared in 1903; *The Devil's Garden*, by W. B. Maxwell, in 1913; *Fortitude* and *Mr. Perrin and Mr. Traill*, by Hugh Walpole, in 1913 and 1911 respectively; *The Passionate Friends*, by H. G. Wells, in 1913; *The Dark Flower*, by John Galsworthy, in 1913; *Bubu de Montparnasse*, by C. L. Philippe (1874–1909), in 1901. *Dans les rues* is not known. J. H. Rosny aîné was one of the pseudonyms of Joseph Henri Honoré Boëx-Borel (b. 1856). Pierre de Lanux (b. 1887) published several social-political studies. Mrs. Herzog apparently did not translate anything of his.
297. The B.C.M.P. is unidentified. Maurice Ravel (1875–1937) and Alfredo Casella (1883–1947), composer and pianist, were friends of Bennett's.

this autumn. My wife says she will never come, because of the voyage. I, however, shall probably come next year. It all depends on God. I have begun the third Clayhanger book. I began it on Monday, some days ahead of time. But whether it will be mediocre or good I have yet no idea. I thought about it a good deal while we were away. We went to Rome in the Yacht, & returned therefrom in the auto. I kept a journal which I shall ultimately sell to some simple minded American editor. I saw Pierre de Lanux in Paris twice. We both laughed at the thought of you searching the folios of the *Nouvelle Revue* for his contributions. What I told you was *La Nouvelle Revue Française*, which is a review extremely different. By this time you have probably heard from de Lanux. I told him you were coming over. Lately I discovered that he has two most agreeable young sisters. I told him that I accepted no responsibility for you, & I tell you that I accept no responsibility for him. You are introduced; that is all.

I now turn to Clayhanger.

Our kindest regards to you both.

Yours sincerely, Arnold Bennett

TEXAS / MS. / 299
(*To Hugh Lunn*)

Comarques
25 June 1914

Dear Mr. Hugh Lunn,

I like your enthusiasm for poetry more than I like your friend's verse. I do not pretend to be a critic of verse, but in my opinion, Mr. Hare is still a rather inexperienced poet, who does not yet know how to manage a rhythm with any skill. Both poems are (always in my opinion) monotonous in effect, & imitative in method. He may ultimately do something admirable, but at present I do not think it would be of much use introducing him to Austin Harrison, especially as I couldn't tell Harrison that I thought a really authentic new poet was at his door! Had I been fortunate enough to be impressed by the verse, I would have written to Harrison with great pleasure. I return the verses.

Believe me,
Cordially yours, Arnold Bennett

KEDDIE / TS. / 300
(*To James Keddie*)

Comarques
July 13th, 1914

Dear Sir,

Your curiosity as to Cyril is very pleasing. I regret to say that this young man turned out ultimately to be an extremely ordinary sort of person. There are probably several hundreds of young artists rather like him in London, and his career presents no interest. Fortunately he has quite enough money to live on, and a sufficient share of the family commonsense to enable him to take care of it.

Believe me,
Cordially yours, Arnold Bennett

YALE / TS. / 301
(*To Frank Vernon*)

[Comarques]
July 22nd, 1914.

My dear Vernon,

I now understand that you are going away to the United States in the middle of August and will probably not be back again until the beginning of October. How you will contrive to obtain a satisfactory autumn production of my play under these circumstances I am unable to conceive. But I should at any rate like to know definitely and clearly whether you intend to give definite commissions to Rickards and to Carter for the designs for the scenery and for the costumes. As you are aware, it is most clearly a part of our understanding that the scenery and the costumes shall be designed by these men, and if there is to be any hitch as regards these extremely important points of the production, serious difficulties will occur. I saw Rickards at the end of last week and he told me that he had received no

299. Hugh Lunn (Hugh Kingsmill, 1889–1949), novelist, biographer, and critic, was at this time on the staff of Bennett's *Hearth & Home*. The poet Hare is unidentified; he may be Kenneth Hare, who published a few volumes of poetry from 1911 onward. On Austin Harrison see page 281 n.

300. James Keddie (1884–1942) was the manager of an American publishing company, and a collector of first editions. He wrote to Bennett to ask what happened to Cyril Povey after the end of *The Old Wives' Tale*.

commission. I believe that Carter is in the same case. If you postpone these matters until you return from the United States, or if you try to arrange them by correspondence from New York, the results cannot be satisfactory. I should not trouble you as to the affair had you not positively assured Pinker that an autumn production is a certainty.

Yours ever, Arnold Bennett

NEW STATESMAN, 5 September 1914 / 302
(*To the editor*)

Comarques
September 1st [1914]

Sir,

In your issue of August 29th, reviewing war literature, you say: 'Almost without exception during the last fortnight our eminent novelists have rushed into print as authorities on all matters of foreign policy and military strategy.' Can you name these novelists? I have noted that H. G. Wells, who has written on foreign policy and whose articles have been of a stimulating and valuable character, was careful to state that he did not write as an authority. As war is preeminently an affair of human nature, a triumph of instinct over reason, it seems to me not improper that serious novelists (who are supposed to know a little about human nature and to be able to observe accurately and to write) should be permitted to express themselves concerning the phenomena of a nation at war without being insulted. You say, as to writing about the war: 'For our popular authors who have made their name and their money already there is no excuse.' The insinuation is clear. My opinion is that this sentence ought not to have appeared in the *New Statesman*, and that some expression of regret is due for it.

Yours etc., Arnold Bennett

301. *Don Juan* was never produced. The play was on the verge of production two or three times. This time the war probably helped to trap it. Carter is not otherwise known.

302. At the outset of the war, Bennett was approached by the editors of the *Daily News* to write for them on it, and the first of a long series of articles by him appeared on 24 August. Wells was writing for the *Daily Chronicle*. Although Bennett was paid for his articles, the sum he received was well below his normal price, and there is no doubt that he viewed his writing of these articles as mainly a patriotic

TEXAS / MS. / 303
(*To M. D. Calvocoressi*)

Comarques
6th Sept 1914

My dear Calvo,

Toutes nos sympathies, mon vieux, I will do anything I can, but I fear nothing can be done. I don't think the Academy will open. *I am exceedingly busy*, doing things for the war. It is very hard for musical critics. I don't know what I can say to you. There is nothing to say. Only don't go and get killed. We should much like to have postcards from you occasionally.

Our kindest regards to your mother & her son.

Ever yours, A. B.

HERZOG / T.C. / 304
(*To George H. Doran*)

Comarques
10th Sept. 1914.

My dear Doran:

That was a great idea of yours to sell my article to the *Saturday Evening Post*. It is the ideal medium for the article. I now have only to thank you very heartily indeed for your initiative, promptitude, and characteristically businesslike handling of the situation. (Pinker, I may say, was ill in bed.) I send by concurrent registered mail one copy of the article. I have sent another copy by registered post, with a personal letter to Lorimer, addressed 'Editor, *Saturday Evening Post*, Philadelphia'. It is difficult for me to judge of the value of the article, but I imagine that it is at any rate readable. You will note that I have refrained from any sort of appeal to the American people. My view is that it is inept in the highest degree to talk to Americans as if they didn't know their own business. Between you and me, there are two English authors who have displayed commonsense in this crisis. One is H. G. Wells. I am not sure

---

service. He would have been opposed on principle to giving articles to editors. See also Vol. I, pp. 212 ff.

The editors of the *New Statesman* expressed regret for their sentence but thought that it could bear another construction than Bennett put on it.

that I even agree with his article addressed to you about the proposed purchase of German ships; but he has written some great articles. I had a long yarn with him the other day. I have only one fear as to the war, and that is that pacifist and financial influences (especially in America and England) may force a peace too soon. If commonsense is allowed to rule, we can and shall finish up Germany's activities in the war department for at least fifty years, and bring about a German revolution against the military caste. When she started out, Germany had no idea what she was arousing in England. I hadn't myself. You know that I am not a Kiplingian patriot, but rather the reverse; nevertheless I have the greatest confidence in the handling of affairs here and in the general spirit of the nation I have been really surprised. We have scarcely begun yet. And with the navy 'in being', there is no reason why we should unduly hurry. For myself I would give every cent and [? acre] I possess, and start again with nothing, in order to secure the overthrow of a handful of men at Berlin. That is how I feel, and how a lot of other people feel. German grand strategy, and German organization, and German guns have handsomely vindicated themselves so far. They are astounding. But the German private soldier proved not to be a fighter; he had neither pluck nor initiative; these qualities have been disciplined out of him if he ever had them. In the end, everything will turn on the private soldier.

If we are beaten—and everything is possible—then you had better begin to build ships and train armies, for you will urgently need them. And don't forget it.

The cost of the necklace was £3.

Marguerite has had an operation—is quite cured.

We join in best wishes to all of you.

Yours, A. B.

P.S. I was forgetting to say that I leave the whole question of the pamphlet issue to you. Make the price so that it will reach the largest respectable-thoughtful circulation. In the title the word 'Liberty' should be large, with a note of exclamation after it—!

304. On George Doran see page 292 n.
Bennett's article, 'Liberty—A Statement of the British Case', appeared on 17

HERZOG / MS. / 305
(*To Elsie Herzog*)

Comarques
10.9.14

Dear Mrs. Herzog,
   Your letter cannot be answered now. It is like ancient history. No doubt you are back at New York. Since it reached me I have had no moment for writing private letters, & I am still completely occupied in war work & in Clayhangering. I thought the war would stop Clayhangering, but it has not done so. I haven't been so interested in life since I was born as I am now. England is full of drilling soldiers, but it is also full of ideas—large general ideas, which overthrow small particular ideas about particular persons. All I can do in the amicable line is to assure you that your friends exist & to hope that in the future friendship may resume its usual course.
   Our kindest regards.

Yours sincerely, Arnold Bennett

GIDE / 306
(*To André Gide*)

Comarques
10.9.1914

Mon cher ami,
   C'est Retinger qui m'a dit que vous êtes à Paris. Je vous envoie seulement un petit mot de rien du tout. A mon grand étonnement je peux continuer mon roman. Mais aussi j'écris maintes chroniques sur la psychologie de la guerre, ou des chroniques purement politiques, ou même guerrières.
   Bref, je suis très occupé, et très intéressé, et plein d'espoir. Je serais très content d'avoir un mot de votre main. La N.R.F. d'août ne m'est pas parvenue, à mon grand dégoût.
   Cordiale p. de m.

Tout à vous, Arnold Bennett

October 1914 in the *Saturday Evening Post*, of which George Horace Lorimer (1868–1937) was editor. The article was published as a pamphlet, entitled *Liberty!*, in the same month. Wells's article is not known.
   306. On Joseph Retinger see page 322 n. He had been a friend of Gide's for several years.

HERZOG / MS. / 307
(*To Elsie Herzog*)

Comarques
15 Sept 1914.

Dear Mrs. Herzog,

Many thanks for yours of the 2nd & the enclosures. I return the print. It is excellent, but not as epigrammatic as some of the morning papers. It is well to remember that there have been many wars quite as ghastly as this one,—only there won't be many more. As no good purpose can be served by letting the imagination loose, it is best to keep it in control. If you were here you would probably say that I was very callous & matter-of-fact. My wife's nerves have now largely recovered, though she has a brother in the French army & a sister close to the fighting line. I have lived, the sole man, in this house with four women (not counting servants) for six weeks, & I have squashed about 1,000 alarms & false rumours every day. For this labour of love I have been well cursed; but the effect up to date is admirable on the household mind.

My wife joins with me in kindest regards to you both. I daresay she would write, but she is busy sending off two little French boys to an English boarding school. Sons of friends of ours (& no relation to each other), they came to stay with us (together with a sister) for a holiday in July, & haven't been able to return.

Yours sincerely, Arnold Bennett

BUTLER / MS. / 308
(*To John Drinkwater*)

Comarques
17 Sept 1914

Dear Mr. John Drinkwater,

Many thanks for your letter. The provincial rights of *W. the P.W.* have been acquired by Vedrenne & Eadie. My policy has always been to use my influence with Vedrenne & Eadie to stand aside in favour of repertory companies. Sometimes they will & sometimes they won't. I have asked my agent, J. B. Pinker, Talbot House, Arundel Street, Strand, to do what he can for you, but I can by no means guarantee the result. You will hear from him at once.

I am *very pleased* you like my *Daily News* articles. This pleasure mitigates somewhat the shock of learning that you ever did disagree with my opinions, so reasonable & so persuasively expressed! However, when you are my age you will probably have my opinions.

Yours sincerely, Arnold Bennett

DAILY NEWS, 24 September 1914 / 309
(*To the editor*)

Comarques
Sept. 23 [1914]

Sir,

I am very glad to see Mr. Wedgwood Benn's letter, with its definite promise of reports as to the work of the Prince of Wales's Fund.

It was, of course, a great pleasure to me to learn, after having written my last article animadverting upon the State's treatment of its defenders and their dependants, that the Government had decided to raise the scales of allowances. I cannot, however, agree with Mr. Wedgwood Benn that the scales have been raised to 'an adequate level'. Nor have I yet come across anybody who agrees with him. The allowances are in nearly every category still grossly inadequate, and at least one capital grievance has not yet been touched at all. Nevertheless, I willingly admit that the Government has done more than I expected it to do, and that in arranging for weekly payments through Post Offices it has done really well.

If Mr. Wedgwood Benn is right as to the adequacy of the new allowances, the following point arises: I said, and I maintain, that it is a scandal of the first order that the Fund should have to be used to supplement inadequate allowances from the State. The scandal would be equally great if the Fund were used to supplement State allowances which the chairman of the Fund's Executive considers to be adequate. Hence either Mr. Wedgwood Benn must choose between one scandal and the

308. John Drinkwater (1882–1937) was co-founder of the Birmingham Repertory Theatre, and was general manager for several years there as well as one of the leading actors. He produced *What the Public Wants* in 1917. See Vol. I, p. 275, on his play *Abraham Lincoln*.

other or payments from the Fund to dependants of soldiers and sailors must practically cease. Will they practically cease?

As to applicants having received better treatment from Poor Law Guardians than from the Fund, my authority was a detailed article dealing with the condition of affairs in Manchester published in the *Manchester Guardian* of the 11th inst. It is too long to quote here, but it more than bears out what I said.

As to the dissemination of the principles upon which the Fund is administered, I would suggest that Mr. Wedgwood Benn might usefully cause to be prepared a résumé for the Press of the White Paper and the circulars of the S.S.F.A. to which he refers. No White Paper will educate the public without the aid of the Press. I am bound to say that my own efforts to obtain first-hand information have met with the usual official reception.

Perhaps I ought to add that, among my correspondence, the most violent criticism of the Fund's methods has come from workers actively engaged in the distribution of the fund. Here is a short extract from a long letter written to me by a helper whose duty it is to visit and report upon needy families:

'I am almost sick already at the "red tape." One family I visited yesterday, wife and six children; absolutely nothing coming in. Two people had already been sent to interview the woman. When I suggested that something more should be given her I was told, "Oh! She had 4s. on Monday!" And seven mouths to feed. Her husband fighting for old England, and this is the way we treat his family!'

In conclusion, let me say that I have no desire to hold fast to a good strategic position for mere dialectical purposes. The danger, when outside criticism encounters an official reply, is that each party will attempt to score points. I do not wish to score points, and I am sure that Mr. Wedgwood Benn does not. My sole desire is that the Prince of Wales's Fund should be administered with generosity and common-sense. I admit the difficulties. Mr. Wedgwood Benn's democratic sympathies are unquestionable, and I hope that they will powerfully prevail.

Arnold Bennett

309. William Wedgwood Benn, later Viscount Stansgate (1877–1960), was Chairman of the Executive Committee of the Prince of Wales's Fund. In an article entitled 'The Fund and the State', which appeared in the *Daily News* on 16

BERG / MS. / 310
(*To John Squire*)

Comarques
25 Sept 1914.

[no salutation]

Yes, my dear Squire, I deeply agree with your objection to that infernal word 'Hun', but I think our objection is literary. The word is a most damnable cliché, especially when used in combination with other words beginning with H. But I think it is a fairly descriptive word. What you say as to the constituents of the German army is true of all armies, & I should say quite true of the English army. A proportion of German feats in Belgium are no doubt due to the riff-raff, but I don't see how it can be seriously argued that the 'terrible example' [?] is not the considered policy of the G.G. Staff. At any rate they have preached it enough. I consider that the entire attitude of the German army is appreciably different from that of the other armies. I will not swear to my conviction, as there can be no certainty till we see the French or Belgians operating in Germany, but such is my notion.

My opinion of the *Daily News* is probably much like your own; but where *is* a fellow to write if he wants to trepidate the great heart etc? I have a contract with the *Chronicle*, but I couldn't whack in there after Wells, nor would the *Chronicle* have desired it. The *Daily News* urgently invited me to step up. So I did. No Tory paper would print my stuff, or Wells's either.

Yours sincerely, Arnold Bennett

September, Bennett belaboured the people who give money to charities and then go their way with their consciences salved, never asking how their money is used. When Bennett tried to find out how the Prince of Wales's funds were used, he was able to learn only that there was a good deal of mismanagement. But the real scandal was that the Fund, which was instituted to relieve the distresses of war, was actually being used to supplement the grossly inadequate pay of the Government to soldiers and sailors. The Fund was thus helping to maintain an evil condition. What was needed was an immediate Act of Parliament to improve the scales of pay.

EDINBURGH / TS. / 311
(*To the editor of* Everyman)

Comarques
September 28th, 1914.

Dear Sir,

In the present crisis Belgium has proved in the most magnificent manner, not only its steadfast patriotism, but also its
efficiency in the exercise of that patriotism. The civilisation of
the whole world is indebted to Belgium for its superb stand
against savagery; and the ample redress of the sufferings of
Belgium should and will be the concern of the whole world.
For myself I feel strongly that the interests of Belgium ought to
be the first consideration when peace-terms come to be discussed. As Belgium was the first foreign country I ever saw,
and as I have visited it frequently and know it pretty well, I
feel a special regard for its territory; but even a German could
scarcely deny the justice of Belgium's claim upon mankind for
the drastic punishment of a horrible and revolting and totally
inexcusable crime. The heroic spirit and the dignity with which
Belgium has borne her dreadful misfortunes are today the
admiration of every race, and particularly of England and France.

Yours faithfully, Arnold Bennett

S. BROWN / MS. / 312
(*To James Brown*)

Comarques
6 Oct. 1914

My dear Jim,

This is a piece of good news & a kind action. I knew that
play would never succeed with any but the élite. It is coming
off, as you may have seen from the papers. You just got there in
time. Don't leave the operation so late next time.

My best to you & yours,

Thine, A. B.

311. The editor of *Everyman*, Charles Sarolea (see pages 316–21), was born and
educated in Belgium, and was active in raising relief funds for Belgium during the
war. Bennett's letter was apparently not published.

312. This note is one of the few surviving pieces of correspondence between
Bennett and James Brown, who were fairly close friends in the 1890s. See pages
33 n. and 60–61. The play referred to is presumably *The Great Adventure*, which
ended its long run on 7 November.

BUTLER / MS. / 313   Comarques
(*To Cedric Sharpe*)   12-10-14

My dear Cedric,
The whole thing is quite irregular. Still, I *think* that if you kept one part & signed it, & had it stamped at the post office with a 6d. stamp, it would count as a contract made by the Phil. Soc., although their signature is only printed. The attached slip would also count as part of the contract. If you tear off the slip & then send the contract signed, it will not count, as the Phil. Soc. would not be bound by it.
You had better write a letter something like this:—
'Dear Sir,
With reference to the form of contract which you have sent me, I regret to say that I cannot possibly accept the terms of it as modified by the attached slip, as the wording of the slip would place me absolutely at the mercy of the Society. If you care to send me the contract without the slip, I shall be happy to sign it.
                              Your loving cellist
                                    Cedric Sharpe'

                                          Thine, A. B.

P.S. The slip is simply monstrous. [One or two further sentences are lost.]

HERZOG / MS. / 314
(*To Elsie Herzog*)
                                          Comarques
                                          6th Nov 1914
Dear Mrs. Herzog,
I can't spoil the simplicity of my novel by letting Edwin & Hilda procreate. They have young George, & he's quite enough for my purposes. I have now finished the second part. There are 3. (The best judges I know are of opinion that *The Price of Love* is A1. This rather surprises me, but it relieves me.) I expect the book will be finished long before the war is. I think the war

is proceeding all right. At present I am devoting $1\frac{1}{2}$ days a week to the prevention of conscription, & the proper treatment of soldiers' dependents, in this country. It is no sinecure. I have made a lot of people extremely angry, but they never argue with me; I wish they would—in print. They only suggest that a shoe maker ought to stick to his last. The British army is really very fine. I am honestly convinced that size for size it is quite unequalled on the continent. This does me good. There may be a few Zeppelins over us one of these days, but the affair will have no importance except that it will aid recruiting. I regret to say that I can't get my articles published in U.S.A. now. Some of the earlier ones were simply pirated & cabled over (by the *N.Y. Times*, for example). Consequence, I can't guarantee to deliver the goods to an American buyer. It is very wrong, but I can't worry with actions-at-law until the Belgian affair is more settled. So you aren't likely to read any more of my articles. I am exceedingly busy. So is my wife (on behalf of refugees). At this moment Belgian wounded, convalescent, are strolling in our garden. Talk about 5 Towns nonchalance. It is nothing to Belgian. These chaps convince me that I am emotional, mercurial, light-headed. Their cheerful calm is an absolutely staggering phenomenon. I am very glad *Liberty* pleased all you people. I shall soon begin to think that I can *write*. Anyhow I have illustrated a book in colour for a friend. My pride in this is very naive.

Our kindest regards to you both.

Always yours sincerely, Arnold Bennett

MAYFIELD, SYRACUSE / A.D. / 315
(*To the editor of the* Daily News)

[16–17 November 1914]

Sir,

The Call for Men

In reference to Mr. Eden Phillpotts' letter published in your issue of the 16th, I entirely deny that there was any error of taste in my remarks as to the late Lord Roberts. I have

314. The illustrations were presumably those for *A Floating Home*, by Cyril Ionides and Bennett's friend J. B. Atkins. The book did not appear until 1918.

mentioned him twice in my articles, & in each case in terms of deep respect & admiration. (I am quite willing that the passages should be reprinted.)

My perfectly courteous animadversion upon Lord Roberts (made, be it remembered, while he was alive and apparently in good health) was based solely on his written prophecy at the beginning of the war that not half a million volunteers would respond to the call of patriotism. I said that such a prophecy was a libel and that it showed that he lacked faith in his country.

I also entirely deny that the fact of me being a novelist impairs my right to expressing views about conscription. Mr. Phillpotts asks what we should say if Lord Kitchener or the late Lord Roberts had published their opinions on my novels. We should consider their opinions, of course, and those opinions, like mine about conscription, would conquer or fail according to their intrinsic worth.

Further, conscription is a matter to be decided by the citizens of this country, not by its professional soldiers. The duty of citizens is to hear all that professional soldiers have to say, and then to decide for themselves. Up to the present the one vital thing that I have heard from a professional soldier is Lord Kitchener's public categorical statement that he has no fault whatever to find with the recruiting. Still further, I do not accept Mr. Phillpotts' 'fact' that had conscription been adopted in England two or three years ago, 'probably' hundreds of thousands of valuable lives would have been saved & this war rendered impossible. My view is that had we decided on conscription two or three years ago a war would have occurred two or three years ago.

Lastly I do not agree that Conservative treatment of women and the disabled would have been better than the Liberal treatment. As to the Liberal treatment, I am very happy to think that Mr. Phillpotts' opinion and mine coincide.

Yours faithfully, [Arnold Bennett]

315. This letter appeared with negligible changes in the *Daily News* on 19 November 1914. Phillpotts's letter was written before Lord Roberts's death. His main point was that he and other pacifists, long opposed to the notion of conscription, had been proved wrong by the inexorable German plunge into militarism. Lord Roberts had been right, and it was time to acknowledge the fact. In an article entitled 'I Told You So' on the 11th, Bennett referred to the excellent results of recruitment, 'a point for meditation by Lord Roberts. . . . I have the highest

FALES, NYU / MS. / 316
(*To Mrs. Alcock*)

Comarques
15th Dec 1914

My dear Mrs. Alcock,

Many thanks for your most sympathetic letter, which I was very glad to have. My mother suffered such constant & acute physical pain (sciatica & neuritis) that her death was a deliverance, & often in her letters to me she would express a wish for it. She saw all her children before losing consciousness. During the last few days happily she had no pain.

We had Freddie up here not long ago; he was as usual intellectually very alert. I gather that he is now having a great time at Falmouth.

I hope that you & all yours are well, & philosophically bearing up against present troubles. The prospects are good, & the grit & commonsense shown by the nation at large is making me quite patriotic!

My wife joins with me in best wishes & kindest regards.

Always yours sincerely, Arnold Bennett

---

respect for the life-work and patriotism of the aged veteran; but, with much deference, I am obliged to say that Lord Roberts is wrong.' Lord Roberts (b. 1832) was best known for his leadership in the South Africa War, and he was Colonel-in-Chief Overseas and Indian Forces in Europe at the time of his death. Bennett used his burial in Westminster Abbey in an early scene in *The Pretty Lady* a few years later.

316. There were four or five brothers in the Alcock family, and whether this letter is to the wife of Fred (see page 43 n.), and 'Freddie' refers to Frederick Marriott, or whether it is to the wife of another brother is unknown.

Bennett's mother died on 23 November 1914. He wrote in his Journal on the 20th:

'She was very glad to see me and held my hand all the time under bedclothes. She spoke of the most trifling things as if tremendously important—as e.g. decisions as if they were momentous and dictated by profound sagacity. She was seldom fully conscious, and often dozed and woke up with a start. "What do you say?" rather loud. She had no pain, but often muttered in anguish: "What am I to do? What am I to do?" Amid tossed bedclothes you could see numbers on corners of blankets. On medicine table siphon, saucer, spoon, large soap-dish, brass flower-bowl (empty). The gas (very bad burner) screened by a contraption of Family Bible, some wooden thing, and a newspaper. It wasn't level. She had it altered. She said it annoyed her terribly. Gas stove burning. Temperature barely 60°. Damp chill, penetrating my legs. The clock had a very light, delicate striking sound. Trams and buses did not disturb her, though sometimes they made talking difficult.

Round-topped panels of wardrobe. She wanted to be satisfied that her purse

STOKE / MS. / 317
(*To Hugh Walpole*)

Comarques
7th Jan 1915

My dear Hugh,
Sorry about this neuralgia. If you [?sit] with Lady M. Paget you will have to be her slave. I suppose you know that. There is only one god where she works. The only thing the matter with me is that I am worked to death with war-charities & so on, & that they are *not my line*. However, will you let us know where & when you are in town. And will you buy a ticket for the Assault at Arms at National Sporting Club Monday 17th inst. on behalf of Wounded Allies Relief Committee Ladies Night. 2 or 3 guineas? Très chic. You can go with Marguerite if you like, but I haven't mentioned this pleasing combination to her in case you could not. I can only join her there as I have a dinner of ex-pugilists before, which I couldn't avoid.
[?Our] love,
Thine, A. B.

P.S. Doran is here.

STOKE / MS. / 318
(*To Hugh Walpole*)

Comarques
1st April 1915

My dear Hugh,
We were very glad to peruse your letter. It took a mere six weeks to reach us! If you do not write a marvellous book about your adventures, all is over between us. I hope, & in fact I believe, that you keep a journal. I wonder what your notion of

---

was on a particular tray of the wardrobe. The Mater has arterial sclerosis and patchy congestion of the lungs. Her condition was very distressing (though less so than the Pater's), and it seemed strange that this should necessarily be the end of a life, that a life couldn't always end more easily.'
The description of the death of Auntie Hamps in *These Twain*, which Bennett finished writing three months later, is based upon his mother's death.
317. Lady Muriel Paget (d. 1919) was associated with Bennett in his work for the Wounded Allies Relief Committee. He was on the Executive Committee. See Vol. I, pp. 226–7.

England must be if you only can read *The Times*! I have been combatting the same in the *Daily News* on the subject of labour strikes & general discontent, upon which I feel rather strongly. The drink question is now agitating us. I have suggested that total prohibition should begin first in the Cabinet, the Reform Club, & the National Liberal Club!! I met three cabinet ministers at dinner on Tuesday, & this scheme seemed to please them. I doubt if they will adopt it. Personally I should be in favour of prohibition as a national act of self-discipline. Everybody high up seems to be perfectly confident about the war, & I have myself laid bets to the sum of £25 that hostilities cease by the end of July. I saw Swinnerton on Tuesday. He has been very ill, & has grown a most dramatic red beard. Also I have had quite a lot of talk with Clutton Brock, who is the most truly educated person, except H.G. Wells I think, that I have yet met. . . . I am just beginning a new novel (brand—humorous). There will be some suffragettes in it, much Paris, and some London. I may go to the French front in order to describe it. The escapade has been officially suggested to me. I said I must have a guide & companion all to myself. It may be arranged. I thoroughly understand your home-sickness. In fact when I think of you I positively *feel* home-sick sympathetically. It is undoubtedly because of the war. We went to the 1st night of Barrie's eccentricity. It was a frost, & most of it extremely poor. Selfridge, the official amant of Gaby Deslys, was in a box with his family! I saw him last Monday at the National Sporting Club. But I did *not* see him at the Bach Passion Music at St. Paul's. (Very noble.) He evidently means to shine; but I fear he is a poor thing.

Our affections to you.

Love, yours, A. B.

You will have gathered from the foregoing that I have had just ten days in London. Last night I returned.

318. Walpole served with the Russian Red Cross at the beginning of the war, and later was in charge of the Anglo–Russian propaganda bureau in Leningrad. His two novels *The Dark Forest* and *Secret City*, 1916 and 1919, are based upon his experiences there.

Frank Swinnerton (1884–) and Bennett met in 1911, and soon became close friends. Apparently referring to his illness in 1915, Swinnerton said of Bennett that 'his shrinking from the sight of pain or sickness in others was so great

BERG / MS. / 319
(*To John Squire*)

Comarques
18 April 1915

My dear Squire,

I have been in telepathic communication with you,—result, I thought you might possibly be saying something about Darton's booklet on me. If you do, you might like to know that his attribution to me of a serial story in *Chatterbox,—Sidney Yorke's Friend*—is entirely baseless, & therefore inexcusable. His bibliography is further faulty inasmuch as though he mentions one privately printed volume entitled *Things*, he gets the title wrong,—it ought to be *Things That Have Interested Me*—, & he omits two later volumes, being the 2nd & 3rd series of *Things*, dated 1907 and 1908. Also he apparently regards *The Feast of St. Friend* and *Friendship & Happiness* as two different books, whereas they are the same book.

Although he has evidently been to the Potteries to study the topography, which is very industrious of him, he was unable to find in Burslem the equivalent of 'Duck Square'. Yet this square exists under the name of Swan Square, just as Duck Bank is really Swan Bank. His suggested spot for Duck Square is incorrect. He does not know that *The Great Adventure* was written a long time after *Buried Alive* (p. 107). He has not perceived that 'Manefold' and 'Axe' are the same town (of which I changed the name), and that the town is Leek. He insists that the first sensational novel was *The Gates of Wrath*, whereas it was *The Ghost*. He appears to think that the 3rd vol. of *Clayhanger* was promised for a certain year, like most people. It was not. I was much too wily to fix a date. Aware of your devotion to the supremely important things of English literature, I felt that

that when I had an operation he could not bring himself to visit me in hospital'. He added, with regard to Bennett's visit to the Front, which took place in June and July: 'So I think he visited the Front as a duty, and was horrified at what he saw and felt that he must not express that horror.'

Arthur Clutton-Brock (1868–1924) was art critic of *The Times*, and had been on the staff of that paper since 1908.

Bennett's new novel was *The Lion's Share*.

J. M. Barrie wrote *Rosy Rapture*, a revue, especially for Gaby Deslys (d. 1920). Miss Deslys was noted more for her physical charms than for her histrionic talent. Gordon Selfridge (d. 1947), owner of the department store bearing his name, worked with Bennett on war charity committees.

you would like to have all this information, especially as you, like all of us, enjoy the opportunity to display exact learning. The Clement Shorters of 20 years hence are very likely to go wrong on *Sidney Yorke's Friend*, & to find traces of my marvellous personality in it, unless you put an end at once to this dreadful legend.

I have been thinking that I might let you have some chunks of the 'Journal' that I have been keeping for 19 years, if you cared. But the copyright would have to be arranged in U.S.A., & this will take time.

Yours sincerely, Arnold Bennett

P.S. I do think the statement about scenery near the bottom of p. 33 is a bit thick. A. B.

HERZOG / MS. / 320
(*To Elsie Herzog*)

Comarques
27 May 1915

Dear Mrs. Herzog,

Many thanks for your letter. I am sorry the other one was sunk. I have very little time these days for writing purely friendly letters. But I am a little more slack now, as I have just finished the first half of my novel *The Lion's Share* for the *Metropolitan*. This half has to be delivered in June. War work takes me 3 days a week. I think that I shall shortly be going to the front, at least as near to the front as a civilian who respects

<hr>

319. F. J. Harvey Darton (d. 1936) was the first person to write a book on Bennett. His enthusiasm for *Sidney Yorke's Friend*, a children's story by a woman who signed herself E. A. Bennett, may have stemmed in part from the fact that he was an authority on children's literature, author some years later of *Children's Books in England*. But also, as he pointed out in replying to the *New Statesman* review on 24 April, the British Museum catalogue ascribed the book to Bennett. It took forty-three years for Bennett's prophecy about the book to come true. In 1958 an American critic wrote: 'His early children's serial, *Sidney Yorke's Friend*, strikes the note which recurs through Bennett's later books, by no means excluding *The Old Wives' Tale* and *Clayhanger*. It is a pure success story, and was followed by other stories of the successful financier or manager.'

Darton was right, and Bennett wrong, about the title *Things That Interested Me* (1906). Darton's statement about scenery reads: 'Nowhere in all Arnold Bennett's novels . . . is the faintest trace of any appreciation or even any perception of scenery or "natural" beauty.'

2 B

his vitality may go. *If* I do go, the resulting stuff will appear in the *Saturday Evening Post*. America will shortly be receiving in large quantities a pamphlet appeal written by me on behalf of 'The Wounded Allies Relief Committee', of which I am a very active member. This pamphlet has had a considerable success in England, & brings in £400 a day by making people feel uncomfortable. I hope it may have a still greater success in America. J. P. Morgan & Co are to act as Treasurers of the incoming money. Our life here is undisturbed, though twice a Zeppelin has flown over the house in the night. The first time I was asleep & the second time I was in London. Our society is almost exclusively military, with a parson or two. The tennis clubs flourish greatly because the officers belong to them. We have much Territorial Cavalry here, & it is not wanted yet— at the front.

Our kindest regards to you both.

Yours sincerely, Arnold Bennett

GIDE / 321
(*To André Gide*)

Hôtel Meurice
rue de Rivoli
Paris
Monday, 5th July 1915.

My dear Gide,

No, I agree with you that it is not yet true. But I regard it as an intelligent anticipation of events. Also, it seems certain that the Russian army is cut in two; and this, according to my favourite military expert (Belloc), will be at least as bad as the taking of Warsaw, if not worse. There was a sale esprit pessimiste over Paris yesterday—and no electricity at the Café Weber! The hypothesis was:

The Germans bring over 2,000 guns from the East.

They break the French line.

They take Paris: which will end the war because all the great war-manufactories are around Paris.

Hypothèse idiote: because what the Germans could not do in September, when their programme was being strictly

320. The *Metropolitan*, an American magazine, began publishing *The Lion's Share* in October 1915. Bennett wrote two pamphlets, *Wounded* and *The Wounded Allies Relief Committee*, both issued in 1915.

followed, and they had a vast superiority of men, and their prestige was unimpaired—they certainly cannot do now.

But supposing the hypothesis were a good one—the war would not be ended. The war can only end unfavourably for France when the British fleet is destroyed.

The British fleet will not be destroyed.

You do not know, but I will tell you as a fact, that 280 new ships of all sorts have been ordered, and most of them have been delivered, since August last. There are even special ships ready to navigate the Danube after Constantinople is taken.

So long as the British fleet exists the Germans are potentially beaten; because without the permission of the British fleet, German international commerce cannot be resumed, and without that commerce Germany cannot live. The greatest factor in the negotiations for peace will be the British fleet.

The silence maintained in England about the fleet is astounding. All France and the rest of Europe know that a British submarine sank a German cruiser in the Baltic the other day. But in England it is given out that a *Russian* submarine sank a German cruiser in the Baltic. It is absurd, but it is sublime. We have sunk 28 German submarines, and perhaps more. But never a word is said in the Admiralty communiqués.

I have nearly finished *Confession d'un homme d'aujourd'hui*. It is very good and helped me to pass a difficult Sunday.

La dernière partie de votre lettre m'a très touché. Pour ce qu'il y a d'artiste en moi, le sentiment est réciproqué. (Ces choses ne se disent pas en anglais!)

Ever yours, Arnold Bennett

321. The Hôtel Meurice was Bennett's base during his twenty-five-day tour of the Front. For further details of the trip see Vol. I, pp. 229–30.

Hilaire Belloc (1870–1953) published his *General Sketch of the European War, 1st Phase*, in 1915. He was a fellow contributor to the *New Age* in earlier years.

Confessions d'un homme d'aujourd'hui was a novel by Abel Hermant (1862–1950). Gide's preceding letter to Bennett is lost.

BERG / MS. / 322
(*To John Squire*)

Comarques
July 29th, 1915.

My dear Squire,

Many thanks for yours of the 28th. Although I am now getting up for a few hours each day, I am absolutely off work.

The interesting question about your first edition of *Le Rouge et le Noir* is :—Are the two volumes in the original illustrated paper covers? A friend of mine picked up a first edition of *Le Rouge et le Noir* on the quays of the Seine in the original covers for a franc, and he gave it to me. I sent the volumes to the binder with the most strict instructions that the paper covers were to be preserved, but they were destroyed. Anyhow yours is a very great find.

How soon are you going to use that contribution by my friend Miss Pauline Smith? I think that last week's issue was an excellent one. It was the first *I* had seen for about a month, as I have just had three weeks at the Front. There are a certain number of criticisms which I could make on the Front, but which certainly would not be allowed to pass the censor over my signature. I am quite prepared to let Sharp know what they are if he cares to use them on his own, incidentally, in commenting on the war.

Yours, A. B.

322. Bennett returned from his visit to the Front in a state of exhaustion.
Pauline Smith (1882–1959), the South African novelist, author of *The Little Karoo* and *The Beadle*, met Bennett in Switzerland shortly after his marriage. Her account of their friendship, *A.B.*, 'A Minor Marginal Note', provides perhaps the best picture of Bennett that there is. He was her literary godfather and her literary agent until his own death. Her story 'The Sisters' appeared in the *New Statesman* on 21 August 1915.
Clifford Sharp (1883–1935) was editor of the *New Statesman* from 1913 until 1931. Bennett became a director of the journal in 1915.

BERG / MS. / 323
(*To John Squire*)

Comarques
4th August 1915

My dear Squire,

Many thanks. I have noticed the Wells phenomenon, & in fact I have got across him in today's *Daily News*. We are still intimate friends, & whenever I see him his talk is absolutely A1, & he seems to improve each time. Hence some of the articles are the more mysterious.

My articles on the Front begin to appear in the *Illustrated London News* on August 21st. But of course all the most interesting things are left out.

Yours sincerely, Arnold Bennett

HERZOG / MS. / 324
(*To Elsie Herzog*)

Comarques
17th Oct 1915

Dear Mrs. Herzog,

Many thanks for your gloomy letter. I wrote you some time ago, addressed to New York, & I suppose that the letter has reached you. I am glad you appreciate the articles. Lorimer does too. In fact, in so far as he is capable of being enthusiastic in a letter, he has been enthusiastic about them. Since I wrote I have had 2 days holiday. I drove over to the Wells residence, about 42 miles from here, on a Saturday morning & returned on the Monday morning. I seem to have played games—including hockey & Badminton—all the time. Wells is not a good games-player, but he is fully aware of their value & of the value of exercise, and whenever there is a lull in the intellectual movement of social relations he turns on a game. His energy is astounding. This 2 days holiday—my only time off since August

---

323. In an article in the *Nation* Wells attacked 'party politicians' and the democratic process that allows them to thrive. Bennett supposed that human nature makes for the same sort of dissension and selfishness under militarism, and he thought that the methods of English government were infinitely to be preferred to German. Democracy was in the tide of evolution, militarism was not.

The war articles were gathered into book form later in the year under the title *Over There*.

1914—did me much good. I still continue to be in a state of surprise that New York women of leisure & wealth and 'Allied' sympathies don't cure their distress about the war by some form of regular organised activity. Our kindest regards to you both.

Yours sincerely, Arnold Bennett

HERZOG / MS. / 325
(*To Elsie Herzog*)

Comarques
9th Nov 1915

Dear Mrs. Herzog,

I am extremely sorry to hear of this physical misfortune. These things have the advantage of drawing out the sympathies of one's friends & that is absolutely all one can say for them. It appears that by the time you get this you will be through the affair, and sitting up at the receipt of congratulations. The amount of superstition abroad is still astonishing. If you had 40,000 husbands & had told each of them 40,000 times that you would die at a certain age, it would not make the slightest difference to events nor would it have the slightest interest as a prophecy for wholly reasonable people. (Not that there are any.) Nor does the strange fact that you resemble your mother add anything to the situation. However by this time your superstition will have had a shock, I hope. Some day it will be understood why women have to suffer so much more in pain & weakness than men, from these diseases in particular. I expect there is some remediable cause. Ignorance as usual is at the bottom of these martyrdoms. My wife sends her keenest sympathy & best wishes for a complete recovery. So do I.

Yours sincerely, Arnold Bennett

324. Lorimer (see page 352 n.) began publishing *Over There* in the *Saturday Evening Post* beginning 21 August 1915.

325. Mrs. Herzog may have had an operation on a tumour at this time. Her mother died of cancer at the age of 37 or 38, the age of Mrs. Herzog in 1915.

BUTLER / T.C.C. / 326
(*To George H. Doran*)

[? London]
15th November, 1915.
My dear Doran,

Many thanks for your letter of the 3rd, which reached me on Saturday. Also the copies of *These Twain* and *Over There*. The latter is a very agreeable object to behold, and I am sure that Walter Hales's illustrations will add to its attraction. As regards *These Twain*, it makes a very handsome volume. My only criticism is as to the jacket, which, although agreeable in colour, bears—so far as I can see—no resemblance to anything in the book. It seems much more like a scene in some small sleepy and clean old English country town. If you had ever been to the Potteries you would understand at once. However, I suppose I ought to blame myself as the artist has in all probability read my description. At the same time it is not my fault that the figures in the picture, and especially the girl, should look as though they have had just a little bit too much to drink!

By the way, in the list of my works printed at the beginning of each of my books, it would probably be better if after the title *Milestones* you were to add in brackets 'in collaboration with Edward Knoblock'. Knoblock would certainly object to the inclusion of *Milestones* among my works without some mention of himself.

On Saturday morning I ventured to telegraph you as follows:—

'Kindly make full enquiries about National Allied Relief Committee Fifth Avenue Building and report when you come here. Greetings. Bennett.'

The New York Committee has made a sort of proposal for co-operation with the Wounded Allies Relief Committee of Sardinia House, Kingsway, London, of which I am a member, and if you could possibly spare time to find out something definite about the New York Committee and report to me personally when you come over, I should be extremely obliged. The official of the New York Committee who corresponds with me is Mr. John Moffatt.

We shall soon be expecting to hear that you are on the way here. Yours ever, [Arnold Bennett]

HERZOG / MS. / 327
(*To Elsie Herzog*)

Comarques
11 Dec 1915

Dear Mrs. Herzog,
This may reach you for Christmas, though I doubt it. We are exceedingly relieved that you have come through so well for yourself & so badly for superstition. But not precisely surprised. You have now to collect a little strength each day. It takes a long time to repay these debts to nature, but the instalment system suits her very well.

If our good & powerful wishes will set you right, you are hereby set right.

Our kindest regard to both of you.

Always yours sincerely, Arnold Bennett

P.S. I think *The Genius* is a pretty good book.

MERTON / MS. / 328
(*To Max Beerbohm*)

Comarques
20th Dec 1915

My dear Max,
I enclose a booklet about the Wounded Allies Relief Committee, of which I am an active member. I am getting up a *high-class* concert at the Haymarket Theatre on behalf thereof. Will you design me a cartoonish-sort-of-cover for the programme? If you can, you will be exercising benevolence, & will live in the hearts of those who are capable of gratitude. If you cannot, I shall understand that you cannot.

Yours, Arnold Bennett

326. Walter Hale (d. 1917) was an American illustrator. On John Moffat see Vol. I, p. 232.

327. Theodore Dreiser (1871–1945) was one of Bennett's favourite American authors. *The Genius* was published in England by John Lane in November 1915.

328. Max Beerbohm (1872–1956) and Bennett had been friends since 1909, when Beerbohm wrote a flattering review of *What the Public Wants*. The concert at the Haymarket took place on 20 February 1916.

INDEX